Sustainable Trade

Sustainable Trade

Changing the Environment the Market Operates in,
Through Standardized Global Trade Tariffs

Zoltan Ban

authorHOUSE®

AuthorHouse™
1663 Liberty Drive
Bloomington, IN 47403
www.authorhouse.com
Phone: 1-800-839-8640

First published by AuthorHouse   12/28/2011

ISBN: 978-1-4685-0595-5 (sc)
ISBN: 978-1-4685-0594-8 (ebk)

Library of Congress Control Number: 2011961107

Printed in the United States of America

Any people depicted in stock imagery provided by Thinkstock are models, and such images are being used for illustrative purposes only.
Certain stock imagery © Thinkstock.

This book is printed on acid-free paper.

Dedicated to
my son and all
those of his generation.
May we have the
wisdom to provide
them with a better
future

I want to thank, my wife and my family for their support. This book would have never seen daylight, without encouragement on their part. Many hours spent by my mother in law, babysitting our son, made it possible to finish this project months sooner.

Preface

Four years after the global financial crisis was unleashed, the western world is still fighting to regain sustained forward momentum. All the classic remedies were already tried, mostly taken out of the Keynesian playbook on how to fight a deep financial recession. The economy's vital signs however all show that North America and Europe are only able to stay alive as long as there is a constant presence of a life support system in place, in the form of private industry and sovereign government bailouts, low interest rates and constant monetary and fiscal stimulus. Given that the current cure does not seem to be entirely effective, and our governments are now exhausted as a result of having to carry the economy through deficit spending, perhaps it is finally time to accept a second opinion on the true cause of the crisis. This book does that, and also offers a proposal for a viable solution, which can help us regain our long term economic health. Most current proposals as solutions for our current economic hardship, center on the same old argument in regards to the share of government as part of the economy, as opposed to the share of the free market, which is a largely useless argument in my view. The sustainability trade tariff is a proposal meant to change the environment in which the market operates, in order to eliminate the flaws that currently treat certain inputs into the production process as free, such as environmental degradation and abuse of basic human rights, thus making it function better. In this way, we can end the current global race to the bottom, before it is too late, if it is not too late already. This way, we can give ourselves a true chance to meet the basic needs of humanity, without having to throw tens or even hundreds of millions more from the developed world into the gutters, like the market did already with about twenty million citizens of the west. Because of the recent rise of Asia, South America, the Middle East, and possibly even Africa eventually, as competitors for scarce, finite resources and for investment capital under the current global trade framework, we are ideally set up for a race to the bottom. Nations are already pitted against each other to offer increasingly obscene concessions to investors. Given the limited demand and potential supply for goods that need to be produced, and the virtually unlimited supply of labor that can now produce most consumer goods, we are left with no choice but to give in to increasingly excessive demands that the owners of capital are in position to make. These demands, they know very well that they can make, given that what they have to offer is very limited and they like it. The reason the west is experiencing such a hard economic time right now, is that we have not fully embraced this race to the bottom yet. Many signs point to this becoming the new reality however, including a surge in the west of the political right, which is vehemently opposed to our current environmental and worker protection policies. The desperate working class is now ready to embrace this revolt against their own long-term well being, because they know that the only way to ensure any long-term future is to first survive the short to medium term, and for that, we need to preserve our means of earning a living. Making more and more obscene concessions to investment capital is the only way they believe that this survival can be achieved, because it is the only option presented to them so far.

A relaxation of our own standards, which is now inevitable, unless we change course, can only lead to a further loosening of already very loose environmental and human protection standards in the developing world. This can only lead to environmental and economic disaster, and it is something I believe to be imminent, rather than an abstract concept about a distant future. The sustainability trade tariff can spare the world and us from the current and expected pain and suffering that generally comes with a collapse of this nature. It is an alternative, which I believe is a last chance for us to save ourselves, given that it is obvious now that we are already experiencing the first symptoms of the coming economic catastrophe, which is likely the last nail in the coffin for western society. Mustering our last resources and global clout, to push for a drastic change in the way we do global trade, which has the potential to transform the global economy, from one being based on consumer demand, to one based on advances in efficiency, product durability as well as improved

2

human rights across the world, is the most sustainable way forward. It is my intention to try to convince as many people as possible, that a standardized global tariff, enforced uniformly based on the ability of nations to produce as cleanly as possible and with as few human rights violations as possible, can re-balance the global economy. It can also provide the market economy with the right price signals to promote resource sustainability.

Book Layout

This book is divided in four parts. Part one contains the introduction and the first two chapters. Chapter 1 is a detailed description of the sustainability trade tariff, which is the central subject of this book. It explains how it would work, if ever implemented as a standardized global trade tariff system, which would eventually replace all current bilateral and multilateral trade agreements. As the discussion in later chapters will move to various aspects of the global market economy, a description of how the tariff I envision will affect these economic institutions, will accompany each theme. Chapter 2 is a brief historical trip through time, which examines the failure and success of humanity in coming up with appropriate answers to challenges of their time and place. The chapter starts with Rome, and its collapse, and then moves on to the disaster from Easter Island. This brief travel through time takes us also to a point, which is often overlooked by historians as a crucial decision moment in 19'Th century Europe, that shaped the modern western world into what it is today, and possibly saved it from a collapse that in hindsight we would now consider premature. A leader, who I greatly admire, named Otto Von Bismarck, founder and first chancellor of unified Germany, managed to transcend his personal conservative ideological constraints, and became the first western leader to propose and introduce the basic social safety net, which in my view provided the necessary social stability needed for a post agrarian society, and the consumer driven economy. Chapter two ends with our return to the present for a brief roundup of the main economic issues we face, and the similarities we can identify between the approach we demonstrated so far, and the one that led

Rome and Easter Island to their eventual disastrous collapse. This is meant to reinforce the need to change direction.

Part two of the book comprises chapters three through five and it mainly focuses on resource scarcity issues. Chapter 3 is very important, because it deals with an important aspect of one of the two main challenges we face that threatens global economic wellbeing, which is increased petroleum scarcity, and the market's inability to deal with it. It also deals with natural gas as a false savior that has been hyped intensively lately. It is in my view the biggest barrier to continued economic expansion. Without this problem, we might be able to deal with the other negative aspects, which are mainly the result of the second challenge, namely the race to the bottom we are setting ourselves up for to compete for investments. The chapter ends with an explanation of the benefit of the sustainability trade tariff in terms of promoting a constant stimulant towards more efficient use of our natural resources, many of which are either finite or too slow to be replenished given our rate of extraction. Chapters four and five deal with the environment and food sustainability in a similar manner as done in chapter three with oil and gas.

Chapters six through nine comprise part three, and they deal with different aspects of the financial and economic systems. An example and/or a discussion of how the sustainability tariff would most likely affect the various financial institutions, is a prominent part of the discussion in each chapter. The main things that I hope that people will come away with from these chapters is an understanding of the financial un-sustainability of the current status quo that got us this far, but is now increasingly a hindrance to moving forward, rather than a positive. The main topics covered in this part relate to; credit, risk management, the stock market, and government finances.

Part 4 is an analysis of culture as the driver of the economy and policy. It emphasizes the importance of having a set of values in place, which helps the collective adapt to current and future circumstances. This part comprises chapters ten through twelve. Chapter 10 is a look at an example of the role that culture played in the varying degrees of success that former communist countries in Eastern Europe had in adapting to the global market economy. The reason that I chose to use people and events from the periphery of western culture is that it should be easier for most to remain impartial, and therefore capture the essence of the lesson we can learn from their recent economic history. Chapter 11 deals with our own cultural shortcomings given present and likely future circumstances. The final chapter of the book is dedicated to a contemplation of western life in the absence of change and the best way for an individual to stand a chance at relative wellbeing in the face of drastic changes to our way of life, which is possibly imminent, given many current signs that point to that being the case.

Most topics in this book are covered in a consumer friendly manner, meant to help those lacking a necessary educational background in economics, cultural anthropology, or history to grasp the essence of the main issues. References to basic economic theoretical models are generally accompanied by easy to understand real life examples that should help most people visualize the concept of the theory as it relates to real economic circumstances. An educational background matching the topics covered here is not necessary. The curiosity and concern for these issues will suffice as the necessary tools to navigate through the pages and chapters, which I hope will bring those who read them, fresh perspective on the problems we face and the solutions we need.

Part One

Introduction

Who says that good teachers cannot make a difference?

The first time I was presented with a glimpse into some of the potential problems facing our society, which I now think we should take very seriously, I was most definitely not the right audience for such a message. I was a high school senior, and the glimpse was offered by my history teacher, who handed out an article about this issue now known as peak oil. The article rightly stated that it is not an issue of running out of crude oil; it is rather, an issue of geological constraints, which at some point will make it impossible for us to continue increasing production of this finite resource. The year they gave as the approximate time that they expected this to happen was 2005. Now that I look back, I realize the worrying fact that the article was technically, in part correct, because it just so happens that the IEA (International Energy Agency) admitted in its 2010 report, that conventional crude oil has peaked, likely forever, in 2006 according to them[1]. Given that the article was written in 1996, while society only started to pay attention to the issue of resource scarcities a few years ago, it is a testament to our lack of ability as a society to preempt our challenges in due time. More importantly, I realize the difficulty that we will have dealing with such a problem given that, even though I was given a chance to learn about it, initially I did not understand it. I expect many others to fail most likely to comprehend the importance of this issue, as well as many others in the absence of further investigation into the matter. Furthermore, there is a real disconnect between what people receive as important information from mainstream media, and what they should be receiving, because let us face it, even though an announcement by the IEA, such as the

6

one made in the fall of 2010, affects everyone, almost no one ever heard about this.

I think back to that day, when a teacher tried to do his small part to make a difference and I realize with sadness in my heart that we are nowhere near as involved in important issues that affect us. In a democracy, we are expected to give a verdict on just such issues on a regular basis at the polling stations. Of course, many prefer things to be this way, because it certainly avoids our elites having to answer hard questions about our present and future predicaments. There are many stakes in current trends, which famous author Jared Diamond identified in his book "*Collapse*" as the main reason we tend to find it hard to change direction from a path of self-destruction. I hope we will not fit that description when the history books will be written about us. I make the optimist assumption here that history books will still be written generations later.

My history teacher tried to make a difference. He tried to get at least a few of his students to think. If I was to venture a guess, I would have to say that most of my classmates did not even bother to read the article, since it was not compulsory reading. Even though I did read it, there was not much of an impact initially. How could there be when there were so many other things that preoccupy a high school senior's mind? The article correctly stated that it was not an issue of running out, but of not being able to increase production, and then eventually production declining relatively gently. I figured then wrongly, that it was no big deal, because it only meant that we will all have to drive a little less, which I suspect would be the initial reaction of many who are unfamiliar with the subject, and are presented with these facts for the very first time. Despite the fact that the article made little impact on me initially, because I in fact forgot about it completely until I came across this issue years later, it helped me focus my thoughts towards a very specific question that has become somewhat of a taboo to raise. It is not convenient for us to talk about it, because it flies in the face of our society's belief that our ingenuity conquers all. The question of course is whether this system of ours is sustainable? It is possible that I would have never asked myself that question if it wouldn't have been for that initial exposure to the issue courtesy of a high school history teacher. Now I find myself putting this question to others.

Reading an article handed out by a high school teacher, or getting a formal education in economics on their own, did not provide the necessary awareness of the vulnerabilities and flaws of our system. The necessary skepticism needed to ask the right questions, and seek for possible answers came from my life experience. There is nothing like experiencing the collapse of a system that seems solid and unshakable on the surface to make one aware that things are not always, what they seem. I gained this valuable life lesson the hard way, as a child growing up in communist Romania. Just a few years prior to the implosion of the communist system in Eastern Europe, the regime seemed poised to survive indefinitely. Few people would have believed the message that the system was on its deathbed then, because the regime was in full control. Yet, very suddenly and unexpectedly from a commoner's point of view, it crashed with a fury, unleashing more than a decade of chaos for hundreds of millions living in the region, despite the stabilizing effect of having a prosperous world to lean on and depend on for investment and other economic activities.

After the initial euphoria felt due to the promise of freedom and expectations of western style prosperity, came the realization that nothing can be taken on faith or for granted in this life. Expectations of capitalism induced prosperity gave way to the realization that we were at the bottom of the pecking order, and it was very hard to achieve a successful emulation of West European and American prosperity, and most people there still do not understand fully, why that is the case. As I watched the argument take place in regards to our own headwinds that we are experiencing, it reminds me of the same difficulties that the place I came from had with finding their bearings. The East Europeans had problems stemming from their own cultural issues, our problems stem from our particular cultural dysfunction. We have a society mainly dominated by the very politically active left and right wings. They both have very entrenched views of things, making it impossible to introduce new concepts to them, given that as soon as any aspect of a new idea contradicts or disagrees with the set of values they already hold on to, they tend to distance themselves. Thus, any new idea that ever makes it on our cultural stage is automatically handicapped by the need to adhere to the set of ideals that either the right or the left holds to be their set of beliefs. We also have the center, which is largely disinterested at this point in economic issues, because they tend to be oblivious to the fact that we have serious problems that will have serious consequences, until it becomes too late to do anything about it. Yet we seem to take it for granted that we have a society that can still manage to identify and tackle new problems, despite the current inability to allow for new ideas and concepts.

We take far too many things for granted, perhaps as foolishly as East Europeans did two decades ago. We take for granted that there will always be plenty of resources on this planet to sustain our current course. If a resource does become too depleted to continue to provide us with its benefits, economists argue that there are always comparable substitutes waiting in the wing to take the place of the depleted resource. Many people also take for granted that there is no amount of environmental damage that can possibly be done by us, which will ever cause enough of a disruption to our way of life. That means that we can go on forever, polluting the air, waters, soil etc, without suffering eventual serious consequences, or put another way, we believe that the net benefit outweighs the net loss. When it becomes harder and harder to deny that any of these above mentioned issues pose a real threat, we go to the last line of defense for our current system. We take for granted that any of these problems can be solved by technology, unleashed by the power of the markets, which like an invisible hand, provides whenever a need is detected. We are therefore living in the most perfectly efficient system ever devised.

The current western living standards are most definitely being taken for granted. It was not long ago that the Bush administration proclaimed "the US way of life is non-negotiable". The market however is doing just that, through its recent transfer of wealth from the developed world to the developing one, and there does not seem too be much that our elites can do about it, nor is there a clear indication that it is in their interest to do something about this. With increased competition coming from developing countries with lower wages, and lower environmental and human protection standards, the western economies are now looking increasingly shaky. Yet we take it for granted that things such as an increase in food prices due to global population growth, ethanol production, combined with limited sources of soil and water to grow more food, will always remain a thing that the poverty-stricken populations of places like Bangladesh or Vietnam have to worry about. We are the lucky citizens of this planet who can always absorb a price increase in basic goods, because we have the buying power to do so. As such, we support the production of ethanol and other bio-fuels out of the global food supply, because the two billion or so people who are currently malnourished globally will never include more than a handful of people who hail from the west among their ranks. With increased pressure to compete globally with the low paid, but increasingly well-educated and well-trained workers of the developing world, can we really take it for granted that we will not end up having a growing segment of our population looking on with an empty stomach, while the corn is being shipped to ethanol plants?

There is currently no question of the fact that the world's living standards are converging as a result of globalization. The challenge we are facing therefore is not only having to compete with the rest of the world, it is also making sure that convergence will happen in circumstances that will allow the world to achieve this convergence of global living standards at a level that can still provide us with a decent standard of living. We should now admit however, that it is impossible for us to maintain the current standards of living enjoyed in the west as we measure it currently. We should therefore refrain from taking it for granted that we will continue living like this. With many of our crucial resources stretched to the limit as it is, the imperative is to make sure that all resources are deployed to achieve the maximum consumer satisfaction when the resource is consumed. As we are becoming a more interdependent global community, we should take care to make sure that we are achieving this maximum consumer satisfaction on a global scale. This is where I take issue with the assumption that the unguided invisible hand can best achieve this. There is no evidence of that when we look back on how the resources have been deployed so far, when the invisible hand of the market was given free reign to allocate certain resources. Government intervention by guiding the market, through their policies, has so far proven to be the more effective tool to deal with vital resource scarcities in the present or for the future.

The worst example of a segment of people within our society who take things for granted, I saved for last. There are many people who do see that we cannot take it for granted that we will solve our increasingly grave problems through markets and innovation alone. Their general response however saddens and baffles me at the same time. The people I have in mind are the ones who see the problems, but rely on people voluntarily giving up their short to medium term potential gains in order to keep from perpetuating these problems as their proposed solution to our problems. They expect individuals and governments to do this in the name of the people, who surely will demand it, if the true horror of the consequences of our ways would only be revealed to them.

During the bloody revolution of December 1989 in Romania, which finally toppled Ceausescu's brutal regime, there were a few stories of soldiers and law enforcement officers being ordered to open fire on protestors on the streets. Faced with the possibility of being executed, some have subsequently admitted to closing their eyes and shooting. I personally admire those few who admitted as much, although I never met such an individual personally. The western workers, as well as their less affluent counterparts from the developing world, faced with the choice of possibly losing their job in favor of stopping the environmental degradation we are inflicting on the planet are likely to close their eyes (actually their minds), and continue on just as the soldiers did.

What the idealists do not understand is that it is not a matter of people not knowing what we are doing to the planet; therefore all we need is more education about the issues as a solution. It is a matter of being stuck in a situation where the citizens of the world are asked to choose whether their governments decide to protect the global environment, at the cost of losing economic opportunities, in favor of those who do not care to protect it. Many people reject the very concepts that environmentalists and others talk about, because of the fear they have in regards to the possible economic ramifications of one's country moving aggressively to combat unsustainable economic practices, while many other countries might actually move in the opposite direction in order to benefit. Therefore, we close our eyes and do what we have to do. If the parameters within which we operate remain, so will the problems. In fact, they may intensify as the competition for providing the masses with work also intensifies.

The failure of the people within our society who correctly see the path of humanity as a flawed one, due to its unsustainable path is in part due to their timidity in challenging the wisdom of the market. Given that the second worst thing that one can be called in western society is a communist, it is understandable why people shy away from making a logical challenge to Adam Smith's theoretical work. As a result, they focus instead on their idealistic belief that the masses can be mobilized locally to push for sustainable development, which so far has produced many unremarkable results, which currently make absolutely no difference in the greater scheme of things.

What these people do not realize is that there can be a challenge made to market economic theory, without referring to Marxist views, and without having to ask people to make uncomfortable decisions that asks them to choose between deferring economic competitiveness to others in favor of being a good global citizen. The challenge can be made based on pointing out the failures already on our historical record, which clearly show that the market cannot be relied on, to make appropriate and beneficial directional decisions in every instance. The alternative to demanding that people make decisions on giving up economic advantages in favor of the greater good is to give the market the opportunity to operate within new parameters set up to give the global economy the right price signals needed to promote the sustainable path. I am frankly astonished that this is not already the predominant message of the sustainability crusaders. They need to finally grow up as a movement and adopt realistic ideas and solutions.

Flawed logic

The main problem we are facing in the present, and what is also obstructing any attempts to adapt to future challenges is that we have a market economy, based on expanding credit as the lifeblood that keeps it going. There is nothing wrong with that model of economic organization, except for the fact that we are endowed with a finite planet. We as a global culture, so far failed to give the market the appropriate parameters within which it can operate in a manner that considers this very important fact. We failed to price in our environmental footprint.

A credit based economy needs constant long-term, infinite expansion to be successful and that means that the financial system and the physical world are on an inevitable collision path. The finite world is a fact that basic economic theory is based on. It is the first thing that students are told when opening my first year macroeconomic textbook, which starts by explaining economics as a social science with an important role to play in our organization of the production and distribution of goods available. "Economics: it is the social science concerned with the efficient use of scarce resources to obtain the maximum satisfaction of society's unlimited wants"[2]. The problem I have with the economist establishment today is that they assume that the market, given free reign, is the most efficient way to exploit the earth's resources, in a way that will maximize our utility and satisfaction as the subject states to aim to do. Somehow, it seems they expect the magic of finance to defy the laws of physics, because as the economics manual states, resources are finite, and we should add to that the fact that many are non-renewable and not easily substituted, while we expect to achieve infinite growth, in the constant struggle to satisfy infinite wants. I am surprised at how flawed economic models treat the subject that is in fact the foundation of economic theory.

The historian instinct in me says that we should examine the past, because we now have a good chunk of past data derived from modern economic activity, which we can compare to the present situation. We can examine whether the market was successful in allocating the world's resources properly within the modern economy, as most economists suggest that it can. The trick is to reframe the question of appropriate allocation of resources to include a longer period than most economic models allow for. In other words, we should ask whether the resource allocations of the 40's, 50's, 60's, 70's, 80's, 90's and the first decade of the new millennia was the best for us consumers living then, as well as today, and tomorrow. That is a question I seldom see being asked in economic circles, but I think it is a question that is very important given that even the first year introductory textbook in macroeconomics tells us the obvious fact, that resources are finite, which I cannot stress enough. We can also examine the response of the market once a problem was identified, such as global climate change, or oil resource limits, and thus we can see the results of our expectations of the market and technology derived from our ingenuity, teaming up to solve these issues and pre-empt their consequences.

Most economists and the models they created are concerned with measuring the wellbeing of the people living in the 50's for instance, in relation to how they allocated resources available to them during that decade. Given that the models were set up this way, the obvious concluding result is as follows: They built many houses, and cars, which they consumed happily. They were much happier driving a car rather than taking public transport, and so were the generations of the next few decades, therefore they reached a maximum utility and satisfaction out of the resources they had at their disposal back then. Therefore, the theory goes, we should also reach the maximum utility and consumer satisfaction out of the resources that are available to us in the present. The generation of my newborn son should also strive to reach the maximum utility given what will be left to them, and so on. We have to realize however that in reading this analysis, we have to keep in mind that just because this is all that economic models are able to tell us, it does not mean that this is the correct picture.

In essence, the flaw I see is that economists fail to consider our collective utility and satisfaction over a longer series of generations. For instance, if we were to take our economic history from 1945, when the Second World War ended, until 2011, will we be able to say that we used up the global resources to the most efficient extent through giving the market the lead in allocating these resources? Furthermore, can we claim with a straight face, that it will be beneficial to the generations living in 2045, in other words, a hundred years after the beginning of the era, where I consider that the modern economy that most of us are familiar with began, with the end of the Second Great War? It is looking more and more like the hundred year period in question is starting to be shaped like a tale of two halves. One half that has reached its peak sometime between 2000 and 2010, and then we have the second part to deal with, which is looking like it is on the verge of taking our average collective utility and satisfaction way down, given what is likely in store for us.

Trying to measure average collective utility over a century's timeframe seems like a very difficult task especially given that 35 years of the period I chose have not even happened yet; therefore, we have to rely on projections. There are many smaller scale examples however, that already happened, which might give us a guide to what we should expect from the market planning of our economy. Take the British petroleum exploration and production history for instance. They discovered massive amounts of oil and gas in the 1970's and made the decision to allow the market to exploit the resource according to what the invisible hand of the market saw fit. Britain ramped up petroleum and gas production, until it became a net exporter during a short period between the late 90's and early 2000's. It had to start importing petroleum about six years ago, as production peaked and then started declining sharply, except now they are doing it at a very different average price than when they were exporting. In fact, the average import price is about 400% higher than the export price they were fetching for their petroleum on average. So here, we have a clear example of the market making a decision that was not in any shape or form in the interest of the British people, or its economy. The net imports at this higher price are starting to act as a drag on their GDP growth, which is out of proportion compared to the net increase in GDP that the exports provided, given the comparatively cheaper price. Compared to what would have been the optimum production schedule, that would have maximized the net benefit to the British economy, the market missed the mark sharply. Clearly, the correct decision for the British people would have been resource nationalism.

Sticking with petroleum, which is a very important resource to the global economy, we can ask the same question about how we used this resource so far, and how is our net benefit from it looking if we were to look out until 2045, from the starting point I chose of 1945. Once again, I have no doubt that people in past decades enjoyed burning the stuff in comfortable cars without worrying too much about any possible consequences to future generations, while driving their hour long commutes from their suburbs to their place of employment in cars that were far larger than necessary. We all enjoyed flying to vacation destinations or for other purposes as a great perk of living in our seemingly wondrous age. Just a hundred years ago, our ancestors on average only ever travelled as far as roughly 20 kilometers from their birthplace. Now the average westerner measures that distance in thousands of kilometers. The black fuel was readily available for most of the period except for two brief disruptions during political conflicts in the Middle East. They used up the easy to get to, and easy to refine resources first, and they used it up with great appetite, because the market made it available through its technological innovation very cheap compared to what we have to pay now, and likely in the future.

I wonder how an economics PhD would justify the righteousness of having burned hundreds of billions of barrels more than was absolutely necessary in past decades. Now we struggle to produce liquid fuel out of the global food supply to add a billion barrel's per year worth (less than 1.5% of total liquids) of extra energy to our otherwise already constrained transportation system. We do this while nearly two billion people on this planet are suffering a certain degree of nutritional inadequacy. Can we even dare to compare the consumer satisfaction derived from past and present generations riding in a bigger than necessary car, to that of a person receiving adequate nutrition, which satisfies the ultimate consumer need, which is the one that prolongs life? This is just one example of the beginning of the second part of the story of our modern global economy. The market, if left unguided on a global scale, will make many more such decisions in the years and decades to come, and this time, the poor of the developing world will not be the only ones adversely affected. The increase in poverty and misery that we have witnessed in the west recently, is only a small taste of what in fact awaits us if we fail to change. Remember that we live in a globalizing, and therefore converging world, therefore misery is likely to be something we will increasingly share in with everyone else on this planet.

Taking stock of our inheritance

The market cannot provide the cheap petroleum anymore, but it left us with three defining aspects of our economy as our inheritance, because of decades of production and consumption of this finite resource. We inherited the infrastructure that is completely incompatible with our current needs, because it is based on the consumption of cheap oil. We inherited as a result of our recent prosperity, the collective knowledge that humanity gained from the past decades of luxury, which is the only good thing that is being passed on, which is what we are putting our hope in to fix our problems. We also inherited the left over reserves of petroleum, which are now increasingly made up of hard to get to, and in many cases very environmentally damaging resources that we can exploit for our needs. Here, the market supporters argue that this in fact shows that the markets work, because as prices spiked, new resources came online. Technological innovation, and capital allocation, stimulated by the market's signal for a need is providing us with new resources, as the old ones dwindle. The cost in energy, monetary measures as well as in non-monetary measures such as the loss of satisfaction to us, due to increased environmental damage is scarcely brought into this conversation. A wounded environment should perhaps be counted as a fourth aspect, because after all, the petroleum driven economy was and still is in large part responsible for creating the heightened level of economic activity that led to so much environmental degradation. We do have to be fair however and acknowledge the role it had also in creating a prosperous society that finally found the extra time and energy to also worry about environmental issues.

The technological know how, which we inherited from past behavior of the market during the cheap oil era is the main source of optimism for most who claim that we are and will be alright, because the market will continue to take care of business. It is true that technological advances that we are able to achieve are helping with the situation, and the market is responsible for that, because the price signal sent by the market is what mobilized increased investment in exploiting harder to get to resources such as ultra deep offshore fields, and Canadian oil sands. The market also signaled the car manufacturers to ramp up fuel-efficient technologies that cut down on our gasoline and diesel consumption per capita. Unfortunately, for the market balance, the market has also signaled the duplication of our lifestyle to the developing world, and they are now duplicating our infrastructure and car culture, which more than offsets current fuel efficiency inroads made by technology. They are also new to this game, so their economies are automatically adapting to the high current prices that we are in fact finding harder to cope with, despite us being wealthier. We are now more than half a decade into abnormally high prices of oil by historical standards, and we are also half a decade past peak production of conventional crude according to the estimates of the official International Energy Agency (IEA). Despite that, there is still a clear trend upward for demand for crude, which now seems to be tempered by only one possible economic force, which is demand destruction, leading to recessions. The role of technology in saving us seems to be completely absent as we are observing a second commodity price spike in less than three years.

The infrastructure we inherited both physical and financial is completely unsuited to high, volatile oil prices, and possibly soon to be declining global supplies. Here we have perhaps the biggest and clearest failure of the market driven economy. This is especially evident if one is to compare infrastructure in the US and Canada, where they tried to allow giving the market as much free reign as possible, with the EU, where they consciously influenced the transport and energy infrastructure evolution by applying penalties through taxes for inefficient technologies. This in effect created a cultural shift that I could not get over when I went to visit Europe for the first time in 2005 after living in Canada for 13 years. While people in Canada and also in the US like to boast about horse power under their hood, Europeans boast about how far they can go on a tank of gas, and generally view those who buy an inefficient car as rather silly. In Europe, an engine capacity larger than 2.0 is seen as excessively big, and automakers have adjusted to having to provide fuel efficient cars that also have some performance capabilities. Aside from more efficient engine technology, this cultural shift also created more demand for public transport by rail, or bus. I was amazed at the level of service public transport provides in places like Germany, or Hungary, where I spent lots of time during my trip. Even in relatively small towns like Zalaegerszeg in Hungary, with a population of only roughly 70,000 inhabitants, living in a still developing economy, bus services were so fine-tuned that upon arrival in town by rail, one can catch three different bus routes, all three buses waiting to be boarded as you exit the train station. That compared to most similar sized towns in the US or Canada is quite remarkable. This culture and infrastructure did not happen on its own however. Very high fuel taxes signaled the market to provide for this, and so it did.

The economic model infrastructure we inherited is now increasingly in favor of building a disposable economy. What I mean by that, is that product durability has become less valued as a feature of marketable products than it used to be. Cheaper, less durable goods are the new trend and it basically creates a situation where our basic needs are met with an increase in resource exploitation intensity. If a pair of shoes lasted ten years for instance, a few decades ago, even if we are now twice as fuel efficient at producing and transporting shoes to the market, it will still mean that we will need to expend more fuel to provide shoes to a consumer, if shoes last only one year on average. The problem is that durability kills consumer demand, while our economy is a consumer demand driven one. Durability also tends to kill innovation, because technological change, whether in consumer products, or physical capital needed by business and governments can only happen at the speed we witnessed in past decades, if products can be assumed to have a lower lifespan. The only way we can restrain this efficiency killer that threatens to morph our economy into one that will eventually meet the basic needs of fewer and fewer members of our global village, is if we give the market an incentive to give the durable economy some competing power again.

In light of the fact that the IEA has now finally admitted in its 2010 report that conventional crude petroleum has likely hit its all time peak in 2006, never to be surpassed in all likelihood ever again, the issue of our infrastructural inheritance should be of major concern. Most people, who looked at this issue, seem to think that preparation for the event when petroleum production will reach a maximum level should have started at least three decades ago. Given that conventional petroleum has peaked, a peak in all liquid fuels cannot be far behind given that conventional crude makes up about 80% of worldwide liquid fuels supply. Many consider that Europe, which consumes only half as much petroleum per capita as North Americans do, is decades behind the optimum level of preparedness. North Americans are in turn decades behind Europe, therefore I think it is now safe to call this aspect of free market economic planning a complete failure, given that it is now obvious that the better prepared economy infrastructure wise is the one that experienced government tampering with people's tastes through its tax regime.

An important point that I want to push home about this important issue, include the misrepresentation of the problem as something that the markets can fix through encouraging the invention and deployment of new technologies. On the efficiency side, I should point out that when the prices at the pump spike, creating demand for fuel-efficient cars, it is generally already too late to deploy the new technology. In 2009, US car sales were only 2/3 of pre crisis levels, and the cars bought were not much more fuel efficient than the old ones that they were displacing from US roads, because by then oil prices plunged by about 75% from their peak. In other words, the price spike has already done the economic damage, including to the market for the very resource that spiked in price to begin with, before the market could react to change consumer preferences. The other important point that needs to be made is that infrastructure investment is unlikely to be high on people's agendas in the west, when their governments are already running 10% yearly budget deficits in order to keep things afloat, due to market failures. Undertaking the construction of new, fuel efficient infrastructure is generally something that should have started decades ago, and as we can already tell, there was simply no market signal in the 70's, or 80's to start doing that, without government intervention to make it happen. The main fly in the ointment in my view, is the relatively low demand elasticity that petroleum as a product has in our economy, which makes market direction for its availability a flawed tool to manage its long-term consumption.

I want to dispel strongly the myth that the market will save us through its efficient introduction of new wander technologies in transport and exploration for resources, because in the current environment at least, it is unlikely to happen. The technology to build a more fuel efficient society has been available, the big difference in fuel efficiency between the US and Europe is proof of that. Americans lack the infrastructure, because they did not bother to create a more expensive environment for fuel consumption; therefore, we currently see a society unable to cope with prices that even at their highest levels, did not come even close to matching the high prices in Europe during normal times.

On the issue of our left over inheritance of fossil fuels and other mineral resources, it is important to recognize some undeniable facts. Most of what is left over has a much lower energy return on production inputs, such as energy and capital expenditures. It takes the equivalent of one barrel of oil to produce roughly 5 barrels of synthetic crude form the Canadian oil sands. In comparison with some of the better quality fields around the world that are now running dry, many fields yielded as much as 100 barrels of petroleum for every barrel of oil invested into extraction. Some liquid fuels have an even lower yield, such as corn ethanol, where the rate of increase on fuel invested is only two to one. It is important to realize that parallel with all the wonderful technologies that are being deployed, which constantly improve efficiency, we have increased demand coming for these resources, from the production process of the resources themselves. That, combined with increased demand coming from developing nations, who currently use far less fossil fuels per capita than we do, makes it impossible to achieve economic growth without the continued expansion of oil production rates, unless we change the way we do business. As a percentage of the world's population, the developing world makes up over three quarters of the total, and most economies are currently increasing average yearly oil demand by about 5%. Without a change of direction on a global scale, it is obvious that we are headed for major disaster one way or another.

The Environment & The "global village"

If the above-mentioned trends do not prove to be enough of a reason to be convinced that we need to change the way we do things, environmental issues, if we can avoid sweeping them under the rug, should be a strong enough argument to advocate a course change. Most arguments of late have centered on climate change related to atmospheric discharge coming from our industrial base, as well as from our transport systems. The issue has been acknowledged for three decades now, and most scientists specialized in studies related to climate around the world are in agreement that climate change is most likely happening and we are the most likely contributor to this change. Many interested parties who wanted to delay changes to status quo policies, launched a strong propaganda campaign, but there is at least in my view no doubt that we are creating a greenhouse effect through increasing the ratio of carbon-based particles in the atmosphere. Some political will was found in some places to push for action, but in the end, the power of persuasion of great potential profits from the abuse of a public good such as the planet's climate, proved too powerful to resist for most major economic players that have the power to affect things.

The ill-fated Kyoto agreement is proof of our shortcomings as a global community when faced with a global problem, if we have to rely on goodwill and voluntary sacrifice as the engine of change. There may be some controversy about the effects of our emissions into the atmosphere on our climate, but one thing that we cannot deny any longer is that in the absence of an economic meltdown hitting worldwide, we are not likely to correct our current behavior in the present economic climate. The market in this case, cannot react in any way to this problem on its own, because there is no price signal to demand technologies that are cleaner, without government intervention. Governments around the world are being blackmailed into not addressing this problem by industries that do not care to deal with a more stringent, emissions restricting environment. An increasing number of politicians advocate a race to the bottom by advocating a further deregulation of emissions standards in their respective countries or administrative territories in the name of attracting investment.

The environmental picture is likely to get worse, if nothing is done. Politically, it is increasingly becoming more and more acceptable to join into a race to the bottom in environmental protection norms. It is always the classical jobs versus environmental protection that is framed as the only two options we have in trading them off against each other. We westerners are being punished for caring about the environment in our backyard and the global situation overall by profit maximizing companies, who do what is in their nature to do, which is to try to maximize profits. If you have any doubts about the political trend of deregulating environmental concerns, just look at the attitude taken by many US politicians in regards to the Gulf oil spill in 2010, or the 2005 decision on the part of the US federal government to exempt the shale gas industry that the US is increasingly dependent on from EPA standards. Little by little, concession after concession, we are increasingly undermining our own well-being through our lack of ability and discipline in dealing with this race to offer increasingly deregulated playing fields for multinational corporations to play in.

It is very hard to defend politically, a tough environmental policy aimed at protecting our local and global environment. Whether it is climate change, loss of natural habitat or water and soil pollution, the side effects are not always as obvious as a policy that may lead to decreased job availability in favor of environmental protection. Reducing greenhouse gases is especially hard to stomach given that others are more than offsetting what some of our politicians are striving to accomplish through local policies, while potential climate change is a global problem, not a local one. The effects of polluting our environment may include increased sickness due to poisoning, lower global food production, increased natural disasters, such as flooding and hurricanes that may cause increased structural damage. All these are things that affect our lives in a negative way, and will likely get worse given current trends. The economic losses in the long term may even outweigh the benefits of tearing up current regulations, but there is simply no other option available, because any attempt to protect the environment through local regulation, causes that region to suffer severe economic hardships, while simultaneously shifting economic activities to less stringent environments. With the human capacity to harm our habitat increasing, it seems like a mad decision to continue on the way we do, yet this is exactly what most elites are proposing.

1

Implementing a solution to the broken system

Many critics of people who criticize the status quo, point out that while many are quick to criticize, few are willing to put forward a viable alternative. If we are to look at most people ranging from environmentalists, to peak oilers who made a perfectly good case for their point of view in the past, few of them actually proposed a solution. Most simply engage in a rant on the reasons we have to change our behavior, or face the consequences of our misguided ways. As to any practical suggestions on how we would make that change in practical terms? Perhaps collective goodwill is a good place to put our hopes in if you listen to most of their opinion forming leaders. I believe that there can be many alternatives as long as we are willing to explore the possibilities, but we have to be realistic about chances for the road to implementation to succeed. We need to have an educated electorate that is actually in tune with what is happening, and somewhat familiar with possible alternatives. Finally, we need to get rid of the current system that automatically places our elected leaders in the indirect employment of special interests, instead of our employment, if we hope to actually change something. These are all good first steps that make any change possible, but then there also needs to be a viable plan ready for implementation.

Given the problems we will identify here, my conclusion is that the only way to redress the problems is through modifying the way we trade on a global scale. It has to be compulsive, not like the failed international initiatives in the past, relying on goodwill, such as Kyoto. Trade can create many positive incentives if properly structured. That is not how it works in its current form unfortunately, because the west has in the past made many mistakes when negotiating trade agreements. These agreements were good for western corporations and for developing world governments, but they are also detrimental to the overall advancement of basic human rights, and environmental protection. The agreements we have in place now allow companies to ship out any job that is not location dependent to places with less stringent environmental rules, and not only cheaper, but also more deprived of basic rights employees. The fact that we tolerate this automatically makes being a bad global citizen, a good strategy for development through attracting investment. The absurd part in all of this is that our leadership saw no danger in allowing free flowing trade, without encouraging the free flow of our standards for basic environmental and human protection. They ditched the crusade for the spread of our standards, without considering the repercussions of transferring production technology to countries that have no inclination of being decent global citizens. They did not consider the race to the bottom that would be unleashed in environmental and labor deregulation. Nor did they stop to think what would happen to the western worker, who is set up to compete against impossible odds, unless his/her job is location dependent.

It seems that our politicians misjudged to even a greater extent than the exodus of manufacturing jobs, the strain created on global resources by the addition of hundreds of millions of new consumers across the world. Much of our vital resource capacity is being stretched. There is very little room left for denial on this one. In 2007-2008, besides the housing and financial crisis, which everyone talks about, there was also a food crisis, which led to rioting in many countries. Together with the rise in the price of petroleum to almost $150 a barrel, this inflationary trend also affected many of the western consumers who lived on a tight budget already, and had a hard time dealing with the higher price of food and fuel. Unfortunately, the topic of actual resource shortages and their effect on the economy is considered a bit of a taboo subject, therefore very little was discussed in regards to what happened during that period, unless everyone is willing to blame it on speculators, rather than actual supply constraints.

As we ended the year 2010, even before we can say that the world economy is back on solid footing, we are already faced with oil prices that are close to breaching the $100 average price, and the global food price index has already made a fresh record high. According to the UN, in December 2010, the world food price index

25

averaged 214.7, which is higher than the previous peak in June 2008, which reached 213.5, and was the cause of protests and food riots from Mexico to Egypt. Barring another recession, which will likely depress prices as it did in 2008, we are likely to see the price of these vital resources spike again, only to be stopped when demand destruction starts to occur, as a large segment of the population is priced out either through the price itself, or indirectly through job loss.

Given these facts, a trade system that stops rewarding the consumer based economy and starts rewarding the efficiency based economy is crucial to our continued stability. Our western governments cannot continue to step in and bail out the economy, and double its structural deficits every time a recession hits as some governments have done in order to temporarily spare us from having to experience the true nature of our position as a result of the last two recessions. The developing world on the other hand is in danger of suffering great consequences if food prices for instance become increasingly volatile, as their low wage population is far more exposed to changes in the price of food than we are now. In short, we have to move away from an economic system that rewards the exploitation intensity of our resources and environment if we are to survive, without witnessing eventual collapse. Avoiding this scenario is a long shot the way I see it, but I believe that it is imperative that we start a conversation on possible alternatives as soon as possible if we are to have a chance at all to change course.

In the interest of doing a small part in igniting a conversation about realistic alternatives to the current accepted, but lately increasingly obviously flawed economic system, I propose that we change the way we do trade as a first and best step towards global economic sustainability. As I already mentioned in the introduction, the sustainability tariff, should replace all current trade agreements world wide, and become an internationally implemented standardized tariff system, which would penalize unsustainable development and the exploitation and abuse of the citizens of nations. I recognize that this at first seems outlandish, unachievable and unworkable. I however intend to show that it is at the very least more likely to succeed than previous attempts at solving major global problems, because once the system were to be in place, there are numerous countries that would see advantages in this system of trade. As romantic as it may be to view humanity through the politically correct notion, that political will is likely to cause people to give up voluntarily certain advantages, I believe that incentives and disincentives are the only drivers towards the betterment of humankind. I should know, because I was born in a system that tried to implement a worker's utopia, and it turned out to cause complete stagnation, and cultural de-evolution, mainly by removing an individual's profit seeking as a motive for innovation.

What this tariff would look like, and what are the benefits?

The first step is to eliminate all previous trade agreements and regulations. This has to include the WTO, which is a failure in my view, because it is in part responsible for the huge trade imbalances created. All free trade agreements would have to go as well. Embargoes are not very helpful in helping implement the new system either, but in the new trading framework as I shall explain, they would become obsolete in most cases anyway. With a clean slate in place, we can then finally implement the new system to govern trade, and thus provide the right incentives for societies around the world to do the right thing by their own members and to all members of the "global village" as well.

Tariffs should no longer be the subject of bilateral, or multi-lateral agreements, but the subject of how each country measures up against a standardized benchmark that evaluates how citizens and the environment are impacted by a country's policies and economic activities. This benchmark can be set up in the form of a point deductions system, where every country is evaluated based on a measure of how much pollution, environmental and human degradation is caused per unit of GDP produced by the respective economy. The importance of setting it up as a measure of GDP will become clear later as I work through the effects it would have through the global economy.

In situations that make it necessary for the maintenance of economic and political stability, existing trade agreements should be maintained. One such obvious example is the European Union.

The only condition for it should be that all EU members agree to be evaluated collectively for being assigned a tariff. In this particular case, they can effectively figure as one country. I do not foresee too many countries wanting to do the same, because they risk paying for irresponsibility on the part of others, therefore current treaties such as the NAFTA would likely end up getting shelved. The EU is a special case because they have the political and administrative capacity to enforce environmental standards and regulations that all EU members have to follow.

The next thing that needs to be agreement on is the maximum level of tariff imposed. This is something that can be changed if there is a new collective agreement in place. Personally, I believe that a maximum tariff does not have to exceed 200%. This tariff level would ideally never have to be applied, because hopefully all governments should be wise enough to avoid such a scenario, when implementing policies that might affect their tariff rating. The minimum tariff would of course be 0%, and ideally, one nation, with no deductions in points would achieve this, at which time, the points deduction process should be made more stringent. Arguments can be made for and against a higher or lower maximum level of tariff imposed on a nation, but the important thing is to implement it in a way that is not ad-hoc, but a true reflection of a measure of how a country does in the field of sustainability and respect for human rights and dignity.

If the maximum level of trade tariff that could be imposed is 200%, for simplicity's sake, the total number of points that a country starts of on should be 200. Every point deducted would result in a 1% increase in tariff on all goods exported from that country, with no exceptions. For instance, if Germany were to be deducted a total of 20 points, its exported goods would be subject to a 20% tariff upon entering any other country. These points would be assigned to two major categories. One would be sustainability and the other would be human rights. The weight of these two categories should be even in my view, but again opinions may wary on this as well.

Environmental sustainability should include and be subdivided into measures of how much air pollution, de-foresting, wildlife habitat endangerment, water and soil pollution, over-fishing of domestic and international waters, and a few other measures as a proportion of GDP is being done. In other words, if a zero point deduction per unit of GDP would require less than a ton of emissions per unit of GDP, and a country surpasses that, it should be deducted points accordingly, in proportion to the magnitude of the lack of adherence. In the case of de-forestation rates, the benchmark should be zero, and if deforestation occurs from year to year, points should be deducted accordingly. In the case of re-forestation, or reclaiming of previously polluted places, bonus points should be awarded, making up for points lost due to deficiencies elsewhere.

The human rights part of the tariff should include freedom of speech, and expression. It should also include a measure of judiciary fairness. Democratic rule should be there as well, because people should be given the right to choose. Gender equality should be there because it is essential to building a prosperous world. Many also believe that it would be the key to stabilizing the world's population, which is crucial to our collective future well-being. Oppression of ethnic, or religious minorities, or of people with certain political views should be sanctioned. The exploitation of workers through lack of protection through law of their right to organize, and a lack of consideration for their safety and working conditions should be sanctioned heavily in my view, because it is currently one of the most dangerous trends that threaten the entire world with a race to the bottom. All these measures need to be promoted because it provides stability. These are values that the west adopted a while ago, but unfortunately neglected to disperse through much of the rest of the world, to our collective detriment, because we are now ready to backslide on these norms ourselves. We are now in fact faced with counter-pressures because of economic conditions to abandon many of these values. This would be our last chance to promote these values, because a decade or two from now, there will be new economic powers who are likely to dominate the world. China, India and the oil rich Middle East, do not care as much for these values and it is probable that with their economic ascent, all progress towards a more just society is likely to be reversed, and that will also negatively affect our progress so far on this front[1].

The evaluation process should be very similar to what the HDI index study does with the world's state of being. The process should be formulated in a way that makes the evaluation as standard as possible, and try to eliminate conflicts of interest. The evaluation process should be done every year ideally, because it would provide an impetus for governments to constantly improve their standing from year to year. Public pressure to do so would come automatically as the new evaluation would come out, likely affecting most citizens directly, or indirectly.

There is the issue of the disruption that might be caused to current levels of trade in the event of the implementation of such a tariff. The way to minimize the shock from such a sharp turn away from current trading practices would be to implement it gradually, while also phasing out all other current trade agreements at a similar pace. The introduction of this tariff perhaps at a rate of 20% every five years would already have immediate effects, especially because markets are forward looking, so firms would adjust to the new reality by positioning themselves not only to dealing with present tariff levels, but also to the increases coming down the line.

Once this process were to be started, there is a need to produce compliance with the system, and as we have witnessed over and over again, expectations of voluntary good Samaritan behavior on the part of most governments as well as individuals, are likely to leave those hopping for it, extremely disappointed. There are some obvious contenders, who would like to sign up for this standardized tariff application, due to its benefits. The most obvious of all are the western governments who were unable to keep millions of manufacturing jobs due to their competing need to adhere to better work safety and environmental standards as well as having to compete with production centers that offer a workforce that is willing to work for a fraction of the price. Japan is likely to be a good contender for this as well. Many other countries would likely shun this new system if it was implemented, because they lack the ability to score well on such an evaluation system, and are unwilling to do what is needed to implement reforms that would help them score better. Ordinarily, in such a situation, our leaders always engaged in horse-trading schemes that end up making the entire endeavor pointless, or simply decide to go on without the collaboration of the entire world as they did with the Kyoto accord. We are unfortunately, no longer in a position to be able to say that any agreement is better than no agreement. We need real results.

The solution to getting the entire world involved is quite simple in this particular case. We need the political will to get the countries on board that would find it a natural advantage for them to embrace such a system. As I mentioned, energy efficient, developed nations would find, it is a net advantage for them. The US the EU, Japan and a few smaller nations around the world would be enough to get things moving. If these countries were to leave the WTO, renege on all existing trade agreements, and implement the sustainability tariff instead, most countries would be left with no alternative but to follow suit. This is not because they will see the light, and move towards it. This is going to happen, because we can force them to do so through economic pressure, which would automatically bear down on the entire world, as long as we would decide to adopt this policy.

The most important piece of the proposal is the part where those who refuse to join the new tariff system will be evaluated collectively, and a commonly shared tariff is to be imposed on all goods coming from these countries as they enter the market of the countries that already agreed to the new tariff system. The reason why this is likely to work is because the above-mentioned, likely voluntary contenders collectively still make up the greatest consumer market. Many of the same countries that are likely to shun such a tariff system are the same ones who depend almost entirely on exporting to us for their continued economic viability. I know this may seem like a dreadful way to go about things, and especially so, given that we have an unfortunate recent history of dictating to some of the same actors. I fear the alternatives can end up far worse for us as well as them however; therefore, this is definitely the least of two evils. In the end, we are all going to be better off by changing course. After all, many of those who are likely to suffer in the event of climate change, food and fuel shortages, are the same people who would resist these changes, that I believe to be the only solution moving forward, which will not involve disaster.

Given the growing dependence that most economies have on trade, this would be a very powerful driver towards changing the behavior of all societies worldwide. The very fact that we have not shaped trade into a driver of good policies so far is an absurd and un-necessary failure of humanity. Good will gestures on the part of the EU, Japan and a few others to produce a more fuel efficient, and cleaner economy has only served to reduce their emissions and environmental footprint on a local scale, while many industries were encouraged to migrate from their shores. An increasing number of people are alleging that the west has only reduced emissions in a real meaningful way in a large part because they outsourced the CO_2 emissions to developing nations[2]. The Kyoto commitment that countries made and many did not keep, was so flawed, on so many levels, that I reluctantly have to admit that former US president George Bush was right in not signing on to it.

This trading system, if it were to be implemented would have many benefits, including in areas that one would think that it has no relation to. The obvious reason to implement this system of trade is to address the ever-increasing pressure we are putting on our resources and the environment. This is very important, as I shall describe in the chapters dedicated to these issues, because our future may be disastrous if we do not address these problems seriously. Aside from that obvious effect, I want to point out that the main effect of this agreement would be to effectively, put a real price on all goods and services around the world. With a proper re-balancing of prices in place, which would take into account the price paid by the environment and the human collective, it is amazing how the global economy would automatically change. Incredibly, this trade system would put an end to any attempts by governments to improve their trade balance through currency devaluation or suppression. I will explain how this happens in later chapters. Governments would also be discouraged from pushing a policy of over consumption, and focus on constantly funding R & D work and infrastructure improvements instead, in order to grow the economy. The net effect will be a re-balancing of the global economy at a healthier point. I will discuss this as well in more detail in the upcoming chapters.

One of the important effects that I hope it would have is to help governments reconsider any initiatives on their territory, which promote population growth rates that surpass the carrying capacity of their environment. One of the main culprits that are currently responsible is the strong presence that religious organizations have in the developing world. A study done recently points to the fact that the world's Muslim population is set to double by 2030, from 1.1

32

billion to over 2 billion people. Christian groups also encourage the swelling of the developing world's population through their policy of discouraging the use of contraceptives. Population stability would be helped in any likelihood by the simple fact that there is a human rights component in the tariff setting system, which includes women's rights. The empowerment of women is thought by many to be the key to stabilizing the world's population. We need to find a solution to this, because our ecological footprint is already too great for the planet to bear. As for its population carrying capacity, there is recent evidence to suggest that we were a little too rash in dismissing Thomas Malthus, and his view that at some point we may reach the brink of a population crash due to resource constraints.

With a system of tariff allocation in place that discourages a large environmental footprint, I am hopeful that governments around the world will adapt. I hope that to hold true, especially for those who currently administer countries with high population growth rates, who will now find it in their interest as a matter of survival to confront this problem. As such, they should see an incentive in finding ways to counteract the teachings of some of these misguided, irresponsible religious institutions, who do not realize that we now live in the 21'Th century, and our problems accordingly, differ from Biblical and Koran times.

In the interest of a positive effect of re-pricing goods and services to a point that is as realistic as possible, I also propose that in conjunction with these initiatives on the trade side, all state subsidies should be eliminated worldwide. An accord to this effect could be reached, and there is already a desire to do so in the current environment. Agricultural, energy, and favorite industrial sector subsidies are in the end harmful, because it distorts the true price, and value of those goods, just as the current trade system does by not pricing in the sacrifice paid by people and the environment. In economic terms, it distorts the opportunity cost of allocating capital to producing these goods to the detriment of other producing opportunities. It also distorts the true national or regional competence to produce certain goods more efficiently than others can. Many developing nations have called for the elimination of agricultural subsidies, so there is already support for this. Developed, industrialized nations are constantly arguing over subsidized steel, aircraft and a host of other products that are hitting the market, helped by government subsidies.

There is also the positive effect that is achieved by the attachment of the human rights component of the points system that sets tariffs. Being authoritarian would become an increasingly expensive habit, and so would the suppression of women's rights. It would also become increasingly pointless to exploit the workforce in an unfair manner, because the very goods that one would hope to export for less than the competition that produces in a more ethical setting, would be taxed more upon leaving the country of origin. The west can now finally have an effective way to close the human rights disparity gap that currently prevails in the world. As the influence of the west diminishes together with its economic weight in the world, the trend towards a more enlightened society, with fewer abuses would still be cemented for as long as the new trade system would be in place. The west can then claim that there was a positive impact on the world as a result of our centuries of hegemony. In the absence of a mechanism to keep the incentives alive for a greater level of humanity, it is conceivable that even we are likely to move backward in our quest for a greater level of fairness as the new dominant cultures in the world will introduce and promote different norms around the world.

Once the global economic system is re-balanced and re-directed to deal with the realities of our time, we can concentrate on aspects of our economy and society that can bring us to the next step of human advancement. This in a way is similar to our step out of the feudal system into the mercantilist system, or from the mercantilist system to the free markets. Now that the free market system has done for us all that it can do and reached its limits, we have to innovate again, if not we are likely to sink.

Closest Suggestions thus far

Many people have identified the problem of resource scarcity and pollution as a threat to our well-being already. There is to my knowledge however, not a single suggestion out there that ties the failure to address the problem of resource scarcity and the environment to our approach to global trade. Some political circles linked the problem of comparatively less stringent environmental and human protection rules to the loss of investment in production means in the west. The typical suggestion to a solution to this is very disappointing, which should not come as a surprise given the political circles that it comes from. I am referring to the right wing political movements that generally tend to favor the interests of business. Relaxing worker treatment and environmental rules tends to favor most business establishments; it should come as no surprise then that these political actors pick up the issue under the populist disguise of wanting to create more jobs.

Some politicians or public officials briefly strayed on to the correct path towards addressing both problems of resource scarcity and the hollowing out of the western economies with trade as the solution. Some European Union members, angry with countries such as the US for not signing up to the Kyoto protocol, suggested imposing sanctions in proportion to the US failure to meet the targets set up in the Kyoto agreement. The idea never really caught on, and we should be grateful for it, because it not only would have failed to address our problems, but it would have accelerated the downfall of western society thanks to an internal trade war, which would have further benefited countries such as China.

If the politicians involved in advocating such a move within the EU would have stopped to contemplate and expand the concept a lot further, perhaps they would have been able to arrive to the more or less same prescription to our current ailments as I did. These people were mainly interested in lashing out at the US, because they felt betrayed in their endeavor to pursue the already highly flawed path of the Kyoto agreement, which became even more flawed with the US opt out from it. Nevertheless, I feel that mention should be given to the instance in which some politicians did briefly touch the right path with their ideas, because frankly there is little else I can point to as an example.

US energy secretary Steven Chu also deserves a mention for an idea he briefly floated around, but never really had a chance of being implemented. The idea was also flawed on many levels, so it would have made little difference. In 2009, as an answer to criticism of the Obama administration's plans for a cap and trade program for greenhouse gasses within the US, Steven Chu suggested a way to soften the blow to the US economy as a result of the increased costs of doing business due to the cap and trade program. He suggested a tariff on products imported from other countries, which may involve an energy inefficient, or intensive method of production.

The main differences between my suggestion and Mr. Chu's include the fact that his proposal only covers a small aspect of the overall problem, by focusing only on greenhouse gasses. Countries such as China, India and others allow for a large range of environmental abuses that make them a more attractive place to invest, not to mention the human rights violations, including worker's rights. The second flaw is that even a country as powerful economically as the US stands to be vulnerable to countermeasures by nations targeted by such a tariff. My suggestion by contrast would entail a large group of countries, representing perhaps over 50% of the global economy, adopting the same policy, causing pressure on smaller global players with extensive economic ties to us to agree to do the same. Remember that countries unwilling to sign on to such a deal would face a collective evaluation. I seriously doubt that countries such as Chile, or Singapore would be happy to share the same level of tariff for their goods entering our borders with countries such as North Korea. The logical thing to do for states that have a chance to get a better rating than the average of the unwilling, will be to sign on as well, leaving those who do not, even more isolated and disadvantaged. This plan would cause some economic disruptions initially, but the benefits of a level playing field, as well as the power of persuasion created by such a plan, would be beneficial to us in the long term. To sum it up in a sentence, the fight would be worth the reward, unlike the tariff plan envisioned by Mr. Chu.

The main problem that I see with ideas such as the one presented by Mr. Chu, as well as the idea floating around in many EU political circles was that they were responding to a narrower problem and their solution was tailored to serve a more narrow purpose. They had the right idea, except they failed to develop it further, and work through the concept. I believe that most of our political elites are guilty of being oblivious to some degree about the true nature of our current situation. They are caught up in arguments that have been fought on our political scene for decades or even centuries in some cases, but which have little relevance currently, since we are facing a very different world right now. The fact that some of them stumbled on the right path, and yet still failed to recognize it, is clear indication of that.

Two years after Mr. Chu floated his idea around, which on its own had little merit for the reasons already given, it is now being reported that the Obama administration has decided to abandon the idea of cap and trade. There is no need to take measures to reduce the negative effects on investment due to the higher cost of doing business anymore[3]. Furthermore, the budget of the EPA (Environmental Protection Agency) is being cut, making it harder to supervise good environmental behavior on the part of industry. In other words, government policy went the predictable way, which we should expect it to go from now, given the current business environment, unless major changes to the global economic system are made.

Environmental organizations, as well as worker's unions were very vociferous in their opposition to liberalizing trade, without addressing environmental and worker's rights issues with potential trade partners, especially in the 1990's when globalization truly took off. They correctly saw the danger that failure to do so would pose to their cause. It was so easy however to silence them back then, because of circumstance, as well as because the proposed liberalization of trade actually meant increased benefits for most people initially, while the consequences are actually only starting to become obvious now. They were ironically painted as people who oppose the wellbeing of the global poor, by trying to restrict trade with them. It was also easy to silence them because they failed to provide a coherent explanation of the downsides, as well as a viable alternative. The unfortunate reality is that it is much easier for me to propose my solution now that the effects of our mistakes are felt broadly within our society, than it was for them back in those days. Very interesting however, that environmental and worker's rights groups are less active in advocating for linking their issues to trade than they were in the 1990's for instance, despite the fact that it would now be much easier to make their case. It is possible that, due to the effect of the idealist left leaning ideas that took deep root already, of convincing everyone to do it on a local level, which is useless, the idea of doing it as a global solution, which would work, has been crowded out.

Perhaps the best chance to avoid the predicament we face currently, due to the resource scarcity issue, as well as the global race to the bottom in environmental and human rights protection we currently are engaged in, due to our need to cater to potential investors was squandered by the US, during the Clinton presidency. President Clinton wanted to tie trade agreements to environmental as well as human rights issues during his first term. Perhaps he did listen to the environmentalists and the worker's unions, and their views, but it seems it was not enough. The idea was not well developed, as a standard policy, like the one I'm currently proposing, but at least it was a big leap in the right direction, or at least it would have been if Clinton would have stuck to his guns. Heavy pressure from industrial interests who had much to lose in potential profits from such an initiative prevailed unfortunately, and President Clinton caved in to these interests. If the leader of the western world would have stood his ground then, we would be living in a different world right now. The part that worries me when I look at this incident is that despite the fact that it would have been much easier then to stand up with such an initiative, our political elites failed to do so. We are currently no longer as dominant globally as we were then, nor are our economies as healthy. It is therefore a much harder fight we would have to pick and win, in order to correct our path.

The fact that President Clinton caved in so easily back then, leads me to believe that he, just like most of our political elites from our recent past, and perhaps even the present did not realize what was really at stake. I think that President Clinton as well as many other western leaders believed that the privilege of producing the high value goods for the world was to remain with us for a very long time. They also believed that through a combination of resource availability that was then estimated by many specialists wearing rose-colored glasses to be still plentiful in relation to our needs, as well as the faith in the power of technology to solve such problems, we would have enough resources to go all around. They also perhaps can be said to have been guilty of some misguided idealism. They probably believed in the theory that prosperity is a natural stimulant of environmental and human rights protection. As it turns out, our developing world economic competitors figured out quite easily that the neglect of these issues is actually a strong magnet for capital investments. It is unlikely that they are willing to relinquish these advantages, without us turning them into disadvantages for them instead.

Aside from these brief accidental strays on to the path of responsible global development, and indeed responsible political behavior on behalf of us; the western constituents who are currently suffering a great deal of discomfort, as a result of the unfair competition coming from irresponsible developing nations, there are no realistic suggestions to deal with the two problems I identified. There are many left-leaning intellectuals advocating various ways to curtail western consumption patterns, which truly take up an unfair share of the global commodities supplies. I should emphasize however that they only concern themselves with reducing western consumption, which would realistically only allow developing nations to pick up the slack faster than they are doing already, which would accelerate our descent down into economic meltdown. As for the resource scarcity problem, it would certainly stop being an issue when hundreds of millions around the world would be told to stay home, because the western consumer is finished. They should however worry about the way that countries; western and non-western alike would approach the rebuilding of their economies in the aftermath of collapse. My guess is that it would be a new world, where human rights and environmental protection would no longer be discussed. These people are simply so filled with contempt for western society that they fail to understand the more recent positive effect that our presence in the mix has on the collective attitude of the "global village".

One of the latest movements that provide for a great example of this brand of immaturity are the degrowth theory advocates. The theory of de-growth is a classical example of left leaning idealism that otherwise great intellectual minds are wasted on. The reason I say that, is that while they have no trouble proving and describing how in theory there is no compatibility between infinite growth, which requires an infinite increase in consumption, and conservation, they fail in my view to propose a realistic solution to the problem.

At the 2008 degrowth conference, Francois Schneider provided a great explanation in regards to why we cannot simply count on technology to provide the solution to overexploitation of our planet[4]. He argued that the rebound effect in the economy causes most of the savings gained through technological innovation to be used up through an increase in consumption. Looking at recent history, it turns out that he is right. The car industry for instance managed to make their engines about 30% more efficient in the last three decades. That gain in efficiency was however more than offset by an increase in the size of cars, especially in the US, as well as a huge swell in car ownership in the developing world. That is why we now consume about 25% more petroleum than we did in 1980. Many other technological innovations of the past have had a similar effect. History is therefore on the side of Mr. Schneider's theoretical model, and not on the side of the current mainstream elites, who claim that technology will kick in eventually and we will achieve sustainable growth under current economic policies.

As great as Mr. Schneider's rebound hypothesis was at proving the one thing that has already been shown over and over again in regards to the current unsustainable path, it still lacks the main ingredient to be able to challenge as a viable alternative. When it came to making viable suggestions on how we should proceed; his answers were typical and overall lacking a logical way to implement. The subheading that introduces the solution says it all "Challenging rebound and growth policy with voluntary debound and degrowth". The contents of this portion of his paper do not disappoint in keeping to the same idealistic model. He starts by arguing for a voluntary change in lifestyle in the western world that will reduce consumption levels dramatically. He suggests that we should all be convinced that we should spend our free time on things that keep us from consuming, such as walking, hiking, biking, taking long meals, sharing a car, and so on. While I certainly agree that it would be good for society to learn to enjoy such activities to a greater extent, I see no hope of this happening on a large scale voluntarily in the current environment.

Aside from the idealistic expectations of achieving such a social change through voluntary means, Mr. Schneider greatly misjudges the effect and indeed the need for such an effect to take place, given current global economic trends. The need is no longer there, because the western economies are being hollowed out anyway through the transfer of manufacturing jobs to the developing world. The true effects of this trend are only starting to be felt now as western governments are forced to start cutting back on the high deficit spending, which has so far blunted the blow to society to some extent. There is absolutely no need therefore for an impossible cultural revolution to take place to achieve Mr. Schneider's dream of a western world on a consumption diet.

Regardless whether the contraction of our level of consumption will happen by allowing the current trend to continue, or whether it would be achieved through the fruition of an idealistic leftist fantasy as envisioned by Mr. Schneider, the effect of such an event is nothing like he or others might imagine it to be. First off, our lives would not be transformed into an ideal portrait of happy co-existence. Many people will become un-necessary for employers, making it very hard to secure a means to earn a living. Governments, which no doubt Mr. Schneider believes should continue to provide a social safety net, and invest in modernizing our infrastructure, would default on their debts, either through an outright default, or through currency devaluation. Either way, pensions or other savings schemes would be wiped out, and we will be left with no way of repairing the financial damage. I doubt that people will be in the mood to do a lot of hiking, and other activities that Mr. Schneider envisioned us adopting, for a more balanced life under such circumstances.

If the hope is that such a collapse would result in a more balanced global economy, which will distribute the wealth more equitably throughout the planet, those hopping for such a scenario will have a chance to be left disappointed if they are young enough to stay alive for the next decade or two. Mr. Schneider argued that commodity prices would drop, making them more affordable to the less fortunate of this planet. I am sure that while the global effect of the economic collapse of the west would keep the entire world in a nasty, brutal downturn, commodity prices would remain soft. When the global economy will start recovering, it will be led by most of the current suspects, such as China, India, Indonesia, Brazil and a host of other currently fast industrializing nations. These developing nations are responsible for adding about 1.5 mb/d in annual petroleum demand in the absence of economic turmoil. If an economic collapse in the west were to wipe out about ¼ of our current petroleum consumption, or about 8 mb/d, the developing world would be able to soak that up in about five years of economic expansion[5]. There is very little chance that some of the less developed regions, such as the ones in Africa will be able to grab a chunk of that extra petroleum consumption share.

The left should also ask the important question of what such disadvantaged regions as Africa will be like when more ruthless capitalist competitors, such as China will take over. Will they have many of their Chinese citizens, question the ethics of exploitation like our society does currently? Will the new global elite, made up of mainly non-westerners be as likely to engage in philanthropic projects similar to what Bill Gates and Mr. Buffet are known for? Perhaps they should have paid more attention as Mr. Gates and Mr. Buffet were politely told to take a hike, when they went to Asia to convince some of the billionaires in the region to give away half their fortune to charity as some of the western billionaires plan to do. In case that some may not be aware of this interesting fact, there are currently almost as many Chinese billionaires as there are in all of Europe combined.

The environment, which is a main reason for suggesting such schemes, as collapsing the western economy, will not have much of a respite either. Many of the developing nations I mentioned earlier are currently using the difference in the level of environmental protection between western economies and their own to attract investment. A western society suffering from the effects of an economic collapse would become extremely desperate for a lifeline to help us ease the suffering. If the left thinks that it is hard to win the environment versus jobs debate now, they should imagine what a society suffering a worst fate than the people of Eastern Europe after communism collapsed there, will think of sacrificing some more in order to protect a relatively "abstract" concept, such as the environment. The relatively mild level of economic pain suffered by western society in the past five years is already starting to turn many people, and politicians against environmental protection issues. The political right in the US, which is using this issue successfully to attract people to their side, is one good example. Poland's refusal to push for much tougher environmental regulations within the EU in their position as holders of the rotating EU presidency is another example of people feeling tired of accepting measures meant to serve the global greater good, which also happens to undermine our own local livelihoods. If things continue down the current trajectory, the only society, which has so far taken global as well as local environmental issues seriously, will likely turn its back on these issues, making it unlikely that the current century will see any significant positive moves towards environmental responsibility.

As westerners will become more ruthless in exploiting the environment and the people as well, it is likely that the global race to the bottom will intensify, putting the multinational corporations firmly into the driving seat. They will encounter no more resistance to extracting from society, whatever they desire in exchange for investment. As basic first year economic theoretical teaching tells us, they always desire the maximization of profit, so they will always push us to concede more polluting rights, as well as the right to exploit the workforce, while paying few taxes to support community projects such as education, sanitation, environmental protection and other necessary things that governments currently do. This is surely not the world that the left leaning idealists imagine to be the end result in the aftermath of the collapse of the "great Satan", responsible for all the world's troubles. Yet, if one is to work through the scenario in a logical manner, uncorrupted by idealism, and political partisanship that serves to blind people, this is the most likely scenario, if we were to follow their advice, or if we decide to continue down the current path for that matter.

It may seem at this point that I am picking on Mr. Schneider on purpose, but it is simply not the case. The same critique can be applied to all the other presentations made at the 2008 conference on degrowth, because they all follow pretty much the same pattern, although the perspective from which the very real problem of sustainability is approached is different, and the various explanations of the problem have merit. Same can be said about most other left leaning critiques of western society and its role in the sustainability problem, as well as for the poor job that they do at proposing a viable and realistic solution.

In the interest of balancing my approach of critiquing the left, right, as well as the center, it would now be appropriate to comment on the shortcomings of the right and center visions for our paths forward. I am not going to do that at this point, not because I want to specifically pick on the left, but because this is simply not the appropriate part of the book to do so. Remember that I set out in this part of chapter one, to present some alternatives to my idea on a solution to our problems. The reason I cannot do that for the center and the right wing of our political spectrum is that they are largely oblivious to the problems that I see as pressing. There is no way to know whether they choose to be oblivious to the main problems we face and their consequences, or whether they are just too entrenched in their dogma to realize what is actually happening to us, but the bottom line is that they do not actually present us with an alternative. In this respect, the left is actually far ahead of the right and the center, because even though they present us with no viable alternative, at least they have a good understanding of the problem, even if their perspective has an anti-western bias, which leads them to misjudge the path to a solution. The center and the right do not get off easy either, because it is important to also examine their shortcomings, especially since they are currently either in power, or have a good chance of getting there, as is the case with the far right movements in the US. I devoted ample room in later chapters to pointing out their shortcomings.

Pre-empting criticism of the sustainability tariff

As is the case with most things in life, my suggested solution to our economic problems is not without its own shortcomings. Just as I argued that, there is simply no hope for the left leaning idealists to convince people in the west to voluntarily adopt a more frugal lifestyle, it can also be argued that there is no hope for people to come around to my approximate point of view in large enough numbers to make a change. My response to that is that the argument is perfectly valid. The current leftists are proposing an idealistic solution that is flawed from a purely economic point of view, as I already pointed out, and if people were to ever be convinced to follow that path, it would lead to disaster. The left is however unified in supporting their views, just like the right is and the extreme wings of society tend to be very passionate and entrenched about the things they believe in. I on the other hand am proposing a new middle road, which may actually be a turnoff for those who believe in the current validity of the center view, because after all I am questioning that validity. In addition to that, the political center has never been known to enthusiastically adopt and fight for a concept or an ideal. The nature of the center is to be more neutral, therefore less reactive and generally less engaged. Aside from that, I am alone currently in proposing my idea for the sustainability tariff, and there is certainly enough in the proposal to turn off the left as well as the right. We should remind ourselves of the fact that the political wings have deeply entrenched values, and generally when people try to get traction on an idea, they try to appeal to one of these factions, by refraining to step over any of their values. The reality is that in the absence of other people with the power to persuade and the willingness to look at my idea of the sustainability trade tariff as a serious proposal, worth considering and advocating, there is little chance that anything will change. I have no doubt however, that many people will change their perspective on the global economy and its prospects as a result of learning about my idea for the sustainability tariff.

There are also valid reasons, based on sound economic theory to oppose this idea. On top of my list goes that it might endanger the current volume of global trade, which has so far served the global economy quite well, by facilitating our collective expansion of GDP, and according to economic theory as well as empirical data, our collective satisfaction, and average well being. The theory of Pareto efficiency, which argues for enhanced collective wellbeing through trade, correctly assumes that through regional or national specialization, and then by trading for the things we neglect to produce, while selling the products we are good at producing, everyone can gain[6].

The gains in production efficiency can best be exemplified by evaluating the typical output per farmer in the western world, where farmers tend to specialize on growing just a few cash crops, or alternatively raise livestock, with places where subsistence farmers try to satisfy as many of their own families needs through their work of the land. Their method leaves very little surplus that makes it to market. The efficiency per unit of labor inputted is staggering. Some societies have half or even more of their potential workforce dedicated to growing food, and yet they still need to import. Western society only allocates about 5% of our labor capital to farming, yet we are net exporters of food. This happens in part because there is farmer specialization, in other words, most farmers do not try to feed their family through what they grow, but rather rely on their cash crop to give them the ability to buy products produced by other farmers, who also specialize in other products. I witnessed these phenomena myself, as I spent considerable time in the Romanian countryside, where most farmers still practice farming that is closer to subsistence than cash crop production. As a result, about a quarter of that country's potential workforce is dedicated to farming, and yet Romania is a net importer of food.

The same analysis can be applied to manufacturing, and the service-providing sector. Through regional or national specialization, we can produce more, and keep prices lower, since we are allocating through this process our labor capital in a more efficient way, which provides more output per unit of labor. It can be argued therefore that my idea is dangerous, because it risks disrupting trade flows, which could in turn cause a drop in Pareto efficiency, leaving all of us less well off than we will be if we continue down the same path we are on right now. On the surface, it is a perfectly valid argument, but there are some problems with it, which become apparent as we dig a bit deeper.

Basic cultural anthropological theory teaches us that in any environment, some adaptations are better than others are. Regional or national specializations in production are also an adaptation to the current global business environment. The west is currently specialized in providing a production environment where capital intensive industries can feel comfortable investing, because we provide a stable political environment, which poses little threat of loss of investment due to political uncertainty. We also specialized in providing a high quality workforce that is relatively healthy, due to access to health care, a relatively clean environment, and the availability of proper nutrition. Access to education made available and accessible to most members of our society regardless of ethnicity, gender, or wealth, allows us to harness the human potential that our population has, which also makes it a good place for companies to look, who want to deploy a high volume of capital, which often requires a highly capable workforce to operate. Our level of individual freedom, and legal framework, which facilitates freedom of expression and entrepreneurship, is a highly desirable trait, because it allows for innovation. Our high-income society is very attractive for people looking to invest in producing location dependent services, which in our high wage society can fetch a better price. There are costs associated with doing business here, including having to adhere to a relatively high level of environmental and labor and consumer protection regulations. Our hope is that the benefits of doing business here will outweigh the costs, in comparison with investing elsewhere.

Our hopes seem to be misplaced if judged by recent developments, because it seems that our main competitors have found a much more formidable formula for specialization, and what Pareto efficiency theory seems to not account for is that it may lead to a phenomenon that happens in nature all the time. It can lead to the obliteration of the competition, which are we westerners in this case. The reason why this is happening is because of the nature of the specialization that they are currently building. They decided to specialize in providing cheap labor, which is increasingly capable of operating hi-tech physical capital, even if they are not necessarily very good at inventing it. Because they specialize in providing cheap labor, they neglect to create consumer demand. They therefore rely on us to consume their surplus production of goods. Their surplus that they gained by not over-consuming is invested in building up physical infrastructure to facilitate the absorption of the high capital means of production, as well as training their workforce to operate the capital invested from abroad. They lack the social infrastructure to provide innovation, but they can rely on our innovative output, which they can absorb through their low cost environment.

In order to provide an investment environment that costs as little as possible, they also neglect to protect their human capital from abuse, as well as their and our globally shared natural environment. As such, they beat us in all but two categories. They do not have a high wage environment, so even though there is a fast growing

47

segment of their population that is affluent, they presently lack in the development of the service sector of the economy. They have to import our intellectual property, and they have to pay for it as their industrial production is highly dependent on our patents. The value of our patent exports is however negligible compared to the value of imports that we get from them. We cannot have a viable economy based on exporting only a few products that are still out of the capability of our developing nation competitors. Recent developments, since the latest recession confirms that fact, because it is increasingly obvious that the western economy is close to collapse. If we collapse however, the developing nations that insist on undermining us the way they do, will lose their consumer market that they depend on, since they lack the means to both provide the cheap labor environment and a viable consumer market at the same time. So the only conclusion that can be drawn from this is that the current arrangement, which leads to a high level of Pareto efficiency, is not a desirable path forward, because in the long run, we are likely to experience far less wellbeing through consumer satisfaction, if we take the negative effect of collapse into account.

The supporters of free trade through lowering all barriers to trade in the pursuit of Pareto efficiency fail in my view to take into account that low regard for environmental and human rights issues can actually become a successful and dangerous specialization. Nevertheless, evidence shows that it has become so in many developing countries. The result is an inevitable intensification of the exploitation of the environment. On the environment, we depend however on the quality of many things we consume. The air we breathe, the liquids we drink, the solid foods we eat are all necessary products that we consume, and the satisfaction we derive from them is dependent in part on how many contaminants we find in the environment. There is currently relatively little attention being paid to this aspect of our consumer satisfaction. In the absence of better controls on the exploitation of our environment, the pursuit of Pareto efficiency through trade is flawed in my view as a result of the negative consequences. Same reasoning is valid for human rights violations as a specialization, which also clearly happens.

The other aspect that needs to be considered is that consumer satisfaction cannot be measured simply by calculating the volume of products being consumed. I for instance took away greater satisfaction from a pair of Italian shoes I purchased more than a decade ago, which lasted me about two years, during which time I wore that pair intensively, than from any two year period I can consider since. Since then, I mainly purchased shoes made in China and other developing markets, which rarely lasted me more than a few months, despite subjecting them to less wear and tear. There is in fact an incident, during a trip I took for a long weekend, when I had to throw away a pair of shoes that I bought specifically for that trip, and only wore during that trip. The synthetic material that the shoes were made of was of such terrible quality, that my feet were sweating more than usual, the material soaked it up, and the chemical compound the shoes were made of reacted with the sweat, producing an awful odor. Paying $25 dollars to wear a pair of shoes for three days may seem like a great deal to some, but the reality is that my Pareto happiness at that moment was not so hot.

The Italian shoes that lasted me for two years, cost me not much more than the shoes I had to throw away after wearing them a single weekend. They were most definitely a better deal, and I received far more satisfaction from them, than I did from any pair I purchased since. I would like to purchase more shoes like that, except there is a problem. The nature of our market is that companies that create more durable goods are displaced by the near-disposable products that cost us far more in the long-run, but are cheaper in the short run. It is in essence more profitable to produce things that are less durable. A Chinese based manufacturing company that produces a pair of shoes that lasts three months on average has me as a potential costumer every three months. If I was to purchase a pair of shoes like the Italian ones I mentioned, they would lose me as a customer for maybe five years, thanks to their high quality product. There are still high quality shoes for sale of course, but the price one pays for them is nothing like what it used to be. The only way that the few companies that still produce high quality shoes can survive is to ask for a much higher price, for a niche product.

So ten years after I started buying shoes made in China, most indications will show that my Pareto satisfaction has been greatly enhanced, because after all, I now consume five times more shoes than I used to. In reality, I have to spend about three times more to put shoes on my feet than I used to, because the only alternative is to walk around with unbearably smelly feet. The strain on the global environment has also become bigger, because more energy and material is expended on putting shoes on my feet, and everyone else's as well. In this case, the disposable economy is displacing the drive to meet other needs that are awaiting the market's attention. In effect, we have become less efficient at providing this particular necessity, as well as many others. The fact that statistically speaking, my Pareto happiness has been improved in this example, while in reality it has worsened, is the perfect example of the kind of factor that makes theoretical economic models that we currently work with quite inadequate, if we do not pay enough attention to consider these factors.

The way to increase our efficiency in providing more potential consumers with more satisfaction is to discourage the disposable economy. Let us face it though; leaving it to the individual consumer to make it happen is not only unrealistic, but also unreasonable. The reason I say that is because the consumer does not have perfect information in regards to what he is buying, and we never will[7]. I for instance had absolutely no way of knowing that a pair of shoes made in China would last me only for a weekend. My ability to make an informed decision as a consumer was not a possibility. We can say the same thing about the purchase of a $200 pair of shoes. We have no guarantee that it will perform in a manner that will make it worth the nearly ten-fold price that cheap near-disposable shoes go for. The logical decision is then to bet on the cheap shoes, because we risk less, while there is always the potential to be pleasantly surprised. So in conclusion, the consumer, when presented with the disposable product option, is inevitably forced to accept it for human logical reasons. One can always count on a handful of conscientious individuals to go against the herd, but that will never make a difference.

The only way to correct for these kinds of theoretical lapses is to put a price on human and environmental exploitation, making the disposable goods, economic development strategy less viable. I have no doubt that many economies will still try to compete through the adoption of such a strategy, but at least the durable economy will once again become competitive, because it leaves a smaller environmental footprint, so it would therefore provide an advantage for the more durable products in international trade. This is how we can free up resources for other needs on this planet, as the left leaning advocates of degrowth have correctly argued that we need to do.

Trade flows would likely decline initially, as a result of the implementation of the sustainability tariff, as it should be expected, because of the disruption of the status quo. There is no reason to believe however that, given a logical incentive, such as improving the competitiveness of their products abroad, governments around the world will not work to bring down their tariff level through improving efficiency. That in turn will boost trade, and this time we will not do it ad-hoc, for the wrong reasons, such as due to political lobbying pressures coming from certain companies or industries. We will do it through adopting a responsible strategy that also happens to serve the common collective good. I believe that such a strategy can create a lot of consumer satisfaction all around the world, given that we will be able to get a lot more out of the allocation of our resources. It might even make up for the initial loss in Pareto satisfaction.

I have no doubt that there are other potential concerns with my sustainability tariff proposal. No idea is perfect, and for every gain that humanity has ever achieved, there have always been some downsides. For the remainder of this book, I will focus mainly on the positive effects it can have on different aspects of our economy, because I am after all trying to convince people that it is an idea worth looking at. It is in fact not only worth looking at, but at this point it should definitely make it on the list of possibilities as an alternative to the way we do things now. We have to find alternatives, because the consequences of failure are worse than any of us, who are used to relative stability can imagine. Some members on the edge of our society are already getting a taste of what is to come, given that due to circumstances of a very wide variation, they already fell through the cracks in the past few years. Just to put things in perspective, the number of people living in poverty in the US has grown on average by one million people per year, since the year 2000. While there were about 35 million people living in poverty when former president George W. Bush was sworn in, there are now about 46 million.

2

From The End of Rome to the End of Us
A Historical, Cultural and Economic Analysis.

A short trip through time

Rome: Imagine yourself in the great city of Rome. Not the modern capital of Italy, with its magnificent ruins, which testify to its former greatness, but the classical Rome, with its toga clad leaders, and the plebs increasingly dependent on food and wine handouts. Imagine that you went back in time, and you get to become a citizen of the great Roman Empire. You my dear time traveler, will witness the actual time of the great Mediterranean classical culture at its peak, as it culminated with the eventual dominance of Rome over the entire region. It was a great achievement indeed for the ancients to build and inhabit such a great urban marvel. By most accounts, the population of this imperial capital reached over one million souls. After the collapse of the Western Empire, which also put an end to that urban marvel of those days, we had to wait more than a thousand years to reach such a level of urbanization again. That of course should not seem odd, because after all, the collapse of Rome was an end of a historical cycle. It was a cycle, which started roughly with the birth of Mediterranean trade, and innovation, and ended with the gradual collapse of *Pax Romana*[1].

The birth of the Roman empire roughly fifteen centuries after the start of the great development of the Mediterranean, which many refer to as *"The Cradle of Civilization"*, a title rivaled by the Middle East, where agricultural societies first flourished, was a culmination of the power that arose from such economic, and innovative advancement that happened in the region. We should not be surprised that the City of Rome reached a population of one million, which is a large city even by our standards. It was the capital of an empire, which was borne out of the legions formed from healthy rural stock, who demonstrated great discipline. They first conquered Italy, which was assimilated culturally to some extent. From there, they proceeded to take the entire Mediterranean coast, with its wealth of goods, and knowledge. They effectively inherited fifteen hundred years of progress. The Romans harnessed that wealth, and directed it towards their Imperial capital, Rome. So if you were to go back in time, that would be the reason that you would find yourself surrounded by another million citizens, slaves, and merchants from all over the old world, sharing in the fruits of empire.

You as a time traveler will be privileged to see a great achievement in Empire, and urban building, so you surely must be quite impressed with such achievement. In addition to that, you get to be treated to many opportunities to be entertained, and you will be privileged with the right as a resident of Rome to consume many of the fruits of Empire. All roads and shipping lanes as well; led to Rome, taking grain, wine, silver, gold, and manufactured goods to be consumed by the privileged citizens. If you as a time traveler would be ignorant of Roman history and how it all ended, surely you would see yourself at the center of a social, economic, and political world, meant to last forever. It would seem like the place with the brightest future. Your fellow citizens of this great empire would most likely see things the same way. They had every reason to, because demographically as well as economically they surpassed all potential enemies many times over. But we do know what the future of that great society held in store, so we know that despite the way it may have appeared to the average Italian at the time, things were not alright.

The farmers who made up the formidable militia, which conquered the Mediterranean and most of Western and Central Europe, were undermined by personal ambitions and greed on the part of the political and economic elite. They were using the time that the soldiers were away on campaigns from their land to disposes them and buy the land out from under them cheaply, which proved to be a very detrimental trend to Roman society in the long-run. The dispossessed independent farmers either stayed on as laborers, working for the new landowners, or were left with no other choice but to seek employment, or other gainful occupations in the city. That was more or less all right for a while, but then came the increased trade in cheaper goods coming from the provinces.

Essentially, the Romans were becoming victims of their own imperial success. The more they expanded, and defended the borders, giving a chance for the provinces to flourish, the more they had to compete with cheaper goods produced in the provinces, and sometimes from beyond the borders as well. Artisans, who had to pay much higher rent for real estate in the Italian towns, could not afford to work for the same low wages that provincials were working for. Nor could the small farmers afford to sell their food on the market, because they had to cover the high cost of land on the Italian peninsula. More farmers sold their land to the large landowners, who were able to produce relatively more cheaply by employing slave labor. The move of the newly landless to the city was no longer easy however. As I mentioned, there were fewer things to do in town because of the flood of goods coming into the Imperial capital. The urban poor became more and more restless, and by the time the Roman Republic, became the Roman Empire through the transfer of power from the Senate to an Emperor or Cesar, urban riots became more and more frequent.

The imperial government did have one tool at its disposal, which was used with increasing effectiveness to keep the urban masses docile. The technique employed was their increased spending on the urban poor. The free handout of grain and wine to the masses became an increasing phenomenon. In addition to that, they thought it wise to keep the masses entertained. That is when they started spending heavily on gladiatorial games, chariot races, plays, and other forms of entertainment. In fact, if you would have been in Rome around the year 180 A.D, and you were to attend some of the festivities of the day, you would have had the chance to see Emperor Commodus slaughter hundreds of exotic animals, such as lions, elephants, and giraffes. That would have been in addition to all the great gladiatorial fights, which Commodus took such interest in, that he even decided to participate himself in them. If re-living scenes from the movie "Gladiator" is not your thing, then perhaps seeing the Coliseum flooded in order to re-enact naval battles would tickle your fancy. Emperor Titus started that in 80 A.D, but soon after, the Romans actually lost interest in flooding the Coliseum, because it took too long, so they preferred to have naval battles re-enacted on lakes instead[2].

The people of Rome became more and more concerned with these sorts of spectacles, and less concerned with matters of the Empire. The economic and military policies of rulers became less important than their ability to put on a good show. The people of Rome remained relatively docile during the reign of the Emperors however, so the trick worked. Unfortunately, for the Romans, they managed to degenerate as a society, into a pleasure seeking culture, no longer able to notice the changes. They were eager to see plays, watch gladiatorial games, and join into drunken sexual orgies. They were in no way eager to join the military campaigns, or engage in other productive work anymore. The only people in Italy who still worked hard were the slaves, but only until they were freed and made citizens, after which they were also entitled to handouts, therefore they could also take it easy. The work of the empire was left to the inhabitants of the provinces. They produced the food and the crafts. They were the ones who defended the increasingly static frontiers. Roman elites were increasingly involved in power struggles, which went as far as removing the legions from the frontier, in order to march on Rome and seize power. This started happening, just as European tribes were moving from east to west and threatening the border, so using the legions for internal power struggles seems a great waste of human resources when looking back in history, but hindsight is 20/20 as always.

Because of the lack of interest, and will of the original citizens of Rome from Italy to run the affairs of the empire, people of foreign descent who were naturalized, obtained more and more functions. That was true especially on the frontier, where often, auxiliary legions meant to defend the borders were in fact made up of foreign elements, which often still had blood ties to the enemy on the other side of the borders. When the time came to do battle, many Roman citizens were sometimes surprised by the willingness of auxiliary troops or allies to just move over, or open the fortress gates in order to let the invading foreigners in. Worst still, towards the end of the empire, the very tribes who settled into the empire for various reasons as refugees from outside, and for a relatively long period served to reinforce the Roman army, in the end carved up the empire among themselves as soon as they realized the poor state of Roman power. In 476, the year that the empire officially ceased to exist, Odovacar, a Germanic chieftain, who for years defended the Italian peninsula, was the one who put an end to the reign of the last emperor. Just like many other tribal chieftains, he started handing out Roman landholdings to his own people, giving rise to Europe's new nobility.

On one hand, many historians view the granting of citizenship to more and more people as a progressive approach to government. They view it as something they can relate to as the ideal of what they believe western society should be like. Yes, the Roman government was becoming more inclusive, and more progressive from our point of view. On the other hand, Rome was first sacked in 410, by Germanic refugees, who asked to be re-settled south of the Danube River, from their lands now known as Romania, due to the push from the newcomers on the scene from east, known as the Huns. Every other sack of the city came at the hands of internal barbarians.

If someone were to tell them back then, that they were hastening the destruction of the Empire, they would have probably been as unreceptive as the tribal chiefs of Easter Island, who destroyed the habitat that supported a population of 20,000 souls in order to build large stone heads. They thought it was more important to have the big heads as a status symbol, than to think and plan about what there was left to eat after they were done deforesting the entire island. In the end, the only thing left to eat was each other, according to archeological evidence. Looking at examples such as Easter Island, which is the next place we will visit, makes us understand that it was by no means a unique thing for leaders to lack foresight, in order to prevent the collapse of their society. This horrific example of collective group failure we will talk about some more in later chapters, because it is important to recognize similarities between us and them.

It should be recognized that Roman emperors, generals and the nobility, would have had a much tougher time recognizing the signs of a crumbling society, which sometimes actually changed very little over the course of a generation. The chiefs on Easter Island should have probably seen the state of their landscape, and yet still they did nothing. The Romans probably had a hard time taking accurate measure of their situation at any point in time[3]. It is true that they were experiencing some demographic decline by the third century on the peninsula, which is always a sign of impending social collapse. Nevertheless, the citizen population of Rome was becoming ever larger with the emancipation of slaves, and extension of citizenship to the provincial population. The soldiers were increasingly no longer Italian, but the size of the army was maintained by drawing on the population of the provinces. The Italian population was no longer the ideal material to mold into a potent imperial army anyways. In the aftermath of the sack of Rome in 410, there is ample evidence that many people still thought that Rome's destiny was to bring civilization and Christianity to the entire world. This just goes to show, just how difficult it is to recognize seemingly obvious signs of decay in an advanced society. Many failed to realize that the western empire collapsed, even after it officially ceased to exist, for decades and in a few regions for centuries. That is similar to the way that we are failing to recognize that we are now living in a world that most likely already reached its limits of its carrying capacity as exemplified by the official recognition that conventional crude has peaked half a decade ago.

The population of the Roman Empire may have reached as high as 100 million, by some accounts, which would have probably included the population of the client states. Their nomadic rivals, who were pushing westwards, often numbered no more than a few hundred thousands, to maybe a million or so people at most taken by individual tribe, group, or coalition. Nevertheless, they made their pressure felt on Roman defenses. In the year 271 AD, Emperor Aurelian decided to abandon the Eastern province of Dacia, resettling the Roman colonists south of the Danube River. At the time, this was seen as a wise move, meant to consolidate the defense lines. In most likelihood, this was indeed the correct strategic move to make, given the circumstances. This however marked the first time that the Romans were accepting their inability to face coming invasion of peoples who were moving west, most likely to capture a piece of the Roman dream. The empire lasted officially for another two centuries after the retreat, but the writing was on the wall already in 271 AD. They had two hundred years to do something, yet they did not.

A brilliant leader of the western empire named Aetius, who is also known as the last leader who tried to put things back together and came close to succeeding, decided to use the Huns as a mercenary force that he occasionally hired to subdue the foreign elements that were increasingly asserting themselves within the empire. Between 410 and 440, they made some progress on this matter, only losing control of North Africa to Geiseric and the Vandals who moved all the way from central Europe to present day Tunisia and Libya in the space of a few decades.

Temporarily; it seemed perhaps like a brilliant move to try to preserve the entire empire, by employing the powerful Huns as mercenaries to subdue the barbarians within the Roman border. In the long-run however it proved ultimately to be the wrong strategy, given that the goal he had in mind was no longer a realistic one. In addition to that, they perhaps helped create a greater danger to their existence than the internal barbarians. With help from the Eastern Roman Empire, they were close to launching a campaign to retake the lands lost to the Vandals, which would have probably helped regain the empire's viability. The Huns, who were previously very accommodating to the Empire's needs however, had other ideas.

It is important for us to understand what happened during the decade starting from about 440, until 451, when the Hunnic leader Attila died in a drunken stupor during his wedding night. Once the Huns led by Attila were unified and bent on taking on the two empires of east and west, they were going to be a potent opponent no matter what. Their cavalry and archery skills were unmatched in Europe at the time. Remember however that the Huns also spent two decades fighting side by side with the regular Roman legions. Consequently, they learned a crucial skill that made them more potent than any barbarian group that ever faced down the Roman Empire. The Huns learned how to lay siege to fortified positions of defense.

The Germans, Vandals, Suevi and many others who torched the empire before, were certainly very destructive in the Roman countryside. Roman society was always kept in place by the local network of fortified towns that many, especially from the upper classes were able to take refuge in. When the Huns invaded the Balkan region that was under the eastern empire, it is suggested by some contemporary sources that they sacked as many as 100 towns in the region, including some of the best fortified ones. The Germans of Alaric officially sacked the great city of Rome in 410, decades before the Hunnic invasions. That sacking was done due to the fact that the gates were open, certainly not because the Germans had the skills to take such a city. Many Balkan fortresses defended themselves fiercely, but it was unfortunately to no avail. The roman world might have been completely destroyed if it weren't for the death of Attila that also signaled the end of Hunnic identity. By the time Attila died, most Huns seem to have blended into the vassal Germanic population that dominated the Hungarian plain and Carpathian region during that period. His sons took over the reins of the Hun Empire, and in the end they started a series of civil wars amongst themselves. With the death of Attila, the threat from the Hunns ended, but for the western empire, it was too late.

The Eastern Roman Empire was able to recover from the destruction inflicted on them by the Hun invasions. The lands they had in possession in the Balkans and in the Middle East continued to provide them with the much-needed revenues to maintain their defenses. Its strategic position as the gate between east and west, as well as south to north, meant that they were able to capitalize on any trade that still remained in the region. Constantinople was only conquered by the Ottoman Empire in 1453, a millennia after the invasion of the Huns. The western empire collapsed however, just two decades after the death of Attila. The fact that the Huns learned enough about taking on fortified positions meant that there was no place left for the upper classes of their society to take refuge to preserve their safety. With the end of any semblance of safety in the empire, the *Pax Romana* came to a complete halt, and the Roman system of trade and economic integration across a continent, as well as trade with outside actors ended.

Now none of this seems like a lot of fun, so perhaps it is time for you, my time traveler to move on. Sure, there is a point to staying on to witness the birth of a new historical beginning. With the end of the classical era, which the collapse of Rome brought with it, a new era was starting to take shape. It was the slow birth of the feudal system of the middle ages. The former barbarian warrior class was gradually transforming into the new elite of Europe. This was a long and painful process however, as one might expect it to be, given that this all happened in the ruins of a collapsed society. The Roman Empire by some accounts comprised up to a quarter of the world's population, and the level of social stability afforded to the people in that region courtesy of the *Pax Romana* was unprecedented at the time. The new system itself did not result in a rise to similar greatness as the one that was borne out of the Mediterranean during the classical era. In fact it took the people of Europe about a thousand years to just come to grips with the fact that there was in their past a great society worth emulating. This was the start of the Renaissance period, a time of rebirth of the vibrancy of European culture, through relearning some of the things that made their ancestors great a very long time ago. At this time, the feudal system, or the system of a collapsed society was beginning to come to its end, as it outlived its usefulness. However, like I said this was a long and painful process, so maybe now its time to move to the next lesson that history has to offer.

Easter Island: On our journey back towards the present, I think it is wise to visit briefly another society that endured a very painful collapse. The reason that I think it is wise for us to do so, is that the Easter Islanders are perhaps the most perfect example where a society most likely saw the impending disaster approaching due to their own behavior, yet they found it impossible to reverse course. As I mentioned, the Roman Empire was a huge entity. Their elites can therefore be forgiven for not being able to take stock of their real situation. The society that inhabited Easter Island numbered only 20,000 inhabitants at the most, at their greatest demographic extent. The fact that they inhabited an island that virtually every member of their society could literally know from shore to shore in great detail, and therefore they could see how the forest that they depended on, for their livelihood, was being exterminated methodically, exposes a weakness we humans have as a collective. It serves us therefore as a warning in regards to the decisions we make collectively as a society, especially in regards to our sustainability.

Your journey to Easter Island should begin about a thousand years before our time. At this point, you would probably encounter a culture with a peculiar taste for building big stone heads. The Easter Islanders were not a united tribe, but a society led by numerous tribal leaders. Increasingly, the accepted paradigm in this society became that the most successful tribal leader was the one who could build the biggest stone head. It is possible that the heads had a religious significance, where the bigger the head, the bigger the expected reward from the gods. What is certain, is that all other considerations became secondary to these people, or at least to their elites.

You my time traveler now have the chance to witness a cold war like buildup of stone heads. Every completion of increasingly large heads, no doubt culminated with a social gathering to celebrate the achievement, and you may experience these euphoric moments, which would make you forget that you are actually partaking in a process whereby a society is committing suicide. Self-destruction is what they were in fact celebrating, even though they did not know it. These celebrations were probably very lavish at first. As the stone heads got larger, and more numerous, no doubt the celebrations that followed were inversely becoming less impressive as the resources, both human and physical were being drained by the huge effort exerted on these societies to build the statues. Some people believe that as the misery of the population intensified, their elites likely convinced them that the answer to better times ahead lay in their commitment to build ever-bigger statues, probably to please the gods. In other words, the very behavior that was slowly draining this society was touted as the best hope for saving it.

There is little reason for you to hang around too long. The path to this destruction of an otherwise well adapted society lasted for many generations, and with each passing generation, the misery likely became more unbearable. At some point, archeological evidence shows that inhabitants of the island revolted against the practice of building stone heads, likely due to extreme starvation setting in. By the time they decided that they needed to do something, it was too late. The means to sustain themselves were largely eradicated. The forest and probably many of the nutritional harvests it provided was gone. They were not even able to build canoes to fish, trade, or move away. Archeological finds suggest that the inhabitants resorted to extreme forms of scavenging, and even cannibalism. The island's population dropped from 20,000 to 2,000 inhabitants. It is possible that those who still had canoes, likely left for other islands, trapping the rest of the population in a barren prison[4]. If there were some who had the means to move away, ironically it may have been some of the very elites who led their population into this nightmare, who were in the end excused from sharing in the misery. You do not want to share in this misery, so let us go to the next historical lesson, I promise that this trip, ever closer to our current time will be less nightmarish in its conclusion.

19'Th Century Europe: This will be our last stop through our temporal odyssey before returning to our reality. The foundation of our current society was laid during the 1800's, and while many may not realize this, it was a time when western society was rescued from a likely path to self-destruction. This period in western history is a wondrous one. The last remnants of the social order that began where we left off at the end of the *Pax Romana,* were being obliterated by a new social order, which is more or less in place even now. The landed nobility of Europe was losing its dominance to industrialists and merchants who were largely responsible for the industrial revolution that changed our livelihoods more than perhaps any event in history since the spread of agriculture. The trend of urbanization took on a great speed, which saw a great societal shift from people working the land as either independent or tenant farmers, to a society dominated by individuals willing to sell their labor in return for wages.

This was the height of European dominance of the world. The only serious competitors in industrial capacity, and therefore military might, were also European offshoots in the form of the US, Canada, and Australia, but only one was in actual fact a true competitor, because Canada and Australia were still under direct British control. Despite this, there were serious social problems that threatened to tear European society apart. Most Europeans saw a disproportionally small level of participation in the prosperity that industrialization created. Lack of political freedom meant that the population also felt disenfranchised. The 1848 revolutions, which rocked the old continent to its core, was in fact about allowing most of Europe's population to participate as full partners in the spoils of European imperialism and industrial might. It is important to realize that many Europeans were themselves the victims of imperialism, as exemplified by many of the subjects under the control of the Habsburg Empire, which was in fact mainly a European empire, as well as the many people under Russian dominance. Most importantly however, we need to recognize the spark of this revolution, which was in fact stemmed from the poor conditions of the working class, mainly as a result of the nature of profit maximizing firms trying to do their best to maximize profits through paying as little as possible for labor related costs.

The lack of trickle down prosperity witnessed at that time led to brutal boom and bust economic cycles, which led to massive rates of unemployment, during a time when there was no social safety net worth mentioning to stem the downward demand destruction cycle, once it started. The lack of social assistance during these downward cycles hit the working urban masses with brutal consequences. The resulting effect of these periods of brutal poverty was the political radicalization, through the dispersion of Marxist ideals, and other competing radical organizations.

It is important for us living today, and listening to rhetoric coming from various political parties to understand that the sorry state of the urban toiling masses, generally and especially during economic down cycles was not an issue of personal responsibility. For one to be able to take responsibility for creating his own social safety net there would have had to be back then, as now, a significant size of spare income available to the wage earner. As is the case for many people now, it was even more so the case then that the base line for starting the negotiation for terms of compensation for one's labor was the approximate amount needed for an individual (not a family) to meet the very basic bare necessities from paycheck to paycheck[5]. As is the case now, it was the case then that one could negotiate a slightly higher wage level in case that the job required skills that were in short supply. But just like it is true today that not all of us can be doctors, back then not everyone could become an engineer. Even if we were all to get such qualifications, we would find that some of us might still end up having to work in a lower paying position as many higher education graduates may have noticed recently. At that point, the higher paid jobs are auctioned off as favors in the shape of nepotism, or outright bribery. Bottom line is that there is always a part of our society who will always be paid just the bare minimum needed to make it from paycheck to paycheck.

Personal responsibility for our well-being is therefore not feasible in the absence of a social safety net to provide stability.

In the absence of a social safety net, that many of us today take for granted, it is my belief that European society would have stagnated and imploded, possibly before the turn of the century. In the absence of a way to blunt the brutal effects of economic downturns on the urban working class, industry would have likely met a powerful foe in the form of the machine operators who made industry possible. The Luddite riots come to mind here, which for those who are not familiar with the reference; they were people who rebelled against automation of production, because of the job losses, it caused due to lack of consumer demand to absorb the extra production capacity. Without the reforms initiated by a historical figure that I regard as the savior of the west, the losses could have become permanent, as production capacity would have far outpaced demand. Industry would have likely found itself in the position of being its own worst enemy. They were so good at producing the goods they made, that there was no longer a market to absorb their products. Their own workers often found it very hard to purchase the goods produced in the very factories they worked in. Good thing that someone had the vision and maturity to see the situation as it was.

The person I am referring to is the great German Chancellor, Otto Von Bismarck. He first made a name for himself during the great revolutions of 1848. Bismarck helped put down the rebellions in Prussia. He went on to unite all the German states into one country, except for Austria. He also managed to preserve peace in Europe through a well thought out system of alliances he promoted, which made waging wars very hard. Historians promote these deeds today as Bismarck's greatest achievements. It is unfortunate that a very important policy started by him, of capitalism with a human face, in the form of a social safety net is greatly overlooked as a defining aspect of European history. It was created not by bleeding heart socialists, as many would expect, if they do not know much about European history, but by a hard core conservative politician, known for uttering such phrases as "to make an omelet, you have to break some eggs". He in fact is known like I said for breaking many socialist skulls during the 1848 revolution. Historians overlook the importance of his social reforms, because they most likely think of them as a political move, without fully understanding the implications to the western economy, past and present.

Given Bismarck's reputation, one might wonder why he would do such a thing. He certainly had very little sympathy for the working class. He was not a believer in social justice, or any other concepts currently associated with advocates for social compassion. One thing he was a firm believer in was *"real politique"*, which basically meant that he was a very strong advocate of getting results. He wanted to transform the newly created German state into a strong power, and for that he needed prosperity. So much for today's right wing rhetoric that government spending does not create prosperity. Bismarck knew better, which is perhaps why this conservative, right leaning politician is not generally counted as one of today's conservative, right leaning movement's role models. Bismarck was the rare breed of politician who had the ability to recognize a good idea, regardless of the political angle it came from.

He recognized that the social safety net had the net benefit of quelling anger and resentment on the part of the working class, due to the uneven distribution of the spoils of empire and industrial progress. The working class in fact saw few benefits up to that point, while during economic downturns, they were far worse off than the peasants who at least could still afford to eat, as long as there was a half decent harvest. Bismarck effectively was one of the first people to realize that the needs of the working masses were now very different from the needs of the rural based masses that dominated Europe up to that point. The relative safety presented to people by owning a piece of farmland, or even those who worked as tenant farmers, sharecroppers, farm laborers, who had some degree of safety by living close to the land, had to be brought into the urban environment.

During bad crop yields, farmers often salvaged what they could, so at least they had food for the winter, and they still had the option of travelling temporarily to look for occasional work, knowing that at least their families had some food stored away. Being close to the land also means that one can also look for opportunities to scavenge the wilderness. The urban workers rarely had the opportunity to save up enough cash to provide their families with more than a month or two worth of necessities. That is often the case still today for a large segment of the working poor and lower middle class of our society. Admittedly, in our case however, irresponsible behavior is actually in part to blame for this, which is something I will elaborate on later in this book. An economic downturn can often marginalize an urban wage earner for more than a year, with only the slight potential to earn some money as an occasional laborer as a source of income. Economic downturns have always happened about once a decade or so. Bismarck recognized the danger that this situation posed to social stability.

It is more than likely that he also recognized the importance of having a consumer base to rely on to purchase the output that industry was capable of producing with increasing efficiency. Much has been made of the fact that Henry Ford recognized the benefits of higher wages for his employees, including the potential to gain them as customers for the very product they were paid to produce. In a world of perceived private enterprise and market supremacy over the role of government, it is to be expected that examples such as Ford should be brought up. Incidentally, few can argue that the Ford Company, or any other private enterprises for that matter, still conduct their business in the manner that Henry Ford did a century ago. The rush to outsource manufacturing, while still hopping to retain the western customer, should be a clue to exactly how firms see things today. Meanwhile, it is simply bad politics in an age when most western countries are looking to slash the social safety net, to reflect back to the wisdom that Bismarck demonstrated more than a century ago, which like I said, is possibly one rare example where society produced a big solution to a big problem. The absence of this wisdom on the part of an individual, could have possibly led to a social collapse that we would now see as premature from our perspective.

The model of the consumer driven economy was born once the social safety net gradually improved consumer confidence, which is a factor that economists today watch very carefully as a prognosticator of future consumption patterns, and therefore prospects for growth. Aside from confidence, the social safety net effectively raised wages for most workers. Unemployment insurance as well as a pension plan is equivalent to having a raise over and above the starting point of the wage negotiation, which as I already mentioned is near the point of what an individual needs to cover basic necessities from paycheck to paycheck[5]. It is true that some of that wage increase if not all of it, is temporarily taken away in the form of taxes, or as an investment contribution. Nevertheless, the money is there for when one might need a few months worth of financial aid in the form of unemployment checks, or in case that one lives beyond the age where one can reasonably be expected to work.

The social safety net also meant that recessions were no longer as deep in part due to panic contraction of consumption, which always accompanies a recession. In the case of uninsured workers, the contraction was more severe, making the recession far more severe as well. Because recessions were no longer as deep, the overall trajectory for long term GDP growth improved dramatically, together with the improvements made to the social safety net. This trajectory was only recently interrupted in the past few decades, due in part to the outsourcing of jobs, which effectively means that our social safety net is now improving other people's economy, because it is our safety net that makes it possible for us to still be the main consumers.

It is unfortunate that firms no longer see us as good producers given our insistence on limiting damage to the environment as well as those pesky labor laws and regulations meant to protect the worker from abuse. Firms do not think that it is in their interest to hang around to help pay for the safety net, which encourages the consumption of the products that they produce. This however was not an issue for the time of Bismarck, because the level of infrastructure and education in the west was so far above the levels found in the rest of the world at that time, that there was simply no practical way to outsource the jobs in a significant way. Transport issues also played a significant role in keeping production of many goods localized. Therefore, unlike our current sad situation that we find ourselves in, European governments did not have to go bust in order to provide this safety net, because firms had no choice but to stay put.

The US did not come on board with creating a meaningful social safety net until many decades later. This was just at the time when it was right in the middle of overtaking Europe as the world's main economic power. As a result, many, politicians and pundits on the right of the political spectrum are tempted to argue that it was precisely this form of pure capitalism, which made their ascent to greatness possible. This is false on two counts. First, all the human and natural resource energy was being harvested because of the large inflow of migrants coupled with high birth rates, which created a fast-paced growth in the country's population, meaning that demand was constantly expanding. The same model is used in Canada right now, which annually takes in about 300,000 migrants, or the equivalent of 1% of its overall population. This creates demand for housing, cars, infrastructure, as well as providing labor to the economy. The result of this can be seen in the current economic crisis, where Canadian home prices are reaching new record highs, while in the US they are still tanking.

The natural resources needed to accommodate such an increase in population also need to be there to create such an effect. In Canada, there is still great potential to expand natural resource production, so the expansion of its population is not a threat to its sustainability just yet. This was also the case with the US, where the amount of farmland, and mined resources were expanding at a similar pace to the expansion of its population. The availability of an ever-increasing amount of farmland is especially an important aspect of the period, which allowed the US to expand without having to implement a social safety net until at least the 1920's. The reality of America during that period is that the bulk of its population was still rural. As you may recall, the need to have the safety net implemented in Europe did not come to be either, until the approximate time-period, when the urban masses started to outnumber the rural population. The exact same phenomenon is being currently witnessed in China, where the government is actually taking the approach of implementing a social safety net of sorts exclusively for its urban population. Even their obsessive drive to keep the overall price of producing goods in their country lower than almost anywhere else is not enough to keep them from having to do what Bismarck realized that needed to be done over a century ago.

The Americans realized the need for a safety net, only after plunging the world into what is now known as the great depression, which only ended with the beginning of the Second World War. In other words, it took the brutal death of 50 million people to get us out of that one. In the aftermath of the war, the western consumer economy took shape, thanks in large part to the now matured social safety net, and we are likely witnessing the beginning of the end of this economic trend at this point in our lives. The sad part is that there is to date no Otto Von Bismarck of our time to embrace new ideas, and be willing to do things differently. Looking at our mainstream politicians, it is obvious that their only plan is to do nothing, and hope for the best. They are rarely result oriented, but rather personal achievement oriented, embracing ideas meant to appeal to the political views of people with an already determined allegiance to a political faction, regardless whether some of those ideas make sense or not. The filter of bad ideas, versus good practical ideas is completely removed from our political system in this way, and is reflected in the lack of reaction to our current increasingly obvious decline.

Back to the Present

Welcome back to the 21'Th century, I hope that you found your trip through the past entertaining and informative at the same time. The present can be a pleasant place, especially if you belong to a European, North American, Some Arab, or Certain Pacific societies. We Westerners in particular have the best of all worlds. We built for ourselves quite a pleasant and open society, with many benefits that allow for the average Joe of our society to enjoy the comforts, which in some ways surpass even the pomp of life at the Imperial palace in Ancient Rome. The ancient ones had the benefit of collecting the yearly production of energy, which the soil of our earth generously gave each growing season. We are now harvesting the yearly fruit of the soils with a many fold efficiency. At the same time, we figured out how to harness the energy that the soils in combination with the sun produced millions of years ago.

From 1,800, until 2009, we increased the global population from 1 billion, to 6.8 billion and we are still growing. There were many skeptics along the way, who said that this could never happen, because we would never be able to supply the resources needed to feed everyone. Thomas Robert Malthus was such a person, who was one of the earliest people to cast doubt on whether we have the ability to keep on expanding our food production. In his publication "*An essay on the principle of population*" he predicted that the world population growth would outpace food growth by the mid 19'Th century, giving rise to famine, and starvation, which would re-establish an equilibrium. In order to avert such disaster, he proposed that charities and government aid programs should be limited, in order to discourage the poor from breeding beyond their ability to sustain themselves. Today we know that to have been wrong, because since he wrote that in 1798, the world's population has grown six fold. Total cultivated area increased roughly four fold during the same period, while the yield of food per hectare increased exponentially as well. The increase in grain yields per acre has been somewhere on the order of 10-12 fold since 1800. This increase was mainly possible because of increased use of motorized equipment for farm work, transport, irrigation, and fertilizer use, which are all connected to the intensification in use of our hydrocarbon endowment. Global energy use overall, mainly due to the onset of the fossil fuel era grew by more than 80 fold since 1800. Most historians and economists, who want to strengthen their argument against any doubter of our continued ability to expand, tend to bring up the folly of Thomas Malthus, who failed to factor in human ingenuity in his forecast of impending global famine.

Geological history was generous enough to preserve plants and animals, which lived and died over the past millions of years, and we are smart enough to find ever more efficient ways to harvest the planetary growth of millions of years in the past, and use it as our source of energy. The addition of this vital source of energy, which we transformed in other forms, including food, was by far the main reason why Malthus was proven wrong thus far. Cars, stereos, computers, refrigerators and other marvels that we came to take for granted may be important to us, but so is the freedom from having to spend most of our effort as a society to grow food. Through a combination of motorized farming, and hydrocarbon-based fertilizers we in the west achieved the feat of leaving the entire food production to roughly five percent of the population. The other 95% are free to pursue other endeavors, such as manufacturing, or arts. It also allows us a lot of free time compared to our predecessors a few hundred years ago, but not as much as probably, we could potentially afford and yet still have our basic needs met. We as a society have converted our productivity gains of the last few hundred years, which we achieved through exploitation of hydrocarbon energy into consumption, rather than leisure time.

There have been other doubters of our ability to continue our economic and demographic expansion. In 1972 a think tank called The Club of Rome, released a book called *"The Limits to Growth"*, which forecast that down the line, the world would encounter shortages of raw materials, food, and an increase in pollution, leading to a further decrease in resources available to us. It is in many ways not much different from the argument I make, with two important exceptions. The first is that we are now already faced with these shortages. Although; many people will deny this, even as countries are collapsing due to the price spikes in food and energy. The second exception is that I only refer to the current situation to point out the benefits to my proposed solution to these problems, rather than simply point out the folly of our ways.

Their arguments were dismissed as Malthusian, which like I mentioned already, has become one of the most potent counter-arguments against anyone wishing to ring the bells about the danger of overexploitation of available resources. "The authors load their case by letting some things grow exponentially and others not. Population, capital and pollution grow exponentially in all models, but technologies for expanding resources and controlling pollution are permitted to grow, if at all, only in discrete increments."[5]. This was the description made by Robert Solow, a renowned economist. I should point out however that Robert Solow is also failing to account for a very important aspect of the argument made by the Club of Rome. They were making an argument about limits to availability of finite resources. Technological advancement may increase the availability of resources, which were previously uneconomical to pursue, and it can also lead to a speeding up of extraction rates. In the end though, finite resources are by the very implication of their name; finite resources. Technology cannot conjure up these resources from thin air. Currently only money and a few gaseous substances can be conjured up that way. Many of these finite resources do not have a viable alternative as a substitute product, which would allow

71

us to maintain our economic order. Many economists fail in my view to understand that they cannot apply the same models for production of finite resources that they would to manufactured goods. For instance, we can easily assume that given available raw materials, and favorable prices, the planet can grow production capacity of shoes exponentially and potentially infinitely. A petroleum field may not respond the same way for geological reasons. There are many mature petroleum fields or regions that continue to decline despite constant new technological inventions. There are many such examples, including US crude oil production, which benefits from the best technology that the world has on offer, yet their production has peaked in 1971, and has not been close to surpassing that peak ever since.

There is also another aspect of finite natural resources, which economists refuse to take into account when projecting future availability. In some cases the technological know how may be there in terms of being able to increase production of a certain resource, given its geological availability. The political will may be missing however, given that not everyone has the same goals for the future as the west does. For us it is essential that we import natural resources, because in some cases we cannot come even close to being able to provide from our own natural endowment. Some countries however may be right in asserting that increased production of a resource may not be in their long term interests. Take the case of Britain, which I already mentioned as an example. They were exporting petroleum in the 1990's, and into the early 2000's. During this period petroleum prices ranged from $10 to $30 dollars a barrel. They turned net importers a few years ago, and now they have to import the stuff at a price range of between $35-145 dollars a barrel, based on recent market prices, which most agree will not go back to the happy days of the 1990's. Their production continues to decline, so they will have to increasingly rely on imports for the foreseeable future. Now how could anyone argue that the market behavior of Britain was in their long term national interests?

At least Britain has an economic structure, which allows it to provide for its citizens even without the availability of natural resource extraction and export. How about a country like Saudi Arabia, which has nothing but oil, sand, and a rapidly growing population? Would it be in their national self interests to exploit their only natural resource in a way that would leave them without anything to export in exchange for the many imports that a country with no agriculture or any other significant resources evidently needs, at a later date? Wall Street economists seem to trend towards arguing that it would be in the interests of Saudi Arabia to double or triple their production, at the cost of being left without oil for export decades sooner. How they figure that this would be better for the Saudis is beyond my comprehension, and it seems that it is also beyond the comprehension of the Saudis recently. In July, 2010 news "broke" that the Saudi king announced a halt to new exploration of petroleum resources in the interest of saving some of it for future generation. This was not news that one gets on CNN, because to my knowledge, not even one major news agency reported on this speech, although its implication to our future is great indeed, if this is true.

Many Economists argued in 2008, when petrol prices reached a record $145 dollars per barrel, that it was resource nationalism and not geologic constraints that was in part responsible for the price spike. I would argue that increased resource scarcity will increase resource nationalism. In other words resource nationalism is a symptom of resource availability constrains, and at the same time it makes the situation worse. Economists should take note that there is currently no resource nationalism when it comes to plentiful resources, which have some industrial application, such as sand for example. I doubt that there will be a fiery speech by some nationalist leader, proclaiming the curbing of sand exports or nationalizing the sand packing industry in the interests of national security any time soon. That is because there is currently plenty of it available, and it is a resource that we can easily adapt to using with less frequency. In Economic terms it is a product to which we have a higher elasticity in consumption. Petroleum, gas, copper, steel, uranium and other finite materials we can hardly hope to maintain our lifestyle in their absence, so they are called inelastic goods. In other words we will continue to purchase and consume these goods with far less demand destruction occurring as a result of rising prices[7]. When demand destruction does occur, it is more likely to be the result of an economic slowdown, rather than through substitution with another product. The increased resource nationalism trend that has been infecting the globe with increasing virulence is a sign in my view that people are scrambling to secure what is left of many dwindling resources. One of the basic assumptions made by economists is that humans should be expected to behave within the economy in a logical manner that enhances their benefits. When it comes to their expectations of petroleum and other finite resource exporters, they evidently think that we should not expect them to behave in a logical, self serving manner.

Aside from resource nationalism, there is also an increasing trend, where resource importing countries are making a clear bid for the resources of other countries and regions. China has been extremely busy in the past decade, acquiring leases and stakes in petroleum and mining operations around the world. They are currently the main players in Africa, where they have been busy building infrastructure and lending funds to countries willing to offer them exclusive rights to their mineral deposits. The Chinese have been known to offer very advantageous deals, where money will be paid and infrastructure built, with no strings attached. There is also a mad dash to try to acquire farm land, wherever it is feasible to buy compact areas for massive farming projects. China, India, Korea, and Arab countries have been busy making such deals. The targets of such deals are generally underdeveloped poor countries, but lately there have been signs that resource rich countries such as Canada and Russia are also becoming an increasing subject of interest. China has secured pipelines from Russia, Turkmenistan, and Kazakhstan, which carry oil and gas to this new resource hungry nation. They are also increasing their influence in Canada, where there are presently many resources that China desires to acquire access to.

The western response to this issue of resource scarcity seems to be confined to trying to convince resource rich counties to keep their markets open to private enterprise. The other move, which in retrospect was a bad one, was the invasion of Iraq. I know that many Americans are finding it hard to grasp, but contrary to the belief of some, their soldiers did not die in Iraq for freedom for the Iraqis, or to protect the freedoms of America for that matter. Those are mainly the talking points of political elites who still try to

74

maintain support for their hawkish policies, but in reality there is no connection between the invasion of Iraq and freedom of any kind, anywhere. The soldiers and innocent Iraqis died for the attempt to free the petroleum of Iraq from political considerations. They wanted to clear the way to let the private companies go in and exploit the reserves of Iraq to its maximum possible extent. The plan was to quadruple petroleum production, leaving Iraq without petroleum decades sooner, but buying the west a decade of breeding room at the same time. Unfortunately for us, things did not shape out that way so far. After eight years of bloodshed, petroleum production in Iraq is still the same as it was under the leadership of Sadam Hussein. The country of Iraq is about to become responsible for its own security in the coming years, yet the central government doesn't actually control the country. Civil war is still a very likely scenario for Iraq, especially if its neighbors decide that it would be in their interest. A trillion dollars later, the west is left with nothing to show for their investment. Failure in Iraq may be something that we will come to regret bitterly in the coming decades.

The most potent argument for the existence of a global tug of war for natural resources is the way that global resource allocation has played out in the last decade. According to the IEA, the organization responsible for advising the OECD developed countries, mainly made up by western nations; OECD petroleum demand has dropped in the first decade of the 21"Th century from 48 million barrels per day, to 45 million barrels per day. The developing world, represented by countries, such as China, India and Brazil have increased their petroleum demand from 29 million barrels per day in 2000, to 40 million barrels per day in 2010, despite the rising prices. Now I know that there will be people out there who will argue that this is actually good news, because we are becoming more efficient, but if you take another interesting statistic from the past decade into account, then these statistics may shed a different light on the situation. According to an article by Neil Irvin in the Washington Post, published Jan/2/2010, there was zero job growth in the US between 2000 and 2010. The net worth of American households has declined, and the average middle class family is earning less than they did in 2000. The situation in the EU is no different. Despite the show of some GDP growth, which was also subdued compared with past decades, since the great depression, the economy of the west can be described as stagnated at best. The growth in GDP that was achieved, went to a few wealthy individuals. Even this stagnation was only achieved through an explosion of personal, corporate, and government debt. As much as economic and other optimists would like to make this into a success story of increased efficiency, the real story is a different one.

The actual story of the 21'Th century is the transfer of jobs, wealth, and power to the developing nations. The cheerleaders of globalization lied to us when they claimed that it would lead to a decrease in poverty in the developing world, while simultaneously propelling us to new heights of prosperity. It did indeed lead to a decrease in poverty in the developing world, but the promise of our prosperous future seems to be very hollow. The 2010 US census shows that the number of people living in poverty in the US has grown by about ten million people. If our current financial situation is a guide, the next decade will look even worse for us westerners. Unlike the past decade, we will no longer be able to mask our decline with an increase in debt at all levels as we did in the last decade. The decline in our standard of living could be even more severe, while the developing powers will be able to capture more of the strategic resources of the planet. Let's not forget that China possesses over 2 Trillion dollars worth of cash reserves.

Remember the plight of the Western Roman Empire, in the 400's, and the solution that their last great leader, Aetius came up with. They managed to buy some time, and thus avoid disaster by employing the Hun tribes into their service to beat their internal barbarian settlers, and pacify them. For two decades, they saw the presence of the Huns at their borders as a blessing. The Huns however were in it for their own self-interests, and when they saw an opportunity in the form of a planned Roman campaign against the Vandals who settled in the financially important provinces of North Africa, cutting off important revenues and supplies from the Romans, the Huns acted on it. As the Romans were busy massing their troops that they gathered from all over the Eastern and Western Empires, the Huns struck. They were more effective than any other previous invader of Roman territory due to their adoption of Roman siege tactics that they learned from the Romans themselves. For the first time, Romans had no place of refuge from the onslaught, because the fortified towns were just as likely to be raided as was the countryside. Ten years or so of these constant wars with the Huns left the western empire beyond any hope of salvage.

The reason that I bring up this important lesson we learned about the Roman era is because I think there is an important parallel that we can draw with current events. We may not be presently in a major defensive war against a potential invader, but we are locked globally in a war among nations for the right to produce and consume things. Until very recently, we westerners had almost exclusive claim to the right to manufacture high value products. Through the adoption of our technology, education system, and capitalist mentality, developing nations are now raiding our shores for the jobs that we thought would always be safe from outsourcing. Millions of manufacturing jobs disappeared from North America and Europe and millions of manufacturing jobs were created in other regions, due to the transfer of technology to those who are more ruthless in using it than we are in exploiting people and the environment. Like the Huns did to the Romans 1600 years ago, the developing world is beating us using our own innovative skills.

As the Romans did 1600 years ago with the Huns, we also made use of the Asian workforce to stave off a very potent potential enemy of our economy that showed its ugly head in the 1970's. We had to subdue inflation. Many may neglect to make this connection, but in reality, our predicament most likely began with the complete abandonment of the gold standard, which happened during the US Nixon administration, due to their default on the promise to reimburse US dollars with gold upon demand to do so. This unleashed the fiat currency monster worldwide, making inflation a very dangerous enemy to our economic system. The 1970's and 80's saw very high rates of inflation in the US and elsewhere, making it necessary to maintain high interest rates to compensate.

The flood of cheaply produced goods helped our situation initially, because it put downward pressure on inflation. A fast paced rate of technological innovation spurred by the introduction of the personal computer into the economy, as well as communications systems, such as cell phones, and the internet, most of which mainly took root in the west, ensured that despite a steady loss of low skill employment, economic growth and low levels of unemployment were maintained. This lasted for a few decades, which meant that our day of reckoning was postponed, thanks to all the hard working people of the developing world, who agreed to work for cheap, and thus provided us with a tool against our inflationary problem. The hard working people of the developing world were not content with only sticking to low skilled manufacturing, they decided to go after our high skilled jobs as well, just like the Huns were not content with merely being an occasional mercenary force that helped put out the fires of barbarian aggression within the Western Roman Empire.

It is very interesting that the issue of outsourcing did not become such a major issue until many middle class, white collar jobs became affected. For as long as dirty, manufacturing jobs were the targets of outsourcing, the issue was easily played down. Similarly in the Roman Empire, as long as their citizenry toiling on the fields were the victims of barbarian invasions, the system continued, as long as the elites were able to take refuge in the defended cities. When the Huns came, and they were not to be denied by a walled settlement, the system was shaken to its core, and the western empire collapsed soon after as a result. In a way, we can look at our loss of the high value jobs as a sure sign that we are running out of places in which we can take refuge; thus, we are also likely close to collapse.

We now face an arguably tougher challenge than the original problem of tackling inflation. We still have a potential danger of inflation courtesy, of the increasing competition for natural resources that we have from the developing world. We are also facing the challenge of keeping our jobs in the face of a leaner, meaner competitor, which is not afraid to break a few eggs and turn our global environment into a very messy omelet. They also have no problem breaking a few human skulls in order to maintain order, instead of our cursed need to try to keep people happy and docile through non-violent means. We are also in danger of losing our basic social safety net due to the need to cut the cost of labor, meaning that our average standard of living is very close to taking a deep plunge.

Maybe I was a little bit hasty, when I invited you back from your time travel. After further considerations, I regret that you had to come back here. Perhaps our future is not so bright after all. It is not as if it is more fun to be our competition. The only reason they are able to get our jobs moved to them is because they work for far smaller wages, in far worse conditions, and many of their governments are far from being serious about curbing pollution and degradation of nature. That does not seem like a lot of fun either.

I wish that we could travel back in time to a better place, such as the 50's or the 60's, even the 90's seem to be alright compared to where we seem to be heading, but then we would be right back in this position eventually, because we can't change the past. Some right wing personalities are hell-bent on trying to convince us that they can re-create those happy times, if we are willing to retreat to some past ideals. I will discuss in later chapters why those ideas are unrealistic. Is there hope for us for the future perhaps? Will there be some technological breakthroughs, which will make everything so efficient that it will allow the developing world to continue their development, without us having to drastically reduce our standard of living? Perhaps we can stretch out some efficiency, which will improve our collective standard of living, while using the same amount of natural resources. Perhaps we will come up with a theory of de-growth, which will wean us of our excessive consumption, without affecting our ability to continue to provide the basic needs of our society. But if we engage in a policy of de-growth, what will happen to our collective debts? Surely we cannot allow our debt to GDP ratio to rise through a drop in GDP. That would lead us to bankruptcy, and only a fool would voluntarily allow for that to happen.

What the future will bring, only the future will tell, but we can look at our current situation, in order to asses our current assets and liabilities of all sorts in order to be able to get a picture of how prepared we are as a society to deal with the challenges of the present as well as the future. We can also learn from the past, because similar problems affected other societies as well. This was my real reason to help you travel back in time for a short glimpse. The unfortunate fact of our society is that the current education system and cultural elites have been discouraging the study of history, so the citizens of our society have very little in terms of points of reference from the past, which they can correlate to our present. We can also extrapolate some of the current trends to give us a sense of our future predicaments.

Future prognosis can be very difficult and imprecise, because each person decides on what relevant current trends and stats need to be incorporated in extrapolations. There are also developments, which are yet to happen, for which we cannot account in any way, but which can have a great impact on future trends. Nevertheless we do know that we have problems and challenges that await us. Some of those problems are already here, awaiting a competent response from our leaders, and society. It is the lack of evidence for this competence in leadership to curb current bad trends, which makes me fear for our future.

Part 2

3

A finite world part one:
Oil & Gas

The crucial role of limited hydrocarbon resources on our economy

The average yearly price of crude oil, adjusted for inflation in dollars, went up by about 450% from 2000 to 2008, when the financial crisis hit. Translated into gasoline prices, the average price of gasoline for Americans went up from $1.50 a gallon, to as high as $4.00 a gallon. For the average American household, this represents an increase of roughly $1,200 in energy bills per year. In addition to that, airline ticket prices went up, because of the increased fuel prices as well. The price of a variety of other necessary products such as food, natural gas, coal, uranium and a variety of minerals also went up in price drastically in the past decade. As popular as it is to blame the speculators for these increases for goods that as I explained already, we have a low elasticity for as consumers, the speculator bit seems to be a very smelly red herring.

Some have argued that the developing world should be affected even more by the scarcity of resources, because of our superior buying power. In many important cases, the opposite is happening. In fact, China has nearly doubled its petroleum consumption levels, even as prices rose almost constantly during the past decade. Brazil and India have also made large gains in consumption, and there are a large number of smaller developing nations, which so far have seen the same phenomena occur, despite the rise in prices. To understand better what is behind this phenomenon we should look at how the

81

price increase has affected an individual US family versus an average Chinese family in the past decade. First, we have to look at the gains in income that both families achieved. The average US family has had almost zero gains in real income; in fact, they may have had a slight decline. The nominal gains over this period are due to wages keeping pace with the inflation rate. In other words, the average US family has had an increase in nominal dollar income of about 20-25%. The gain of the average Chinese family income nominally has been over 200%, given real and inflationary gains. The average Chinese family had wage gains that actually almost kept up with the increased rate in petroleum prices. The US family did not even come close to making up for the price increase; therefore, it was much too hard to cope with it. The slight decrease in consumption by American and other western consumers stems from us, the richer people actually being priced out of the market. That may seem counterintuitive; nevertheless, the past decade has proven that this happened with a large number of developing versus developed nations. There are some examples of exceptions, however this trend should be expected to continue as long as there will be a relative tightness in resource availability.

To exemplify just how serious the problem of resource scarcity is on our planet, given our current needs, I have chosen two resources that best represent the problem on which I shall concentrate, although I will mention a few others as well. I picked petroleum and natural gas, because they are very important to the running of our world. Because of our dependence on these products as consumers, the elasticity or the substitution ability of people to renounce on their consumption is very low in the short term at least. There is some hope of adapting somewhat to scarcity in these resources in the long run, but as we are already facing this problem for almost a decade, very little real initiative has been taken to confront it, which would give us reason for optimism. Despite the recent hype about renewable resources, and how they may gradually decrease our addiction to these crucial finite resources, as some like to see it, I remain somewhat pessimistic about our chances of success, without resorting to drastic redesign of our lifestyle. There is also a reason to discuss these two important resources, because there are increasing credible voices that are starting to ring the alarm bells. Unfortunately, in many cases they end up paying for it by having to withstand sometimes-brutal attacks on their credibility and livelihood by the establishment.

A recent example of such a person who paid dearly for braking ranks with the chorus and daring to speak up, is Canadian economist Jeff Rubin. He published his book *"Why Your World Is About to Get a Whole Lot Smaller"*, which deals precisely with the problem I intend to deal with in this chapter. His reward was that he was let go from his job with the Canadian Imperial Bank of Commerce (CIBC), despite the fact that he was recognized for many years as Canada's top economist. The reason they had for letting him go, and this is just a personal guess, is because he committed the ultimate taboo in the field of economics. He is an economist who dared to say that North American society would most likely face a decade of economic contraction, due chiefly to the lack of availability of resources, more specifically petroleum. He argues that there is not enough to go around satisfying, the growing thirst of the developing world, and at the same time allow us to go about our business as the society that is already the largest consumer of the fuel per capita by far. The reason for a bank to be angry about such a statement made by their top economist is obvious, just as they would be in regards to the contents of this book. A shrinking economy in the long term is one that can no longer meet its debt obligations. This is debt, which banks have taken upon themselves to allow consumers, producers and government to incur, without calculating the true long-term risk of us defaulting. As a result, this line of credit was awarded to us as it was awarded to the sub-prime customers a few years back. Perhaps they should have been more careful to ascertain whether we are worthy borrowers or not.

As I write this book, I myself am wondering whether it might one day be used against me at some point in the future. As I realize the fear that one can potentially experience to speak out, I am reminded of the fear experienced as a child, living in a brutal, autocratic system, where the threat was seemingly more serious, as one was actually risking his/her life. My parents were constantly reminding me to avoid speaking about certain things as I went to school in the morning. Most of us have become accustomed to think that we had to fear our government's potential autocratic reaction to free speech.

It is increasingly the case however that it is private enterprise who screens potential or current employees in order to effectively punish them, in case that they exercised their free speech in a way that they do not agree with. Since the rise of the information age on the internet, it is increasingly easy to single out people for political, economic or social views. I also recognize the fact that in a world where most of us sell our labor for a living, facing employment persecution because of one's views, may be as effective in deterring true free speech, as was the threat of imprisonment and violence. The main difference being that one mode of persecution leads to one being viewed as a martyr, while the other as just a failure. As a result, we may get a very unrealistic, but dominant view of what our future holds in terms of commodity constraints, based on people's desire to keep their positions rather than based on fact. This is not a new concept to most that experienced communism in Eastern Europe. Those wishing to keep their job, or even their freedom constantly fudged reports on agricultural or industrial production. The value of those reports was experienced by most in the form of shortages because of bad decision making on the part of government in terms of export volumes, in part based on the fudged reports. I realize that there may be repercussions because of what I write, but I think we should also realize the price we can end up paying for not exercising our right to speech, whether it is demanded by our government or private enterprise to do so.

Petroleum: (The resource we are most likely to go to war over, yet we sometimes deny its role as the main pillar that sustains our current lifestyle, without too many real alternatives).

The issue of petroleum availability is one of utmost importance to the global economy. Most of us think of petroleum as energy, which is a major use we have for it, since we use more petroleum as an energy source than any other competing source. It is vital to the transportation industry, as it powers about 90% of it. Petroleum is also important to the synthetic materials industry. Roughly, half of global petroleum production goes to the chemical, rubber, plastic, and other important industries. Even some of the big potential contenders as substitutes for transport fuels, or plastics, such as ethanol for transport, or soy-based plastics require a lot of petroleum based energy input. In fact the energy return on ethanol is thought to be as low as 1.5. That essentially means that it takes roughly 10 litters of gasoline to produce 15 liters of gasoline equivalent in ethanol energy. Not to mention the possible side effects on the environment, as more land is cleared to accommodate bio substitutes to petroleum. We can lose more forest cover, squeeze the wildlife habitat even further, and our water systems can end up becoming more poisonous as a result of fertilizer and pesticide runoff, but we will not succeed in replacing a relevant portion of our current petroleum consumption.

Given all these concerns I listed, I am amazed that the left leaning politicians and activists are inclined to be in favor of these industries. My personal objection to using food in our gas tanks is that we still have on a global scale, a few billion people who are still malnourished, and many of them are actually dying of starvation on a daily basis. For me, the ethics of this resembles the ethics of starvation camps. In other words, we will allocate food to transport in the more industrialized world, while a child in Sudan is deprived of having a bowl of rice per day because he/she had the misfortune of being born there (the starvation camp). The availability of this very precious commodity and the ethics of its allocation will play perhaps one of the most important roles in shaping our future. I do not mean to underestimate the importance of many other resources, ranging from fresh water, to steel, but if we were to pinpoint the most important resource that has shaped the past 100 years, petroleum seems to be the clear winner. Since we currently do not have many alternatives to replace its use with, I think it will equally shape the next few decades at least. If I were wrong, would there still have been a war in Iraq in 2003?

The top 20 petroleum-producing countries in the world are responsible for 70 million barrels per day of the total output of 85 million barrels in liquids. That is roughly 83% of the grand total. This total production includes condensates, synthetic crudes, such as oil sands, bio fuels, and refinery gains. Among the countries that make up the 17% remaining in production, most of them are in decline, although there are some promising prospects for increase in a few of them such as in Sudan. The overall health of the industry hinges on the 20 top nations that make up the bulk of production. As

85

a result, I decided to take a brief tour of the situation in each of these countries in terms of current proven reserves, past discovery history, and future prospects for future discovery and production based on current knowledge about their geology as well as political situation. Before I do this, it is important to define and clarify a few things regarding reserves and production on a global scale.

It is generally accepted that petroleum reserves can be referred to as such in the situation in which it can be ascertained to be feasible to produce the field, given current technology, and at the current range in prices. Not all countries count their reserves in the same manner, and there is still a lack of independent auditing of these reserve claims. OPEC members that adhere to production quotas, have a stake in overstating their reserves as it allows them to claim a larger share of the production quota. Some international private companies have competing interests in both understating their reserves, and overstating them as well. They may overstate in order to improve their balance sheets. They may understate for taxation purposes in some cases, depending on where they operate.

Other facts of note, regarding global reserves is that the peak in discovery volumes happened in the 1960's, and there has been a general decline in volume of new finds since. The world has been producing more petroleum than it found since roughly 1980, depending on whose data we choose to use. In the past two decades, production has outpaced new discovery volumes by a rough margin of 2.5 to 1[1]. In other words, we have been producing two and a half times more than we managed to discover. Some will claim that reserve estimation tends to be conservative, and the discoveries of the past decades are actually much larger. Even if they are right, and they were to double the reserve size of each discovery from the past decade, which is somewhat absurd, it would still mean we are consuming one third more than we are finding. There is also ample evidence from fields that were discovered and have already entered production that quite often the opposite is true. In the case of the Thunder Horse project in the Gulf of Mexico, it is quite clear based on its field performance that it is unlikely to yield the full amount that has been claimed as reserves in that field[2].

Of important mention should also be that not all reserves are equal. For example, there is a great deal of difference between producing petroleum from Saudi Arabia's biggest fields, and producing it from Tar Sands in Canada. There are approximately 1.3 trillion barrels in proven reserves claimed on the planet, and in addition, more than one trillion barrels has been produced already. Of the petroleum that has been produced so far, most of it was the kind that was easy and accessible to get to. The energy input to output ratio for many fields in the Middle East and good quality fields elsewhere was sometimes as high as 100 to 1. It is estimated that it takes the equivalent of one barrel of petroleum in energy inputs to produce five barrels in the Canadian oil sands projects. The energy return ratio for many deep ocean fields may also be somewhere in the ten to one range.

In terms of economics, it was just a decade ago that many financial analysts were predicting petroleum prices ranging from as low as five dollars a barrel, to highs of fifteen dollars a barrel. Here we are a decade later, and we are already stuck with a price floor in the $55 to $75 per barrel range. A sustained period of prices bellow this price range would shut down many current extraction operations, and postpone many new projects for the duration of the lower prices prevailing. A price floor of fifteen dollars, which was the upper end of most predictions ten years ago, would effectively mean that the global economy has suffered near complete collapse, and we only have pockets of economic activity, therefore we only need maybe 20% of current production.

The last piece of basic information in regards to petroleum production has to do with recovery rates from individual fields. At the beginning of the 20' Th century, roughly 15-20% of the original oil in place was considered recoverable. Currently that recovery rate seems to hover at around 35-40% of the original oil in place, thanks to enhanced recovery methods. The primary recovery method, which allows for about 15% of the oil in place in a field to be recovered, depends on the field's natural pressure to get the oil to the surface, so drilling a hole was all that was needed. Secondary recovery methods have been used for many decades now, and that is what allows us to reach the 35-40% average recovery rate. These modes of recovery include; water injection to increase pressure, electric pumps, chemical injections to dissolve tar walls and a host of other creative techniques. Most of these secondary recovery strategies require a much higher investment in terms of money and energy.

The net energy return on energy invested is much lower once a field starts producing through these means.

It is possible that there will be many more innovative techniques that will be employed to increase the ultimate average recovery rate of fields, but the essential part that we have to watch aside from the monetary costs is the energy cost. The energy return on energy invested for many old fields that are still producing is sometimes as low as the net energy return that we get from oil sands in Canada, or from the Bakken field in North Dakota, both of which yield only about five units of energy for a unit of energy invested. This decline in net energy return is one issue that is perhaps more important than watching the total liquids production from year to year. Even if we register an increase in total liquids production, if we have to allocate that increase to the production of these liquids themselves, we really are not increasing the net energy available to the public.

A quick look at the main petroleum producers

Keeping in mind the general information I mentioned above, here is a brief roundup of the top twenty petroleum producers and their prospects for the future. I decided to focus on crude oil exclusively, which accounts for over 80% of total liquid fuel production, because that is the true measure of what our future holds for us[3]. I think it is worth having a brief look at each individual producer, because that way, we can better understand the challenge of these countries in trying to maintain or even increase production. It is also worth questioning whether all of these key producers even have the long-term interest of trying to achieve maximum production that geological factors may allow.

1) Russia:

Average production in 2009 was 9.5 mb/d, or 3.4 billion barrels per year according to the EIA organization. Their proven reserves stand at roughly 80 billion barrels. Looking ahead at the next decade, if they keep their production at current levels, they will produce 34 billion barrels from their current reserves. Essentially, this means that they would have to find another 34 billion barrels in new reserves during the decade ending in 2020, to keep their reserve base from decreasing. Alternatively, they would have to find ways to enhance recovery from current old fields. The geologic potential for this to happen is there, but the political will and interest, may be lacking. There is no reason for Russia to strive to increase their current production levels, as they already export more than two thirds of their production. My current view is that a decade from now, Russia's production levels may be down from current levels by more than 5%, as many of the older fields continue their decline, while new projects will not make up for that depletion. I should stress however that given the immense size of this country, and the relatively large areas of territory that are still left to be completely surveyed, there could still be some upside surprises.

2) Saudi Arabia:

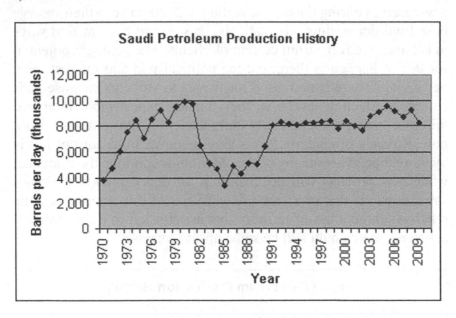

Average production in 2009 was 8.3 mb/d, or 3 billion barrels per year, according to the EIA. Their official proven reserves stand at roughly 260 billion barrels. The accuracy of these numbers is contested, because Saudi Arabia inflated drastically their reserve numbers after OPEC introduced the production quota system correlated to their official reserves. Furthermore, they failed to account for the roughly 90 billion barrels that they already produced since the reserve inflation occurred in the 1980's. They did not announce any discoveries of giant fields since the 1970's; therefore, it is hard to imagine where these extra reserves come from. Many industry insiders, including Mathew Simmons, who wrote the intriguing book on the issue of Saudi reserves and production, entitled *"Twilight in the Desert"*, claim that Saudi Arabia may be close to reaching a terminal decline in their production levels. The Saudis currently claim that they have roughly four million barrels per day of extra production capacity, which they could utilize if the need arises. It should be noted however that even as prices were marching upwards almost uninterrupted in the past decade, the Saudi's failed to surpass their previous yearly average production record of 9.9 mb/d. Their highest production levels in the last decade were recorded in

2005, at 9.5 mb/d. If they truly had a total sustained capacity of 12.5 mb/d as they claim, wouldn't they use it to settle the nerves of the markets when prices were surging uninterrupted for the most part of the decade?

Looking at their future potential for production, it should be noted that most of their giant fields have been in production for decades already. Their largest field Ghawar, which by some accounts still contributes about half of current production levels, has already produced 65 billion barrels. Despite their claim that there are still plenty of reserves waiting to be squeezed out from that field, and there is no danger of decline, most evidence points to the contrary. More than 90% of their production comes from a dozen or so giant fields, all of them discovered more than three decades ago, and they only have one more giant field in reserve named Manifa, which is still waiting to be put into full production. In the last decade, they re-tooled some of the old fields, which were not producing at their full potential in the past due to technical difficulties. Many of these fields cost a lot more to develop in monetary and energy investment, and due to their geological complexity are more unreliable than Ghawar has been up to now. They also have a portfolio of almost one hundred small fields, but all of those fields combined will probably not be enough to make up for the decline of even one of the old workhorses.

The political environment regarding future production should be of note as well. In a recent speech by Saudi king Abdullah, he stated that it is time to think of future generations when it comes to petroleum exploitation. That is not surprising since it is their only meaningful natural resource. They have to import most other natural resources and products from abroad, and that includes food. They also need massive amounts of energy to desalinate water, since the natural resources of water in Saudi Arabia cannot sustain its population. They also have one of the highest birth rates in the world; therefore, all these needs will most likely intensify with time. Given these considerations, it is hard to imagine what will move the Saudis to deplete their reserves faster. The geological realities of fewer recent reserve additions through discovery, and rapidly depleting old fields, combined with the political and demographic realities, will most likely inhibit the Saudis from ever producing above their original 1980 peak in production. In fact, I would not be surprised if a decade from now they will produce less than the current production levels, which are already 16% bellow the peak of three decades ago. In my own personal opinion, the 260 billion barrel reserve claim reflects the approximate amount that will ultimately be recovered in Saudi Arabia, and not current reserves. During the next decade, they will produce roughly 30 billion barrels at current rates. If they would truly have as much left in reserve as they claim, this level of depletion would not be so painful for them. Their real situation however is that they probably have only roughly 150 billion barrels left in reserve, given that 120 billion barrels were already produced; therefore they have to start thinking of reserve preservation.

3) United States:

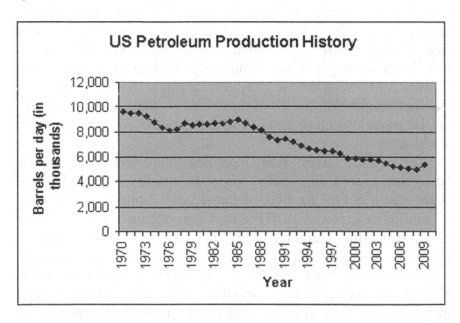

Average production in 2009, was 5.4 mb/d, or 1.93 billion barrels per year. Their current proven reserves amount to roughly 20 billion barrels, so at current production levels they would exhaust almost all their current reserves in the next decade. Only to maintain current production levels, the US would have to find and bring into production another 20 billion barrels of petroleum by 2020. Given that the last great frontier of discoveries and production is the Gulf of Mexico, where they already explored and produced for a few decades now, I would have to say that achieving this feat would require some luck. It would also have to involve a government more concerned with petroleum production than with the environment, since many future potential prospects lie geologically in environmentally sensitive areas. Given the recent BP disaster in the gulf, and its possible future effect on public opinion in regards to oil exploration and production, there is a good chance that it will not happen. Given most of these considerations, it is most likely that the US will resume its gradual production decline, which started in 1971, from a peak of 9.6 mb/d to the current temporary plateau of just above 5 mb/d. As I said however with a bit of luck, some great discoveries could still prolong this current plateau for another decade or more.

US hopes also lie with the shale oil fields that recently were proven as producible with new technologies. These fields only yield 1-3% of the total oil in place using current technology, but the oil in place is estimated to be at hundreds of billions of barrels, so even a slight improvement in extraction efficiency can mean billions of barrels in additional reserves. At best however, these fields will likely only make up for declines expected to happen in other older fields, therefore any increase in US production stemming from tapping these fields is likely to only offer temporary bumps in production at best.

4) Iran:

Iran's 2009 average production levels were 4mb/d, or 1.43 billion barrels per year. Official reserves stand at 138 billion barrels. This is yet another one of those OPEC countries that decided to inflate its reserve estimate by a relatively large margin in the 1980's, and like the Saudis they forgot to account for production in the last three decades. Unlike the Saudis, they do seem to have had more success with new discoveries. This country could easily produce more than it currently does, but it cannot, due to external political pressures. Their standoff with much of the western world and Israel over their alleged nuclear ambitions, which might include a desire to produce nuclear warheads to counter their main regional threat Israel, which is believed to posses 200 warheads and the means to deliver them, is the main obstacle. These considerations will most likely prevent Iran from increasing its production in the next decade. There is hope however that the current issues will be resolved (hopefully not through war), and maybe they will start developing their fields in the medium term. For now however, it seems that Iran can be expected to start decreasing its exports, even if it does not decrease production, because their internal consumption from its population of roughly 70 million is increasing rapidly.

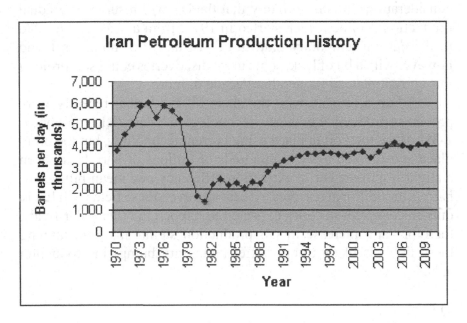

5) China:

China: 2009 average production levels, 3.8 mb/d, or 1.36 billion barrels per year. Their official reserves are at 16 billion barrels. If they were to maintain production levels at the current rate, they would need to add a minimum of 14 billion barrels of new reserves during the next decade. The odds of this happening are rather low, given that most of the potential places to be explored have already been surveyed, and as is always the case, the big finds have most likely already been found. What remains now are the smaller, and more challenging projects. My personal view is that they will have a very gentle decline until 2020 from current production rates, followed by a steeper decline in the following decade after that. Perhaps by the end of the next decade their production levels will be down by 20%.

The Chinese government controlled petroleum exploration entities will most likely work very hard to prevent this from happening, but in the end, their plan B seems to be a lot more likely to pan out for them. The Chinese are currently working very hard to secure petroleum reserves across the planet. Their move into Africa with massive investments with no political strings attached is yielding good results in terms of securing mineral rights privileges. They will need these resources if they are to continue down their current path of economic growth fueled by the same frontier mentality that was the engine of growth for North America some generations ago. Except for their frontier is made up of the urban, industrialized, versus the poverty-stricken rural line. Given their limited resources of domestic petroleum reserves, I expect that their policy of securing foreign reserves will gradually become more aggressive.

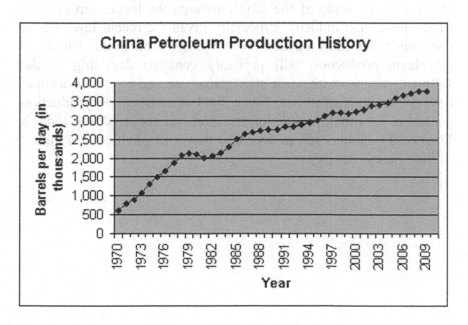

6) Mexico:

2009 production levels were at 2.6 mb/d, or .93 billion barrels per year. Their current reserve base is 10.5 billion barrels. They would have to find and develop at least another 10 billion barrels over the next decade in order to avoid disaster. Given that, they have access to the same gulf that the US has access to, it cannot be excluded that they might get lucky and find some major deposits still. Given the political reality of having to adhere to the law passed in 1938, regarding foreign ownership of exploring and production rights, which forbids such activity by multinationals, it is not likely to happen. The state run company Pemex, runs the show there, and they do not have the necessary technological and technical abilities to go for some of the harder to find and develop fields.

The Mexican government also depends largely on money made from petroleum production to fund its needs. By the most recent estimates, the state budget depends on Pemex for 40% of its revenues. This is money that could be used to modernize the company, but the short-term needs of the state outweigh the longer-term health of the petroleum industry, especially given the recent lawlessness the country has suffered from recently. My view is that Mexico's petroleum production will probably continue declining in the following decade with some short pauses caused by the occasional new project coming on-line. Since 2004 when Mexico's production peaked at 3.4 mb/d, production has declined about 30% to today's level of 2.6 mb/d. Perhaps by 2020 they will produce less than 2 million barrels per day.

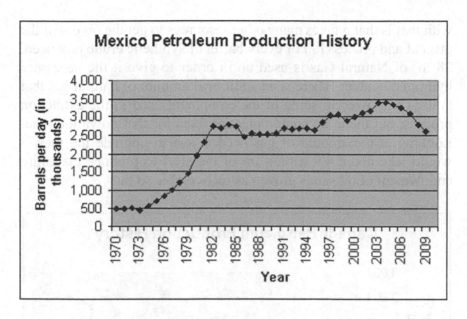

I should also note here that back in 2000 most official petroleum-forecasting agencies like the USGS and EIA were forecasting that Mexico's petroleum production levels in 2010 would be around 3.5 mb/d. It seems their forecast missed the target by a very wide margin. Some of the same organizations that missed the mark in the case of Mexico and many other countries and regions currently continue to forecast that we are free of concerns regarding petroleum availability for the next two decades at least. That is despite the fact that it seems that we have been dealing with this problem for half a decade already. Perhaps these agencies are yet another example of failed institutions that we continue to depend on, despite the already obvious shortcomings of these people. Then again, maybe their purpose is not what we may think it is in which case maybe they are performing admirably.

7) Canada: (The place, I consider to be home)

Canada's, 2009 production levels were at almost 2.6 mb/d, or .92 billion barrels per year. Canada's official reserves stand at 178 billion barrels, the second largest reserves on the planet. Here we have a special situation however, because most of that is in the form of oil sands from Alberta and Saskatchewan. The main problem with that is that it takes many other resources to get the oil out of the ground and process it. For every barrel of synthetic crude produced, 28 m³ of Natural Gas is used up in order to give it the necessary hydrogen content. There is an additional amount of natural gas that is used in powering some of the equipment used in the extraction process, but there are some potential fixes for that down the road. Looking at the amount of gas needed just to upgrade the fuel; it would take about 4.9 trillion m³ of the stuff to produce the entire endowment of oil sands proven as recoverable so far.

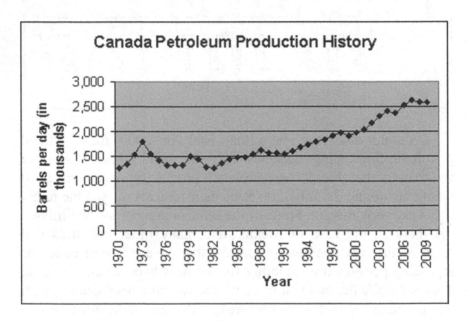

Canada's current proven reserves of natural gas stand at 1.3 trillion m³. That is less than a third of what is needed just to produce their oil sands in the next decades, never mind that Canadians are among the highest per capita users of natural gas on the planet due to the cold climate, and the need to produce fertilizers for their agricultural needs. Currently, Canada uses about 93 billion m³ of gas per year, more than 16% of which goes to the oil sands. If they are to triple their production of synthetic crude, as many forecasters believe will happen in the next two decades or so, Canada will soon become a major natural gas importer. While I have no doubt that, many new potential natural gas finds will greatly enhance Canada's capability to meet its needs, it is increasingly unlikely that they will be able to cope with future demands caused by the oil industry.

The other issues tied to oil sands production have to do with the environment. Alberta and parts of Saskatchewan are the most arid regions of Canada. I have driven through these provinces many times and every time, I was amazed at the lack of tree growth in that region. Sometimes you can drive for over an hour, without seeing one naturally occurring tree. Given the arid nature of the region, the oil companies are competing with the needs of Alberta's growing urban population, and with the farmers involved in irrigation supported farming, and cattle ranchers. There have already been issues concerning river systems that were either overdrawn by the oil industry, leaving nothing for some farmers, or in some cases the pollution of water systems by runoff from recycling ponds. Despite the great effort that the oil industry has gone through to limit water use, the process continues to remain somewhat water intensive. Currently the oil sands industry requires twice the amount of water that is required by the city of Calgary, Alberta, with a population of over one million inhabitants. There is also the issue of CO_2 emissions, but that on its own is unlikely to threaten the industry's progress, because the need for the petroleum outweighs the concerns of the emissions in our cultural values.

The overall trend for Canadian oil production should be up for the next two decades at least. Reserve depletion is not an issue on its own, but associated reserves of other resources involved in the production of oil sands is a big concern. Water availability may continue to pit the industry against other interests in the region. The natural gas required to produce synthetic crude out of the bitumen being mined from Alberta can potentially restrict the ultimate recovery levels of the oil sands reserves. To put things into context, the often-hyped shale gas reserves that have been proven so far in North America equals to roughly the amounts of gas needed to produce the synthetic crude from the bitumen. It is in a way ironic that the production of one unconventional fuel source cancels out the availability of another unconventional fuel source. Unfortunately, to date the financial and political elites have chosen not to point out the correlation that exists between the availability of one resource with the other. For now, they seem to be content with engaging in a game of double counting. Despite the boom in oil sands mining and processing in the last decade, Canada's petroleum production increased by only 500,000 b/d during that period. The following decades should be not much different; therefore Canada is by no means the next best hope. Given demographics in Canada, fueled by immigration, and continued economic growth trends, this production increase rate is only enough to satisfy growth in domestic demand and not much more than that.

8) Iraq:

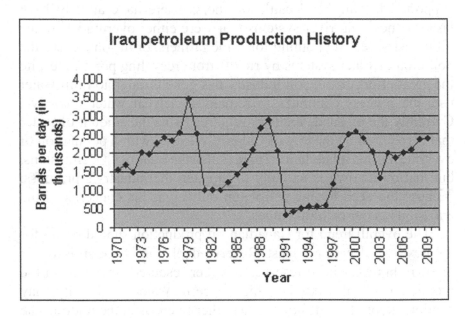

Iraq's 2009 production rate was 2.4 mb/d, or .86 billion barrels per year. Official reserves stand at 115 billion barrels, but here we once more have another one of those OPEC members that were at one point tempted into raising their official reserve count for political reasons. In the 1980's their official reserves stood at about 32 billion barrels, yet now they claim to have 115 billion, without announcing any major finds in the last decades. For the past few decades they also produced about 18 billion barrels, so even if they did have some success in new finds in the past decades, it would only make up for petroleum already produced. Even with the recent price increase, and advances in technology, it seems incredible that they should be claiming such a high reserve base. Incredibly, official energy statistics organizations like the IEA and the EIA, which are charged with the responsibility to monitor the overall global energy situation, accept these claims as fact, without any reservations. Like the vast majority of Gulf States, Iraq does not get independent audits in regards to their petroleum, so what is going on in that country is anyone's guess.

My personal hunch is that they do have at least the original claim of resources of 32 billion barrels originally claimed in the 80's. There is ample evidence to suggest that many gulf region reserves were somewhat underestimated before that decade. The true amounts that are still left to be recovered most likely amount to somewhere between 40-60 billion barrels. Given the lack of technical data to rely on, these remain only guesses. Even if they only have the amounts that I think they still have, it is still a very significant potential energy source for our future. The world's hopes lie chiefly with what will happen in Iraq in the following decade or two.

Recent news articles that quote Iraqi and American officials have informed us that they hope to increase Iraq's petroleum production levels from the current 2.4 mb/d to as much as 12 mb/d, or 4.3 billion barrels per year. Former US president G.W. Bush stated that history will ultimately judge him, whether he did the right thing or not by invading Iraq in 2003. As much as critics like to dismiss that in light of the trillion-dollar price tag of this on-going adventure, perhaps he may have been correct in his assessment after all. Given the bleak situation faced by the planet in terms of future energy supplies, it is not too hard to understand that ultimately the value of that war will have to be judged on whether it will yield a 10% or more increase in global petroleum supplies or not. That 10% increase will be crucial for the economic well being of the world in the following decade. Given recent trends of the west deferring their use of the stuff to the emerging markets, it is increasingly obvious that this increase in supplies will be especially crucial to us. If it will not happen, we will most likely go through another round of economic contraction, similar to the 2007-2010 period, when we transferred 5 mb/d of consumption to the rest of the world. This time it could be worse, as our governments are already out of policy options due to the surge in negative numbers on their balance sheets.

9) United Arab Emirates:

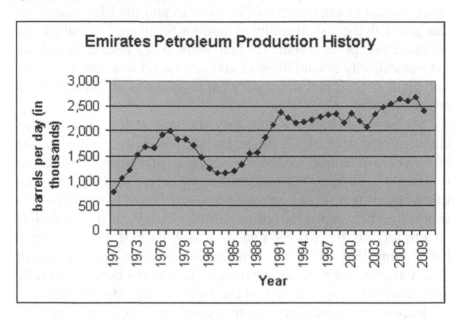

The Emirates 2009 production average was 2.4 mb/d, or .85 billion barrels per year. Their official reserves stand at 98 billion barrels, but this is once again dubious to say the least. The Emirates increased their claim of proven reserves from 33 billion barrels to 97 billion in 1986 without any explanation. They kept this claim despite producing about 16 billion barrels since then. Effectively they are claiming an increase in their reserves of about 340%, without evidence of any new significant finds. I could understand a doubling of reserve claims based on some improvements in technology, a less stringent method of counting potential reserves, and some new finds since then. Based on that, they could claim a maximum of current reserves of maybe 50 billion barrels, which is half of what they actually claim to have. Once again, due to lack of transparency, the truth can be anyone's guess. I do not expect the Emirates to be very eager to increase their current levels of production significantly. Like Saudi Arabia, they have no reason to rush to deplete their reserves, whatever their size, just to satisfy the needs of the rest of the world. Like the Saudis, they also have a fast growing population, which demands to live relatively well. They both also share the unfortunate situation of being endowed with not much else besides oil and sand as natural resources. Some tourism has evolved in the country, but it would not likely survive without the presence of petroleum wealth in the region.

10) Kuwait:

   Kuwait's 2009 production rate was 2.35 mb/d, or .84 billion barrels per year. Their official reserve count is about 112 billion barrels. Given that in 1983, they increased their official reserves from 67 billion to 97 billion barrels without explanation, and despite the fact that they produced since then another 20 billion barrels of crude, without any major finds that would replace the depleted fields that official number, seems like a fantasy. A 2006 report by the Petroleum Intelligence Weekly, (PIW) claims that official government reports from the turn of the millennium in Kuwait showed that at that time their petroleum reserves only amounted to 48 billion barrels at the beginning of the decade. Ten years later, given that not too many new fields were discovered in Kuwait, that figure could be as low as 40 billion barrels. Even those reserves apparently do not all qualify as proven reserves, as some are only probable, or p50 reserves, where there is only a 50% chance that the reserves are actually there in the abundance assumed. If they are right, then more than 60% of Kuwait's reserves exist only on paper. Even if we were to assume a much higher price in the future, which would increase the incentive to drain their fields to a fuller extent, their ultimately recoverable reserves would not be much higher.
   In the case of Kuwait, we have a potentially accurate picture of the original oil in place in that country from 1995 made by the USGS (United States Geological Survey). In that survey, they state that their original endowment was about 170 billion barrels. Recovery rates around the world are on average just under 40% of the original oil in place. Even assuming that with future technological advances and higher prices as an incentive to try to recover more, it is doubtful that they can reach a recovery level higher than 60%, or 102 billion barrels to be produced in the end. They already produced about 45 billion barrels cumulatively over the years. That leaves them 57 billion still to be produced in the best-case scenario, for which there is no guarantee that it will materialize. Incredibly, they wish to claim

that they will ultimately produce 157 billion barrels cumulatively, or 92% of the oil in place. That is more than twice the global average recovery rate, and there is no evidence to date that a recovery rate more than 50% will ever be possible for a producing region. Besides, official reserves are what is considered possible today, not in the possible distant future.

Just like in the case of the other five OPEC members we visited so far, the "prestigious" energy analysis organizations, like BP, EIA, USGS etc, continue to report the official, un-audited reserves that Kuwait puts forward every year. The economic analysts in turn take those same reports, and they estimate that the world has nothing to worry about in terms of petroleum availability, because the Gulf States could add another 10-15% to global production and maintain that level for decades. Given their massive official reserves, there is no reason to doubt that. If we pause for a moment and look at the details for these countries, their behavior seems to defy all logic in terms of economic theory. Despite a steady increase in prices from 1999 to 2008, that ultimately resulted in an increase of more than 400% in annual price average, if you notice, most of these Gulf petroleum states collectively flat lined after 2004 or so, despite prices continuing to move up almost uninterrupted. Perhaps some Harvard economics graduates out there should pick up a first or second year textbook and review the theory of supply & demand, and how prices encourage production levels of a good. Recent behavior by these states that also happen to be the official stewards of our global spare production, supposedly ready to kick in when the need arises, seems to be further proof that something is not all right in the desert.

Most of these countries could still put in an effort to increase their production capacity by significant margins. If they truly had the reserves that they claim to have, they should not worry about having to ration production just yet, after all Kuwait for example could produce at the current levels for another 100 years before declining, according to the official reserve estimate. More realistically, they can hope to produce at current levels for another few decades, before declining permanently. If they attempt to increase production by a significant margin, they risk depleting their reserves too fast, and the day of reckoning would come fast indeed.

I cannot stress enough the reality facing the Persian Gulf states. Once the petroleum will be gone, at least three out of the five states we looked at will have absolutely nothing left but sand. Iraq and Iran do have some other resources, including more fresh water and agriculture, but even they would be left having to rely on outside imports for most of their basic needs. All five states have a fast growing population, which is already 10 to 20 times higher than the carrying capacity of the land they inhabit. The expectation that people have of these countries accelerating towards their own doom in order to slow our march towards the abyss is incredibly unrealistic. Perhaps as unrealistic as the people who thought that sub-prime mortgages were AAA investments. These are decisions and views coming from a group of people often referred to as the best and the brightest. They are the elites that received their Master's, or Doctoral degrees from the best schools. Given their failure to see many of the bad trends, especially in the last decade, and their oblivion to many of the problems that are starring us in the face currently, that will hurry us if we do not at least make an attempt to tackle them, I'm a little worried.

I am left wondering whether the things that are being taught to us in the primary and secondary education system leaves us well adapted to current realities. Then again, maybe it has more to do with censorship. Jeff Rubin, who was recognized as Canada's top economist was pushed out from his job with the CIBC, because he tried to warn the world about possible calamity down the road. The "best and the brightest", working for other companies perhaps are taking note and keeping silent, because they love their fat paychecks, more than the urge to tell the truth. If they are required to see 112 billion barrels of petroleum in Kuwait, and therefore expectations that petroleum production capacity in that nation should double in the next few decades, it is exactly what they will see. I see many parallels between this sort of mindset and the one that prevailed in the system that I already experienced the collapse of, and it worries me greatly, because after experiencing such a traumatizing childhood as I experienced in Romania in the early 90's, my appetite for such "interesting" times is greatly diminished.

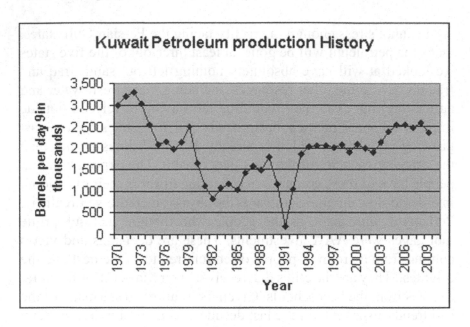

The bottom ten producers from the top twenty

11) Venezuela:

Venezuela's 2009 average production rate was 2.34 million barrels per day, or .84 billion barrels per year. Their reserve situation is murky, given the fact that they are in the process of upgrading their unconventional petroleum to their official reserves. As an OPEC member, however they also inflated greatly their official reserve claim in the 80's. They went from 28 to 55 billion barrels in 1985, without explanation and they have been growing the claim of reserves as the years passed. They currently claim to have some 98 billion barrels of conventional reserves. If they will claim their unconventional fields of extra heavy oil, they will be the number one oil reserve nation on earth. As a producer however, they probably will remain somewhere where they are currently, maybe move up a few spots at best.

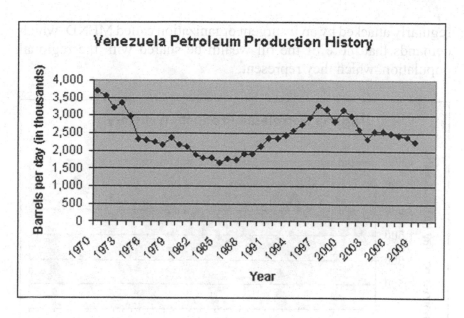

While there are plans in place and currently being executed to start producing and refining large amounts of heavy crude, it will most likely prevent Venezuela's overall production from declining further. The ultimate price of producing and refining the stuff is not very clear yet, however the refining part seems to be particularly costly. In any case, this will most likely be another one of those situations where reserve availability will in no way reflect production capacity. The current political environment in Venezuela will also inhibit the expansion of production of this heavy oil. Hugo Chaves, the current president is very skeptical of western companies, therefore investments in increasing capacity have to come from internal resources, or a select list of partners from China, Russia and a few other places.

12) Nigeria:

Nigeria's 2009 average production was 2.2 mb/d, or .79 billion barrels per year. Their official reserve estimate is at 36 billion barrels. Nigeria is one of the few OPEC members that are thought to have a relatively accurate reserve estimate. The main problem facing Nigeria's petroleum industry is the lawless nature of the country, which inhibits investments in new projects. Current projects are regularly attacked by an insurgent organization called MEND, which demands that more of the oil wealth be shared with the regional population, which they represent.

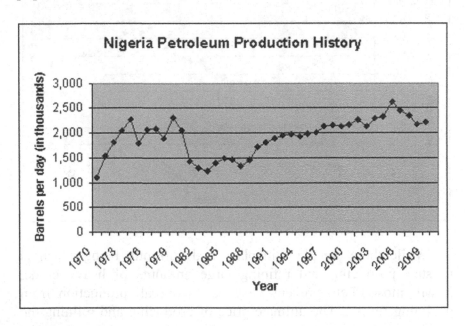

They regularly steal petroleum and sell it on the black market, and engage in capturing petroleum workers for ransom payment. Occasionally they actually disrupt the operation of production platforms by doing damage to them. Nigeria is also faced with the always-dangerous prospect of civil war between Muslims and Christian inhabitants living in the country. Nigeria's corrupt government has also ensured that the country's 120 million inhabitants remain one of the world's poorest, contributing to the country's instability. If they will be able to maintain relative calm, Nigeria may manage to deliver a few hundred thousand barrels per day more than in the present, in the next decade. The downside risk is very steep, because an all out civil war, which could break out any time just like in Iraq, could completely disrupt production.

13) Norway:

Norway's 2009 production average was 2.1 mb/d, or .75 billion barrels per year. Their official reserves stand at 6.7 billion barrels.

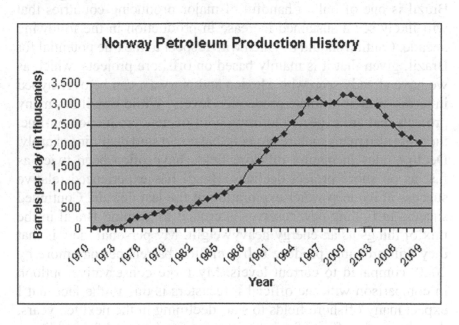

There is little doubt that Norway will continue to decline in production as it already has done for a decade already. Here again we have one of those mainly offshore producers who were forecast to provide anywhere from 3.5-4 million barrels per day by 2010. As you can see from the graph, the optimistic forecasts missed the target here by an even larger margin than in Mexico's case. It seems to me that there is an emerging pattern here, which tends to over-hype the production potential of offshore drilling. Recent lack of success on Norway's part to replace their produced reserves suggests that they are likely to decline even further in the following decade. It is even conceivable that they may drop in production rates to less than one million barrels per day. Even the Norwegian government admits as much.

On a side note, I admire the way that the government has handled the issue of petroleum wealth. The petroleum was largely extracted by the state owned company, and most of the profits from petroleum sales ended up in their trust fund for its five million citizens. They should be able to enjoy the proceeds for decades to come.

14) Brazil:

Brazil's 2009 average production was 1.95 mb/d, or .7 billion barrels per year. Their official reserve estimate is 12.6 billion barrels. Brazil is one of only a handful of major producing countries that will likely see a sustained increase in production in the following decade. Caution should be taken with respect to the true potential for Brazil, given that it is mainly based on offshore projects, which as we have already seen with Mexico and Norway, can be over-hyped in terms of their ultimate production levels. While Brazil has many projects that are expected to bring a lot of new production on-line, there are also many mature projects that could start declining sharply. Decline rates in mature offshore fields have often been twice as fast as on shore project declines. Brazil has experienced relative success in its deep-water exploration in the last decade. Continued success in finding new reserves is crucial to keeping Brazil in the mix of things as an energy heavyweight. My personal view is that they will probably produce half a million barrels per day more by 2020, compared to current levels. My more conservative outlook in comparison with the official forecasters is due to the fact that I expect many offshore fields to start declining in the next ten years, dampening the effect of many of the new projects coming on-line.

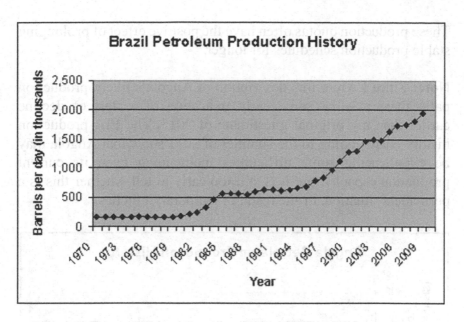

Brazil Petroleum Production History

15) Angola

Angola's average petroleum production in 2009 was 1.9 mb/d, or .68 billion barrels per year. Their official reserves stand at 9 billion barrels. Angola has seen a lot of success in the past decade with exploration of their offshore region. That success is also reflected in the increasing oil production levels seen since 2000. Continued success would hinge on continuing success in exploration, which would bring a lot more projects on-line. The likelihood of continued expansion in production will most likely not mimic the previous decade, as many projects brought on-line in the last decade will start declining, in a similar fashion as the other offshore projects have done so far around the world. At some point during the following decade the decline rate of old projects will most likely outpace the growth rate of new projects coming on-line. At that time, which I believe to be around 2015, a gentle decline in production will set in until about 2020, followed by a much faster overall decline after that time. By 2020 however, Angola should still be producing at least as much petroleum, or even slightly more than it does today. Given that Angola is a new OPEC member, it may even have to comply by production quotas at some point.

These production quotas often have the positive effect of prolonging stable production schedules for longer.

Note: Since I wrote this description of Angola's likely production path, there may be some early indication of a start of decline earlier than my original guestimate of 2015. The EIA production history charts, going to the summer of 2011 show that Angola may be experiencing some difficulties maintaining even its current production capacity, but it is still too early to tell whether this is a permanent situation, or the result of temporary glitches.

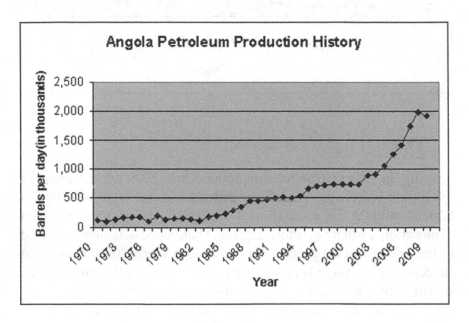

16) Algeria:

Algeria's 2009 average petroleum production level was at 1.8 mb/d, or .64 billion barrels per year. Their official reserves stood at 12.2 billion barrels, and despite being an OPEC member, it seems to be the real deal. Exploration activity in the past decade has had modest success, so the reserve base should continue to remain stable for now. Algeria should continue in most likelihood to provide the current level of production at least until 2020. That will depend on the government's ability to avoid the violence and unrest experienced more than a decade ago. Exploration for more resources also needs to continue to show results in order to replace depletion from older wells. There is little prospect of Algeria achieving much higher production than it did in the past few years, so this OPEC member should not be counted out if hopes are that OPEC will deliver for us increases in the near future.

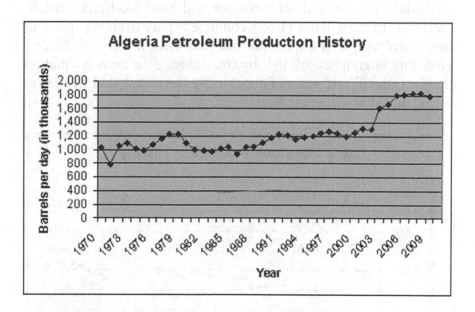

17) Libya:

Libya's 2009 average petroleum production level was 1.65 mb/d, or .59 million barrels per day. Their official reserves stand at 43.5 billion barrels. Despite being an OPEC member there is no reason to doubt that this amount is actually there. Here we have a nation that could greatly enhance its oil production capabilities, the question remains however if that will happen. Their colorful leader Muhamar Ghadafi has much larger dreams than simply becoming a major energy player. He was often quoted as saying that he is hopeful about the slow, but steady growth of the Muslim population in Europe. He effectively claims that peaceful colonization will work, where the sword has failed in the past. Given his tendency to consider things for the longer term, it would not surprise me if he also sees his country's petroleum wealth the same way. Given the speed with which some OPEC and many non-OPEC producers are depleting their resources, he probably figures (correctly) that Libya is in a good position, given their relatively small population, and the longevity of their resources at current levels of production to be future exporters of a very valuable commodity. Things may change if Ghadafi will die, and his successor will have a different vision. Until then, Libya will most likely continue to pace itself in exploiting their petroleum, after all, it's not like they have much else. Since I wrote this, ongoing events in Libya may change the current situation greatly, Ghadafi's 42 years of dictatorship has ended, and we are yet to find out what will come next.

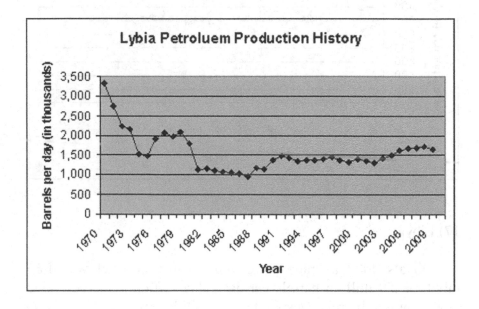

18) Kazakhstan:

Kazakhstan's 2009 average petroleum production was 1.46 mb/d, or .52 billion barrels per day. Their official reserve estimate is 30 billion barrels and it includes the giant Kashagan field discovered in 2000. It is estimated to hold up to 15 billion barrels, which makes it the largest field to have been discovered in the past three decades. This giant is a very troublesome field however, and production is yet to commence after a decade of work. The latest news is that production will finally commence at a slow rate in 2014, but the startup date has already been rolled back so many times that, if it will be done again, it will surprise no one. If the project will finally start showing results, Kazakhstan will most likely see a relatively robust increase in production. Everything hinges now on one troublesome field.

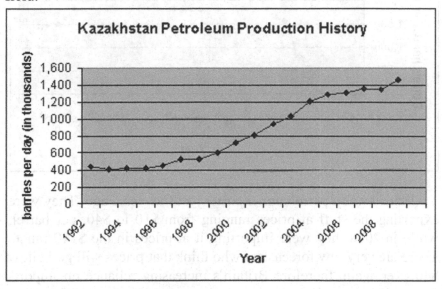

19) United Kingdom:

Britain's 2009 average production was 1.33 mb/d, or .48 billion barrels per year. Their official reserves stand at 3.4 billion barrels. At this rate of production, they would exhaust all their reserves in seven years. Britain shares the North Sea petroleum province with Norway, which is also experiencing steep declines. If exploration efforts will continue to be poor, Britain could end up having production of no more than 3-4 hundred thousand barrels per day by 2020. The region has been thoroughly explored now, so the chances of hitting the jackpot by continuing to explore the North Sea are very remote. Britain's petroleum exploration policy is an interesting example of why it might not be wise to exploit this resource to its maximum level from an economic point of view, as I already mentioned earlier.

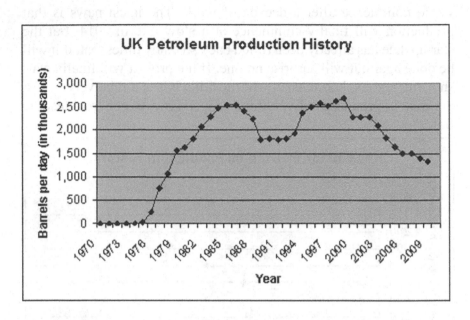

Britain was a petroleum exporter just five years ago. They were exporting the stuff at prices ranging from $10 to $40, per barrel, while in 2008 they were importing it at prices in the $140 range. There are very few forecasters who think that prices will go bellow $40 ever again, therefore Britain's increasing reliance on imports due to dwindling domestic production seems like one of the worst possible policies one could make. Perhaps Libya's Ghadafi is not so backwards after all, despite his image as a traditional Bedouin, who still likes to live in a tent. This is yet another example why perhaps we westerners need to start a serious re-evaluation of our values and concepts. When a North African dictator is able to promote wiser policies than our democratically elected leaders, it should be obvious that something is seriously wrong.

20) Azerbaijan:

Azerbaijan rounds out the top twenty producers of petroleum on the planet. Its 2009 average petroleum production was 1.01 mb/d, or .36 billion barrels per year. Their official reserves stand at 7 billion barrels, and there are remote chances of finding many additional reserves in the future. Azerbaijan's region is part of the Caspian

Sea neighborhood, which was one of the first petroleum production provinces on earth. There are some indications that they want to increase production further in the next couple of years. Most of their fields are already very mature however, and any increase from this point on will be accompanied by a faster decline, and fewer reserves ultimately recovered due to field damage. I do not expect Azerbaijan's production levels to be much higher than the current levels by 2020, and sometimes during that turn of the decade, they will most likely decline.

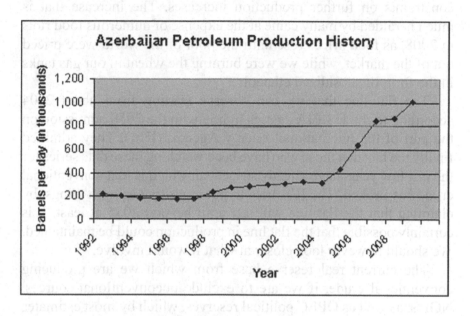

Global petroleum production: (excluding lease condensates, LNG, ethanol and other unconventional sources)

The last chart I want to include is the one for global petroleum production as a whole. The previous twenty cases were meant mainly to help visualize on an individual case level, why there are serious constraints in future additions to petroleum production capacity, whether it is for geological, political or a combination of reasons. This chart allows us to consider the behavior of global production in response to the phenomenal rise in price witnessed in the last decade. Of particular concern as far as I am concerned is the flat lining that occurred after 2004, as the chart clearly shows. Despite prices rising as high as $147 by 2008, production remained stagnant. The only reason overall fuel supply grew was because many alternative liquid fuel supplies such as ethanol and Natural Gas Liquids increased in availability. Because of these increases, the total liquids supply increased from 84.6 mb/d average production in 2005 to the present 86.0 average running so far in 2010 according to the latest available stats from the EIA. This will be the number you will most likely hear being quoted by the ones attacking the peak oil advocates who argue that the world has reached its production capacity due to geological constraints on further production increases. The increase that is much heralded by many came at the expense of numerous food riots in 2008, as food prices rose until the poor of the world were priced out of the market, while we were burning the wheat in our gas tanks in the form of subsidized ethanol.

The flat line that we can observe starting from about 2004 according to the US EIA data, is in line with the 2010 admission on the part of the International Energy Agency, (IEA). They admitted finally the fact that those who have been watching these data series for the last few years have already suspected, which is that conventional crude has peaked. The IEA tries to put a positive spin on things, by claiming that the flat line will last until beyond 2035 at least. It is certainly possible that the flat line in production could be maintained. We should however look closer at what it would involve.

The current real reserve base from which we are producing conventional crude, if we are to exclude unconventional sources, NGL's, as well as OPEC political reserves, which by most estimates adds up to 300 billion barrels, we in fact have a current proven reserve base of conventional crude of 800 billion barrels. At a yearly extraction rate of about 25 billion barrels per year, by 2035, roughly 625 billion barrels of crude will be produced. That means that if we are to maintain current production rates to 2035 as the IEA claims that we will, then it obviously means that we have to find ways to bolster new discoveries, as well as improve field recovery rates. Based on historical data of the last two decades, it seems we are finding less than 10 billion barrels in new conventional reserves per year. That means that the best we can hope for from new discoveries is about 250 billion barrels in new reserves by 2035. That leaves us with 400 billion barrels that will have to be found through increasing extraction rates from currently producing fields. This in effect means that we are entirely dependent on technological improvements to increase current recovery rates from about 40% currently to 50% in the space of 25 years. There is absolutely no way of knowing whether this will happen or not, but if it will not materialize, sometimes between now and 2035, the world will undergo some very painful changes.

The IEA projects an increase in total liquids production, based on the assumption that unconventional sources will almost double in production from current levels. There is no guarantee that this increase will materialize, but if it will, while conventional crude production will not maintain a plateau, there is the possibility that there will be no increase in liquid fuel availability. It is furthermore important for us to remind ourselves of the fact that not all fuels are equal. NGL's and bio-fuels do not have the same energy content as crude, as they only yield 2/3 of the energy per volume that crude does, and there is also the issue of the lower energy return on energy invested that is associated with the production of many of these unconventional fuel sources. Enhanced recovery techniques from conventional fields also require a higher net energy input per volume of crude recovered. Taking all these considerations in evidence, there is a very good chance that sometime between the present and the 2035 date that has been examined by the IEA, will see a decline in net energy available to the consumer, regardless of what the data will show in regards to the volume of liquids available to us.

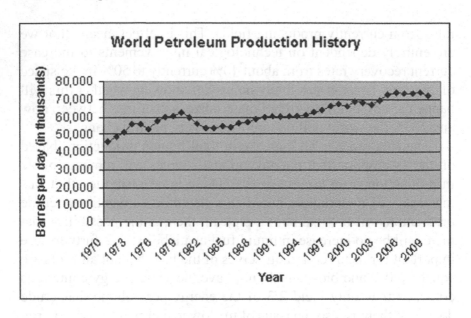

Note: The decline in production shown by the chart in the 1980's period is due to a pullback for economic reasons, which cut petroleum demand drastically. The flat line in the early nineties is also due to an economic event, mainly having to do with the collapse of communism in Eastern Europe, which cut demand by a few mb/d. The small decline shown on the graph form 2000-2002 is also due to an economic event, known as the bursting of the dot.com bubble. The flat line formed from 2004-08, is in fact a geological and political event, in other words production could not be increased for geologic, political or a combination of the two reasons. Demand was definitely not the constraint as it was in the previous events I pointed out, and that is the reason why this most recent plateau should definitely give us cause for worry.

The flat line continues presently, despite the fact that we are now in an economic recovery mode.

Reality versus Public Perceptions

An article in "The National" on August/16/2010, entitled *"Peak oil theory has peaked and there is no apocalypse now"* written by Robin M Mills, argues in a sinister way that we are saved from peak oil, because one of its advocates Mathew Simmons died recently. Mr.

Mills may not know it, but he provided me with a great example of media manipulation that is most definitely at work to try to ease the fears of the masses on this issue. In trying to prove that everything is looking rosy, he invoked a statement made by peak oil advocate Kenneth Deffeyes, who jokingly predicted a precise date when crude oil production will peak, "The former Shell Oil geologist Kenneth Deffeyes put the peak date, rather precisely, at December 16 2005, which again has been proved wrong.". Perhaps Mr. Mills should do a little more research on the subject before publishing, because the exact day may not be known, but the record in global average yearly petroleum production, is in fact found about 6 years in the past. In 2005 crude oil production, average was 73.7 mb/d according to the EIA. Crude production has not surpassed that mark in the past five years, and it is unlikely to do so in 2010. While my personal belief is that the 2005 levels of production will likely be surpassed in the next few years, as of today, Kenneth Defeyes has not been proven wrong just yet. There is also the slightest of possibilities that he may never be proven wrong about his humorous prediction. Even if a number of events will come together to help beat the average production record set in 2005, the likelihood that it will be beaten by more than one or two million barrels some time in the future is starting to look more and more remote, as I exemplified in the individual country situation.

The article continues, taking on the peak oil crowd by Mentioning how flawed the predictions and analysis of Mathew Simmons was in comparison with the reality. "Simmons predicted "a collapse of 30 or 40 per cent of [Saudi] production . . . sometime in the next three to five years—but it could even be tomorrow", yet the kingdom's production capacity has risen significantly since 2005." To begin with, Mr. Mills made the first mistake when he mentioned the officially stated production capacity that Saudi Arabia claims to have as fact. In 2007-08, when petroleum prices spiked as a result of global supplies held in reserve around the world being quickly drawn down as a result of demand outstripping supply coming on the market, the reserve capacity of Saudi Arabia, which they claimed was somewhere around 1.5 mb/d, never showed up in the market. In fact, according to the EIA the opposite may have been the case. When prices crossed the $100 per barrel threshold, Saudi production in fact started declining slightly, demonstrating that the maximum monthly average they reached of 9.7 mb/d was in fact not sustainable by the fields. In the end, 2008 production average was 300k barrels lower than the 2005 average, when Mathew Simmons became famous for his book entitled *"Twilight in the Desert"*. What kind of journalist believes everything they are told as fact? Are they not supposed to investigate and dig into the facts a little?

Taking the official capacity estimate for petroleum production in Saudi Arabia as fact was by no means the last poor assumption made by Mr. Mills. He made the mistake of assuming that somehow the Saudis have an interest in increasing production capacity in any significant way, therefore depleting a non-renewable resource at a much faster rate.

"Saudi Arabia was always a strange place to start with peak oil: even if we believed peak oil protagonists' contentions that Saudi reserves are overstated by half, the country would still be pumping less than 3 per cent of its reserves annually. When the UK's production peaked in 1999, it was extracting more than 20 per cent of its reserves each year".

Actually, Mathew Simmons was right to start with Saudi Arabia. Aside from the already mentioned fact that many of the stats coming out of that country on reserves and production capacity are highly suspect, given recent events as I already exemplified, there is also the issue that neither peak oilers, nor peak oil deniers are eager to tackle. That issue of course being long term political and economical considerations that each country has to contemplate in order to assure a stable future for generations yet to live. Britain allowed private companies to exploit the country's resources as they saw fit. The fact that Britain was not as concerned about the quick depletion of its resources, which is to be seen in the current production and reserve situation of that country means that petroleum production was not as essential to the country's future as it is in Saudi Arabia. Britain has many other developed industries besides petroleum production, which have the potential to provide a decent future for that country. They produce a very wide range of manufactured products, while they still have the ability to be almost self reliant in food production and fresh water. I'm sure however that there are at least some Britons who realized by now how much of a raw deal the people of that country got by exporting the stuff at $10-40 a barrel, while they recently had to pay as much as $145 to import it.

Saudi Arabia has oil, some gas and a lot of sand. The expectation on the part of most analysts that they are likely to follow on the British footsteps of hyper resource depletion boggles the mind. King Abdullah already made a public statement in 2010 regarding his intentions in this matter, which unfortunately made very little news in the media as I already mentioned. I only hope that policy officials around the world took him seriously on the matter, because if not, we could be in for a very big surprise courtesy of the Saudis, and a few other like-minded desert oil producers in the very near future.

This once again proves that sometimes dictatorships succeed where democracies fail. I am hard pressed to think of many major incentives for future well being that came from a major democracy lately. Most often policy is determined on the basis on how well the policy will feature in the short term, or before new elections are set to take place. The thought of sacrificing in the present in order to reinforce stability for the future rarely goes down well with an increasingly shortsighted electorate that is generally a feature of western society. The British could have decided to limit exploitation of their fields to a level matching their own consumption. Instead, they opted to let the royalty paying companies exploit at the maximum rate possible, which indeed helped their budget situation and their trade balance for about a decade, but now they are importing at more than triple the average prices they were exporting at. Due to extreme levels of depletion in the North Sea, within a decade they will most likely have to import most of their petrol just like most other European countries. There would be nothing wrong with that except for that Britain's economy is used to petrol improving its trade balance and government budget, while now the trend is turning negative.

Robin M Mills and many more like him will have you believe that we should expect a one trick pony to yield its only trick to us, just so we can go on living our western dream life. Perhaps he is right, and a country such as Iraq will pull off the great miracle of peace and stability in the very near term, and then somehow manage to quadruple their production by 2020 as many analysts expect, or hope. That would imply that there is indeed a government in place there, which cares little about the long-term future, and will sacrifice it for the short-term gain. Perhaps Iraq's government will remain a democracy, prone to changes every few years, in which case maybe they will deplete as fast as technology and investment will permit. That will most definitely buy us a decade, and in that case, you can put this book away and worry about the future later. We will still have to deal with continued job loses to the developing world, an ageing society, other resources we are short on, climate change, runaway budget deficits and a host of other issues. Those are all problems that can cause us real headaches, but we will most likely manage, even if not to such a great extent that we will be able to usher in a new era of renewed prosperity. Or perhaps you are wiser than that and despite being conditioned to search for instant gratification, you decide that it is time to stop the consumerist binge, where you are consuming products and services like there is no tomorrow. A decade might sound like a long time, in our instant expectations world, but it is amazing how fast it can fly by. When the decade is up, you might look back, and wish you had piled some money into more useful investments such as some farmland, or some gold. You will wish that you would have done that, rather than waiting in line to be the first to get your hand on a new "I" something or other that periodically tickles the fancy of tech enthusiasts.

Perhaps the idea of having a full decade before acute petroleum shortages might seem like there is still plenty of hope to readjust to the new reality through investments into the new renewable technologies, coal to liquids, natural gas adapted to transportation needs, more public transport and other such remedies. If Iraq does not manage to pull off the awaited miracle, be it for political, geological or safety reasons, then that decade, which would be a very tight schedule to adapt anyways, especially due to lack of political will, may not even be there. We may only have two to five years before a similar price shock to the 2007-08 periods, or even worse will occur. According to three recent studies done by reputable organizations with a stake in stability of the oil price and supply, in the absence of such a miracle as is expected from Iraq in the next decade, by 2015 at the latest, we will have severe shortages of petroleum.

In early 2010 an industry taskforce in the UK, made up of Arup, Foster + Partners, Scottish and Southern Energy, Solarcentury, Stagecoach Group and Virgin, came up with a study that warns of impending hardships for OECD countries that were used to free flowing cheap oil. They state that the era of cheap oil ended in 2005, and by 2012-13, when they think the effects of the recession on recent petroleum consumption will wear off; we will have serious price shocks due to production constraints. They also concluded that petroleum production capacity would reach a plateau as soon as 2011, and last until about 2015, when production would start declining. I should note here that they are looking at total liquids production, which they see reaching a maximum global capacity of 91-92 mb/d. As I illustrated already, crude oil already made what could turn out to be a final plateau, beginning in 2005, which has been hovering at 72-74 mb/d. If there will be significant increases in the overall flow of liquids, we can expect that the food riots seen in 2008 will most likely be repeated and perhaps even rise in frequency and intensity. Ethanol does not come free; it comes at the cost of pricing the more vulnerable segments of the "global village" out of the market. The study concludes that the UK government should take urgent action to help cope with these changes, in order to avoid major disruptions to the economic well being of its individual and corporate citizens.

The conclusion that I found to be the most interesting, especially as it relates to the topic at hand is that developing nations stand to be at a strategic advantage when it comes to dealing with price increases in energy. The argument is that since their economy is currently already developing under the hardship of higher prices unlike the OECD, which mainly developed structurally after the Second World War, they are already adapted to current reality. In other words, our economies in the west are adapted to cheap petroleum and the change in the paradigm means that we are more vulnerable than the countries that are just evolving into industrialized societies in the present. This gives further cause to consider that my guess that major companies in the present are sitting on their collective trillions in currency reserves, not because of any policy coming out of western governments, but because they are waiting to invest the money in the better adapted, fast growing economies of the emerging markets. Despite the claim on the political right, that our companies would invest in our backyard if only government would just see the light and stop collecting such a high level of taxes from them, I do not believe that lower taxes will do the trick this time. The argument is flawed from the outset, because these companies are not refusing to invest for the lack of funds. They already have the money necessary to invest and more. Tax brakes would only add to their piles of cash, and eventually it will end up as investments in the more lucrative markets.

This theory of being out competed for resources flies against the prevailing idea, coming mainly from the political left that worries that the increase in commodity prices will mainly affect those who are already poor. The poorest of the poor, like the people living in failed states such as Haiti, or most African nations can indeed end up suffering the most. They are already lacking the tools necessary to compete in the global economy no matter what the prevailing situation. The second most affected people will be the citizens of developed nations, who are already giving up on their unhealthy consumption patterns to some extent.

A warning is the appropriate thing here, to those who, feel that the current global patterns of consumption are a crime and needs to be changed, and therefore the current trend is a good thing. This is not a decline in consumption that will cut a little off the top, from most households in more or lees uniform manner. This decline in overall consumption is presently being achieved through a general loss in jobs that is creating pockets within our society of extreme poverty, while the bulk of the population continues on living as they did before. Poverty within a relatively prosperous society can be just as painful in some cases as poverty in less prosperous nations. In Europe where there is a relatively well developed social safety net, there is still the benefit of those down on their luck from taking advantage of many government services such as education, health care, welfare and the surrounding infrastructure. In America however, a loss in employment also means that eventually health coverage becomes out of reach, education is very uneven from neighborhood to neighborhood, and welfare is much harder to qualify for than in Europe. Lack of maternity leave means that a family with a newborn and only one parent employed can easily end up in dire straits if the second parent happens to loose his/her job as well.

This coming shortage will change our lives forever. Besides the report made by the UK industrialists taskforce, the US defense department did a study that reached similar conclusions, and insurance company Lloyds, together with Chatham House concluded that a failure to diversify into non fossil energy in the near future will be catastrophic. All three studies that came out within the first six months of 2010, forecast a serious energy crunch around 2011-13, yet neither one of these three studies received much interest in the media. On the other hand, there is never a shortage of what I call empty information. For instance, today August 28/2010 while watching television; I came across four or five reports about the fact that Paris Hilton was caught with possession of cocaine, within half an hour of channel surfing. I call this empty information, because it does not do me or anyone else any real good to know these facts, yet there is always it seems a plentiful supply of this information.

I am not ignorant of the fact that the masses like to be kept entertained, and the elites who allow it to happen tend to benefit from the mass content that is created. As you may have already noticed I like to try to learn lessons from history, whether it is in regards to society, politics or economics. I dug as far back as the Roman Empire to help with a better understanding of the concept of the need to entertain the masses as a measure against them being too concerned with issues in relation to their present and future well-being. I am of the view however that we no longer have a global situation where we can afford to keep people disengaged from the realities of our planet. In the case of oil shortages as it is with many other issues, it may be painful to face the reality, least of which being that it would create market and social turmoil. People will have to re-adjust to many new realities in the present and in the future. In my view, it is far more dangerous to proceed along this path, and hit the wall full speed when we come to it. That will likely mean a total destruction, probably in the form of society as we are used to thinking of it, collapsing to near complete annihilation. The rule of law will likely become the rule of force, by either government entities, corporate interests, or a combination of both. This issue is something worth coming back to, and I will in the last issues I will cover, which are cultural aspects.

Natural Gas: (A false savior?)

I will not go into a detailed survey of the major natural gas producers and reserve holders on the world, as I did for petroleum. Main reason for this being, that currently petroleum is a much larger energy source than natural gas for the planet. Petroleum consumption accounts for 37% of all energy use, while gas is 23%. For that reason, gas is not as critical. Natural gas is also a resource that can easily be replaced in its functions with other sources of energy such as coal, wind, or hydropower. The principal uses for gas are electricity production, and household heating needs in the colder climates. It is also important in the chemical industries, especially fertilizers, as a cooking fuel and increasingly as a transport fuel source, or as an additive for unconventional petroleum recovery and preparation. As I already mentioned, Canada's needs in the Tar Sands recovery industry exceed the current proven reserve ratio of this country by 3 to 1. Natural gas plays a very insignificant role as a transport fuel in the present, but that could change.

Many hopes voiced recently, such as the one of T Boone Pickens, who made his billions in the oil industry, point to natural gas as a possible savior from impending shortages, which even this old industry insider sees as a coming reality. He proposed a few years back to transform America by switching petrol guzzling transport vehicles into a natural gas run fleet. In order to make up for the lost natural gas, he proposed a massive investment in building and connecting windmill farms to the grid. To my surprise, he even put up some investment money himself, but so far, there has been very little movement on this front. The US government is dragging its feet, and petrol prices have dropped due to the recession, so the pressure to invest into this infrastructural shift has abated for the moment. This is in line with my assumption that as prices spike in these important commodities, a recession creates a fast plunge in prices, diminishing incentives for more expensive substitutes such as wind farms.

My personal view is that they should have taken his plan more seriously. If you choose not to believe my analyses of the petroleum situation worldwide, try to read about changes in recent projections by organizations that are more reputable, in terms of belonging to the official hierarchy. Try to find the IEA projections for future production, where they revised downwards their predictions every year since 2007, which also paints a growingly pessimistic view. For instance, their 2007 projections to 2020 had production levels for all liquids at 103 mb/d. That has been trimmed back year after year, and now it stands at only 92 mb/d. That is only 6 mb/d more than 2010 production. There is nothing to say that further revisions will not come year after year, until we actually reach 2020. If that will be the case, Americans will most likely regret not listening to the old man.

On the face of it, natural gas is a far less critical resource than petroleum. At current consumption rates, the proven reserves of the world could last about 55 years. The reserve resources being reported are also somewhat more credible than the resources touted by the petroleum industry. There are also more chances that resource depletion will be replaced by new discoveries, or by bringing on-line old discoveries that were previously beyond our technological or financial means. Going from that to making it into the savior from petroleum depletion is a long stretch however. On the supply side, considerations just as with petroleum have to be accounted for such as geological availability, political willingness to exploit at higher rates, and increasingly, there are ecological concerns. On the demand side, we have to recognize that there is an increasing demand for it in retrieving petroleum, water desalination needs in the Middle East and elsewhere are an increasing part of the equation. The desire to replace coal fired plants that emit far more CO_2 than natural gas for the same power output is also a big source of new demand. The continued increase of the world's population coupled with the increase in affluence of many citizens of the developing world will increase the demand for fertilizer, based on natural gas. Once those new needs are addressed through the increase in production, then maybe there might be a little bit left to deal with transport issues, and other needs in industry that are currently met through petroleum use. Given all these considerations, I am not even certain that there is new production available to satisfy the needs already listed, never mind the sharp increase in demand that would come from gas being used as a transport fuel.

Reserves and Production

The three largest reserves of natural gas, which accounts for about 45% of the world's total, are currently found in Russia, Iran and Qatar. If there were to be a massive increase in production, this would be the most likely places to look. In all three cases, there are serious barriers to significant production increases. The fact that all three countries currently produce way under their geological potential of extraction is no accident. Aside from the usual barriers such as politics, price, technical-geological difficulties that are posed by the production of petroleum, there is also the problem of transport method that plagues this industry. Until recently, the bulk of natural gas was transported through ducts, and it is only recently that they figured out that the stuff can be liquefied and transported in containers like petroleum. This is a very pricy method of delivery, and it most likely disqualifies many projects around the world, if this has to be the method of distribution to the market. That is why we prefer to rely on petroleum rather than on gas, because it is more versatile.

Russia does not have a problem of delivery for its gas, unless you want to include some of the political problems associated with some of the transit countries, which feel entitled to lower prices for their gas imports as former soviet members. Russia sends most of the gas to its domestic and foreign market via pipelines, which makes for steady and affordable delivery to its European and Asian customers. Despite the blackmailing extortionist behavior of some of these transit countries, such as Ukraine, the Russians took most of the blame for this issue. Other than that, the only major issues are the political considerations and some of the technical and economic challenges related to the hostile, cold environment where this production must take place.

The political and economic issues are mainly related to resource nationalism, embodied in the near monopoly that Russian state owned giant Gazprom enjoys in the production and delivery of natural gas. The Russians rightly figured that they stand to gain from keeping all the proceeds from the sale of their resources rather than having to settle for a royalty from private firms. While it may be true that private firms would be able to exploit the resources faster and maybe at a better price, the overall political view in Russia is that there is no reason to increase their already highest rate of production on earth, at the price of losing pricing power. Depleting the resource base faster, which will leave the future generations with nothing, is not very enticing either. Once again, the example of Britain comes to mind, which went from being a net gas exporter, as it was the case also with petroleum, to becoming a large importer. In fact, they will have to import 75% of their gas by as early as 2015.

Russia currently produces similar volumes of natural gas as the US; whose reserves are six times smaller (43 trillion m^3 Vs 6.7 trillion m^3). Russia produced over 660 billion m^3, while the US produced 580 billion m^3 of natural gas in 2008. Currently Russia is working on its potential as a transit country for Turkmen and Azerbaijani gas rather than focusing on developing its own fields. By keeping these countries from reaching Europe directly with their gas deliveries, Russia maintains its pricing power in Europe. The Europeans currently have very few alternatives, therefore this is a very lucrative situation for the Russians, and they are not likely to jump to flood the market with more gas in order to drive prices down.

Iran could possibly be the most potent competitor in the Natural Gas market in Europe to the Russians. Thanks to the not so wise diplomatic choices made by the EU towards this nation, Iran will be a long way from becoming a meaningful gas exporter anytime soon. Presently the US led campaign to isolate Iran is actually picking up momentum, and the Europeans are dutifully following the lead of the US. To better illustrate the shortsighted stance of the Europeans, I give you the proposed Nabucco pipeline from the Caspian to Europe project, as the height of stupidity. This was supposed to be the pipeline that would break the dominance of the Russians in European markets by excluding Russian gas supplies, and avoiding Russian territory as a transit country. Potential suppliers were Caspian area nations such as Azerbaijan, Turkmenistan, and Kazakhstan. The other two Caspian Nations are Russia and Iran, of course and they lie at the north and South shores respectively. Turkmenistan and Kazakhstan lie east of the Caspian Sea, and there is presently no agreement in place in the region that would allow one Caspian nation to build a pipeline through the Caspian waters, without the agreement of the other Caspian nations. Any land-based pipeline would have to go through Russia, or Iran. As a result, Azerbaijan is the only country left to supply all the gas, and Azerbaijan already has many other contracts to fill. There is the possibility of war torn Iraq also helping in this matter by contributing to the Nabucco project with some supplies, but that proposition is risky and insufficient on its own. The only way Nabucco could ever become reality would be to agree to include Iran in the Project. In other words, Nabucco is dead.

The natural gas reserves of Iran account for over 10% of the global reserves. Not to mention that they also account for 10% of the petroleum reserves, which we need even more. Although, as I previously mentioned, those may be political reserves. Still, the potential to help alleviate many energy related problems that will most likely plague us in the coming decade and beyond, by trying to get along with them, should not be ignored. I really fear a very ironic end to the current stance of the west and Israel towards Iran. They are ratcheting up more and more pressure in the form of sanctions, while at the same time they are probably wondering privately on a constant basis where the energy will come from in the next decade or two. The worst case scenario aside from an all out military confrontation down the line, which would be a huge gamble with our collective future, I envision a turning point, when the western powers will have to negotiate some sort of end to the sanctions and a resumption of petroleum and gas exports. That should be a scenario that should be feared, because after years of bitterness following the isolating policies, the Iranians might be inclined to offer very humiliating terms for the resumption of energy deliveries. If this turns out to be the case in the next decade or so, it will be a very painful experience for us, and we will have no one else to blame, but ourselves.

An alternative to the current policy, through a show of goodwill, and offer of mutual assurances would yield a much better situation on balance. For instance, a treaty comprising all nations with weapons of mass destruction that would commit all to a policy of no first use, might be just the ticket in easing the real fears that Iran has in regards to being attacked with a nuclear arsenal by either Israel, US or even Pakistan. A resource hungry China might even be a cause for concern for the Islamic republic. We have to remember that other nations have security concerns that matter to them, as much as our concerns matter to us. To improve overall global security, initiatives like making the Middle East nuclear free have to be looked at seriously, which would have to include Israel coming clean, and Pakistan and India giving up their arsenals as well. The established nuclear powers should continue to aggressively reduce their arsenals as well. A move to reduce global uncertainty is also one that could enhance our ability in the near and long term future to produce nuclear power. As hard as it is to stomach for many that we actually have to abandon hypocrisy-based policies, it is more and more clear that it is necessary to do so. If current policies continue, Iran might indeed get the bomb, and we will be left enforcing trade barriers that will be increasingly more painful for us rather than for them. The alternative of starting an actual war is really not a credible option. Another costly war will most likely be the last nail in the coffin for the US. The danger of having petroleum shipping from the Middle East disrupted for months or even years is something that we are currently not prepared to live with. As much as the right wing smash and bash crowd would like to see Tehran bombed, in the end we should all hope that cooler heads will prevail.

For the sake of the European population that depends every winter on those crucial gas deliveries, a new policy should be implemented. This new policy will bring Iran's gas to the Nabucco project, and diversify European gas suppliers. What should happen and what will happen are two very different things however. We no longer live in the old western culture that saw the leaders we chose, embrace changes meant to make us prosper and advance. We have been riding the status quo ever since the end of the Second World War, and I fear that there is no force strong enough to convince any of these leaders to show initiative. Without change, we cannot adapt to the new realities. The West's policy towards Iran is a case that makes that point.

Qatar, which rivals the gas reserves of Iran, is not under any such political pressures. It is very unfortunate that this small Gulf country is faced with such a hard task of getting their gas to market. Despite having the third largest reserves, they rank only eleventh in production. It is unclear how they would feel about massive increases in production levels, but it is almost certain that they want to export more than they currently do, except they have to liquefy it and ship it via container, and there are few facilities to accommodate the delivery of this product to date. Work on expanding facilities is ongoing worldwide, so in the future we should see more gas from Qatar on the market. It is possible however that most of it will ultimately stay in the Middle East, because of increased demand in the region for a relatively clean energy source needed to power desalination plants as well as an increase in electricity needs.

A new gas revolution?

In recent years, there has been a large enthusiastic chorus in regards to the miracle of shale gas, which has been touted as the energy savior of the 21'Th century in America. It is an industry that started producing this unconventional resource of gas through fracturing techniques, which some say will provide half of all gas produced in the US by 2030. Based on some rather optimistic assumptions a media advertising campaign was started, stating that this is a resource that can provide the US with its gas needs for the next hundred years. It is worth noting that this estimate is based on the estimate of natural gas being there as a 5% chance. They are not basing that estimate on the proved or even possible (50% chance) reserves booked so far. The proven reserves of shale gas that are currently booked by the industry represent about seven year's worth of US consumption. Incidentally, it is also comparable with the amount of gas needed to produce the entire reserve of tar sands in Canada as I already mentioned, which will have to happen in order to lessen the effects of decline in conventional oilfields. So in effect, one unconventional energy source almost cancels out the other. There is no doubt that more resources will be booked, as proven and new fields will be discovered in North America. There are still plentiful potentially promising sites of exploration in northern Canada and Alaska. The claim of a hundred years worth of gas supplies, when proven reserves only amount to roughly fifteen years in North America is a little bit of overreach to say the least.

A study made by the United States Geological Survey (USGS), recently downgraded the largest Shale Gas play in the US. The

Marcellus Shale was thought to hold as much as over 400 tcf of recoverable natural gas by some optimists. The energy industry was trying to push a comparatively more conservative estimate for the field of over 200 tcf. The USGS in August of 2011 released a study that shows that the most likely scenario for recoverable gas from this field will be 84 tcf[4]. That is still enough to cover US natural gas needs for four years at current consumption, which means that this is still a huge resource. There are also an estimated 3.5 billion barrels worth of NGL's associated with the Marcellus shale play[5]. The main point that we have to understand from this downgrade is that the previous claims have already made it into our calculations for our energy future, and those calculations are most likely wrong. The other shale gas plays are most likely just as overhyped as the Marcellus. The Barnett shale play in Texas has already reached a peak in production, and despite what the gas industry claims, it will likely start declining soon, which means that ultimate recovery rates have been overhyped as well. It is still early to draw final conclusions in regards to this still young industry, but if the USGS survey is correct, then we may only have a fifth of the gas available from this resource. That, compared to some of the more, optimistic views previously taken as plausible, which gave rise to the claim of the one hundred year supply at current US consumption rates.

Given the relatively early stages of life of this industry, there is still to be determined whether the economics of extracting gas through this rock fracturing procedure are sound. There are many indications that the majority of these extractive operations are losing money. Many operations, which are currently profitable, are only making money because of very wise hedging bets made a few years back. The main indication that the drilling projects are ultimately set to fail in returning a profit is the fact that so far the decline rates in production were underestimated by a relatively large margin. In other words, there is a great risk when drilling for shale gas, that the value of the gas that will ultimately flow out of the hole will be less than the price of drilling the hole in the first place. Overestimated flow potentials also point to an overestimated reserve base as well. It will take maybe until about 2015 to get a clear enough picture of just what kind of prices are needed for this resource to at least break even. Some early estimates put that price range to be double the current prices.

A 2005 decision on the behalf of the Bush administration has exempted the shale gas industry from EPA regulations. There are currently very few scientific studies that we can rely on to understand what the possible environmental side effects could be as a result of this kind of drilling activity. Until we get a better picture, it is impossible to determine just how much of this resource will ultimately be recovered. Opposition to drilling for shale gas is already intensifying because of the feeling of helplessness in determining the true side effects; therefore, there is no reason to expect that all state legislatures will approve drilling projects. If mounting evidence will show that, there are indeed many unpleasant side effects, including the possible poisoning of the underground water table, which millions of people depend on for potable water, a large chunk of the already proven reserves may become off limits potentially forever. Given the many hopes that were created by taking the routinely pushed message that there are now enough supplies of gas to take the US to 2100, major disappointment, which is still a very probable reality with this young industry will be crushing to our sense of safety of our economic future. Given these implications, the environmental effects will most likely be ignored for as long as possible. In a way it can be paralleled to, the same government mentality, which led to declaring the Gulf area safe for fishing only two weeks after the leak stopped from the BP debacle. Will there be more cases of cancer half a decade from now, because people are eating contaminated seafood? Most likely yes, but the link to the poisoned seafood may never be made.

There are of course many more factors and players in the gas industry, who are likely to affect the future availability for this crucial resource. Based on the analysis of the main players in terms of production and reserves, it is hard to envision a major shift of the energy mix from petroleum to gas as a substitute in the conditions of growing global demand for both resources. Natural gas can most definitely soften the blow of lack of petroleum availability, for some nations it may even be a way to potentially prosper in the event that new fields will be found, and an increasingly valuable commodity will be available for export. In terms of making up for possible shortfalls in petroleum production, the likelihood of keeping up with a possible 10 mb/d gap that can easily develop between demand under normal economic conditions, and supply under the assumption that Iraq will not deliver, it is doubtful. It takes 164.2 m³ of gas to displace the energy of one barrel of oil. In order to make up for a one million barrel per day shortfall in petroleum production, the world would have to add about 60 billion m³ (2 tcf) of new gas production per year. If the very real possibility of a 10 mb/d shortfall by 2020 materializes, the much hyped shale gas production ramp up would only make up for about half the petroleum shortfall. Not to mention that much of that shale gas production increase, if it even materializes, will be used to make up for forecasted declines in conventional gas fields across North America. There are some hopes for production increases in the Middle East, Africa, and South America, but that will most likely only keep up with consumption increases and make up for declines elsewhere, such as in Britain.

Economic considerations: (A hypothetical global economic scenario to 2050)

There is no denying that given no interruption to the current dominant trend in global economic trends, the likelihood is that we are facing a converging world. If the current rates of growth continue in the developing world, we will likely see a world with the average standard of living, similar to the range that one sees within the EU, by about 2050. In other words, there will be some countries with a real per capita GDP of $40,000, like Britain, or Sweden, and others with about $12,000 in per capita GDP, like EU members Romania, or Bulgaria. If we are to confirm whether this is possible or not, we should ask ourselves how much oil and gas would be needed to achieve this global convergence? The EU's 500 million citizens currently consume roughly 7.5 billion barrels of oil equivalent in oil and gas. The world's population will most likely surpass 9 billion people by 2050.

At this point, most optimists will proclaim that surely by 2050, the world can reach an average standard of living that the EU currently has, all the while, far surpassing the Europeans in efficiency rates. Logic and history would in fact dictate that as time passes, human ingenuity would be able to increase the amount of GDP that one can get out of a unit of energy. I most certainly expect electric cars, more efficient combustion engines, windmills, solar panels, better-insulated homes and other innovations to help indeed cut our use of oil and gas in certain sectors of our economic activities. It would be sheer folly to ignore this trend towards better efficiency and more productivity, which has been the case for centuries now.

It would be in my opinion just as foolish to ignore the effect of the low hanging fruit pattern of production of most of our resources, as I already mentioned. Few can deny the fact that if we were to achieve whatever production rates of oil and gas will be needed by 2050, if we are to achieve the average standard of living of the EU globally, we will have to rely increasingly on unconventional sources, such as tar sands, shale oil, and shale gas. Conventional fields are already, stagnated, there are fewer and fewer new discoveries and the current fields will be largely depleted by then. Producing the unconventional fields, even assuming some major improvements in techniques, will still be far more energy and material intensive than the current conventional fields. Squeezing out more and more oil out of conventional fields is also far more energy intensive than primary production techniques. Production of most other mined resources, are similarly likely to become progressively more energy and material intensive, despite constant improvements in extraction technologies, because the ore quality of many of the crucial minerals we depend on is degrading rapidly.

A perfect example of the increasing path to energy and materials intensity in commodity production is the shale gas industry. Shale gas is likely to become a significant or even dominant part of overall global gas production in the coming decades. Wellhead productivity rates that have been observed so far appear to show a very fast drop-off in production within the first year of commencement. Some studies suggest that the rate of decline can be as much as 60% within the first year. This effectively means that the industry needs to drill this year at least six wells only to make up for declines of ten wells drilled the year before. This means that many wells need to be manufactured, brought into place, and then a lot more energy is put into drilling and fracturing the rock. Given that this study was made about an extractive industry in its early stages, where the most prolific sites are drilled first, it is a very worrying sign about the industry's long-term prospects, as it will progressively move to tapping less prolific potential drilling sites.

Providing the world's growing population with a more protein rich diet, similar to what the developed world likes to consume will likely push demand much higher for fertilizers and pesticides, which are derived from oil and gas. Similarly, demand for synthetic material products, such as plastic goods, car tires and many other items will also mean a growing per capita demand for oil and gas. The increased need for countries in the Middle East and perhaps elsewhere for water desalination also means there will be a huge increase in energy demand, no matter what form it is produced in. There is currently a huge infrastructure deficiency problem in most of the developing world and all that is creating a big demand for petroleum. The list of things can be extended of this type of demand, for which there is little hope that electric car technology can help much with. In other words, there is in many cases, very little that technology can do to curb demand.

Lastly, we have to be aware of the fact that there is currently very little appetite on the part of governments to engage in trying to push for regulation, or tax policies that would help curb demand for oil and gas. The EU is in fact currently one of the most fuel-efficient economies in the world. Even on a per capita basis, many countries around the world use far more oil and gas than the EU. The US, Canada and Australia for instance use twice as much oil and gas per capita than their European counterparts, despite having relatively similar standards of living. Some countries like Saudi Arabia and Kuwait use four times more energy per capita than the Europeans do. This relative advantage in fuel efficiency that Europeans enjoy over most other countries is in large part due to their government policies, such as energy taxes, and environmental regulations. The mood in most of the world currently is actually one of deregulating, and cutting energy taxes in order to stimulate the economy. There is also currently very little appetite, especially in the developed world to invest in infrastructure and technological developments that might help with fuel efficiency. There are already many other pressing needs that they need to budget for, such as taking care of the growing number of elderly people.

Assuming that no global scale policy will be in place to actively encourage fuel efficiency, it is not unreasonable in my view to expect that if the world economies were to converge to a level similar to what we have within the bounds of the EU currently, the world's per capita consumption will likely also match current EU levels. This in fact would mean a many fold increase in efficiency on a per GDP output basis for most countries around the world. The developed world would have to do a great deal on the efficiency front, because like I already mentioned, some countries are very far behind the EU currently on this front. If the world were able to achieve this convergence at let us say a level of efficiency that is better by 20% than what the EU has managed so far, I would have to say that under current trends that would be a huge achievement. To put it into perspective, the US would have to cut its oil and gas consumption by about 55-60%. China would have to achieve a fivefold increase in GDP output, per unit of oil and gas input.

Keeping us in an optimistic mindset, let us assume that the world will manage to achieve the level of convergence that it would be likely to do if current trends were to continue, at an efficiency level in oil and gas use that beats the EU's current level by 20%. That would in fact mean that the world would have to supply roughly 108 billion barrels of oil equivalent in oil and gas per year. The world currently supplies and consumes about 45 billion barrels of oil equivalent of these two fossil fuels combined. On the supply side therefore, we can conclude that one would have to eat many optimism pills, and put on some very thick rose-colored lenses in order to be able to be optimistic about the world achieving this.

On the demand side of the equation, assuming a more realistic, but still very optimistic view that we could increase production of these fuels by about one third from current levels, we would have to achieve a great deal in energy efficiency if we were to still reach an approximate global convergence with current EU living standards. Living on approximately 67.5 billion barrels of oil equivalent per year in a converged world would mean that the US for instance would have to make do with roughly 2.75 billion barrels of oil equivalent per year. That would be a significant decline from the current consumption rate of almost 11 billion barrels per year. China on the other hand would have to improve its output per unit of oil and gas input by at least eight fold, from current rates of consumption. Even the EU, which cannot be reproached for not having tried their best to achieve energy efficiency, would have to dig deep, in order to find a way to cut their oil and gas consumption in half from current levels. In effect, this would mean that we would have to almost eliminate the role that oil and gas currently play in fueling transport and electricity production. To put things into perspective, we would have to almost cut all combustion engine production by about 2035. This would also apply for air travel. Currently, combustion engine production worldwide is on an increasing path. It will likely continue to be the case in the absence of further fuel price spikes and deep recessions for a long time to come. The use of natural gas for electricity production and as a transport fuel is also picking up steam.

Achieving a converged world, as I described, by 2050, which is based on current growth trends, under the optimistic assumption that we will have about a third more fuel to play with than we do currently, is unlikely to happen in the absence of a global effort to promote efficiency. The market if left to its own, will promote the continued production and marketing of combustion fuel technology, which will be made increasingly affordable for the emerging markets. They may produce far more fuel-efficient cars like the "Nano" made in India by Tata Motors, which beats average US made vehicles' fuel efficiency by a factor of three. The problem however will be that they will also outsell vehicles made in the vest by a similar factor, increasing demand for transport fuel and especially infrastructure. They will do this because the market signal to do otherwise in this case would be way above the level at which we trigger an economic contraction. In the absence of a market signal to do otherwise, they will continue down the path of maximum profit maximization. In this case, when the price signal will be given to the market, it will be too late. This remember is a discussion about a hypothetical world, where we still have a one third increase in fuel availability coming our way by 2050.

My personal view is that we do not have such an increase in oil and gas availability coming our way. By 2050, we will be lucky if we will still have the same rate of fuel supply that we have presently. Furthermore; there will be far less oil in the mix, and a lot more natural gas. Facilitating the consumption of natural gas is more difficult, because it does not have the same energy level per volume as oil does, so that will mean there will be further complications. Given these considerations, I am inclined to believe that sometimes between the present, and 2050, by which time the current economic trends would have brought us to a level of global convergence as I described, the current trend will be broken in the form of a calamitous economic collapse[6]. The exact timing of it is hard to pinpoint, because it depends on many factors, including geology, and many economic decisions made by countless actors in the private as well as public sectors of the global economy. The effect of reaching this breaking point however, will likely be much worse, and much longer in duration than the great depression of the 20'Th century, which ended in a global war, which took 50 million lives. Tens of millions were raped, injured, displaced, occupied and condemned to decades of communist dictatorship, and many other miserable effects that war has a way of creating.

Conclusions about the energy situation

It is fitting to end this brief study of the energy situation by summarizing the finds of a recently leaked German Army report on threats on the horizon stemming from expected oil shortage on the global strategic situation. Anyone who owns a German made car, or wishes to own one; does so, because of the perception that the Germans can be trusted to create good products. I therefore see no reason why anyone should find reason to discredit the findings of the German army, which was meant as an advisory study for the German government to take into account when instituting public policy. Despite the source of this report coming from a leaked document from such a prestigious organization, it is amazing that the report flew so far, under the mainstream media radar. I myself first came across it in a Romanian language newspaper, and the only way I was able to come across it in an English language version was by doing a Google search for peak oil. There was nothing on TV, or on any of the major on-line news outlets. Given that this report goes as far as predicting a high likelihood of the global economic system experiencing outright collapse in the event of a peak of oil production, which the report claims to be a certainty at some point in the near future, one would think that it was important enough. The news outlets have been going for weeks about Paris Hilton being caught with some cocaine in her purse during the same time. It is a sensational piece of news that the media successfully managed to inform the majority of the population of, and made us all more aware of the things that "truly" matter. The news that the German military is predicting hell on earth given current trends within the near future reached most likely no more than 1-2% of the total population in the west[7].

In the hopes that a few more people will be made aware of the contents of this report that evidently cannot compete with all the other important items that made the news lately, here are some of the main conclusions. The idea that crude oil production rates will soon experience a steady downward trajectory is taken as given. The precise date of this event is not certain. Things that are seen as likely hastening that downward trend are things like the doubt in regards to the true reserve status of fields in the Middle East and other OPEC members. The report also concedes that new technology and prices probably serve as a factor moving the ultimately recoverable volumes of oil up. Consequences of a catastrophic nature could take from 15 to 30 years on a global scale.

Possible effects could include a heavy toll on the industrialized west dependent for 95% of industrial activity on oil at some level. Price spikes can be disruptive to the generally heavily industrialized, but poor in resources western nations. As prices rise, and lack of availability of resources gives power to those who have it, the open market in energy supplies will diminish in importance, while bilateral deals will be more prevalent. This can greatly diminish the political and economic influence of the west on a global level, and western ideals such as democracy, individual rights, freedoms of speech, religion and other things taken for granted by us will retreat globally. Energy exporters will be in a position to dictate to importers on a large variety of global and bilateral issues. Consumption will increasingly shift to energy producers, as the trend is to subsidize or shield local consumers from market prices. Energy production is seen as becoming an increasing government led activity across the world, as it already has been trending that way for the past decade. Resource nationalism may play a further disruptive role in supplying key markets with the needed energy. A rise in food prices will affect everyone globally. Such resource availability pressures will most likely lead to conflicts, further restricting the free flow of energy worldwide.

Aside from the gradual risks, the report also identified systemic risks, where a recessionary environment will topple the global economic system built on the assumption of continued economic expansion. I already explained the need for continued long-term growth trends in order to sustain the current financial system. My personal feeling is that we are more likely to be faced with the effects of the systemic risks rather than the high-energy price scenario, where we will experience a gradual deterioration of the situation. To be more precise I expect the systemic risk issues to disrupt the global economic system, before we are faced with the onset of dictatorship, rationing of goods, or in other words a more severe version of what I experienced in my place of birth in Romania, while growing up under one of Europe's most brutal communist regimes.

It was a world I hoped that I never had to experience again, since I really enjoy breeding the free air. I've known for a long time already that one way or another control will always be established, whether it is through keeping the masses docile through gladiatorial shows, or whether it is at the point of a bayonet and a very ruthless secret service. I still remember my mother's sadness triggered by the death of one of her co-workers, who officially died of a pulmonary infection, but the body was bruised up. Given the choice, if it has to be one way or the other, I prefer the gladiatorial games that keep the majority of the population numb. Those who do awake will be branded paranoid schizophrenics. Perhaps Paris Hilton and her constant media grabbing behavior has a role to play after all. She is the modern day gladiator that makes it possible to avoid more coercive aspects of mass control.

The German army report gives a period of up to 2040 for these things to happen, and they have an obligation to report the worst-case scenario, given what they know about the present direction of things. The reason that their timeline differs from mine is that they most likely underestimate the forward-looking nature of investors and markets. Market panic will always precede any economic event, if that event is bound to happen down the line. When the reality of peak oil will settle in and become hard to deny, markets will sell off, and banks will cease most long term lending activity, out of the realization that they are very unlikely to be able to collect in a shrinking economic environment. Soon after, there would either be a strong government hand attempting to control the population, or there will be a civil war perhaps as the result of some wealthy individuals or corporations believing that they can challenge the monopoly of violence that the weakened governments hold. Either way, the life as we know it will be changed forever.

The only wild card that could change things is the fate of the thousands of nuclear warheads that can end up either in the hands of governments desperate to survive, or in the hands of non-governmental organizations. Either way, I see failure to prepare for this event as a much greater danger than the German government does. I also see failure to prepare as an almost absolute, because of the flimsy financial situation in which most western governments find themselves.

Effect of the Sustainability Trade Tariff on resource scarcity

The need to prevent this likely disastrous scenario should be considered even by those who believe that we can easily dismiss the findings of our potential future by the German military. In my view, the simple fact that such a disciplined and efficient organization as the German military sees this as a possibility, means that we need to look at alternative paths urgently. If the chance of this catastrophe happening is 50%, should we ignore it? Would we feel comfortable ignoring it even if the likelihood was only 10%? I personally do not think so.

The path proposed here of redressing the situation through the sustainability tariff is likely to be one of the best ways to ensure that we will not have to live through the dark days envisioned to be upon us by the Germans. This is a great opportunity to examine the effect the new tariff system proposal, would have on consumption of oil worldwide. While the restraint on consumption is not direct,

145

it would happen due to the need to lower the tariff point deductions through the curtailed use of petrol as a transport fuel to avoid CO_2 emissions. To visualize this I decided to take two countries that are similar economically in most ways, namely Germany and the US. Currently, if a firm was to desire the production of widgets for export, they would find that between Germany and the US there is one main difference, which is fuel efficiency due to environmental policies. A firm might see the difference between the two countries mainly in cost of keeping to the more stringent rules in Germany, against higher energy costs in the US, mainly due to the likelihood that in Germany, rail transport per unit of GDP is more readily available. In the US, the transport of their products might be done to a higher degree by truck[8].

Widget Production US & Germany in present conditions:

US Costs per unit		Germany Costs per unit
Labor:	$10	$10
Capital:	$10	$8
Environment:	$0	$5
Taxes & Tariffs	$10	$10
Total:	$30	$33

Widget Production US & Germany in future, assuming Sustainability Tariff:

US Costs per unit		Germany Costs per unit
Labor:	$10	$10
Capital:	$10	$8
Environment:	$0	$5
Taxes & Tariffs	$20	$10
Total:	$40	$33

146

Explanation for this is the fact that Germany's tariff rating based on sustainability would be much better thanks to their better environmental policies, which also encourages lower fuel consumption as seen in their per GDP unit energy use, which is currently half of what it takes to produce a unit of GDP in the US. The extra costs associated with maintaining the more stringent environmental policy that Germany currently has and is being punished for by investors, would be offset by the higher tariff that the more *laisez fair* competitor, in this case the US would have to pay due to its larger ecological footprint. The most likely result of such a situation would be that the US would try to reduce petroleum consumption to reduce CO_2 emissions in order to catch up to its competitor Germany, which in their turn would also refrain from remaining idle.

Extrapolating this over a period worldwide, the effects would likely be great within just a short decade of implementing the new tariff system. Most countries would think twice before allowing the love affair with burning gasoline in luxurious cars to ruin their tariff ratings. Research and investment into new infrastructure to reduce the burning of this fuel would become a priority for most countries, and there would be a definite incentive to tax gasoline at a much higher rate, changing the taste of the consumer. Economists generally frown upon changing consumer tastes as a policy, because they argue that it decreases the consumer's overall satisfaction through consumption. The Europeans have been doing this for decades however, and there is every indication that they did find other consuming patterns that make them as happy at least as Americans are. There could also be a new pattern emerging because of this, which is the increased consumption of leisure, given that human labor is increasingly productive due to technology, and yet we are still unable to cash in on that increased efficiency through more leisure time. We in fact increased per family work hours through the past few generations through the encouragement of women to enter the workforce.

Many countries would find it also to be not in their interest to continue with certain production practices, such as is the case with Canada's tar sands. The government might be tempted to increase royalties imposed on the industry to match the loss in export ability due to the increased tariff levels due in part to the large ecological footprint left by the tar sands industry. Rail transport would become far more popular than it is in the present, and electricity prices would soar due to the dirty generation of coal. This all sounds like it would be a recessionary force on the global economy, but in fact, it would save it in the end, through encouraging better efficiency at every economic level. This perpetual quest for efficiency would replace the current trend of carelessness towards our commodity consumption levels. We currently cannot afford to contemplate even the probable pain we are setting ourselves up for through our careless use of our resources. The $100+ per barrel that petroleum fetches on the market currently is in large part due to careless use of the resource in the past, and our lack of adaptation to the high price to begin with is what makes that price so painful to bear. The pain we will feel five, ten or twenty years from now if we do nothing to remedy this, will be many times greater than the relatively shorter term pain felt due to the economy needing to change course due to a new tariff structure.

One thing that we can be certain of is that local production would be greatly encouraged through cost reduction measures companies would seek to find. Avoiding having to pay a tariff alone would be a great incentive for this. Transport of goods over long distances would thus be cut, saving the world more fuel. In this case, economists would argue that this is a bad thing because it prevents us from achieving Pareto efficiency through trade. This concept, shortly summarized basically to remind us of this concept that we already went over, argues correctly that by everyone concentrating on producing goods that are best at, and then trading with others who do the same, we all gain more consumer satisfaction. The model in no way accounts for the long-term costs of using up finite and largely un-substitutable resources to facilitate this trade.

One thing that we can say for certain is that in the absence of such an incentive as the sustainability tariff, or maybe some even better ideas, we are headed towards a far worse future than the one available to us in an environment that encourages more efficient resource allocation. Our current behavior is in many ways no better than that of a swarm of locusts that expands until it runs out of food. Unlike the locusts however, we are endowed with very powerful weapons with which we are likely to threaten each other in the event of discontent experienced due to lack of resources. The recent violence in the Middle East, triggered in large part by rising food prices is a good indicator of what is in store for most of us in the event of diminished resource supplies. We will likely become violent, disrupting the flow of resources even to a higher degree, as is the case with the situation in Libya and elsewhere. We can easily become so destabilized that we will suffer far beyond what would be the case if one were to simply take commodity shortages on their own as the main source of our misery.

4

The finite World part two:
The Environment

An ignored disaster

As a Canadian citizen, who spent most of his life in that country, I may be forgiven for not having given much thought to environmental issues for most of my life. Canada has one of the lowest levels of population density among most nations. I lived most of my life in Winnipeg, which is a prairie town isolated from most other large urban centers in the country, and south of the border. If traveling south by car, one would have to drive seven hours continuously to reach the first town with a population of over a million, which is Saint Paul-Minneapolis. Going east, it takes about 24 hours to reach Toronto. If heading west, one would have to drive about 13 hours to reach Calgary. There are no urban settlements north of Winnipeg. The southern part of the province has mostly been claimed by farmland and urban residential settlements, but there is plenty of pristine nature to be enjoyed, if one heads north. Most importantly, it is really cold in that part of the world.

Given the reality of my personal life, there were very few environmental issues that I thought should give me personally reason to worry. Global warming does not sound all that bad, when one lives through a six month winter every year. Canada has plenty of land; there is therefore less cause to worry about potential coastal flooding due to the melting of the glaciers. There may even be some potential positive economic effects if the crop-growing season is extended, and farming can gradually creep north. The fact that global climate change may potentially displace hundreds of millions of people worldwide was the kind of consideration that needs some

150

reflection in connecting it to one's own reality, and how it might be altered due to such a phenomenon.

The fact that the salt-water fisheries may experience complete collapse within the next few decades was equally irrelevant to my reality[1]. There are plenty of lakes in Manitoba, and fish is plentiful if one is willing to go out and catch it. I happen to be a good angler, so lack of fish based protein from the oceans was not something that kept me up at night. There are also local fresh water fisheries that can keep the local market supplied to some extent. The dependence of hundreds of millions of people on the coastal fisheries around the world for their livelihood and as the main source of their nutrition was not all that clear to me even a few years ago. The fact is however that people living in coastal areas and on islands around the world are highly dependent on the ocean's ecosystem. For many people in places like Africa, Asia and Latin America, the presence of abundant fish and crustaceans is literally a matter of life or death by starvation. Even for millions of people living in developed countries, the fisheries are the main pillar of economic stability in some of the coastal areas, including in Canada. I am not even certain that we can farm the amount of protein that will be lost globally on the land and water we have available to us if the global oceanic ecosystem will collapse as an increasing number of scientists prophesize that it will likely happen in the next few decades. Here we once again have a problem that could potentially adversely affect hundreds of millions directly and all of us indirectly.

Walking through many of Europe's old towns, some of which were spearheading the industrial revolution, like Dresden, Germany, where I visited a few years back, one has to appreciate the strides we made in cleaning up the air. The marks of the initial industrialization drive are etched in the building blocks of stone that still remain standing in many towns that made sure to preserve their historical inheritance. In Dresden, this is especially obvious, because many of the medieval churches and palaces had to be rebuilt after the brutal bombing that the city received during the Second World War. They tried to re-use as much as possible the old stones, but in most cases, it was not possible, so new stones were also used. The contrast between the newer, lighter colored stones and the black stones that absorbed all the CO_2 that coal burning machines from more than a century ago spewed into the air, could not be greater. We most certainly made a lot of progress through the introduction of new technologies over the many decades since the great industrialization began, yet we still have many cities and regions that suffer from a great deal of air pollution. This causes many health problems for hundreds of millions around the world. However, I lived in Winnipeg, where air quality issues were not a major factor given the relatively low population density of the region, although I often thought that authorities were being rather neglectful by allowing many cars that spewed obnoxious smoke from their tail pipes to be on the road.

Water quality was a somewhat more serious issue in Manitoba, because there is a great deal of farmland that produces chemical runoff. There are also many hydro dams, which allegedly release mercury into the water. The mercury then ends up in the fish we eat. The level of contamination is not considered dangerous as long as only moderate servings of fish are ingested. Many lakes and rivers around the world, including a few in Canada are considered to be too polluted for many uses such as drinking water, for swimming or as a fish supply. There are already many people around the world, who do not have access to clean drinking water, and some find themselves going thirsty altogether. This is also considered to be a great catalyst to human migration.

At some point, if we take all the ecological reasons for people to migrate in the next few decades, it becomes obvious that the gates to Canada and a handful of other nations that still have the surplus environmental carrying capacity will be inundated by the great masses trying to get away from the misery associated with ecological collapse. At some point, the carrying capacity of these countries can quickly become overwhelmed as well, especially if the influx is greater than the social absorption rate that these countries are capable of. Canada's immigration rate currently experienced is already beyond the coping capacity of the native-born population in cultural terms. In other words, the immigrant communities are no longer absorbing enough of the cultural institutions that make Canadian society be what it is (a European offshoot). What this means is that a place like Canada, despite its seemingly natural resistance to adverse global ecological trends that have the potential to throw humanity into global chaos, cannot maintain stability in most likelihood either in the event of global upheaval. If for no other high-minded reason, for that reason alone, me and most other Canadians should care about the global environment, as should everyone else.

Making the case for action

The sustainability tariff is directly set up to influence our environmental policies; there is therefore no doubt about the effects it would have on environmental protection. Pricing in environmental damage as part of everything we will produce globally can finally create an economic incentive to reverse our current destructive path. Rather than focus on the effects that the tariff would have on the environment, it is in my view far more important to re-classify the environment as a mostly non-renewable resource that we depend on. We should pay attention to its degradation in a similar way that we should pay attention to the dwindling reserves of other non-renewable commodities.

My choice for treating the environment as a natural resource stems from my belief that the only effective way to connect with many people on the issue of the importance of protecting our habitat, is through voicing our potential loss as consumers of the environment and the products it provides us with. Many people try to create awareness about the plight of ecosystems or endangered species, with mixed results. The main reason why they achieve less than full social backing for collective action on environmental protection is the old debate, whether the environment or the economy is more important. There is simply no way for environmental activists ever to win that debate, because ad-hoc sacrifice on the part of society is never a practical proposal. A system that automatically prices the environmental price into all goods and services produced is the only practical way to deal with this, yet there is to date no such proposal put forward by any of the interested organizations.

The reason that I call previous attempts to deal with this issue ad-hoc is because most often national, regional or local governments are asked to independently decide on measures of environmental responsibility on behalf of their constituency. That most often leads to local economic sacrifice in the short-term and quite often in the long-term as well, while the benefits are often universal, as is the case with air pollution. Most international attempts to implement a new direction were based on voluntary goodwill as I already mentioned, and the results so far have been extremely disappointing. There are sometimes exceptions, as is the case with Europe's insistence on pushing for fuel efficiency through structuring their tax system in a manner that discourages gas-guzzling vehicles, and through stringent enforcement of emissions standards. There is no question of the wisdom of pushing for a more fuel-efficient economy in light of the high, volatile petroleum prices, we have been witnessing for over five years now. The cut in net imports due to the more efficient economy alone contributes greatly to growth in GDP where population growth is no longer a driver of economic expansion in their particular case. This is just one exception however, while most can agree that stringent rules on environmental protection have an overall long-term effect of pushing away investment in manufacturing of many products. Many politicians and lobbyists who push for removing these regulations tell us so.

Take textile manufacturing for instance, as an example of the clear effect that environmental protection has on the economy. Most westerners believe that the only reason textile production is no longer an important manufacturing activity in the west is because it is a labor-intensive activity, which can be done much cheaper by investing in a developing country such as China. I should point out however; that there are other developing markets, which are also being outcompeted by manufacturers in countries like China, and it is done mainly on environmental grounds. Take my country of birth, Romania for instance. Wages are only marginally higher than in China, yet Romania is an importer of textiles itself. Main reason is that Romania is now a member of the EU, and thus it must abide by EU environmental regulations.

A private firm however also needs to abide by a regulation, which may not be as official, but is equally powerful in its effect. A private firm needs to pursue the maximization of profit, because if not, it will be outcompeted and eliminated from the market. If the firm is in the business of producing blue jeans, then the logical decision is to produce in China, because there, they can dump the blue dye used to color the jeans in a nearby river. That is less likely to be overlooked in an EU member country, so despite Romania's relative advantage of being closer to a great market in which China also competes on in textile exports, meaning that there is a benefit in transport costs to producing jeans in Romania, the winner of this competition is nevertheless China.

Many developing nations either have weak environmental protection policies, or are less likely to enforce them because of lack of funds, political will, or corruption. They do however increasingly posses the necessary human capital and physical infrastructure needed to attract increasingly complex manufacturing activities. There is of course also the labor cost advantage that is not negligible. Faced with such a powerful challenge to the right to produce things, western elites are left with no choice but to adopt a less active approach to legislating and enforcing environmental standards. As competition intensifies and things become more desperate in the western economy, the race to the bottom also tends to accelerate. In the US for instance the political right, is now advocating more or less to do away with federal environmental standards on the ground that it is unconstitutional, like many of the government activities they oppose. Leaving individual states to legislate environmental regulations means the end of meaningful environmental protection, because business can easily play individual small states against each other, just as they are already doing to some extent with nation states. The rise of the right, which is especially evident in the US, is in effect a revolt on the part of many who are tired of shouldering the burden of responsibility for the environment, while others take advantage.

It is becoming increasingly clear in my view that one of the first victims of the current economic competition among countries is likely the environment. Many reports, such as the one claiming that fisheries will be depleted globally by 2050, due to overfishing and pollution are sending a clear message that we are likely to inflict serious damage on the environment due to the current competitive framework. It is hard to imagine any significant measures becoming a reality in the absence of a change in the rules of the game being currently played worldwide. In the short to medium term interest of all of us to win the right to produce and consume cars, computers

IPods and a host of other goods, we are in fact committed to leaving the next generation with a scorched earth and waters as well. There are few indicators, which show the worldwide trend of an increased rate of environmental exploitation slowing. If the condition of the working class worsens as it is trending right now to do, environmental considerations will be neglected even further.

In order to grasp truly the meaning that the loss of environmental balance and its pristine pockets still left to us, we have to look at it as a commodity we consume. We did the same with petroleum to measure the effects of consuming this finite resource through time. The environment is even more crucial, because it is not only finite by any practical measure, because most negative effects of our actions can take decades or even centuries to heal, but also because it contains things within it that are far more crucial to our basic survival than petroleum is. The water we consume comes from our ecological system, which means that it is technically renewable, but if the riverbeds, or underground aquifers become contaminated, it means that the water we collect for personal or agricultural use are also contaminated.

We inevitably end up consuming the contaminated water, even if it contains substances that may be potentially harmful to us. Measuring this activity in economic terms, it is still of course a net benefit for us to consume the water, because we can stay alive by consuming it. There is no greater net benefit to a consumer than consuming a product that provides for the maintaining and prolonging of one's life. The net benefit is diminished however for those who end up suffering side effects because of ingesting the pollutants. The net loss now becomes a shortened and lessened quality of life for many individuals whose body may be less able to effectively deal with the toxic and harmful substances. The net loss to society is an increase in the cost of caring for the sickened individuals. That is unless, society is set up to simply ignore the unlucky individuals as is the case to some extent in many countries.

A study made by the EWG, or Environmental Working Group, came to the conclusion that there are currently about 300 pollutants in US drinking water. About 2/3 of those contaminants are currently unregulated, in other words there is no law or guideline to how much of these contaminants it is safe for us to have in our drinking water. Of the regulated substances that were found to be present in the drinking water, almost fifty of them were over the legal limit. Furthermore, it is estimated that over fifty million people are affected by the contamination that is over the legal limit by at least one contaminant, yet very little action is being taken to correct the situation. There are currently few economic models that take into account the negative side effects of the consumer as a result of drinking contaminated water. It certainly does not show up as a negative drag on GDP, or any other indicator. If this situation becomes five, ten or a hundred times worse, it might only show up as a positive indicator because of increased demand for health care services as a result. Our consumer dissatisfaction is not priced in as we consume all the goods that we managed to produce by doing the economic activity that created the pollution that contaminated the water we drink.

The market in response to an increase in water contamination came up with a solution that is less than optimal, given most choices in my view. Given the lack of direction coming from authorities, markets reacted by identifying a need and devising a way to meet it in order to reap the profits of their activity. The demand naturally came from individuals not willing to ingest the harmful substances increasingly found in our water supply, and with the means to afford an alternative. The market provided the alternative in the form of a wide range of sources of drinking water. One can choose to drink bottled water coming from natural springs, or purified tap water. Water purifiers mounted on to the tap water system, provide us with some protection from a number of harmful substances, but many other substances remain. Some more affluent individuals choose to buy property in areas that are still relatively pristine, where the local source of water is not yet contaminated. The positive effect is that fewer people get sick from water impurities. There is also the positive benefit to the economy in the form of hundreds of thousands of jobs worldwide, which currently rely on providing the world's interested customers with clean drinking water. On the face of it, it is an optimal solution to a problem caused by our economic activities. Some may even venture to claim a net positive, due to all the new jobs that were created, due to new demand being created thanks to pollution of our water supplies.

My view is that there is absolutely no question that water pollution is a net loss to society, even with the response of the market factored in. The bulk of the world's population cannot afford bottled water as an alternative to tap water. Many people do not even have access to tap water, never mind purchasing bottles of Perrier. As a result, we can expect to see more people getting sick from ingesting contaminated water. All other market based solutions, such as providing with new technologies in water purification have so far had a limited impact in limiting the rate of water contamination, especially given the financial squeeze faced by local governments in implementing some of these solutions, as well as price pressures causing private utilities to shun investments in improvements.

The market is in fact aggravating the water contamination, because there is an expansion of industrial activity associated with an increase in demand for bottled and filtered water. The transport demand alone should be counted in as an increased demand on transport fuels, which in turn causes an increase in ethanol and other bio fuels demand. That is in fact a great contributor to fresh water contamination due to runoff, stemming from the heavy use of pesticides and fertilizers needed to provide the required increase in crop yields, needed to accommodate the increased demand for crops used in the bio fuels industry.

On a side note, this is also a great example of the negative effects that we can expect on fuel efficiency within the economy because of this economic activity. The fuel efficiency of providing drinking water via pipeline into people's homes versus trucking it into supermarkets from great distances should be obvious to most. If the increase in bottled water demand is due to increased water contamination, due to industrial activity, which is caused in part by the increase in demand for bottled water, then this is a clear example of a vicious cycle that affects both the environment and our overall economic fuel efficiency level. Just try to picture the environmental impact as well as the increase in fuel demand if an ever-larger proportion of the Chinese, Indian and other developing market populations demand to drink clean bottled water as well. This should not come as a great surprise considering their increasing buying power, as well as the rapidly deteriorating environment in which they live.

If we are to measure the full impact of the increase in bottled water demand, we should also take it a step further and also examine some indirect effects of this demand as well. Consider for a moment the increased demand for transport fuels needed to transport bottled water to the market. The fuel needed to transport the bottles to market might be the equivalent to one tenth the ethanol produced in the US[2]. The production of ethanol causes runoff that pollutes the waterways, as I mentioned. This runoff flows all the way to the ocean. There are now many dead spots around the world that have been identified at the point of river outflows into the ocean because of this agricultural runoff. That in turn causes the fisheries to suffer, increasing loss of harvest. The resulting loss in the supply of protein, which is essentially almost free, courtesy of our ecosystem, is increasingly compensated with farmed supplies of protein, causing even more agricultural runoff. I am not suggesting that this is all due to the bottled water industry, but it cannot be denied that it makes a small but not insignificant contribution to the vicious cycle it derives its potential customers from.

The market does not offer a way out of this vicious cycle, in fact it encourages it, because as we saw with the example of bottled water, the degradation of our ecosystem often offers the market a new opportunity to supply consumers with new or improved products and services. The owners of capital are in fact the main cause of lack of regulation and enforcement of environmental standards. We are nevertheless told that the solutions are found within the market economy. The market economy however already has a historical record on this problem that we can refer to, and there is so far no evidence of it being the solution, but there is plenty to point to as it being the main problem.

The environmental record of command economies is no better in any way compared to the market economy in the developed world, but it seems to have been more successful in its protection than many, market driven developing nations such as China. I still remember the fact that the Birzava River that flowed through the city where I was born in Romania, was so toxic that I never saw one fish, frog or any other creature swimming in it. One of my friends fell in once, and the clothes became oily. She got rid of the clothes permanently, and had her hair shaved off in order to get rid of all the chemicals that she became contaminated with. That was not the case with most waterways in Romania, but there were definitely many polluted spots within the country. If we are not careful in guarding our environment, we might end up having many more Birzava River like situations in our own backyards. Most people might not be familiar with this reality, because fewer and fewer people work in an industrial setting, and most of those who do, care very little about what they witness. I worked for a small company that was throwing industrial coolants, together with metal dust down the drain. The sewer system does take care of many pollutants, but I am certain that many of the chemicals found within the coolant cannot be neutralized, nor are most of those chemicals healthy for us. I am absolutely certain that they were not the only company that engaged in such behavior. Furthermore, there are many guidelines worldwide, which are inadequate, given the industrial realities we currently have in place.

The results are already a sad reality. A recent study done in the US, shows that most drinking water supplies contain toxic chemicals. The news came with the reassuring explanation that poisoning was not imminent, in other words you are more likely to prolong your life by drinking the water than by not drinking any water at all. Perhaps if the only water supply on the world would be as polluted as the Birzava River was during my childhood, most of us would decide to drink it still, despite its highly toxic properties. It would still have the effect of prolonging life, but not by much. If there happened to be one spring that still had relatively clean water, I'm sure that the market would do its trick in making it available to the consumer. The price of such a water supply would become prohibitively expensive, only accessible to a small minority of the world's affluent. There are of course other ways to get clean water, such as through distillation, but that takes vast amounts of energy, which once again brings us back to the original question, whether we are headed for a more fuel efficient economy?

To many people, it may seem that we are still a very long way from reaching such a dire situation, where the value of our earnings might be measured in terms of how much uncontaminated drinking water we can afford. Remember however that we are currently not headed in the right direction in terms of environmental protection;

in fact, the opposite is clearly the case. Take the 2005 decision made by the Bush administration to exempt the shale gas industry in the US from environmental regulations. Millions of people can potentially find themselves in the situation of having their drinking water contaminated by the process of underground rock fracturing involved in the shale gas production process. Our desperation for energy to continue running the global economy as we currently do, is pushing us to ignore the potential dangers. Our desperate need to respond to fierce economic competition, has so far only produced calls for extreme de-regulation as the best way to respond.

I was six years old when the Chernobyl disaster hit neighboring Ukraine. We were told to drink only water coming from underground reservoirs, or in the absence of such supplies, we were told to boil the water before drinking it. It is still unknown how many people either died, or were made sick from that accident. Many people maintain that a higher rate of birth defects, cancer occurrence, and infertility is prevalent in the region, but few serious studies attempted to quantify it. We prefer not to do so, because if we ever would, then we would have to go to the next step of justifying why we do not change course in order to prevent any more such disasters. There are now even more nuclear power plants in the region than there were then. The US gulf coast will similarly see many additional attempts at reaching the deeper fields, as the shallow ones run dry, increasing the likelihood of additional environmental disasters in the region. The Japanese will not stop using nuclear power, despite the realization that they live on very unstable ground. The seafood in the Gulf area has been declared safe to eat, and so will the radiation-contaminated seafood from the Japanese coast. It is no different from farmland close to the Chernobyl disaster also being brought back into use. In the end, we have to eat and drink, no matter how contaminated the supplies will get. As long as it prolongs life, it is a net benefit.

My sister has a re-occurring brain tumor. She already went through two brain surgeries, and chemotherapy. There is a very good chance that she will need additional interventions in the near future, and even so, it is not certain how much longer she will live. It is impossible to know whether the nuclear disaster in Ukraine is responsible or not. She started having headaches right around the time of that accident, but we cannot know whether or not that is just a coincidence. That is in fact the way most cases of harm done by contamination go. There may be an increase in diseases such as cancer, asthma, or any other disease in a particular region, or globally. It is likely caused by a particular contaminant, or a combination we are exposed to in our air, water or food supply, but we will never ever identify for certain the main culprit. When we will look back at the gulf oil spill from 2010, most will recall the eleven workers who died a violent death due to the explosion. The direct economic damage will be recorded and repeated over and over. The number of illnesses and deaths caused due to short term or long term exposure will never be recorded, or quantified, nor will the full tally of the environmental impact. Those things we will squabble over endlessly, because the real bill can never be paid for such an environmental catastrophe.

It is hard to get people excited about such issues, despite the potentially great magnitude of the problem. This all goes back to our human nature. When the disastrous tsunami hit Indonesia, we all came to life in trying to help. A few hundred thousand people died in an instant, which shocked us into action. The same numbers of people die every week worldwide, because of lack of basic needs, such as nutrition and clean water. Despite that, it is hard to imagine us ever being shocked into action over this, as we were over the tsunami, or the Haiti earthquake. In fact, I do not think we would be shocked into action even if the number that currently dies in a week from poverty and contamination would start dying every day instead, as long as it happens gradually enough. We react similarly to changes in our environment. If a chemical spill would kill a dozen people, as it did in Kolontar, Hungary in 2010, it would be all over the news for a few days at least. Millions might be dying every year as a result of exposure to various substances that we released into nature, yet we remain unmoved. If the millions were to turn to hundreds of millions in a gradual manner, would we take notice? My personal view is that we would most likely not. At most, there would be some people trying to raise the alarms about it, and those with an interest in keeping the status quo would likely challenge the findings as unsubstantiated, because we can never know for certain whether or not we are the cause of the great increase in illness and death. Invoking the argument of jobs versus environmental protection would inevitably be brought up again, and we already know which side wins the argument, because we have seen this play out repeatedly.

As consumers of the environment, we are badly neglected by the Economic establishment. They rarely bother to measure the loss in consumer satisfaction resulting from the fact that we increasingly have to think twice before ingesting tap water, fish; land-based farmed food, or even breathe the air. We have to be increasingly careful where our children go swimming. More and more cities around the world are witness to the site of people going about with their mouth covered, due to smog. There is little doubt that our climate is changing, however there are still many, who claim that industry is not responsible. Year after year, we are increasing the likelihood of major ecosystem collapse, which could disrupt food supplies to millions, such as is the case with the world's fisheries, or the potential loss in agricultural yields that would result from a destruction of the bee population. In intensifying the current global competition for the right to produce toys, cars, electronics, and other consumer goods, we are creating a situation where we are given no choice but to endanger our right to consume the ultimate consumer goods, namely food and water. The mainstream economic establishment tells us that environmental protection is a hindrance to the right to produce and consume manufactured products, which is what they are able to measure from year to year. Unlike the satisfaction gained from drinking clean water, and breathing clean air in the present and for future generations, which is something they cannot measure, and therefore they tell us that we should not concern ourselves with.

Just because Economists have a hard time measuring our loss of consumer satisfaction due to environmental degradation, it does not mean that we are not adversely affected by it. The fact that we currently think the way we do scares me in this current economic situation that we find ourselves in, because it can become a disastrous combination if coupled with our economic misery. In the past few decades, some progress has been made on environmental protection, mainly spearheaded by western nations, with some mention due to a handful of non-western countries such as Japan. With the global economic situation becoming more fiercely competitive and an increasing number of countries desperate to just keep it together financially, it is likely that we are headed for a quick reversal of the progress made so far. In fact, we may surpass the point where progress first started to be made in lack of care for what we are doing to the environment and ultimately to ourselves. The first signs of this trend are already apparent in the crucial energy industry, where imposing on industries like the Canadian oil sands, more stringent constraints on pollution levels or the US shale gas industry is out of the question, despite evidence that these industries are far more dangerous to our habitat than conventional sources of energy. I fear that we might only realize what we are collectively losing as humanity when we rush to scramble to produce many disposable and non-essential goods, when it will be too late to do anything about it, except live with the awful consequences as the Easter Islanders did. Over the past decades we globalized trade, travel, communications, economic interdependence, there is no reason to assume that we did not also globalize the potential for environmental disaster. That is why we need the global solution.

5

The finite world part three:
Food

The most basic of needs, which us westerners have forgotten just how important it really is, thanks to generations of relative plenty that we managed to achieve might be in danger of no longer being met for an increasing proportion of the world's population. That is not news for about two billion people around the world, who currently do not get all basic nutritional needs satisfied. The part that is increasingly difficult for us privileged developed world citizens to grasp is that some portions of our own society are increasingly facing the danger of malnourishment. We have to wake up to the reality of globalization and its effects on everything, including nutrition. Globalization means convergence remember, and as the means of production are increasingly transferred to the developing world, and there is a rising middle class, ready to feast on the fruits of harvest in a similar fashion as we do, an increasing number of us will lose our privilege. The middle classes of Asia and other places are increasingly ready to outcompete some of our less privileged western citizens. The optimists may claim that it is in fact possible to apply technology and chemical fertilizers to achieve a level of production in food that should satisfy the needs of a converged world. The same optimists tell us that we can use technology to allow us to drastically cut our use of oil and gas. The same oil and gas that we have to transform into fertilizers meant to provide the plants we grow for the necessary nutrition. Mined phosphate production may have peaked already as well, which means that more marginal sources need to be tapped, which also require an increase in energy inputs, namely oil and gas[1].

The overall picture that emerges when we look at the resources we already examined, namely oil, gas, and our environment, as we combine their interactions with the other crucial commodity we need, which is food, it is a system, which engages in double counting. The oil industry in Canada claims that we have 170 billion barrels of oil we can extract from the Alberta oil sands. At the same time, the North American gas industry claims that we have about ten trillion m^3 of shale gas in proven reserves. Thus we all assume that we have about 230 billion barrels of oil equivalent in these two unconventional resources. No one mentions the fact that it will take about half of the current proven shale gas reserves to produce and upgrade all of the oil sands deposits. Thus we realistically should say that we have about 200 billion barrels of oil equivalent in these unconventional fuels. That is before we factor in all the other aspects of producing these resources, which are both actually very thirsty in their demand for oil and gas in the production process.

Similarly, we look at the farm acreage we have in North America, but we fail to subtract the amount we stand to lose if we go after the oil sands and shale gas resources. Both industries are currently in the process of displacing farmers. The farmland lost can be counted as an opportunity cost, which basically means that we lose the opportunity to produce something in order to produce something else. The means to produce food seems to be increasingly an opportunity cost that we are willing to pay in order to produce many other goods that we like to consume. We allocate farmland to urbanization, road construction, bio-fuel production, mining and a host of other needs we perceive as important.

The worst thing of all is that we consume our means of food production parallel to our consumption of the environment. The industrial accident at Kolontar, Hungary polluted a river, and also rendered about 40,000 hectares of farmland beyond use for decades. The nuclear disaster at Fukushima will probably produce even more damage to both the fisheries and to nearby farmland. Bio-fuel production also greatly affects the fisheries because of chemical runoff from the farm fields. These are just some examples that I chose to mention, because they are beyond debate. Many argue however that we are losing larger agricultural surfaces and yields do to effects of climate change. On this particular issue, we can argue until we are all blue in the face, because just as with the possible health side effects of Fukushima, Chernobyl, or the Gulf oil disaster, there are always other possible factors that one can put the blame on. It is like trying to pinpoint my sister's brain tumors to the Chernobyl incident, thus trying to disprove the possibility that it may only be a coincidence. One thing that we can be certain of is that there is a change in climate occurring, and it will most certainly change the farming prospects worldwide, regardless whether climate change is human caused or not.

Some have argued that climate change can be a good thing, because a warming trend may provide some extra farmland in places such as Canada and Russia as the crop and grazing line moves further north. The last 20 years or so have been among the hottest on record globally. My own personal observation, having lived just a two hour drive from the northern line where farming is no longer practical, is that the phenomenon of farms creeping north has not happened yet. On the grain growing, and animal grazing prairies of Canada, climate change seems to have made the province of Manitoba a little cooler and wet in the crucial summer growing months. Saskatchewan and Alberta became drier. There is no evidence of increased yields on the current northern frontier of farming in Canada anyway. While the farming frontier does not seem to be moving north in a hurry, the current farming regions seem to be experiencing an increase in droughts, floods and generally more unseasonal weather. In 2009, in Winnipeg, the hottest month of the year was September, which actually helped rescue that year's harvest in the region.

The UN has estimated that by 2050, the demand for food will double as a result of both population growth, and an increased appetite in the developing world for western eating habits. If we were to reach a global economic convergence that would be similar to the EU average, which like I said, given global economic growth trends, should happen in the absence of major interruptions to this trend, I think the UN may have underestimated the growth in food demand that it would generate. I think therefore that we should take a closer look at the tools and resources available to us, which we could use to at least reach a doubling of the food supply, which would help us avert catastrophe on this front.

The first thing we should consider is available cropland still left in the world. We are currently utilizing an estimated 1.5 billion hectares of farmland to feed the current world's population. The potential amount that could be added is uncertain, but with some exceptions, it is marginal land. In other words, for various reasons, the yields would be hardly worth the effort of farming the land. There are still some good quality potential farming fields left, but many places are the victims of economic or political upheaval, which is likely to actually increase with the recent trend of spiking energy and food prices. Parts of Eastern Europe are still not fully recovered in the aftermath of the dismantling of the collective farming system. In Romania for instance, it is estimated that about three million hectares of good quality farmland remain idle. Doubling the world's food production would probably require hundreds of millions of hectares of additional farmland, while the idle land in Eastern Europe only counts towards a fraction of that.

A sure way to gain more farmland is to cut down more forest cover, wherever suitable farmland can be gained through doing so. The lesson of the Amazon rainforest, which started shrinking rapidly a few decades ago as a result of the wish on the part of Brazil to become a cattle grazing powerhouse, was that when the loss is added up, it is hardly worth it. The loss of biodiversity is just a small part of the equation. Losing the global air filter is a far more dangerous trend that deforestation can bring about. When one looks at the issue of producing and extracting commodities for our increasing appetite to be satisfied, it becomes more and more clear that there is no way of getting them for free. Most of these extractive processes require a trade whereby, we give up the opportunity to enjoy another commodity. My guess is that in the next few decades, we are likely to lose more hectares of farmland to weather related trends, as well as to an increased encroachment by mining, urbanization, contamination, drought, or flooding and other causes. On the other side of the equation, some deforestation, as well as bringing some farmland back on line, where political upheaval previously prevented the maximization of area use, will not make up for the above mentioned losses.

Given that the opportunity to increase global active farmland is rather limited, the only thing left is to increase yields, per unit of farmland. In past decades, yields per unit of land allocated to grain had a tendency to increase at a rate of about 2.5% per year. At that pace of growth in yields, a doubling of production was achievable from existing landmass dedicated to farming every three decades or so. There is growing evidence that the rate of yield increase in grains is now in a slowing pattern. In the last twenty years or so, yield growth has slowed to about 1.5% per year. That is still not too bad, given that it would still provide us with a doubling of grain yields every 50 years. The most recent data, on the past decade shows a further, if only slight slowdown in yields. Grains production worldwide increased by roughly 17% in the 2000-09 periods, according to UN data, but we had a bad year in 2010, making that increase less robust for the full decade. The main problem I see is that the declining trend of yield growth per unit of land can actually lead to a peak, where yields will plateau, and stay there, or even worse, decline. There are many reasons to expect this to be the case.

It is true that there are many parts of the world, where an increase in pesticide, and fertilizer use, as well as an improved infrastructure for irrigation can still produce great gains in yields. Many other parts of the world, where potential for good crop yields was always the best to begin with, are already at a saturation point in the use of crop yield enhancers, so there is not much hope for continued spectacular gains. If anything, there might be a chance of a drop in yields eventually in those places due to some of the negative side effects of modern farming practices, as well as climate change. Crop yields in the developing world, especially in places that are rather poor, and are typical of subsistence farming practices will likely continue to stay with their current traditional practices. Fertilizer and pesticide additives are often too expensive for these farmers, and they lack the ability to invest in farm machinery. We should remember that western farmers are greatly helped by government subsidies that help pay for their inputs.

The introduction of stable, capital intensive farming is not always feasible everywhere on this world. Many parts of Africa for instance are prone to long drought seasons, where a farmer can easily be wiped out financially, in case that some loans were taken out in order to buy farm equipment. Western farmers, despite all the support they receive from government are often defeated and forced to throw in the towel because of a few bad harvests. It is hard to imagine many people willing to take the risk in a place like Kenya or Ethiopia, where droughts can last over five years.

I did not forget about GM crops either. In some cases, they can be a blessing, especially given that many crops are re-designed to withstand drought. Underground aquifers are being depleted very fast in many parts of the world, which makes it imperative for us to accept GM crops. Scientists will continue to work hard at creating better and better GM crops, and there will likely be some increase in crop yields as a result. These crops may be able to alleviate some of the pressures put on increasingly strained water supplies. Crops with natural resistance to pests and disease may reduce the need for pesticide use, which itself is derived from finite resources. GM crops are likely to be the great tech savior, if there is to be one. This technology already showed its potential in places like the US, and many dry regions around the world, where it helped increase crop yields dramatically in many cases.

I want to start my roundup of the many negative potential factors that might push the trend of food production down worldwide by highlighting one of the possible dangers of GM crops. We currently have some genetic variation globally of our crops, meaning that if one variation happens to fail for any of the many reasons; it can easily be replaced with another variation that can be adapted to a certain region. GM crops have a tendency to kill variation. If for instance a farmer decides on planting GM crops, he inevitably ends up contaminating the crops of the neighboring farms with GM seeds. That in turn forces the neighboring farms to adopt also the GM seeds, because their own crops are no longer considered GM free, and can no longer be sold as such to customers who are willing in many cases to pay a premium for natural. If the GM seeds happen to fail for any reason, it might lead to a situation where it would take years for the diminished amounts of natural seeds still found in some remote areas to replace the loss. The level of food disruption could be catastrophic.

Take corn for instance, as a good example of the potential for catastrophe. GM corn currently provides great yields wherever it is planted; therefore, it is present in many regions. The initial loss would be huge, because if it were to fail worldwide, total world grain production would suffer a double-digit percentage drop during the year of failure. To make matters worse, the second year would also see diminished production, because the high yielding GM crop would have to be replaced with natural or other less productive seeds, which might not be properly adapted to all the regions that would see a failure of the GM seed. There is currently absolutely no way to make up for such caloric loss, except by allowing for many people around the world to starve.

Water availability is another reason we can expect to see lower yields around the world. The capacity of the environment to provide irrigated land is decreasing. Places like India, where the green revolution produced magnificent results initially, are seeing their underground aquifers depleted at a very fast rate. Farms have to compete for water increasingly with a growing urban middle class, who have pretentions such as having a daily shower, or bath. Industrial expansion is also increasingly cutting into their rapidly shrinking water supplies. Under our current consumer driven economy, food is seen to have less value than other consumer goods such as electronic or other manufactured products. Saving an underground aquifer for the purpose of having that water available to us a decade or two later is not a concept that the market understands, or agrees with. It is true that in many cases, these aquifers undergo natural replenishment, but once the aquifer is drained, what is left over is only the amount that replenishment provides. Here again we see the market behaving in a manner that does not concern itself with long-term welfare of the consumer. The market's main concern is to deploy capital in a manner that is satisfactory to the owners of capital. In this case, as in many other examples the interests of the long term welfare of the consumer, and the interests of the owners of capital are not aligned, therefore if we allow the interests of the owners of capital to prevail, which is in effect what allegiance to the market does, our long term welfare will suffer.

Soil erosion and depletion can affect not only caloric yields but also the nutritional value of our crops. Fertilizers can often make up for most potential losses to caloric yields. Many question for how much longer we will be able to continue spraying the fields with fossil fuel derived fertilizers, as well as mined phosphate and potash.

For now however, we are able to do just that. Soil erosion does pose challenges to caloric output, but there are some remedies.

A far larger problem is the loss in nutritional quality of many of the crops being grown. Many minerals that are a natural part of the soil's chemistry are being depleted as a direct result of industrial farming. The proof of that is the increased need for people to ingest nutritional supplements. At the rate we are going, perhaps we may see a new trendy cultural norm develop, where at the dinner table; a plate with supplements might be included with the rest of the meal. This may seem unreal, but the reality of it is that many nutritional deficiencies can have very serious health consequences, it is therefore not out of the roam of possibilities that culture may adapt to make sure that people do not forget to ingest the proper supplements in order to stay healthy.

While many people can adapt to deal with nutritional deficiencies by making sure to take some daily pills, the reality for most of the world's population is that pill popping is just too expensive. For them, it is therefore clear that in the absence of proper nutrients being found in common foodstuffs, they can only cope with the negative side effects and nothing more. A large portion of our population can also be classified in this category. As economic convergence is likely to continue, so will the ranks of the ones suffering from improper nourishment within our society. Caloric needs will still be met for a while yet for most, because cheap carbohydrates can easily be provided by the industrial farming system. The cost to society in terms of negative health effects, and even deterioration in the developmental abilities of many within society can easily cost us more than we can presently afford. We need to keep a healthy, well developed physically as well as mentally society in order to compete on the global stage. Soil depletion does not help with that. If the trend of soil depletion continues, we will likely see deterioration in our health parallel to it.

An increase in soil salinity is another problem that we have to be aware of. One of the worst hit areas right now is Australia, where it already affects 9% of all farmland, and if trends continue, it may eventually affect a quarter of all farmland on that continent. Salinization of cropland can either diminish crop yields, or even render the land useless. For all practical purposes, the damage is irreversible, because it takes hundreds of years for the land to purge the salt from the soil. One of the main culprits in this case is irrigation of the land. In the absence of careful irrigation practices such as drip irrigation, excess water seeps beyond the depths of the crop's roots, absorbs the salt layers often found under the soil, and then finds its way back towards the top layers of the soil. If a quarter of Australia's farmland will eventually be affected, that is bad enough, but the truth is that soil salinization is a problem that affects most continents of the world to some extent[3].

The last potentially negative effect that can affect our ability to feed the world's increasing, and increasingly demanding population is the effects of climate change. I will not get into the controversy of whether it is human caused, or a natural phenomenon. I will instead admit to the fact that it is happening and thus focus on some of its possible effects. The shift in global climate patterns is in fact causing disruptions to farming activities already. Some areas are seeing unseasonal temperatures affecting the growing season. In Winnipeg, where I lived most of my life, and is the capital of a grain producing Canadian province, I noticed a definite increase in precipitation during the summer months, accompanied by cooler temperatures. Wild temperature fluctuations, ranging from way above average temperatures during the traditionally bone chilling cold months of January and February, to summer months devoid of summer-like temperatures have caused disruptions to crops in Manitoba. Flooding has also disrupted farming practices in many parts of the province with an increased frequency. As I mentioned, the reverse has been the norm in the other two prairie provinces of Canada, where Saskatchewan and Alberta have been experiencing an increase in drought conditions.

It is possible that some parts of the world that are seeing a worsening of potential crop yields due to climate change, many other parts might become a better place to farm, where it was previously not a practical undertaking. Here we have to recognize however that farmers tend to be rather sedentary in nature, and generally, when faced with an increased rate of crop failures, they are more likely to give up and move to the nearest urban location, rather than chase after better farmland. Some areas may indeed become more farmer friendly, but it can easily take generations for the opportunity to be exploited. In the meantime, disruptions to current farms around the world will likely register as disruptions to our food production, which may become more acute in the event that the weather continues to defy our needs.

The shortcomings of our crop farming in conjunction with the likelihood of a complete depletion of the fisheries as I already mentioned in the previous chapter concerning the environment, can easily outweigh the potential gains from introducing technological solutions such as GM crops, and a potential increase in chemical fertilizer use around the world. We have already witnessed two periods of political upheaval as a result of food price spikes in the past three years. The first price spike was alleviated by a combination of steady crop outputs and a drop in demand, due to the negative effects on people's buying power around the world as a result of the 2008 near economic meltdown, while the current one is still unfolding. We have already seen a few North African governments get toppled as a result of it, and there is no telling yet what effect it may have in the end. Much will depend on this year's harvest and harvests of grain crops from here on, as the one thing that can alleviate the current turmoil. Given the events of the past few years, I find it hard to accept the optimist view that we are likely to experience smooth sailing in the next few decades, when it comes to global food security.

Governments from Asia, Middle East, Europe as well as private interests already purchased millions of hectares of prime farmland in Africa. Various interests are also probing the purchase of land in other parts of the world. Farmland seems to be the new strategic resource that an increasing number of interests around the world seem to believe that they need to have some control over, in addition to fossil fuel reserves. Recently, the UN has declared the era of cheap food to be over, like many organizations also declared the obvious, which is that the era of cheap oil has ended in the past decade[4]. While many still prefer to put their full faith in technological innovations that will save us, I believe we have to wake up and start looking at this problem in a sober manner.

How would the sustainability tariff help alleviate the food problem?

There is no easy answer to the food dilemma, and that is why few politicians ever try to address this problem seriously. Ensuring our food safety for the long term is especially tricky, when the market tells us to destroy portions of our food production capacity in favor of producing goods that currently demand a better price, create more financial wealth, jobs, and economic power as a nation. Economic power as a nation is in fact one of the best ways to ensure food availability in the current global environment. It provides citizens with more buying power, which allows them to outbid others, especially hailing from societies that do not engage in the process of forgoing the opportunity to produce food sustainably in favor of allocating resources to the production of manufactured goods, and high priced human dwellings. Those who do not choose the current market trend, in fact risk destruction in the present, as is the example of African countries, which currently are experiencing a case of mild re-colonization, because foreign interests are able to use their financial might to purchase the rights to use their farmland as well as mining their mineral wealth.

So, given that doing the right thing for the long run is not an option, as is also the case with environmental protection, even though it is increasingly obvious that the current road leads to eventual disaster, why should we expect the ones in charge to do the right thing? The answer is that we should not, as long as doing the right thing regionally, leaves us vulnerable globally to becoming economic prey. We should expect them to change the rules by which we play this game of economics, in order to eliminate these conundrums, and thus giving us real choices. The sustainability tariff can do that by forcing societies to pay the real price for current practices in respect to the means of food production. It does have its unpleasant aspects, but it is no more unpleasant than having to ask society not to borrow excessively so "our children won't be saddled with our debt". I am sure that most have heard a variation of this slogan pushed by a politician at some point in order to make the case for spending cuts. In this case, the sustainability tariff puts a price on us spending the means of production of food in the future. I was going to say, "the means of producing food for our children in the future", except, we are already seeing trouble brewing due to food shortages, therefore we have to think of the future as something starting from the present and no longer an abstract concept about a time period far away, and at an undetermined time of arrival.

For many reasons, this will not be a pleasant proposal at first sight, because when the real price of producing food industrially, versus responsibly is priced into the economy through tariff penalties being priced in, the inevitable outcome will be a re-pricing of food in relation to other goods, and it will go higher. Remember that I am also an advocate of eliminating all farming subsidies, due to their market distorting effects, which leads to a mispricing of food in the global economy. I am a strong believer that the best way to make the global economy prosper, is to price all goods we consume as accurately as possible. Looking at food as an example, I believe that we can all be better off.

To start with, the most vulnerable people within our global village, we should look at how this would affect the poor starving Africans. At first glance, a rise in food prices due to the re-pricing effect that the tariff would have, one would expect that the one place where we should expect major misery to occur is Africa. If we look closer however, we realize that the opposite is true. For one thing, the small farmers there would be finally able to compete with the industrial farms, which like I mentioned are heavily subsidized. Yes, prices would rise, but so would the income of the local farmers, and with the rise in the value of their products, so would their GDP, through both an increase in the value of the goods they produced, as well as through an improvement in trade balance as industrially produced food loses its ability to penetrate the market. The African city dwellers, who have to pay for the higher food price might seem to be at a disadvantage at first sight, except, we have to remember the local farmers, who now have more spare income. That translates into more demand for basic manufactured goods such as clothing, farm tools, and many other things that the previously unemployed masses of the urban communities can now, produce and earn an income that will let them afford the food.

The governments would also have to abandon the policy of relying on cheap labor, and unregulated mining and industry to attract economic activity, because if you remember the tariff as I proposed it, it is based on measuring the environmental footprint and the level of human rights observance as a percentage of GDP. Essentially, it would force currently corrupt, lazy and incompetent governments to work harder and smarter to produce results, instead of relying on crutches. This should in fact help kick start many dysfunctional economies around the world. Incomes would inevitably rise as a result of eliminating the distortions caused by currency manipulation that suppresses local buying power, making the local food more accessible in price.

Coming back to the effects that we should expect to see as a result of implementing such a tariff in our own community, we might be surprised by how well it could in fact suit us. The proof of the unsuitable nature of the current arrangement is found within our demographic reality. We now rely on less than five percent of our workforce to grow the food we eat, while in the urban areas, we see unemployment rates in the double-digit zone. So in other words, the few ageing farmers who are left to do the work are forced to find increasingly environmentally damaging solutions to feeding us through introducing increasingly mechanized and chemical reliant means of production. Meanwhile, we have a rising tide of youth sitting idle in the city, because we have run out of things to do. Some things that do have to be done, we can no longer afford to pay for, as more and more government cutbacks are taking effect all over the western world.

The natural reaction of our governments because of the effects of the sustainability tariff will have to be to discourage the dominant position of the industrial farming system. The reality is that the cost to the entire economy as a result of being subjected to tariffs incurred as a result of the environmental damage that industrial farming does, would outweigh the benefits of allowing for these practices. In effect the industrial farming system would go from being the most favored segment of farming through subsidization, to being the least favorite through taxation. Sustainable farming on the other hand would have to be encouraged as a mode of providing food, because it leaves a much smaller footprint if it is properly done, so it would most likely benefit from lower tax rates.

Sustainable farming, preferably done on a more localized scale, in order to prevent incurring costs of transport, both direct and indirect through the sustainability tariff would necessitate a much more labor intensive approach, meaning more people would have to be self employed or employed in the process of growing the food, and providing it to the consumer. In economic terms, this would not be a bad misallocation of our potential labor force, because like I already pointed out, we already have too many people being kept idle within our economy. If current trends continue, and more job transfers to the developing world will occur, we could easily reach a level of youth idleness that will surpass the threshold that ensures basic social stability. We could in fact be just one more major recession away from catastrophe.

I am fully aware of the unappealing aspects of this proposal. It involves higher prices for food in relation to other products. It also involves an increasing number of us having to make a choice that few had to make in the last few centuries. It involves a reverse in trend from one of urbanization, to one of re-adopting a more rural lifestyle for some. It is not at all an appealing prospect, I know, but we have to take an honest look at the alternatives. Holding the current course may not have any better outcomes either, in fact they are most likely worse, and we are already witnessing the first signs of it. Food prices have already gone up, because of both increased global demand, as well as a large increase in the price of transport for a food delivery system that is very transport intensive. It has been suggested by many studies that the average food item on an average North American's table most likely travelled more than 1500 kilometers (about a thousand miles). With fuel prices spiking, it is naturally to be expected that we may see a rise in the price of everything that has to be transported for long distances, including food. The rise in prices of farming inputs such as fertilizers derived from fossil fuels is not negligible either. Despite these higher prices, it seems that we are still far from having the ability to provide a proper volume and quality of nutrition. In other words, market forces are yet to bring more product to the market, in order to start pushing prices back down.

The effect of no longer having cheap affordable food on our economy, is that demand for many other products is set to slowly get squeezed, as we increasingly work to outbid each other globally for the right to eat properly. If the economy crashes as a result of decreased demand for non food items, the government will lose its ability to continue subsidizing industrial farming. In this event, many farmers who still owe money on their property will likely be forced to declare bankruptcy. At the same time, the lack of demand for non-food products and services will cause unemployment in the urban areas to skyrocket. At some point, the masses of unemployed, and the idle farmland left over by the bankrupt farmers will have to be matched up. The difference from my suggestion and the one I described here is the level of pain suffered by the masses in the process. I personally think that the managed approach would be more pleasant than the complete crash approach, but there is no doubt that there are many who would contest that, as well as rebuke anyone who dares to say that what we have going now is not sustainable.

It is entirely possible that speculators will pick up the foreclosed properties making the unemployed masses looking for work a source of cheap farm labor, ready to be exploited. It is also possible that governments will step in, and take over the running of these farms in some cases, transforming them into cooperatives, not dissimilar to the ones found in Eastern Europe during communist rule. In either case, the fate of both the urban population as well as that of those who will choose to go work in the countryside will be much worse than if we were to fix the current system like I suggested. A more nightmarish scenario could develop if we were to experience a large influx of investment into farmland from countries like China. In this case, the large masses of urban unemployed may look on with envy as Chinese farm workers would take the place of ageing and increasingly bankrupt local farmers. The Chinese were already probing the possibility of buying farmland in Canada. With our increased financial dependence on this country of savers, who have thus far built by far the largest financial reserve on earth, our ability to resist their desire to purchase our farmland will decline as well; therefore, I do not think we should dismiss the danger of such a thing happening so easily.

These are the alternatives as I see them if we continue down the current path. I did not even include the effect of the demographic reality of our farmers, who in most western societies average in the mid to late fifties. Even without any other considerations in place, such as the ones I already touched on, we have to find a way to replace these farmers gradually as they age. Some may think that Chinese or other colonists would be a desirable solution, which is what the market would dictate in most likelihood. I think we have to convince cool coffee shop dudes and ladies that there is no future for us, if we are not willing to do more hard work. We cannot all go to university and become philosophers, historians, anthropologists, psychologists, or other wise guy, "we refuse to get our hands dirty", well articulated snobs. I wish someone would have worked harder to convince me of this fact a decade ago, rather than having to find out myself the hard way.

Convincing people of this is not enough however; we have to present them with the opportunity. That cannot happen if we are not willing to change course, in order to re-shape demand from the consumer, as well as the shape of capital investments. This is perhaps more important in food production than in any other field, because if we do not take care to maintain a society that is willing to produce what we need to survive, we will likely end up surrendering the means of production to others. There are many around the world that are also desperate to make sure that they have what to eat in the near and distant future. The fact that we have Chinese investors, who are already engaged in this type of colonialism in the developing world, kicking the tires in our own neighborhood, should be a great cause for alarm to our society. This is one current, undirected market based solution we westerners might end up regretting bitterly, and it may come sooner than many might think. Having worked in a retirement home, I know firsthand just how quickly that farming demographic is helping fill the ranks of the retirement home demographic.

No matter how we will organize the future crop growing system, there is no getting around the expected demand, which is likely to come from both an increase in the global population as well as an increased appetite for protein in the diet of a converging world. Continued farming practices that degrade the soil, increase the danger of major food disruptions, and thus severe misery for humanity. Introducing more sustainable farming practices will not improve the level of food output greatly however, therefore the solution lies in both sustainability and dampening demand. Dampening demand is by far the greatest of challenges, but I hope that the new trade structure implemented as a result of international acceptance of the sustainability tariff could help somewhat.

Part of the new demand for increased food production comes from people in the developing world who increasingly have the financial ability to support a more protein rich diet. As the world economy continues on a path of convergence, which will be the case no matter the trade structure in place, this trend becomes unavoidable. The only thing that we can do in order to counteract this increase in demand is to make sure that we implement measures meant to reduce waste of food, which is a major problem in western society, and anywhere where there are pockets of prosperity for that matter. Some recent studies suggest as much as 40% of the food sent to the market in North America is wasted either through the distribution or the consumption process. If we can cut down on this waste dramatically, we can help cushion the impact of the demand surge as a result of this new global middle class. If the price of food rises in relation to other prices as a result of the shifts in crop growing practices as a result of my suggestion on the trade tariff, it should have enough of an impact to change the behavior of food merchandisers as well as consumers to see some tangible results in cutting food wasting habits.

The other main driver of food demand for the next 40 years or so will be population growth. On this issue, I have a diverging opinion than that of the current consensus among economists and population experts, who seem to be in general agreement that population growth is inversely correlated to growth in general affluence. They seem to think that in a converging world economy, where an increasing number of people will gain affluence, and better education, population growth should level off. My observation is that affluence level is probably less of a factor than religious beliefs, especially among the great three monotheistic religions, which together encompass about half the world's population. Religious belief has the power to override personal financial considerations, as well as knowledge gained through education. Current religious doctrine is to encourage a family model that is devoid of family planning or Planned Parenthood.

Evidence of the effect of religion on family size can be seen even in places like the United States. The prevalence and intensity of religious allegiance among people living in different states is positively correlated to family size. I currently live in South Carolina, and the difference I noticed in family size is very visible compared to the more secular leaning Canadian norm, or what I have seen in places like Illinois, and other more secular leaning regions of the US and Canada. The high rates of birth in places like Israel, and affluent Persian Gulf region states are further proof of affluence being swept aside as a deciding factor in birth rates, in favor of religious guidance. The low birthrates in Europe and a few other places are in fact a result of a more secular society rather than affluence. I frankly do not see this level of secular culture penetrating in many of the places that currently serve as the engine of global population growth for a very long time to come. I therefore foresee that in the absence of economic catastrophe, or a targeted policy towards discouraging large families, global population growth is unlikely to be stemmed during the current century, and the rate of growth will likely be somewhat higher than most predictions that are currently floating around.

A fast growing population currently has appealing aspects, which is why Canada for instance is very active in accepting immigrants at a very high rate. The payoff is that it can maintain a high growth rate in consumer demand. It is in fact responsible, more than any government initiative during the 2008 economic crisis for keeping the housing market stable. This in turn kept the construction boom going, against all expectations to the contrary, including mine. Consumer demand growth is a key factor in maintaining stable and steady GDP growth, and population growth is the easiest way to achieve that. There are some downsides as well. For instance, in Canada's case there is a steady erosion of benefit per capita from the nation's natural resource exploitation. Given that the overwhelming majority of the immigrant population is now coming from Asia, Africa, and the Middle East, there is also an issue that Canadians are generally very uncomfortable and reluctant to discuss, which is the change it can have on cultural institutions, which up to now were dominated by the fact that Canada was a European offshoot. Some Asian communities have very strong cultural institutions of their own, and given the growing size and increasing cohesion of their communities, it is unlikely that they will abandon them. They may instead look to introduce their cultural values to the wider population. In the long-run, this can become a source of friction, which is not apparent yet; because the still European dominated population of Canada has taken an attitude of accommodation, going as far as introducing discriminatory measures against the majority, such as affirmative action, which currently seems to have at least tacit consent from the vast majority of Canadian citizens[5]. The results of these possible cultural changes are uncertain, but in economic and living standards terms, it can result in losing the values that made Canada the attractive place it is to migrate to. There is no certainty that the new values adopted can provide for the same avenues towards a prosperous future.

The issue of social and economic friction because of a shrinking of available natural resources is also relevant in all other countries that currently experience a high rate of population growth. The higher the population density, the more likely it is that people will step on each other's toes. Differences in opinion stemming from cultural, ethnic religious, regional points of view are harder to avoid given an expanding population, increasingly forced to deal with each other. In most cases, however, the shrinking availability of resources can be the main source of friction, and on a local level, it has already proven to lead to disastrous consequences. Jared Diamond's insightful description of the genocide in Rwanda, as he presented it in his book *"Collapse"*, is an example where increasing friction over farmland availability in fact caused the implosion of that society. A fast growing population, coupled with cultural norms that encourage the division of farmland among siblings upon becoming adults, meant that an increasing number of people were reduced to subsistence farming that could no longer even provide subsistence for many of them. The end result was a willingness to trim the population through genocide[6].

The pressures of population growth are having a similar effect on a global scale. The ongoing food revolutions witnessed in the Middle East recently are just a precursor to more major confrontations that are likely to occur in the absence of a concerted effort globally to discourage population growth that is overwhelming the planet's ability to provide sustainable nutrition supplies to all[7]. The effect of putting a price on the footprint that we leave on the environment nationally should serve as a dampener on policy to tolerate fast population growth, which inevitably increases the level of environmental degradation. My hope is that governments will consider a stable population policy, where replacement rate becomes the optimal choice to aim for. In the case of population growth, as is the case with many other things that have a potential economic trajectory benefit in the short to medium run, we cannot expect the majority of world governments to go against the wishes of the religious establishment, especially when there is no short term political gain to be had. As is the case with everything else, we have to make sure the right incentives are in place.

Part 3

Our economy from past till present

How well adapted is it to deal with current and future problems?

Humanity's history, paraphrased in a paragraph, would have to start with the first great revolution, which was the breakaway of humans from nature, symbolized by our ability to change the shape of objects, and the use of fire. They used these simple tools to harvest nature. This first chapter in humanity's history is also by far the longest. It lasted for roughly 2.5 million years. The next great chapter in humanity's history started with the agricultural revolution. This started about 10,000 years ago, and it is a point where the way humans lived changed fundamentally. It gave rise to complex societies, organizing to build settlements, infrastructure to allow an ever greater number of individuals to co-habituate. A surplus of food allowed for a small portion of society to pursue other specializations, giving rise to acceleration in innovation. This chapter lasted about 10,000 years and it ended when our own current chapter started. At some point during the last few hundred years, humanity made a seemingly permanent break with the old lifestyle we had from the beginning of the spread of farming communities, till sometime in the 18'th or 19'th centuries, depending where we want to look and how we wish to see things. This break is not uniform worldwide as a phenomenon, because different regions around the world developed differently, and, arguably, there are still some regions such as in parts of Africa, where this break with the past is not as obvious. The most important aspect of this new chapter is that it started with our removal from the land.

This change that makes our lives no longer comparable to the past manifests itself in numerous ways. One aspect of great importance is that most regions of the world are now removed from a lifestyle where the great majority of the population is engaged in growing and harvesting food. Only two hundred years ago, most of the world's regions had some form of feudal or even slave system in place, which encompassed as much as 95% of the population in some cases. In other words, only about 5% of the population was involved in other pursuits, which were not directly related to farming or a form of forced labor. In western society, this rate of involvement in agriculture is now completely reversed, where now only about 5% of the population is involved in food production, while roughly 95% of all people are urban dwellers.

This situation does by no means describe the entire planet's regions and populations, but it is fair to recognize that there is presently a trend where most regions are trending towards rapid urbanization of their population. Even Africa is set to see a point of having a greater urban dwelling population than rural in the next few decades, if current trends continue. I emphasize the word "if" here, because in my view, there is far too little recognition of the fact that we made this transition based on harvesting the life of our planet's past in the form of hydrocarbons. Without the implementation of a harvesting trend that started with coal in Europe roughly four hundred years ago, and then spread to petroleum and gas over time, we would have never broken ourselves free from toiling on the land to grow our food. Our dependence on fossil fuels has constantly grown since then, and despite reassuring voices who tell us that it is just a matter of wonder technologies making their way through the economic system, which will likely break our addiction to fossils, I see no evidence of that happening so far.

Not all credit is due to fossil fuels on their own as the main element of change in humanity's latest historical chapter. The financial system, which can best be described as a means to organize the production of goods, through the deployment of capital, happened to be well suited to organizing the harvest of life from the world's past, which was transformed through geologic circumstances into the hydrocarbon fuel and material we use today to produce a variety of crucial goods. Without the financial system, we likely would have never embarked on this great project of removing humanity from its natural habitat through urbanization, made possible by fossil fuels. It is the purpose of this part of the book to weigh in on the argument of whether the current financial system is still adequate to meet our needs. It should help us answer the question of whether we need to make significant changes to it, or to the environment in which it operates. I believe that we should focus on changing the environment, because there are still many positive aspects to the financial system itself, which can benefit us greatly.

The unfortunate reality we find ourselves in is that we are wholly dependent on finite resources, which will reach at some point a peak in production, and then start declining soon after. There have been a great number of arguments over when this is likely to happen. Some argue that it is happening right now, or is imminent. Others like to argue that we are decades, or even centuries from such a cataclysmic event. There is also the dominant argument in this question, which is that even though the limits to the continued growth in production of fossil fuels should be acknowledged, we should not worry, because we are able to transition away from it, without making major changes. Our technological knowhow is just itching to tackle such a challenge, and it is only waiting for the price signals given by the market to go into action. These optimists see us moving to the fourth chapter in human history. The next logical one being colonizing other worlds, like we did in the Star Trek episodes and movies.

As I pointed out in chapter three, on the finite world, I do not believe that those who claim that we are many decades or even centuries away from having to face with declining fossil fuel production are right. The past ten years have shown that while technology combined with higher prices can lead to new reserves being discovered or harnessed, unfortunately, the net return on energy invested is declining as we replace old conventional fields with unconventional sources of energy. The net gain from undertaking these unconventional projects are not substantial enough to keep up with demand coming mainly from developing nations that are in the process of claiming their fair share of the energy endowment, as well as replacing production losses from conventional resources that are dwindling. I believe that we have one or two decades at the most before we reach a crisis of declining fossil fuel inputs into the global economy. If we collectively choose to become utterly ruthless with the environment in the process of extraction of these fuels, we may gain an extra decade, but the environmental damage will most likely be more costly to humanity than the net benefit from the increased fossil fuel supply.

The technology and market worshipers, who believe that these two forces combined together can conquer all obstacles to human progress, are also being proven wrong by recent global economic history. We already saw how price spikes in crucial commodities such as petroleum cause the global economy to contract, and thus the price of this crucial and very inelastic fuel plummets as a result. As we discussed in previous chapters, the market would need to be able to sustain high prices for many years and even decades in order to spur on the capital owners to invest in fuel-efficient technologies and infrastructure. Nothing symbolizes this lack of ability on the part of the market to create a fuel-efficient future for us as does the fact that in the US wind power generator installation was down in 2010 by roughly 50% compared to 2009 according to the American Wind Energy Association. This is largely a side-effect of the natural gas price having declined precipitously over the past few years, due in part to increased production thanks to shale gas in the US, and also due to soft demand courtesy of a weak economy. I am willing to put my bets on technological innovation being capable of dealing with many technical challenges. The main hindrance to us having a chance of adapting to a declining fossil fuel production environment that may be upon us sooner than most would like to believe is the faulty assumption that the market mechanism is a good enough driver for increased capital investments in alternative energy. Recent history clearly demonstrates that I am right about this; therefore, it is clear that we have to re-tool the system to start giving the right signals to the wielders of capital.

This part of the book concerns itself with the nature of our financial world. It describes how it evolved into what it is currently. It shows why it was a clear advantage for us to stick with it until recently. It explains why it no longer works, and what we need to do to fix it in order to have the market do what we need it to do. I hope that we are not too late as many of the pessimists who believe that the key ingredient that made the current chapter of human history possible, namely an expanding fossil fuels supply is likely to reverse its 400-year trend and plateau soon, and then start declining. The IEA already acknowledged that conventional petroleum production has hit its plateau, which makes up over 80% of total liquid fuels supply. If this is the case, we need to implement a solution that will fix the market economy in the hope to avert complete social breakdown as the global economy freezes up as it already almost did in 2008. If we do have a decade or two, before we have to face this inevitable event, then let us hope that humanity will come up big by displaying some un-characteristic collective wisdom on a global scale, by adopting a financial mechanism that will work at helping us adapt.

6

Credit

A brief history

Time to take another short stroll through history, but this time we will move through the centuries a bit faster, and focus not on a place, but rather on financial evolution. In order to understand our current financial system, we have to understand a little about how it developed. The beginning of the modern financial system has its roots in the collapse of the Roman Empire, where we left off during our short leap through time, to go to the next historical lesson. When the social and political structure of antiquity Europe ceased to function, increasingly the Christian church moved in to fill the void. They secured increasing support from the new feudal warrior class, and established supremacy in the field of ethical questions, and in politics. One of the many ethical issues that they demanded the population to respect and follow were the rules regarding usury.

As many of you may have noticed, the religious establishment always picks its ethical battles that need to be fought in order to save our souls. These days, they tend to fight against birth control, abortion, assisted suicide, sexual promiscuity, normalizing our views towards the gay and they are of course, for abstinence. Some of these issues were also relevant back in the early middle ages, but equally important was their stance on money lending. They considered it a grave sin; therefore, no Christian was allowed to engage in it. Some think that this lack of credit flow was in part responsible for the lack of rebound in economic activity post antiquity. It is fascinating to watch televangelists today preach about how righteous that person must be, who manages to accumulate a lot of wealth through their business dealings. The contrast with the attitude of the church in the early middle ages could not be any clearer.

It is somewhat puzzling to me that the church establishment decided to take such a harsh stance against money lending. I am not an expert on the bible, but in Luke: 19, I found this interesting parable allegedly told by Jesus about a lord, who gave a pound to each one of his ten servants before leaving on a prolonged journey. After his return, he demanded to see all the servants, and he praised those who managed to invest the pound and to multiply their wealth. One servant decided to take the pound and hide it for safekeeping, in case the master shall want it back. The master chastised him for his folly, and took his pound. He argued that the least he could have done, would have been to lend the pound out for interest returns. This parable is meant to teach us that we should find ways to increase our wealth through investing it. In the same chapter of the good book, there is the story of Jesus throwing out the moneychangers from the temple of his father, which could be interpreted as being a sign that he disliked business dealings perhaps. Luke: Six, also suggests that lending money should not be done in the interest of receiving the money back with interest. The Old Testament forbids Jews from charging other Jews interest.

It is not clear how the church came to the very constricting conclusion that Christians should be forbidden from money lending. Scripture can be interpreted either way. The historical reasons for the beginning of the church ban on usury stems from the fact that many, of the moneylenders in the Christian communities in the early centuries of their existence were in fact the priests. At the first council of Nicaea in 325 A.D, hosted by Emperor Constantine, which shaped the Christian movement into what it is today, they decided to forbid the clergy from lending money to their parishioners for an interest rate greater than 1% per month. This did not forbid usury, but it did regulate it. Things escalated from there as they often do. The clergy gradually extended the rule and made it harsher, so in the end no Christian was allowed to lend money anymore.

This opposition to financial dealings went on for centuries, where Jews and Muslims were the only source of credit for investment ventures in Europe. The church figured that their souls were already lost to the dark side, since they did not recognize the true faith as the path to salvation. Feudal economics as a result consisted mainly of subsistence farming and a barter system of exchange. Any projects that were undertaken had to be financed through funds and resources already available. Cash money, mainly made up of precious metal coins was very hard to come by. As a result, very little was being done, in terms of structural and technological advancement. Economic activity picked up mainly thanks to Italian city-states, which managed to break free of feudal and papal hegemony to some extent. They became a commercial link between the still thriving east, where economic life never ceased despite the fall of Rome, and the backward feudal Europe, which was mainly trying to survive, with little chance of comforts of many luxuries that they enjoyed centuries earlier. Some of the feudal lords still liked to enjoy some luxury items, such as spices and perfumes. The Italian merchants increasingly filled the needs for these luxuries, and in the process revived trading fare tradition, where buyers and sellers regularly met. One of the most famous locations for these fares was the Champagne region in France, where merchants and buyers from the north of Europe came to meet up with merchants and buyers from Italy. The church was still opposed to money lending however, so the capital the merchants used was still only their own, which placed some real limits on expansion of trade.

The beginnings of revival of money lending started with the *commenda* partnership practice, which essentially involved merchants who were too old or sick to continue on their former travel adventures, lending their money to a younger merchant, who would pay back the loan, and a share of the profit at the end of the venture. Through the revival of trade, there was an increased need for monetary liquidity. Currency was still based on precious metal coins hoverer, so there were still some severe constraints on economic activity. It took the intervention of some crafty goldsmiths to change all that.

When the merchants needed to park their gold somewhere for safekeeping, they appealed to the people with the most secure safes in town. Those of course being the goldsmiths, who needed to keep their gold in lockdown, until it was sold to customers. The merchants figured out eventually that it was much safer to get depository notes from the goldsmiths as proof of the gold, and then sign over the notes to other merchants, rather than traveling with physical gold. The goldsmiths created networks across Europe, where they would recognize these promissory notes to be as good as gold. The goldsmiths also realized in turn that there was very little chance that everybody would show up with promissory notes to redeem the gold at the same time, so they started issuing promissory notes, which were greater in volume than the actual physical gold in their possession. The promissory notes issued by them carried an interest rate similar to lending out physical gold. By this time, there was also a decreased objection on the part of the church, which also found itself in increasing need of credit due to expensive crusades, and other projects. Therefore, goldsmiths increasingly became bankers, and monetary liquidity increased with the appearance of paper notes, that could be re-deemed for a set amount of gold. This was the birth of modern banking, and by the 16'Th century, it transformed Western Europe, from a backward place in the preceding centuries, into the most dynamic society on earth. They were ready to conquer the planet, and by the end of the 19'Th century, they largely did just that.

The central bank system

The goldsmiths were the first to conjure up money out of nothing by transforming themselves into banks. The second source of money, which did not necessarily have to include the minting of precious metal coins, came via the central banks. In 1664, the bank of Sweden, which is still in operation today, was founded, and in 1694, the Bank of England came into existence as. These banks were not operating as fiat money operations initially; they still adhered to the gold standard. To be more precise, money in circulation could be exchanged for gold. Since the gold standard has collapsed, after WW1, most central banks went on a system of monetary supply, which is legal tender. In other words, if you go to the central bank with a one hundred dollar bill, you are only entitled to receive another one hundred dollar bill in return, or the equivalent in smaller denominations. There is no intrinsic value to our paper money, aside from the value of the paper itself. The only reason that a banknote can function as a medium of exchange, is that we all agree to use it.

The main purpose of the central bank is to control the country's money supply, and influence interest rates. Aside from that, they also act as a lender of last resort, when government or other institutions have a hard time securing funds. Central banks are also responsible for regulating the private banks. One important thing that should be noted is that the central bank is only responsible for issuing about 5% of the total money in the economy. That money is the one that most of us are familiar with, because we use it every day when we purchase goods. The other 95% is money that is created through the process of money lending. Central banks are perhaps the most powerful tool of a semi-governmental organization to control the direction of the economy. Fiscal policy, which is the government's decision on how much to spend on goods and services, is also very important for sure, but recent history has shown us that the central banks have tools that are more potent at their disposal. As an example, the US government has injected 800 billion dollars into the economy as part of a stimulus package meant to keep our system from total collapse after 2008. The Federal Reserve on the other hand has printed money, which it used to buy up many delinquent mortgages; it also bought US government paper to help finance the deficit. It lent money to private banks at low interest rates in order to provide financial liquidity. The operations of the Federal Reserve have amounted to trillions. It seems that banks also preferred to lend their money to the federal government more than to anyone else as well, keeping the real economy subdued, but making it easier for government to finance itself. Bottom line, the Federal Reserve has had more effect by printing a few trillions than the government had with its stimulus.

The role & importance of credit

Whenever a mortgage or any other lending and borrowing agreement is signed with a bank, money has been created. That is where that 95% of all money in the economy comes from. In other words, money is in a way just as it was centuries ago, a promissory note. It should be important to mention also that whenever a loan is paid back, money in circulation in the economy is erased. That is a major feature that people like to leave out of a conversation whenever they want to present this system as something sinister, or as a fraud, where we are all being fleeced. Any loan that a bank makes has to be covered by a percentage of liquid assets on their balance sheet. In other words if the percentage of required reserves is 10%, then the bank can make a $10,000 loan whenever someone deposits one thousand dollars in savings with that bank. Taking that into consideration, money really is not just conjured up out of thin air, there is in fact some backing for it. The only thing that may be sinister in our current position is the fact that bankers it seems have so much influence with government officials that these requirements for bank reserves have become less and less stringent in recent times, and as a result, we are currently stuck bailing them out. There have been other moves towards deregulation as well, which many blame for the current financial crisis. There is some evidence for that, as we witnessed the 2008 financial meltdown, there was an unmistakable trend, where better regulated financial institutions such as the Canadian ones, fared much better, than their less regulated British and US counterparts.

Understanding the basics of financial flows is important, because it is in fact the main issue, which affects your everyday life, even if we do not see it directly in our day-to-day dealings. If you have a house, and you are like most people, you have a mortgage loan, which you are currently paying to the bank. If the bank would no longer issue mortgages, you would not have the house, or at least not at current prices. The house construction companies, and subcontractors, would have never built the neighborhood you live in. They in their turn would not afford their own dwellings. The furniture you bought on credit perhaps would not have been assembled either without a loan, and the $30,000 car, would have been beyond reach as well without financing. Of course, I do not mean to say that we would all be homeless. Nevertheless, without credit, house prices, furniture prices, car prices, and many other items we consume would have never been able to fetch the price we pay without credit.

As good as, it may sound to a prospective house buyer to think that house prices could in fact be a lot lower than what we are currently being charged, that may not be the as good as we might think. It is precisely our ability to charge a quarter million for an average family home, which sets us apart from the third world. Because a new family home costs a quarter of a million, a plumber can charge $35 dollars per hour, when working on building that home. He then takes his wife to the restaurant where a college student works part-time, so he will not starve while getting an education in order to become an engineer. However, since the wife gets food poisoning, and she suspects it was from the restaurant where her husband took her to, she decides to divorce. The lawyer who handles the case on her behalf can afford to charge her thousands of dollars, which will be more than a Chinese plant manager, who is in charge of the factory that made the lawyer's suit will make in a year. The small clothing store that sold him the suit, which the owner imported cheaply from China, can mark up the price in order to make enough profit to afford a mortgage on a house, which our plumber will be grateful to help build, because he earns $35 per hour as I mentioned. As for the Chinese plant manager, he has to make due with a much smaller dwelling in Shanghai. He has a car, but it was cheaply built, so it only cost him $7,500 brand new. That is all the bank could give him based on his yearly earnings. He is happy though, because before they were able to export so many goods to the west, he only had a bicycle to get to work with.

Credit does not only finance private consumption; it is more importantly responsible for financing private enterprise, as well as government projects. Private firms usually benefit from a line of credit with one or more banks. They use those lines of credit in order to finance a variety of projects. To illustrate this, I chose the example of a construction company where I worked. Secure Firestop LTD, is a small construction company in Winnipeg, Manitoba. When I started with the company in 2006, they were undertaking a large renovation project, which required the financing for wages and material. The way that these contracts work is that, the project is divided into a number of stages by percentages. For instance, a company could get a 20% payment from the total value of the contract for the completion of 20% of the project. Until the first milestone is met, a source of financing for operations is needed. Like many companies, Secure, did not have the cash to complete the first stage of the project, so they used a credit line that they had with a bank. The owner, of course had to sweat a little, at least until the first milestone was reached in the project.

Companies routinely use a line of credit with a bank, in order to meet wage payment obligations, or to finance the purchase of product and equipment necessary for operations. Consumers also tap credit lines on a regular basis in order to finance the purchases that they desire. The current financial system can be seen as a very well thought out system if viewed from far. Credit becomes available to entrepreneurs who want to undertake a project, which will yield a profit, which will cover the interest due to the banks, and still have a profit left over. Interest rates will reflect in large measure the risk of investments, which weeds out many potential losing projects. The money supply will always reflect the needs of the economy for liquidity. In theory, this is the foundation stone of limitless economic expansion. There will never be a shortage of financial capital to restrain economic growth, because since most transactions are done with borrowed money, economic growth will always conjure up more money. Remember that every time a bank writes a loan, money has been created. When the loan is paid back, the money, which was lent out, has been destroyed. What remains is the gross profit, earned from the collection of interest, which is reflected in GDP growth. The gross profit of those who invested the money is also added to the overall wealth as measured in GDP. The wages of the workers and the profit of other suppliers of material and equipment are also part of the growth story. The only thing that is imperative in order to continue this system on a national, and global level is to maintain a steady growth rate in GDP, which allows loans to be paid back with interest.

An increasing GDP over prolonged lengths of time allows banks to lend based on expectations of low rates of default, thanks to increasing amounts of wealth, which allows people to pay back with interest. That should not be a hard thing to visualize. Just think of an economy made up of 100 households, and one bank. The bank lends everyone money to buy the houses, and expects to be repaid with interest, which ads up to paying for the house twice. That would not be a problem if the economy expands at a rate, which allows it to increase by, at least as much as the total interest to be paid on the loan, by the time the loans are due. If there is no economic expansion, and the only money in circulation remains the money created by the original loan, then most people would be unable to pay for their loans, and they would default. If a bank would have the foresight to see that there is no prospect of economic growth on the long horizon, then it would keep lending to a bare minimum, and at very high interest rates. I hope that through this illustration I achieved my goal of explaining the need for ever higher peaks in GDP in the long term. This explanation should not be confused with the prevalence of low interest rates during periods of slowdown, which at first sight contradicts what was illustrated above. In this case, banks continue to lend some money, because they believe that economic growth will pick up. They can also do it at lower interest rates, because central banks also lowered the rate at which they are lending the money to the banks.

Banking gone wrong

My own personal opinion is that the banking system in the US and elsewhere produced economic growth, where real growth was not due in the past decade. In other words, banks themselves became the engine of growth. They did not do it alone of course; they had help from Alan Greenspan and the Federal Reserve. In order to make the 2000-01 recession more shallow, the Federal Reserve decided to lower interest rates, and kept them low for the better part of the decade. Some refer to this as bubble economics, where a new bubble is created as the old one, in this case the tech bubble deflated. In order to avoid the pain of a much deeper recession, it was decided that an even bigger bubble than the tech bubble should be created as the new engine of growth. The move worked for the better part of the decade; until interest rates had to be raised to combat growing inflation, and even though it is not popular to mention it, surely the high price of oil and other natural resources were a big part of what punctured the bubble monster by 2008.

The banks did their part as well, by lending money in increasing proportions to people who would not have qualified under normal circumstances. They did not want to keep those mortgages on their books, so they decided to package them and sell them as investment bonds called "mortgage backed securities". The "trusty" rating agencies put an AAA stamp on these faulty mortgages, and so unlimited lending was achieved. Housing became the new engine of growth, as more and more people bought houses they could not afford to pay off in 30 or 40 years. Millions of construction work jobs, and financial jobs were created directly. Millions of jobs added to the economy created increased demand for everything, creating millions of additional jobs[1]. Given that over the whole last decade, zero net job creation has occurred, I would have to say that the whole thing was really just a waste of time. No doubt, many people profited from this bubble, but even more people were burned. Unless someone will come up with a similar scheme, which will buy us another decade, we probably will have to face up to reality now.

When the governments of US and Europe intervened in 2008 to save banks, and other industries, they did it because they had no real alternative, and the bankers knew it. I get a real kick out of political outsiders, hoping to convince the electorate to make them insiders, bashing the power elites of 2008-09 for the bailouts. In reality Mr. Bush, the republican US president of 2008 and Mr. Obama, the current democrat president, both faced the same choice. They had to allow for the printing of trillions in un-backed dollars, and they were forced to borrow hundreds of billions more in the name of the taxpayer, and hand all that over to the bankers. They did that not because they may be corrupt, or because they do not care about the American taxpayer. They did it, because the alternative would have been the complete drying up of credit. The ceasing of lending activity in America would have led to a collapse in the standard of living, which would have made the US and the EU members into third world countries. The situation is as I emphasized already, in regards to the correlation of credit and our standard of living. Without the flow of credit, we would not be able to afford to pay a janitor three times the wages that a Chinese engineer, or software designer earns.

I hope that I am able to illustrate here the essence of the system that allows us to live better than others, without having to work harder. We westerns have the historical advantage of being the first ones to evolve into the credit-based economy. In order to keep up the system, we are caught in a cycle where we cannot afford to slip from our current rates of credit flow. Therefore, we have to continue consuming at the same rate that we currently do at the very least. An expansion in consumption would be even more welcome in economic terms. Perhaps now it may be clearer to us, why it was that after the 9/11/2001 attacks in New York, and Washington, the most important message that President Bush had for the nation was to encourage them to continue going about their business, and consume as they did before. We are locked in a ferocious battle for the right to consume more than others do. The developing nations, who up to now had the historical disadvantage of being latecomers to the game, and therefore have been entitled to a disproportionately smaller piece of the pie, have managed to make inroads on us. If I am right about the current global trends unfolding, by the end of the next decade, they will have turned the tables in terms of overall proportions.

The sustainability tariff as a fix and recent signs of the urgent need for a solution

The surprising turn of events would be if we were to defy history, and thus defy those who learned from it that they should expect our demise to come soon. Let us imagine that we were to adopt the new trade tariff as I described it. The new engine of growth would no longer be fueled by the increasing trend of resource exploitation, which we cannot keep up forever, because of natural constraints and increasing environmental damage. We would instead be fueled by a drive towards more efficiency, protection of the environment, and respect for human dignity would also be rewarded.

In such a scenario, one of the main drivers of growth would be an acceleration of technological innovation, spurred on by policies meant to reduce the impact on the environment in order to gain an advantage in trade. Fast-paced economic growth has often been the result of innovation. One of the latest global expansions was sparked by the revolution of information technology. This revolution allowed me to take pictures and qualitative measurements on construction sites, when I worked for Secure Firestop in Winnipeg, and send them to an engineer in the US via e-mail. This allowed him to review the situation and get back to me within hours if needed for us to be able to go on with our work. Now, try to picture this situation and other similar ones where we are now dependent on fast communication on a worldwide scale, and try to size up the level of efficiency that it created. I can just imagine if all this would have been done through regular mail. It could potentially cost firms worldwide, hundreds of billions in delays and other inefficiencies, if we did not have access to today's information technology. The internet is a US government innovation, derived from defense spending.

Now imagine if the US were to be spurred on by the new tariff regulations to upgrade it's outdated and energy inefficient electricity grid. More could be done with less electricity. The upgrade itself would require many new jobs to be created. The coal and gas saved would be an attractive new source of potential transport fuel, displacing the immoral use of food. The switch to the new fuel sources would require additional changes in infrastructure, giving rise to more employment demand. The food that is now burned in our fuel tanks could be exported, increasing the total export volume of US and EU goods, cutting the trade deficit. Alternatively, some farmland could be re-claimed as woodland, where feasible, increasing the appeal of US and EU goods even further, which would similarly help re-balance the US trade deficit. Remember that I suggested re-forestation efforts should be rewarded with bonus points in the tariff evaluation scheme. Remember also that expectations of future economic expansion are necessary for maintaining the availability of credit. At this point, we can only grow at a significant pace if we can achieve a much more effective use of the resources available to us, because making more resources available, which is mainly what we depended on so far, is no longer feasible.

The worldwide effect is similarly positive in this instance. Take the availability of resources, and its effect on expectations of growth. We cannot expect global economic expansion to happen in the absence of the necessary resources to make it happen. If banks realize that there are resource constraints in achieving this growth, they naturally have to cut back on lending due to lower expectations of loan re-payment rates. The credit tightening itself can precede the recessionary effect of resource constraints, giving rise to more recessionary pressure. In the event that these recessions become deeper and more frequent, lending institutions have to adjust their long-term outlook on risk of delinquency of borrowers. This in turn would force them to raise interest rates, even as the economy would continue to limp along, or worse during a recession. I believe that this is likely to start happening in the next decade or so, if we continue with business as usual.

An effort on better efficiency being promoted around the world due to trade incentives would most likely lessen the pressure on our planet's resources, removing the increasingly real prospect of shortages. This would remove one of the most significant threats that we currently face in terms of financial stability. This is counter to the market argument, which assumes that all is well as long as the market prices out demand on goods, in case that there are shortages, maintaining a balance and stability. I would advise economists, most of whom think that way to re-examine their views. As I write this, there are a number of global instability tremors being felt as people are reacting angrily to being priced out of the food market. The government in Tunisia already collapsed, while Egypt's Mubarak is holding on by a thread (Since I wrote this, he too has been deposed). The unfortunate reality is that no matter what governments they will have in the very near future, those people still have to deal with record high food prices.

This is all very relevant to financial markets, because while economists may have missed this very important fact when looking at their supply-demand models, there is a very important fact that needs to be considered. Sovereign states that can no longer afford to provide food to most of their people tend to go into crisis brought on by the reaction of its citizenry. People may revolt by starting a general strike, or simply taking to the streets as they did in Egypt. If peaceful protests of starving people are put down brutally, it may lead to guerilla warfare. None of this bodes well for the ability of these sovereign states to manage their sovereign debt. A number of emerging or even developed countries defaulting on their debt outright or through hyperinflation is not healthy for the overall economy for various obvious reasons. Sticking with the financial system though, it is a real threat, because if many countries start to default, it may be the end of the credit fueled economy altogether.

It is very unfortunate that we have elites, including in the economic field who fail to stay in touch with the real world.

Failed states, or financially constrained ones such as Greece, Portugal, Ireland and others also cut the availability of customers on the global scene. Same thing is currently witnessed in the US as individual state and municipal governments are locked in a fierce competition with each other to provide lower taxed, and a more deregulated environment for potential investors. Texas alone is rumored to be eying cuts in their government workforce, and projects that will lead to direct and in-direct job losses in the state of up to 600,000. Credit cannot continue to expand, or even stay at current levels, nor can the rates of interest, in the event that schools and infrastructure are neglected, giving rise to a gradual loss of human and physical capital.

Reneging on social obligations such as health coverage also kills the ability of the consumer to continue spending and servicing their credit lines. I am personally surprised that banks are not cutting back on lending more drastically in places like the US and the EU, given the grim prospects of many personal consumers to have a healthy and steady income flow. At present, central banks are making the availability of relatively cheap credit possible through their low interest rates that they offer to financial institutions. When commodity driven inflation will drive prices up too much, they are likely to cut off that lifeline to our economy, and then we shall have to deal with reality.

There is no alternative currently proposed locally and internationally that can deal with the incompatibility of having to expand credit, while at the same time we are facing the type of problems described in the chapters describing the finite world and its implications. Bismarck saved the world from stagnation over a hundred years ago, when he recognized the need to create the consumer that could match the production capabilities of an industrializing world. The social safety net is what made the credit driven consumer economy possible, because in the absence of an economically stable consumer, credit would have been just too risky to award to the consumer at the present affordable rates. Deeper recessions would have meant a steeper increase in default rates. Pricing in more default into interest rates, would have made access to credit too prohibitively expensive. We would have never reached this level of economic advancement.

At this point, we need a repeat of a Bismarckian moment, in the form of a game changing initiative. We have to realize that the consumer driven economy that Bismarck helped start more than a century ago has run its course, and it can do very little for us going forward. Credit markets are telling this to us through their refusal to continue providing growing volumes of credit to costumers. Credit will only flow in the long term if we can avoid hitting our heads against a raw material availability ceiling that we seem to bang up against whenever the economy picks up. We already witnessed this situation for about half a decade now and there is no indication that things will improve. Prices will be volatile, and every time oil and food prices will crash down, people will proclaim that we are saved, and there are plenty of resources. As we saw starting with late 2010, and going into 2011, despite a relatively weak recovery, food prices already hit new records, and oil prices were just one rally away from hitting new records as well. The only way we can avoid hitting our heads against the ceiling repeatedly in the near and long term future is to jump-start the efficiency driven economy. Based on my analysis of market reactions to this impending commodity crisis, it is safe to declare the hope that market forces will take care of this on their own a badly mistaken leap of faith.

7

Risk assessment and risk management
(Complete failure of the system)

The importance of proper assessment of risk

A very important aspect of lending and borrowing is risk assessment. It is important to factor in risk when a loan is created, because a default on a loan has an amplified effect through the financial system, due to leverage issues. If you remember, I already explained the fact that banks do not actually lend out money, they can fully account for in their volts. If they are required to keep a 10% reserve ratio in the bank, they are in fact entitled to lend out $10,000 for every $1,000 in internal resources. If a $10,000 loan goes bad however, they have to take the full brunt of the loss on their balance sheet. In other words, it comes out of their overall reserves made up from their cash reserves, made up through profit. Alternatively, they can socialize the losses has been the case since 2008 in many instances, where governments had to cover bank losses on toxic assets. If too many loans go bad at the same time, as the sub-prime mess did just recently, the reserves of the bank become inadequate. That is why the Federal Reserve had to print trillions and take some of these bad loans off the balance sheets of the banks. In addition, the governments in the US and in Europe borrowed money in order to fork it over to banks to repair their balance sheets. All this was essential to be done, despite the rhetoric currently being pushed by the likes of the Tea Party movement, and other organizations that tend to be on the fringes politically. Failure to act would have had dire consequences. The complete seizing up of credit would have thrown us back to the dark ages in no time. The world of Mad Max would have been realized very fast.

205

To understand risk assessment and management, we should look at the way it worked before the sub-prime debacle, and try to understand how it went wrong. First, we have to understand that in order to be able to lend out money in such a reckless manner as mortgage brokers did in the US and elsewhere during the past decade, they had to find a way to neutralize the risk. They did that by departing from the traditional model of a bank lending out money to individuals investing into purchasing a house, or expanding a business, and then keeping the I.O.U in their volt until full repayment. With sub-prime mortgages, they found a way to transform them into bonds, which were sold on the market in the same manner that government or corporate bonds are being traded. Other banks, pension funds, sovereign governments, and private investors bought these bonds worldwide. They claim that this was done to make more room on their balance sheets in order to increase their lending potential. My suspicion is that they knew the stuff was toxic from the outset. The fact that Goldman Sachs, was selling such products, and at the same time shorting them on the market is a great example of the real opinion of these banks towards the stuff they were saddling the world with, even though they deny this. Goldman was able to justify this policy by implying they were just following the time-tested method of creating a balanced portfolio. In order to pull this off, financial institutions needed two accomplices to play ball. These are two institutions, which we depend on for our financial safety, and they failed.

Before selling these bonds, they had to be rated by the rating agencies. There are three main rating entities in the US that most investors around the world take their signals from. These rating agencies are the S&P, Moody's and Fitch Ratings LTD. The Securities and Exchange Commission designated them as "nationally recognized statistical rating agencies". Many funds have it within their charter that they may only invest in bonds if these rating agencies rate them above junk status. These rating agencies calculate the risk of an asset, and assign it a grade on their scale.

The sub-prime mortgage related holdings were given an AAA or equivalent designation by all three organizations. They argued that they were completely safe, since these financial assets were fully backed by the value of the houses. They had a good point, as long as house prices were trending up, or at least keeping stable. As soon as the re-possessed house would be resold, money would be recovered fully, therefore no loss was the general consensus. How many economists in their right mind would believe that an asset price would have the potential to move up forever, without ever coming back down? If you choose to believe the excuses made by the financial "gurus", also referred to as "the best and the brightest", then it should be normal for an economist to believe that. After all that time spent at Harvard, or other reputable teaching entities, they should know what they are talking about.

Failure to recognize that millions of people who signed mortgages that they never hopped to be able to repay, and therefore would end up defaulting would end up throwing millions of extra homes on the market, driving prices down is also hard to understand from my perspective. It is not as if no one saw it coming. A group of investment advisors called "Wise Research" had been sending me newsletters since 2005, many of them warning about the impending housing bubble collapse. After looking into it myself, I realized that they may be right, back then already, and that was years before I received my B.A in economics. Yet, once again we are told by the likes of Alan Greenspan, and the talking heads invited to speak on finance related shows on television, that they had no way of knowing. Economics is not a precise science, mainly because there is one ingredient, which people can predict with very little success, and that is human behavior. There are also just too many variables that one can look at in order to come to a conclusion, which will reflect the variables that the economist chose to examine. I can see how some economists may get a major prediction wrong. I have done it myself in the past, and I surely will do it again. The rating agencies however, that first rated the toxic sub-prime assets, and then kept their ratings level from dropping even as the impending collapse was becoming obvious, resembles an honest mistake less and less, if one is to look at it closely.

The rating agencies that we all depend on and who have the power to declare which, bonds are worthy of investment, and which are not, have a dubious recent record of accomplishment. Aside from the sub-prime debacle, where they were full accomplices, they also demonstrated a lack of foresight, and outright bias in some of their recent dealings. In the recent Greek government credit crisis, they were definitely off the mark, as the Greek bonds were kept above junk status for way longer than it deserved to be. On the other hand, they recently declared their desire to downgrade Hungary's debt rating to junk, mainly because the Hungarian government did not want to renegotiate a deal with the IMF, which would have included painful spending cuts, on the part of the Hungarian government, rather than the bank tax that the Hungarian government implemented. When the Hungarian government refused the IMF recommendations, this other dubious organization came out and publicly repudiated the Hungarian government's stance and warned of impending financial Armageddon for the small nation. That is despite the fact that in 2010, the Hungarian government will only have a budget deficit of 3.8%, which is the third lowest in the 27 member EU, and compares rather favorably with the over 10% budget deficits of the US and Britain[1].

The rating agencies quickly joined the cause of "doom on the Hungarians", stating their intentions to most likely downgrade Hungary's debt to junk status in the same year. Even many traders seem skeptical of the posturing of the IMF and the rating agencies, together with many media outlets. Despite all the commotion, demand for Hungarian government paper remains relatively robust, and their currency, the forint has re-stabilized soon after the initial storm. Most likely, however, if the rating agencies carry on with their threats, given their vast influence, the real economic fundamentals will probably lose out, and there is a good chance that the IMF will be back in Hungary. This seems like a highly politically motivated move, designed to squash a rebellion against Reagan style ideology of riding the poor as hard as possible, while treating the rich with the utmost tenderness. It also works in the favor of the IMF, which was almost obsolete as an organization before the 2008 financial crisis. There was a recent suggestion made by the Czech government that they actually created the financial turbulence in Central and Eastern Europe in order to create new clients for their lending facilities. If that is the case, then the rating agencies are most likely working towards helping with that goal. I wonder when the transition of these ratings agencies went from economic fundamentals to reaching political objectives.

Political Ratings

Perhaps they were never meant to be impartial entities, after all they do have a US government charter. No wander then that Hungary's deficit spending level is attacked even though it is only a third of the size of the US and British deficits lately[2]. Despite the impending deficits that stretch into the horizon for as far as the eye can see, these two above mentioned countries still enjoy the AAA stamp on their government paper (S&P downgraded the US, due to political instability since I wrote this). In June 2010, a new establishment from China has done the unthinkable, and downgraded US government bonds. However; as I said, no one is supposed to pay attention to that, because they do not have the pedigree of the US rating agencies. However, if we are to look at their recent record of accomplishment, perhaps these rating agencies should be downgraded. The fact that they are still seen as reputable, independent organizations after the sub-prime fiasco should make everyone who uses their ratings as an investment guide wary of what this free advice is worth. I think the phrase; "you get what you pay for" in this case is very appropriate. This is one of many examples; I will give in this book of organizations that are supposed to look out for us in an official or semi-official role, and is proving to be a failing institution. We generally like to think of failing institutions as the kind of entities we find in the developing world, where society is held back from flourishing thanks to the interests of some of these institutions. In our case, we seem to have more and more of these institutions that are poised to drag us down while we continue to follow blindly their leadership.

Hundreds of millions in the west are counting on good analysis being delivered by these institutions. It is important, because we all need a safe investment path to be able to retire after our minds and bodies expire as real productive assets useful to society. If these ratings are indeed more political, than based on economic fundamentals, we could all end up having a very unpleasant surprise down the line, when our time will come to cash in. These ratings also serve as a risk assessment of various other paper assets, including private debt. For the wider economy, there is a definite destabilizing effect from multiple gross misjudgments of risk. As I mentioned, risk is one of the main components of rate setting activity. Overstating risk can have negative effects, as is the case of Hungary. They end up paying much more in interest, than the real fundamentals dictate. In the case of the US and Britain, where risk to government paper assets is grossly understated, the risk is that the interest paid is too low, given the fundamentals. This affects the saving activities of those who want to stash some money away for retirement, or for a rainy day. Understating risk can even have the effect that we witnessed in 2008, when paper assets, previously thought to be squeaky clean, turned out to be so toxic, that nobody wanted to be left holding the bag they were in, leaving it to government to use its resources to contain the toxic waste. My worry is that the damage is already permanent and terminal. Western governments used up so much of their resources on containing this crisis, that they will not be able to deal properly with the challenges facing us in the following decade.

I mentioned that it took two accomplices to achieve the sub-prime fiasco that many of us are still suffering from. This is another one of those institutions, where it is possible that it no longer serves our best interests in the western world. This is valid to a more or lesser extent, depending on the country in question, but it seems more and more that democratically elected governments are no longer able to provide us with the quality services we need, in a responsible manner. The US government had a very vital role to play in the sub-prime mess. They first allowed it to happen, without thinking too far ahead about the possible consequences. Through the actions of the Federal Reserve and regulatory laws past by lawmakers, they made sure that nothing stood in the way of banks to push these mortgages. They did not do this because they are evil beings, who like to take it out on their own country of course. They did this because they are politicians, and they care a lot about making things look good, while they are in office. Unfortunately, the same politicians and their supporters and political allies often understate the consequences of their actions, which is the case with the two recent US presidents.

They overstate the responsibility of the person currently in office, who had nothing to do with the fact that the economy is in bad shape, and is trying to fix it. Bush was served very well by the housing boom, which lasted through most of his presidency. Economic growth was achieved at least on paper, and the unemployment rate was kept low after the dot.com collapse of 2000-01. He gratefully moved over to make room for the next person, who is now being pounded politically for the bad shape of the economy. If you are an American, I am sure you have seen by now a Republican politician making the argument that it is no longer an excuse to blame the state of the economy on the previous administration, since the new one has had now plenty of time to fix it. It seems that they try to present a view of the world, where each leadership cycle operates in a separate reality, completely unattached from the past leaders and their actions. If that does not seem like a "realistic" proposition, I do not know what does. Perhaps here we have another example of a failing institution. Maybe democracy itself in its current form is failing us. A good temporary way to paper over the problems is to understate risk, and thus afford to keep interest rates artificially low.

Hedging and Insurance

I will briefly mention here the sophisticated tools available to manage risk in economic activity. Hedge funds are investment funds, which as the word hedge implies, they try to reduce risk in their investments through various strategies such as short selling, and derivatives. Derivatives of course are another asset class, which are often hard for people to wrap their mind around. Hedge funds have an accepted status of unregulated entities, as they are very narrow in their appeal to investors. Most of them only accept large-scale investors, and they charge a percentage fee for performance. Due to their outlaw status, they get to operate in markets with very little supervision. The overall size of Hedge fund activity seems to be hovering around 2 trillion dollars, which effectively means that a few of them together can easily create upward, or downward momentum in global markets. They can often defy the fundamentals by simply using momentum trading. The 1997 Asian financial crisis is often blamed on George Soros and his hedge fund, which apparently caused the panic that threw the entire region into years of financial turmoil and increased hardships for millions of people. As the Greek financial crisis hit the markets in the winter of 2009, many Greek and other European officials blamed the crisis on hedge funds operating in the markets to increase the financial turbulence. The issues revolving around hedge funds are very tough to tackle. For our purposes, it should be enough to recognize their nature as being independent enough from regulators, and big enough to affect financial asset markets, without necessarily relying on fundamentals as market drivers. We need to be aware of these sorts of market forces that operate in order to understand better our own personal investments. Perhaps this sheds a little more light on the concept of the irrational markets.

There is nothing wrong with insuring oneself against misfortune. People insure themselves for health, weather, financial, and against any other possible sources of misfortune, and it is a good way to keep people from going through life strapped to a financial rollercoaster. Farmers insure themselves against commodity price fluctuations by purchasing forward contracts for fuel, or by selling futures of their crop. They also purchase insurance for their crops in case that there are any weather related misfortunes. Manufacturers who need to keep a steady price for their commodity inputs also try to insure themselves against price spikes by buying futures. Companies who do many international transactions also buy currency futures as a hedge against wild fluctuations, which lately have become more volatile, and are likely to continue to be so.

Bond investors purchase credit default swaps in order to insure against possible default. With the increasing debt burden in the west, and an increased danger of default of many emerging economies around the world, due to the wild fluctuations in commodity prices, the cost of insuring sovereign debt as well as private sector debt will eventually skyrocket. With insurance increasingly unavailable, many economic activities around the world can cease to function properly, because in many instances the risk would be too great given the size of the potential reward. There is also an increasing trend of sovereign debt being insured automatically by other states in some cases. Greece is one such example, where the Credit Default Swap issuers are essentially earning free money, because they are not on the hook for Greece, because the collective of EU governments are providing the funds to cover the losses.

Reducing volatility through the sustainability trade tariff

Many among those who like to make people believe that everything is still all right will tell us that this is all just the fault of market speculators who drive up the price of commodities, while there are no actual shortages. That is an interesting take on things, but there are many who argue that there are other forces at play here. The more realistic answer is that we are running out of resources we can continue to expand our productions of, and we are running out of environmental tranquility. Food prices can become especially volatile if the armada of scientists who are predicting a shift in our climate due to CO_2 and other greenhouse gas emissions will turn out to be right. Many argue that the many adverse climate related effects are already being felt in the form of disruptions to our food production. Given our increasing global population, and increasingly tight supply/demand relationship, these disruptions can no longer be absorbed and compensated for, by the global food production system, which is stretched to the limit. The only real solution is to implement a system that cuts waste and puts a real price on this commodity as well. The results would benefit everyone on the planet in the long term.

The real price of food should include any deforestation that took place to clear farmland. It should also include the damage to the environmental well being of the agricultural region by drawing down underground aquifers faster than they can be replenished, and the fertilizer and pesticide runoff that results from production. This is also, why I mentioned that I would like to see an end to farm subsidies in all its forms. The relative price of food would rise in this condition, but there are actually some real benefits to that, in terms of reducing financial risks.

For starters, it would give, as I already mentioned in the chapter on the finite world (part three) governments around the world something to think about in terms of their population policies, which is actually part of the problems that arose in the Middle East. Many governments around the world are influenced, or even dominated by religious zealots, who do not think in terms of 21'Th century sustainability issues. They generally oppose contraception methods, including education in this regard. With new ways of thinking in place, stability can be achieved, because there would be a very high price to be paid for allowing unsustainable policies and trends to dominate, including excessively high birth rates as is the case in the Middle East. This would reduce the risk of default in developing countries. It would also reduce price fluctuations. The main reason for that being the case is, because there would be no glut to shortage movements driven exclusively by short-term market speculation. Governments deciding what sort of farming regulations to implement given that the real price for cultivation would be reflected in their overall scorecard that would determine tariffs on all their goods would dominate the price instead.

The overall effect of this would be a leveling out of farming competitiveness around the globe. This will likely reduce the risk of disruption to the food supply generated by local weather anomalies. The obvious result being that political instability caused by food price shocks like those that we have seen in 2008, and now again as I write this book, would diminish, helping reduce risk. A study made by the Fund for Peace organization, ranking countries by how close they are to failed state status, in other words, a state where there is no more authority and collective government run programs, has found that there were 7 states that were close or at the point of being a failed state in 2005. By 2010, it has found that the number of these states has doubled to 15. The implication to the rest off the world is the prospect of a breakdown in global stability through the eventual spill over effect from these states. Somalia is a great example of this, where the absence of a stable government in that country has meant that eventually some of its citizens have started resorting to piracy. The effect has been that shipping in the region of the horn of Africa has become much more costly, in terms of insurance and in terms of the expenditures, we are incurring by having to try to keep a lid on the pirates through our deployment of armed forces. The recent price and supply volatility of many vital resources has increased the likelihood of failed states like Somalia threatening global security through their failure. I believe that this is a strong enough argument for promoting commodity price stability through my suggestion, in order to avoid a potential breakdown in global security, and an explosion in the price of insurance as a result.

The most unexpected result of the tariff regime proposed here, would be a reduction in currency instability. The reason I say this is, that there is an increased cost, and a diminishing of the benefits of currency de-valuation built into such a scheme as the standard tariff. The best way I can explain why this would be the case, I chose to give a hypothetical example of two countries manufacturing the exact same good. One country is Germany the other I picked is China. This example serves very well in providing a good overall picture of the long-term effect on the behavior of states.

Under the current system, if Germany were to produce these generic goods, called widgets for export to the US for instance, it would be at a clear disadvantage compared to a country like China. One of the reasons is that China is not allowing its currency to float freely; it pegged it instead to the US dollar, a currency that has little reason to appreciate rapidly, because the US is a developed country with one of the worst trade deficits among major nations. Countries that have trade deficits tend to see a downward pressure on their currency, meant to stimulate exports, and discourage imports, which is how the market is supposed to re-balance unhealthy trade relations. China is a major net exporter of goods, so its currency should appreciate to encourage imports and domestic consumption. So let us compare Germany and China presently as opposed to if we were to implement my idea. The current prices I estimated approximately based on current economic and political realities in these two countries.

Current Situation.

	Germany cost of widget production:	China cost of widget production:
Labor:	$10 per unit	$5 per unit
Raw Materials:	$3 per unit	$4 per unit
Regulations: (Environment, Labor etc)	$5 per unit	$2 per unit
Capital investment:	$2 per unit	$2 per unit
Tariff:	$10 per unit	$10 per unit
Total cost:	$30 per unit	$23 per unit

Assuming that US tariffs on both sources of widgets are equal, and all else held equal, China has a clear advantage due to its policies towards the environment, labor protection, and its policy of keeping its currency low. Conversely, Germany is at a clear disadvantage, which is the price it pays for being good to its people, environment, and generally being a good global citizen. It does not take a genius to figure out that the widget plant in Germany would either move, or close down.

Situation with new Tariff

	Germany cost:	China cost:
Labor:	$10 per unit	$5 per unit
Raw Materials:	$ 4 per unit	$5 per unit
Regulations: (Environment, Labor etc)	$5 per unit	$2 per unit
Capital investment:	$2 per unit	$2 per unit
Tariff:	$5 per unit	$20 per unit
Total cost:	$26 per unit	$34 per unit

Explanation: Remember that the tariff would be based on observing environmental and basic human rights norms. Germany is one of the most efficient and clean economies on the planet, and has a great human rights record. The exact reverse can be said about China. The increased cost of raw materials comes from a readjustment of the global market. The reason I assume a greater cost in China is because it is a less efficient economy, before and after. The best part in all of this is that the environmental and human rights infringement cost is calculated as a proportion of GDP. In other words if Germany pollutes and infringes on peoples rights on a small scale per unit of GDP, while China does so as a larger proportion, China pays for devaluing its currency twice. If for instance they were to let their currency float, and it would double in relation to the Euro used by Germany, its GDP would double, and the tariff would be cut in half. Working through the exercise again, it turns out that they would regain some competitiveness in this hypothetical case, because the final price would become $29 for China, while it would remain $26 for Germany. In that case, I assume labor costs doubling, the tariff dropping to half.

The bottom line is that, unlike the first scenario, which is an approximate interpretation of the present situation, Germany, which is already doing the right thing for its people and the planet, would still be able to compete. China on the other hand would not be granted any advantages by its currency manipulation and its terrible record on the environment and human rights, as it is being rewarded now. Under the new tariff regime, both countries would be compelled to do the right thing, because it would be the most effective way to gain an advantage. At the same time, it would automatically benefit the people of all trading nations, and the environment as well.

I have to admit that there is one potential flaw in this plan. There would be a definite advantage for an importing country to favor buying from another country, which has high tariffs imposed on its products. The tariff would be a good potential source of income for the government. One way to dampen such an effect would be to allocate automatically any tariffs collected above a certain rate to financing the cost of administering and maintaining the tariff. There is also a case to be made for financing the UN from those funds. Other than that, there is no reason why such a tariff system should not be agreed to, because it solves many of our problems, and puts us on a sustainable and stable path. The main opposition to such a trading system would come from obvious corners. The private interests that are currently making a large profit in this system are an obvious obstacle. Many regimes around the world that would have to change their current lack of respect for their citizens through their oppression, corruption, and their overall lack of ability as leaders would also be against this. As long as we accept the concerns of such people as legitimate, and we buy their arguments for keeping the status quo, we will continue to support a system that is in the long-term detriment of us westerners, the entire planet, and its environment.

A stabilizing effect on trade relations, commodity prices, and an increase in efficiency levels would all benefit a better global risk environment. We currently see developed nations struggling with balancing their books, the danger of it only being hidden by under-stating the risk to their long-term finances, which can come back to haunt us, as we saw with Greece. Commodity price spikes affect most countries, rich and poor, but the poor can easily see a worsening of social stability, because food prices especially, tend to bite much harder into the budgets of the poor. Currency fluctuations would be more predictable, and their management more responsible. If risk management becomes better, and less reliant on political considerations, as is the case now, investment trends may improve as the risk premium decreases.

8

The stock markets
(Another troubling sign)

A brief history

I explained how the monetary flow system, mainly the private and central banks work, and how they affect our situation. The stock markets are at least equally important in the evolution of our society, from past, present, and into the future. We could in fact argue that they are the most important aspect of the market economy, because it provides the tool of pricing all aspects of the economy. The history of the stock markets is not clear-cut, but the first actual official stock exchange took shape in Amsterdam in the 17'Th century. The Dutch East India Company started trading in 1602. The London stock exchange started operating in 1688. Stocks started trading on Wall Street, in New York in 1792.

The main reason to have stock exchanges is to be able to raise capital for expansion projects. If firms would have to finance expansion through their own inner means, it would take forever to expand in any meaningful way, and the expansions would only be in small increments, as a reflection of the lack of sufficient internal resources. I think that it is safe to say that without this financial innovation, there would have been far less globalization, and economic development would be far below today's levels. Just take the Dutch East India Company as an example. As I previously mentioned, it started trading in Amsterdam in 1602. It was the first official multinational corporation, and the first company to issue stock offerings. The stocks were a great way to raise capital, which was put to work, through financing ship purchases, and the payroll needs of the company. This corporation was in operation for 200 years, during which period it constantly paid 18% dividend yield to

219

its stockholders. At its height, the company operated roughly 4800 ships, which were responsible for connecting Europe to Asia by trade, and colonization. During this 200-year period, it is estimated that the company sent 2 million Europeans to Asia as employees. It shipped 2.5 million tons of goods to Europe, which was roughly three times more than the rest of the European government and private entities in Europe combined during the roughly same time.

With the expansion of this first pioneer in globalization also came the first victims of globalization. This company had such powers that it was given a charter to act as a quasi-state institution. It was allowed to among other things act as a colonizing power. This of course meant that there were people who were being subjected to all types of inhumane acts meant to bring populations into compliance. They needed the local populations of Asia where they operated to remain docile, allow for the removal of their resources, and "volunteer" their time as laborers on the company plantations, and mines. The Dutch East India Company also employed strong-arm tactics in order to gain advantageous terms of trade with many Asian populations.

For many Europeans however, this was a great company, which improved the lives of countless people. There were of course the primary beneficiaries, the major stockholders, and the Dutch government. There were the ship builders, and manufacturers of trade goods and equipment for colonial development for the needs of the company. At a dividend rate of 18%, any shareholder could double his money if the dividends were reinvested into the company within roughly five years, depending on the evolution of the stock prices. An investor looking to save up for retirement back in those days would have been very happy to invest his life savings into such a venture, unless this would have been at the approach of 1800, when the company went bankrupt. Certainly, very few companies today would be able to offer such returns in the best of times on a steady long-term basis. If you have invested into stocks in North America or Europe, as a buy and hold investor in the past 10 years, chances are that you have gained nothing or nearly nothing as a broadly diversified investor.

For the broader European economy, companies such as the Dutch East India Company and other companies that followed on its footsteps, it meant greater manufacturing activity, through greater global demand for European goods, and ships. Retail activity also picked up as the inflows of Asian goods were being distributed and sold. The great returns that these companies brought to their shareholders were to become a further stimulus for product demand in Europe, as more people were made rich through stock ownership. Stock issues were also an economic stimulant as I mentioned, because the companies that issued the stocks were able to draw on the savings of the broader population in order to produce large inflows of cash. These large cash flows could be mobilized in an efficient manner to finance the projects that seemed to be the soundest ideas made available by companies. In a way, it almost sounds like a form of democracy, where people choose the industrial and other investment projects by enabling companies to raise the money to engage in the project. In reality however, back then a very small proportion of the population actually owned stocks, so stock trading insured that Europe developed the way that a few investors desired it to develop.

Bank loans could perhaps replace through their loans this surge in cash that can be achieved through the issue of stock in a company, but there are a few drawbacks. The main one being that unlike stockholders, bankers will demand the same amount of funds back, in a set period of time, and with interest. The terms are a lot more rigid, which would give companies less wiggle room to innovate, because they would have to be mindful of the monthly financial obligations, which come with a bank loan. Legal action can often be forthcoming, if monthly obligations are not met. Firms may be forced to liquidate assets. Shareholders on the other hand can only buy or sell the shares. In practice, that means that if a firm will undertake a project that will diminish its profit for the following three years, a shareholder who may have bought the shares of the company years before, may decide to sell the stock, due to lack of prospects for stock appreciation and/or dividend returns. However, the firm has already profited from the initial stock offer, when the shareholder initially bought the stock. The money raised was already put to good use through various investments into the company, which made it more profitable. If a company decides to implement a plan that might strain profitability for a certain time, but increase the company's value and profitability in the longer run, stocks may fall initially. The next step in the company's evolution would be a re-evaluation by investors, who would be looking to invest in future growth of a company, and would like to maximize profits by investing early and beating others to the opportunity to buy a stock with a lot of potential. Therefore, the company gets another inflow of money from stock sales, or new stock offers. In theory and up to recently in practice as well, this has become the best way for a nation to allow for industry to develop and prosper through the best possible system of mobilizing capital for project plans.

The current situation

The reasons to go public with a company are essentially the same in the 21'Th, century as it was in the 17'Th. Companies are looking to raise cash through the issue of stock. What is different for us, compared to the Europeans who pioneered this sort of financial activity, and later the Americans as well, is that the expansion of these companies no longer favors us necessarily. Between the end of WW2, and now, there has been a convergence of education, infrastructure, and general know how between the OECD, and the developing world. Wages have converged at a much slower pace however, as a fast growing population absorbed a lot of development. This fast growing population is already massive compared to Europe and North America, so despite a lot of flow of western capital, and development, there was only a relatively small change in the standard of living so far. There are many nations that fit in this category, but China, India, Indonesia, Brazil are some of the main ones that come to mind, because of their massive population size. China alone has a population much larger than North America and Europe combined. Same can be said for India, so for those who hope that convergence in living conditions will eventually spare us from the current trend, are badly mistaken, because convergence will happen at a much lower level.

Firms in a market economy try to be profit maximizing, as it is their economic definition, which favors them over government owned entities, which tend to be less efficient. As profit maximizing firms, there is no reason for them to extend production facilities in a high wage society. They invest in less developed nations that offer lower wages, less stringent employee protection laws, and most often more relaxed restrictions on pollution. At first, there was mainly low technology intensive production that went to other countries. Production of clothing, kitchen utensils and dishes, were things that could be produced abroad, without much loss of economic activity for the developed world. While the low tech nations produced less tech intensive goods, developed nations moved on to produce higher value goods, such as cars, mineral mining technology, electronics, software, industrial equipment, including the type needed to produce the lower tech goods in developing countries. That was a very good arrangement for us, because it offered us the best of both worlds. We got to keep the higher value jobs, in high tech, including much of the research and development, while our high wages allowed us to purchase an increasing amount of consumer goods such as clothing, toys, hand held calculators, and stereos, just to name a few.

In the past two decades, things have changed dramatically. GM has just announced that in 2010 they will produce and sell more cars in China than in the US. Brazil is increasingly challenging the west in aeronautics, petroleum extraction, and bio-fuel technology. India is increasingly capturing the IT jobs. Workers in all these countries I mentioned, earn on average at least three times less than their counterparts in Western Europe and North America. Yet we continue to hear the same old story that if we are presented with a level playing field, we can out-compete any workers on this planet. Try to tell that to the recently unemployed manufacturing, or IT workers, some of whom were faced with the humiliating task of training their own cheaper replacements. The strategy so far to stay ahead of the newly industrializing economies was to stay ahead with the production of the value added products, which used to be out of the reach of their technical expertise.

Recently, China has put a man into space, and they are working hard to make it to the moon soon. If they have the knowledge to pull that off, they surely have the ability to become increasingly self reliant in products currently made in the US, or Germany, such as bulldozers, tractors, CNC machines, and other such products that were formally known as the exclusive domain of the OECD world.

We still have a strong lead in R&D, but that lead is fading fast, as Chinese, Indian, Brazilian and other places where universities are becoming stronger, and steadily increase their share of activities, are catching up. Furthermore, there are more and more foreigners coming to western universities to conduct their graduate studies, and an increasing number are headed back to their own country. R&D, which is the last level of specialization where we are still in the lead, is not exactly the field that is ready to absorb the millions of lost jobs in manufacturing and other fields and even there, our supremacy is increasingly being challenged.

There are only two sectors of the economy, which have seen a drastic rise in employment in the last decade, in most western developed countries. Those two sectors are retail and construction of course, but those two sectors had nothing to do with the classical model of publicly held companies raising money through stock offerings, and then investing that money into local projects. Construction boomed for as long as the taps were kept open for everyone and their dog to get a mortgage. Retail boomed for the same reason. Those two sectors were hit among the hardest after the 2008 financial meltdown. Perhaps granting a mortgage to the neighbor's dog was not such a hot idea in the end. It may not have been a great idea for the long run, but for the short run, our financial industry, in complicity with the government managed to keep the economy floating for another eight years. That was despite the fact that in most sectors, the west was already being out competed by the newly industrializing world in most economic sectors.

Going back to the question of whether it is still a good model for us westerners to continue with the stock market system, without innovating it or giving it the right incentives to do the right thing, let us consider a few things. We know that increasingly, capital that is being absorbed from our investments is no longer invested in projects that develop our infrastructure, human potential, and into jobs here in our backyard. The resulting outcome is that we are increasingly losing jobs, which previously supported the national budgets, through taxes. We are losing the ability to provide for ourselves, and our governments are increasingly dependent on deficit spending to make up the difference, but that will not last forever. We are increasingly losing infrastructure that could at least provide for a possible revival. Very importantly, we are losing the human talent needed to compete in the global economy. As the jobs of the future are increasingly found in lower paid regions, our ability to produce many goods is hampered by a lack of experience in many fields. It would take years, if not decades to re-learn certain trades that have now gone extinct in our society. We are close to reaching a point of no return, where we will reach a tipping point, and go down, without the possibility to stop.

There is ample evidence that this is now in fact happening. I already mentioned the IEA reports, which clearly show that the developed OECD countries have been ceding ground in their demand for natural resources, which cannot be attributed entirely to gains in efficiency. In fact, improvements in efficiency might be near the bottom of the list of reasons, of why this is happening. It should be noted that Europe and Japan already have by far the most energy efficient economies on the planet, and they make up the majority of OECD nations, and further gains in efficiency are now harder to achieve as a result. A decade without net job growth is partly responsible, as is a net drop in manufacturing activities. In the year 2000, OECD countries consumed 63% of petroleum products. As of the end of 2009, they consume 53% of all petroleum produced. Correspondingly, the non-OECD nations, led by China, India, Brazil and the Middle East in consumption growth, went from 37% of consumption to 47%. If this trend holds, they will consume more petroleum than the OECD nations by around 2012. On one hand a fair development on the consumption front, given that non OECD countries in fact make up the greatest part of the world's population. On the other hand, it demonstrates that the western world, which is the main component of the OECD population, is definitely losing out on actual economic activities, aside from finance, which requires very little petroleum to run.

Current investment levels into expansion of industrial capacity and other activity in the EU and North America seem to continue a similar trend as it did in the last decade. Recent news broadcasts in the US have been very vocal about firms listed on the stock exchange, which have been reporting solid profits for a few quarters now, but are still reluctant to hire. Despite the increasing cash levels on the balance sheets of these companies, few US projects are expanding, or starting up. Many pundits, especially on the right are arguing that this is in fact a reflection of the misguided efforts on the part of the Obama administration's desire to let the tax cuts for the wealthy, instituted by Bush to expire. The health care bill, which still does not cover everyone, unlike in most other OECD countries is another reason given for this reluctance. Finance reform, which it seems is a very much, watered down bill, also enters the conversation quite often. In short, they want to paint a picture of companies eager to do business in the US, but too timid to do so because of the uncertainty in regards to these new measures. The same reports also point out that the cash pile that these companies are sitting on collectively amount to up to two trillion dollars.

There are no logical ways to connect tax hikes, and perhaps enhanced health care costs to a lack of interest in investing as opposed to sitting on cash, which given the low interest environment cannot earn much of anything in interest. Personally, I doubt that investment levels would rise in the US even if they would scrap the health bill, the financial reform bill, and extend the Bush tax cuts. They could even try to introduce new tax cuts, as many people on the right would like to proceed. I am sure that most of you have heard this old argument by now. "If they (the government) would only get out of the way of free enterprise", and then it goes on to make the point that jobs would be created, and prosperity would break out. In theory that might be the case, but in reality, there is only one reason why so many companies are willing to sit on so much cash instead of investing it. They are slowly feeding it into the still developing economies. The only reason that they did not invest all of that money already is, because many of these developing economies, some of which never slowed down significantly even during the 2008-09 period, cannot absorb it, because there is already domestic investment happening on a relatively large scale in these countries. They have to be careful not to overheat those economies, so in some circumstances, like in China's case, measures have been taken to limit the growth rate, and thus their ability to absorb investment. The argument that somehow these companies would necessarily be interested in investing in expanding operations other than some new retail outlets perhaps, or some more chain restaurants, rings hollow and is most likely false. No amount of tax breaks will convince a company to produce widgets in the US or the EU, when widgets can be produced at one quarter the cost in India, or China. The gap in competitiveness is just too big.

If I were to be wrong, then perhaps GE, who it turns out did not have to pay any federal income taxes in 2010, would have stayed in the US with the core of its operations, instead of cutting 20% of the US workforce in favor of investing in new facilities elsewhere in the past decade. I doubt very much that there are many other places on this planet, where a company is exempt from paying taxes on their profits, where they can hire somewhat competent workers. It is true that the headline US corporate tax rate is one of the highest in the world. The net intake however, when you factor in all the loopholes provided by the tax code is one of the lowest as a percentage of corporate profits. If there are some who still choose to invest in North American and West European manufacturing facilities, they do so because they have other considerations that need to be factored in.

The ugly kid that even dogs will not play with

I am sure that most of you have heard of this joke about the kid, that was so ugly that his/her mother had to put some bacon around the poor kid's neck, just so dogs would be interested in playing with that poor creature. That joke is increasingly what comes to my mind when I think about some of the initiatives that our western governments have engaged in to save some of the manufacturing jobs. There are still some great manufacturers in Europe and North America, who did not quit on us yet. Boeing in the US is one such example. They are not only producing for the domestic market, they also export their planes around the world. Car manufacturers still hang around to some degree, although there has been some leakage of manufacturing activities on that front in the favor of the developing world. Most often, people like to tell the story line of the great western worker, who is just so darn valuable to these high tech operations that these companies just could not part with us, despite lower labor costs and other benefits elsewhere, as the reasoning behind company decisions to stay. If one looks closer at the real situation, it is not such a pretty story after all. It is in fact the story of the ugly kid.

The operations that are still around in North America and EU in manufacturing are not necessarily continuing to operate here because they would not find it more profitable to move. They are here because it allows them to maintain a more positive image by continuing to provide employment to the population that is also still a major consumer of their goods. Such is the case of the auto companies, who know that they can find a cheaper place to build their cars than US, Canada, or Western Europe. The quality can be maintained, while labor costs can be cut by as much as 2/3. They look at that option with envy, even after the latest concessions made by the trade unions. Let us face it though; Ford would be hard pressed to get American consumers to buy its products if they were to move most of their manufacturing operations out of the country of its initial birth. The American consumers would never forgive them. However, if you expect to hear that Ford will open up new manufacturing facilities in order to export cars to the newly growing markets of the developing world; do not hold your breath. In fact, they are just like their competitors, outsourcing an increasing amount of work even for cars and parts meant to build the cars that are sold in the US or Canada.

Evidence shows that even political and consumer pressure is failing to keep some of these high profile companies from the pressures of outsourcing. According to a report in the Economic Populist, GM apparently is planning to shift some of the production meant for the US domestic market to cheaper labor locations. In fact, they intend to bring in roughly 50,000 vehicles built in China and sell them in the US in 2011. They apparently want to have up to 1/3 of the vehicles that they sell in the US to be produced elsewhere. Now I admit that a lot of that one-third figure might include cars being built in Canada, which is also a western country, but they in fact intend to cut production in Canada as well, while shifting it to Mexico, China, South Korea and Japan. I bet the Canadians must be kicking themselves at this point, since they also participated in the grand GM bailout. Incidentally, GM is also planning to cut jobs in Australia and Europe, in order to shift production to the above-mentioned countries. I am sure you can see a pattern here.

Four countries, none of which belong to the west culturally, will gain jobs through GM's investment policies. Four other countries, or regions all of which are culturally western countries, as they are either Europeans or European offshoots, will be losing jobs. It is interesting to see that they are actually also investing in a non-western industrialized nation such as Japan. My guess is that they want to gain a foothold into their market, so they are doing the same thing that Toyota does in the US and Canada. They will build some assembly plants to gain local producer credibility. If they will make it in Japan, I am thinking they will export some of their car production from China to supplement the Japanese production, so that way they will keep the overall price low.

The GM example is not unique in these sorts of practices. Microsoft, who does not feel the same sort of pressure to keep jobs in the west, is busy hiring this year in India, after they laid off thousands of people in the US. They just signed a new contract with outsourcing firm Infosys from India in March 2010. I guess those IT people who thought that they would be back in business once the economy recovers were overly optimistic, but word is that fast food joints are expanding this year. I could go on and on about this, but I fear that I might end up sounding like Lou Dobbs (former CNN employee). Bottom line though is that if people expect that the high quality jobs, which were lost in the past two years or so, will be back, they are going to be sorely disappointed. This is not because "evil" Obama, or Prime Minister Steven Harper of Canada do not want to bring the jobs back, as some of their political opponents would have you believe. It is the very simple formula of the profit maximizing, private enterprise firms, trying to earn the most money in the short term, because it will give them a better chance of survival in the long term. Given the current global trade formats, this is the profitable trend, and as long as we stay with the current trading system, the trend will continue.

Perhaps the best symbol for the ugly kid syndrome is Boeing in the US. The main reason that they are still heavily invested in the US is because the reward is currently greater than the downsides. Even though they could find other places around the world, where they could hire a capable workforce, their loyalty to the US workers is greatly rewarded by the US defense department. Boeing has clearly received preferential treatment over the past decades over their potential rivals from other parts of the world in receiving US defense contracts. There are now many reasons why this convenient marriage may have to end, and with that, so will the Boeing loyalty to American workers.

For starters, the US government is reaching the point where it has to face up to the fact that they cannot continue the level of defense spending that they are currently engaged in. That means that fewer defense contracts will be available to continue to entice firms such as Boeing to stay in America. With the recent rise of many potent potential rivals to this aerospace giant coming from China, Brazil and possibly Russia, they may have no choice but to start moving many of their production facilities to other shores in order to remain competitive. Most of these countries are either producing a new potential competitor to Boeing models, or are in the process of delivering passenger planes for the first time, that are likely to compete in quality with Boeing. The price of these new planes is going to be a gap that Boeing and its European rival Airbus will never be able to come close to matching in competitiveness. This means that by sometime in the 2020's, producing airplanes in Europe or America will become an insurmountable disadvantage in the current trade environment.

Many supporters of the current status quo argue that a complete desertion of the west by large manufacturers will never happen, because they do not want to kill the goose that lays the golden egg, in other words the western consumer. That may be true, and firms may indeed be aware that their actions may contribute to the overall destruction of the buying power of westerners. If they are aware of that however, it still does not mean that they can do much about it. Firms have competitors, and if their competition is lowering product prices through outsourcing, then the firm that is aware of the problem will be faced with either outsourcing as well, or face collapse through the lack of ability to compete.

The thing that we need to understand is that the developing world is increasingly becoming a consumer power as well. They may not have as many resources to purchase luxury items on a net basis yet, but their appetite for low budget cars, cell phones, computers, and internet access is already very well developed and growing at a very fast pace, since they still have a few billion people collectively who aspire to become the planet's newest consumer. As this happens, the advantage that the western consumers have over the large profile firms to force them to keep some of their operations in our neighborhood is diminishing. As that power to compel diminishes, our position will become even more desperate, as companies will increasingly continue to accelerate their move out of the less profitable environments, and into the fast growing, young, vibrant population environment.

Our governments who are actually fighting to put some pressure on these companies to stay, or try to bribe them into staying through increasing concessions, are already showing the strain, because they have already been doing what they can to keep our economy from being deserted. The Bush tax cuts are one such example, the Reagan era, trickle down economics policies were actually the beginnings of this battle. Our governments are now so loaded with debts and obligations however, that they have to choose increasingly between providing its citizens with the very basics such as security health and other needs or alternatively continue bribing these companies, but then they have to neglect the immediate needs of the citizens. The latter alternative which involves lowering the taxes on the wealthy even further, thereby convincing them to continue keeping some of their production facilities here might work partially in the short run, but we will most certainly lose an increasing volume of government services. I should also point out that a decrease in government spending on offering the public services will further exacerbate the unemployment situation. Jobs in health, diplomacy, safety, education and other government related jobs will eventually become a shrinking proportion of total employment positions, further weakening our consumption power.

Investing in the most lucrative markets

An increasingly prominent aspect of stock investing these days is that western investors are increasingly looking to buy into developing market exchanges. In the past decade, the stock markets in China, India, Brazil, Russia, and other developing nations have greatly outperformed their western counterparts. In fact, the tech heavy NASDAQ composite index, which reached its peak in 2000 at over 5100, currently trades in the 2000-2500 range. The Dow Jones index is essentially trading in the same range as it was a decade ago, however it should be recognized that unlike the NASDAQ composite, it did reach some higher peaks in 2007. The German DAX index suffered a 13% drop for the decade. Most other Western European indexes have shared the same fate, with some slight variation. The main Shanghai index in China has achieved a gain of 26% as of August 2010, compared to its high point 10 years ago. It is not much, but at least it did provide some positive returns. Brazil's main index the Boavespa, has managed returns of 394% compared to its high point in 2000, so it had a good decade, and so did those who invested in Brazil for the past ten years. Among the better performing western stock indexes, the Canadian TSX managed a 5% gain for the decade. These results have to be adjusted somewhat for currency fluctuations to get a more precise picture, if one wants to be more precise. For our purposes, the straight analysis of these various stock index results around the world paint a clear enough picture. The future for stock market gains is plainly in the developing markets.

Investing for Retirement

Remembering the analysis of the Dutch East India Company, which was the first publicly held company on this planet more than 400 years ago, I mentioned the second major role that publicly held companies are meant to have. With the improvement in health, sanitation, and food supply in the western world, we now have the ability to live a life that on average surpasses in length that of our ancestors 400 years ago, by roughly 100%, or double what it used to be. This means that we are increasingly dependent on pension schemes, be they public, or private to take us from the time that we retire because of our lack of ability to cope with the work environment, all the way to the grave. We retire also, because we have a desire for a bit of peace following a struggle that starts from early childhood when the pressure is on to get educated, and ends with our retirement, from a job, which most of us struggle to hold on to in our later years in our professional career, and few of us enjoy doing. There is of course the other reason as well, which is that we tend to become increasingly obsolete knowledge and ability wise, and it is hard to teach old dogs new tricks. To be able to provide for this luxury currently enjoyed by our citizens, governments, private entities and individuals have to engage in investment activities meant to increase the size of the initial contribution made by individuals through taxes, or through private employee/employer pension funds. Stocks are one of the main investments for these funds, and there is a definite need to see a steady, constant growth in these investments. At the very least, the growth rate should exceed inflation rates; ideally, there should be a real growth in these assets, if they are to provide for the increasing longevity of our golden years.

As I already conveyed the information in regards to the major western stock indexes for the past decade, the newly retired senior citizens are in for a rough ride, if they had their private savings invested in a large proportion into stocks other than some of the emerging market stock exchanges. If the past decade is a sign of things to come, our baby boomers, who are increasingly getting to the age where it is time to throw away the work boots, or that silly tie that many had to wear for the past few decades, will have to reconsider their retirement strategy. They will have to invest abroad to get the returns needed for them to obtain a somewhat comfortable retirement. The stock market system still works, but not for most of us. We have a choice, between being patriotic, and investing at home, and financing the development of other countries as the price of getting the chance to retire in a decent fashion.

For individuals currently in their midlife, this is very much like being told to cut the branch off from under your own feet. We have to invest wisely, in order to secure a decent retirement for ourselves. The only way to invest wisely is to pursue foreign companies, or local companies that expand in other places, while cutting jobs in our communities. Thus, both private enterprises, as well as our struggling governments neglect investment in our home base. Our children are therefore facing a much dimmer future than our own, and we ourselves are threatened to live out our old age in a society that will be less safe and pleasant, due to lack of prosperity. Even if some of us are investment savvy enough to secure some income for our own post retirement needs, our surroundings will make that retirement less pleasant. Our children will likely have to forget the concept of retirement altogether, and be happy if they will be able to sell their labor to someone else. That is the case for most, unless you are one of the exceptionally successful investors who will be wise enough to leave enough behind to take care of them as well, in which case they will likely do the hiring of the poor souls forced to bid down their own wages more and more aggressively.

Buy and hold Vs frequent trading

Another thing worth mentioning, when assessing the benefits of the stock market in our current environment, is the fact that the duration of investments may no longer provide the capital that companies need to finance expansion and modernization projects as it used to. The days of buy and hold investing are ending. As more and more investors realize that the market no longer has the steady upwards momentum that we became used to for the last decades, they increasingly choose to join the frequent trader program. As I mentioned, very few people made money in the stock market by, buying and holding on to stocks in the past decade. Plenty of people however won or lost money by playing the day-trading game. Those who have a good understanding of short duration trade do well. For example if you are a person that inherited $100,000, you could choose to buy a house, blow the money, start a small business, or if you have the instinct for picking the up and down days, you can secure for yourself a good living by buying stocks in the morning, and selling at the end of the trading session. A 1% gain on a daily trade on the market will net you $1000. Do that once a week on average, and do it successfully, and you could easily create an income for yourself, which most likely will trump the income earned from starting a small business enterprise with that same amount. I am sure you are thinking as you are reading that it seems risky. The truth is, if you are disciplined, and on the good months you put some of the money earned aside in case one of your trading days goes bad and you loose a few thousands, you will have the reserves to make up for it, therefore keeping your original $100,000 intact. Now that you know this, start hoping that someone will leave you $100,000 or more in their will. While you are waiting for that to happen, brush up on your knowledge about securities trading so you can later take advantage of your good fortune. Who knows, you might realize down the road that by reading this book, you received the best advice ever on how to live well, without the 9 to 5'ver.

The good news here is obviously that there is a way for some to make easy money, by buying and selling stocks. In other words, you make money without producing anything of value to society or to the economy. The bad news is that this in effect is nothing more than capitalism inspired monetary redistribution. Who said that Communists and Socialists are those who like to redistribute the wealth? Here we have a capitalist institution that encourages redistributing wealth from those who still engage in more traditional investment practices, meant to benefit both investors and the firm that issued the stocks, to those who only lend their capital for a day, or two. A day or two is not nearly enough for a company to take that money and invest it into a brick and mortar operation that would also create jobs. Increasingly, we are becoming a society that encourages increased financial activity and decreased real economic activity. It is true that those day traders who pile in the benefits of their knowledge and luck in their short term trades, also make good consumers, therefore they stimulate demand for real goods. Many of those goods are no longer being produced in the west however, so there is no reason to pat them on the back for that either.

If a person happens to have a million dollars instead of only $100,000, the benefits of the daily 1% gain on trading are multiplied ten fold. A smart day trade would net around $10,000. Ten to twenty such successful trades in a year and it is; hello good life!!! A really lucky individual, who may have been endowed with a ten million dollar nest egg, can do this same trade maybe five times per year, and live a very privileged life, even after paying the capital gains tax, which in most cases amounts to less than the collective taxes paid by an individual who owns a small business operation. Trading in this manner is aided by the fact that increasingly, the world markets have a trend of reacting to each other. For example, if Asian markets have a sharp up day, chances are that so will the North American and European Markets. A person that does nothing else except to follow the markets is also able to react to the daily economic news on a moment's notice. That is not the case for the poor schmuck, who works from nine to five, contributes into his or her retirement plan, which is invested sometimes into long duration trades, and which lately are losing money. That money as I already mentioned is picked up by the day traders, who mostly do better.

This trend towards the slick day-trader investment environment is also supported by our cultural norms and values. We live in a society, where everyone wants to be the "wise guy" who gets to be the winner. Obviously, the image of the stock trader, who through a few trades can afford the posh apartment in New York and the fast car, is that of a winner. So why anyone in such a position should give that up, and start a ten million dollar private company making widgets for sale? First, running such a company takes a lot of an owner's time, especially in the beginning. That means not too much time for driving around in that fast car. Other than that, it is actually riskier to pile $ ten million into one investment of long duration, which could be hard to liquidate in case things go bad. Potentially, the whole investment can be wiped out. Pilling the money into the stock market, on the other hand only carries minimal risks. Thanks to the stop loss option in a trade, a sell offer is made as soon as the level of the stop loss is breached. A one to two percent loss is much easier to stomach than engaging into an action that could jeopardize everything. The other aspect of a small to medium size business is that it could take months or even years to see a profit return on the investment. The profit return on a trade is instant; therefore, a real wise guy will choose the sexy option.

I met an individual a while ago, who owned a trucking company. I will not name this person, as I do not want to breach his privacy, and I am sure he would not want to gain fame through my revealing his misfortunes. His wife convinced him in 1999-2000 to liquidate his physical assets, and get in on the tech frenzy. She wanted him to be more hip, while the poor guy was a simpler, and from my perspective a very likable fellow, who started out as an honest truck driver, and was smart and disciplined enough to grow a company out of his occupation. Unfortunately, the tech frenzy turned into a tech rout, and from my understanding, he was wiped out. His wife, who just married him, a few years prior to this event, left him soon after, because as we already know, this society can only embrace a winner, and so should we as individuals. He did not make the cool and sexy club of successful stock traders.

My guess is that he did not really know what he was doing. He was just a person in love with a woman who wanted to make him into something he was not. I bring up this example, because it is a very good measure of the values of the society we live in, in regards to one's economic activities. Here was a man who had a solid asset business, that was providing him and his family with a good standard of living and employment for others, yet the manner in which his money was made was considered to be lowly by some standards. A speculator, who makes money through strictly financial dealings, but unlike our unfortunate former trucking company owner does not even provide jobs for people, or offer a service, is seen as something we should all aspire to be. So if you are asking yourself, where the jobs are, you now know what happened to them. The jobs are not there in part, because the capital that is meant to create the jobs that we depend on is increasingly stuck in financial speculation.

Benefits of the sustainability tariff to the investment environment

The benefits to having the tariffs I proposed in place should be rather clear. The market will no longer punish countries that are willing to do the right things such as cutting greenhouse gasses, which is something that benefits everyone, while rewarding the countries that continue to employ policies that do the opposite, which more than offsets the cuts achieved by a few responsible global citizens. Factories will once again be built in places where human dignity and environmental responsibility are observed, because the benefits of outsourcing to dirtier and more inhumane places in the world are automatically erased. I recognize the disappointment that would be felt by many companies that have enjoyed in the recent past this great race to the bottom in which they managed to pit us against each other in, but at some point, we have to say that enough is enough. This trend has to be reversed for our collective good, and we have to put an end to the punishment of those who try to do right by their citizens and humanity.

It is true that governments would end up playing an ever bigger role in the overall economy. Taxes would have to be raised in order to fund projects that would encourage more innovation to improve efficiency, and better education in order to promote competitiveness. This does not mean that private companies would necessarily be squeezed out. They can still play a contractor or subcontractor role in projects such as building new power grids, or fast rail transport. They can still build the schools that the government funds. They can still design and manufacture most consumer products. The difference is that they will now be obliged to pay their taxes to help build the things, which make it possible for them to operate and thrive, because governments that will not invest in these things will be left further behind. Operating in such environments where investing in the people, environment as well as improved infrastructure are neglected will be more expensive due to the import tariffs I am suggesting; therefore we will no longer have to fear that if we dare to tax business, they will leave us. The ability of firms to pit governments against each other in pushing for lower taxes, less environmental regulation and more relaxed human rights standards is taken away. We should not worry however that this might kill business, because private companies can easily adapt to new business environment, and they will learn to compete within the new framework.

Firms are in fact currently being corrupted by the way we try to cater to them by providing an easier environment for them to function within. They no longer have to look for constant innovation in efficiencies within the structure of the firm, or even for improvements in technology as much as they should. Money can be made by trying to extort governments for concessions. Firms that provide good employment opportunities often do just that. They ask for subsidies, tax breaks, or for the relaxation of regulations of all sorts. Governments are obliged to accommodate them, because if not, the firms go on to knock on the next door that they can knock on, where they will eventually get the concessions, they are looking for, setting the bar lower and lower. Every time such concessions are made, governments lose the ability to finance much needed improvements in infrastructure, education, technological innovation, and other things that make up a modern economy.

Poor countries that make the concessions to attract these firms lose a lot as well. They lose on government revenue, more pollution leads to an unhealthy population that ends up being a drag on long-term sustainability. Many governments in the developing world also underperform by not providing an avenue for all people in society to attain a path to education. Giving up on providing a basic social safety net has meant that countries such as China have become over reliant on exports, because they were never able to provide the basis for creating a widespread consumption pattern within their society. Failure to work with us to solve many of the environmental problems that can lead to increased food production volatility is not in their interest either. As recent events have shown, with food rioting disrupting the status quo in developing countries, they are more vulnerable to environmental degradation than we are at the moment, because they have a greater proportion of their population that lacks the buying power to cope with even slight price spikes.

Governments increasingly give up on basic research, making it more and more unlikely that a new engine of growth such as the internet, or many pharmaceuticals and hospital equipment innovations provided in the past. Stock markets can only function properly if there is some expectation of progress that should give reason to believe that there is a path, which can lead stock values higher. Between stagnation in infrastructure, technological and human development deficiencies firmly setting in, in most of the developed world and limits to growth and development being imposed on us because of nature due to limits to resource availability, firms do not have a reason to cling to the status quo in the end any more than we do.

The system that they depend on, in order to be able to operate, comes from the collective resources that governments spend on providing that business environment, and overall system. Do they think that they really have much to gain if we as a society lose the ability to provide for basic safety and crime suppression? Do they think that they stand to gain if transport infrastructure is left to crumble away? If only the very wealthy families of this world get a chance to purchase an education for their children, will we be utilizing our full human potential? Will firms have the ability to find well educated people, with the right skills they need to operate increasingly sophisticated business models? I personally think that there are plenty of smart kids being born in lower class families, which fail to realize their potential, due to economic circumstances they were born into, even in current circumstances. Cutting the ladder from under their feet by further cutting support for their education means that the potential will only be realized from among the ranks of the wealthy. It should also be mentioned that not all wealthy families produce gifted offspring, despite all the resources available to raise them. This is not a viable plan for the long haul, yet the markets are acting as if it is.

With the destruction of the western consumer, which is an inevitability if we continue down the current path, for the many reasons I have already mentioned, perhaps they believe that they can rely on the thin strata of middle class citizens that is rising in the developing world. With conditions not being favorable for entire developing countries reaching a situation where the majority of the population is poised to reach middle class status, the thin top strata may be all there will be. Leading CEO's may be mistaken in believing that such a social structure can be maintained successfully, without producing instability. If there are any doubts about that, I think the recent situation with the revolts in the Middle East should clear things up. I am sure that in their mind, it would be a way to keep social leverage, by maintaining the constant threat for the thin middle class strata, that they may join the ranks of the extremely impoverished. A position of advantage over others is always desirable, but in this case, it would be a very unstable position, which may in fact have no winning parties in the end.

Business cannot thrive without a certain level of stability, and it is for this reason that I expect that many business elites may not be so hard to be persuaded of the benefits to my proposal. Perhaps with a reinstatement of some market stability, we can return to a state of affairs, where companies once again are able to use stock offerings to promote long-term projects. Pension funds can once again hope to achieve some stable market returns for the future retirees. Most importantly, however, is the fact that countries will no longer have to face brutal punishment by the markets for trying to do the right thing. The markets are essentially a pricing mechanism. All the tariff system would do is to promote the right kind of pricing. Good behavior leading to sustainable growth would be priced positively and bad behavior, promoting the bulldozing of the environment and human rights would be affected negatively, as it should be.

Widget producer deciding between investing in China, or the US under present and potentially future circumstances depending on our decisions

To illustrate the way the behavior of the firm may change in the event that we go from the present state of affairs, to a new trade scheme, like the one suggested here, I picked a widget factory, making production decisions in the present, compared to the same widget factory making its decisions in a new environment for trade.

Costs and benefits of producing in China:

-Cost of capital 10% less in China due to cheaper property and building construction prices. Capital investment is $100,000,000.

-Cost of labor per unit produced is four times cheaper, cost is $5 per widget produced.

-Government taxes are same, property tax, 100,000 per year, and income tax is 30%.

-Cost of environmental compliance, which could be added to capital costs, but I prefer to keep it separate for the purpose of highlighting the cost that we pay to protect the environment is $1 per widget produced.
Wholesale price of a widget in this case is $15, and I assume that at this price the company can sell 10,000,000 widgets per year.
Yearly revenue in this case is $150,000,000, while profit before taxes is $90,000,000.

After paying the taxes, company is left with $62,900,000, which they can use to pay down the initial capital investment, pay for interest accrued during these investments, and pay dividends, CEO bonuses and so on.

Investing in the US:

-It would cost $110,000,000 to build and equip the production plant (10% more).

-Cost of labor is four times more, as I mentioned per unit produced, in other words $20.
Government taxes are the same, $100,000 for property taxes, and 30% on income earned.

-Cost of environmental compliance is $5 due to the more stringent rules in place.

Wholesale price of widgets in this case is $30.
Because of the higher wholesale price, there is only a market for half as many widgets, due to demand destruction occurring at the higher price, so only 5,000,000 widgets are sold per year.
Total revenue in this case is $150,000,000, just as it was in the China scenario.
Profit before taxes in this case would be only 25,000,000.
After tax profit is $17,400,000, which is 45.5 million dollars less than if they would have invested in China.

Notice also the income tax that China can collect at the same level of taxation as the US. China collects in this case 27 million dollars; as opposed to the 7.5 million collected in the US (Set rate is 30% in this example). It is also true however, that given the far larger incomes of the workers in the US; the government can make up for that shortfall through income taxes levied on workers.
The numbers I chose are hypothetical, but they are not far from the approximate situation that is the current reality. There is no way that the US workers can compete in the field of the hypothetical product

called widgets, although the patent most likely originated in the US or Europe.

The investment choice of the widget-producing firm under the new tariff regime:

In this case I have to include two separate scenarios for China:

The first scenario is the same, except the cost of production is changed due to a tariff of 100% due to deficiencies, and I assume that the main market for the widgets is found in countries that chose to comply with the tariff regime.

The cost of selling the widgets in effect becomes $30 per unit.
The market will only take half as many in this case, as was the case with the US production scenario.

Revenue is thus cut to $75,000,000. The before tax profit is $45,000,000.
After tax profit is $31,400,000, which is still more than what profits would be in the US, but it is no longer such a big difference.

The Chinese government feels a huge difference however. Their tax intake drops significantly here, since they only take in half as much in taxes. We should remember that unlike in the US, Chinese wages are relatively small; therefore, they cannot make up for the shortfall by taxing worker's incomes. The decline in government revenues would mean that the Chinese government would have to cut on infrastructure and education spending which are all necessary in order to attract high quality investments.

In the event of compliance, the 100% hypothetical tariff would still be in place initially, but the difference is that it would most likely get reduced every year as progress on environmental as well as human rights issues would be made in order to gain a more competitive rate of taxation on their exports. At the same time, firms would find themselves in a business environment increasingly resembling ours, complete with more stringent environmental laws, and higher wages and benefits for their employees. The playing field would be leveled eventually, but convergence would most likely be towards increasingly evenly matched countries in terms of efficiency rather than converging towards more equal rates of poverty and overall human misery as we are currently headed towards just such a convergence currently.

You may have noticed the fact that in the example I gave of non-compliance, the Chinese may still hold a slight advantage in appealing to investors looking to find suitable places to invest, in order to maximize their profits. I believe this to be the case initially. In time however, as you may remember, the level of government revenues in China would take a hit, due to lower corporate profits as a result of higher tariff costs associated with exporting from a non compliant country. That means that they will lose the ability to invest in their human and physical infrastructure. Initially, the main threat to the Chinese would come from countries that work far cheaper than us, but would choose to comply with the new tariff regime. These countries would most likely attract much of the investment that initially would have gone to China and other such, hypothetically non-compliant places. In the long-run, the cheap labor, but tariff compliant countries would most likely converge in their wage levels as well as in environmental standards with us. Countries that would choose non-compliance as a strategy would most likely see their competitive level become much diminished.

What this all means for us is that the playing field in international economic terms would be changed drastically. Instead of us having to compete for corporate investment through deregulating our environmental and labor standards, because others are outdoing us in the rape of their environment and people, making their economy more attractive for investment in the process, we will be rewarded for the opposite reason. Our current competition would be divided into two camps. One camp would choose to compete with us in environmental and human respect. That camp would be forced to find new ways to compete, such as outdoing us in efficiency. In other words we would finally become engaged globally in a healthy competition. There would also be many countries, which would choose the other way to compete, which is through status quo policies. They will forego the tedious efforts to become a less corrupt, more open, innovative, and more efficient society, in favor of trying the course of undercutting us through their current methods of no environmental or human protection, currency manipulation to keep wages low, irresponsible exploitation of their natural resources and so on. This strategy is not one that would work in the end, for the reason that I mentioned in the hypothetical example. With diminished government resources that these countries would have at their disposal for investment in infrastructure and human resources development, these countries would be missing the key ingredient that is currently responsible for making it possible for them to beat us.

9

Western governments; the ultimate
sub-prime borrowers
(The Fiscal Situation)

A piece of a smaller pie: (The declining influence of western governments as the tax base they depend on is shrinking as a percentage of global GDP.)

Just 35 years ago, western governments were in control of 80% of the world's economy, and they were the lenders to the developing world, through the World Bank and the IMF. Now they find themselves borrowing heavily from banks, international investors, and developing world governments such as China's. The only reason they even have the ability to borrow the amounts needed to finance their needs is that they have the historical advantage of being the safe haven of stability in the financial markets. This is only so because of habit, and not so much because of fundamentals. The same S&P rating agency that is a step from downgrading Hungary's debt rating to junk despite them being on track to run deficits in the 3% range, as a shameless political move, continues to rate The US and UK as AAA despite their well known problems. According to the IMF's own study, the US needs to redress a budget gap of 14% of GDP right now, in order to achieve long-term viability. It currently collects only 17% of GDP in federal taxes, so they would have to either double the tax rate, cut spending by about 2 trillion dollars per year, or do a combination of both. None of those moves would bode well for the economy. A sharp move along that front would be nothing short of suicide. A slow, gradual move into that direction may not be a fast enough course for re-balancing the economy, and would act as a drag on economic expansion.

Rating the US as AAA at this point is equally shameless politics as is their punishment of Hungary, for their strong stance on making banks share more in the burdens of the recent hardships, as opposed to taking it out on the poor. The fundamentals will catch up with them eventually though, or the S&P and other current establishments will lose all credibility, and it will no longer matter to anyone what they have to say[1]. Based on their failure to see the danger of the sub-prime mortgages, we should already have realized that we should have stopped listening to them years ago, because it would have saved investors hundreds of billions in losses.

The importance of these above mentioned facts, aside from telling us that many western countries are insolvent, and have very little chance of making it in the long run, given their structural financial situation, is also to help us understand our capacity to tackle the future. As a democracy, our collective will is supposed to be reflected in the actions of our politicians. The actions of the politicians at this point need to reflect the urgency of fighting for our right to maintain our economic activities, such as the right to manufacture products. Many corporate interests are preventing the government from taking a stance, to redress the current imbalance, which is making it prohibitively expensive to produce in the western developed world compared to developing nations such as China. We expect them to do that, but we also prefer to pay a lower tax that makes it imperative for countries like the US to borrow money from some of these same nations that they need to take serious measures against.

The many challenges that have already been identified in the previous chapters are currently coming together, making it harder for western governments to continue to provide the standard of living that people are used to, and have come to expect as a birthright. A big picture review of the situation can be summed up as one, where the global outlook for growth is looking grim due to constraints caused by limits on resource availability growth. Within this situational trend, western economies are finding themselves at a competitive disadvantage compared to many developing nations, for the reasons already mentioned. Lack of economic viability is in turn forcing governments to hide the true nature of our situation by engaging in large-scale deficit spending.

Short-term considerations that led to a disastrous economy

Reagan and Thatcher: In the 1980's right leaning, politicians became the trendsetters in the western world. The concept of small government as a means to create jobs and prosperity was adopted as the main established wisdom of the elites. It was argued that cutting taxes and the role of the government in the economy was the way to economic prosperity for all. Taxes were slashed, especially for the wealthy, who they argued that is actually good for us, because the rich are the ones who can invest and therefore create jobs. The second part of the equation was to slash government spending. This proved to be harder said than done. Not because the elites find it hard to hit the poor and desperate due to their conscience, as many would have us believe. Charity and decency is not at all at the heart of this issue, but as we saw during our tour through 19'Th century European history, when we met historical heavyweight Otto Von Bismarck, it is rather an issue of economic and social stability, which is imperative in a post agrarian society. As the drive to slash taxes to become more competitive became a race to the bottom in the western world, we slowly made our way to the current situation, which we should all admit is not looking good at all. In fact, it is hard at this point to envision a western world, which can avoid massive government defaults in some form, through massive inflation, or outright default.

The main reason we came to be in this situation is because I believe there is a serious deficiency in understanding where the drive to cut taxes in order to grow the economy leads us in the long run, and in the wider picture. There is little evidence that low corporate and business taxes lead to the creation of many jobs and economic growth. What is in fact happening is that as an administrative district, be it a country, or a regional entity, cuts its taxes, it becomes more competitive in relation to other administrative entities that did not follow suit yet. In effect, what happens here is that investment and jobs are siphoned away from other places. The argument goes that this leads to fast economic growth that will in fact lead to higher revenue in the end, despite the low tax rates. This is the main argument that is used to explain the wisdom of Reaganomics, and at first glance, it seems to make perfect sense, and initially it works[2].

The problem arises when the other administrative districts are left with no other choice but to follow suit and also slash taxes. At this point, it no longer has the desired effect of creating jobs by attracting investment, because there is nowhere left to siphon jobs from. The administrative entity that initially went ahead to undercut everyone else, also finds itself stuck with a low tax rate that no longer provides the growth that was witnessed initially, which brought in more tax revenue than was lost through the tax breaks. The end result is that the ones who already have the capital win, because they just received generous tax breaks. Government loses, because now they in fact are bringing in far less in revenue than what they expected to get through the expected but never materialized long-term growth. Remember that low taxes themselves do not create many jobs. If that were the case, we would have a high flying economy, because current tax rates are much lower than they were in the 50's and 60's, when the economy was flying high, despite the much higher tax rates than we have presently[3].

Despite the fact that now we have a historical reference to measure the true effects of tax cuts, when all factors are included, including the effect of engaging in a race to the bottom, which is what undercutting each other in effect does, we still have mainstream politicians who advocate a new round of undercutting each other. Given the debt and already huge deficits that most governments are running, while already under-investing in human and physical capital for the long run, I believe this round of undercutting each other will be the last one we will engage in. I fear that we will do just this, because politically Reaganomics is a far simpler concept to explain than trying to explain the necessity of having a basic social safety net, since the end of the agrarian dominated era, as we saw during our short stroll through history, as we met Otto Von Bismarck. It is also harder to explain a historical reference to earlier decades when taxes were higher and yet we are now growing slower, which disproves the claims of the right. As a result, many people, especially in the US were converted to this belief, including many for whom it is a concept that does them great disfavor when implemented. In Europe, there was a proposal by some members of the EU to introduce a union wide rate of corporate taxes. The measure is bitterly opposed by a few states, such as Ireland, who use these lower corporate tax rates to undercut the other members of the union. At some point, it is inevitable that they will engage in a race to the bottom within, as well as with other industrialized powers such as the US, Japan and others who compete at the same level.

Misguided trade policies

As you noticed, I did not include our developing world competitors in this analysis on tax policy. The reason being that they may very well compete on taxation level as well, as they try to undercut each other. They do not need tax policy to undercut us however, because as we already saw, they are already able to do so, on wages, lack of environmental protection, as well as almost non-existent worker protection laws. When US president Bill Clinton decided in 1994, with pressure coming from many business interests to stop the policy of tying economic relations to human rights and environmental issues; that is when the green light was in fact given for the developing world to do this to us. Business interests won in this case, to the detriment of the working class in the western world, which had no choice but to follow the lead of the US for economic reasons, as is the case with the race to the bottom unleashed in taxation policies.

For decades now, our leaders have been engaging in a frantic race to improve global trade flows. Globalization was not just a means to improve the lives of millions across the world, as pro-globalization advocates correctly point out, given that hundreds of millions across the world did indeed benefit from global trade by getting a chance to join the global middle class, and many people even joined the millionaires or billionaires club. The increase in global trade flows has indeed facilitated this overall increase in global wealth. Aside from politicians serving the interests of a few very powerful individuals or corporations, who were the clear beneficiaries of what has transpired so far more than any other interest group, we have to realize that we more than anything had to move towards globalization due to circumstances. We made huge leaps in technological progress, and it was only possible to do so by drawing on a wider resource base, human and physical. We westerners were the main innovators thus far, but bringing many products to the market as fast as they penetrated it, was only made possible by making the prices of many of these goods affordable. Achieving that was possible thanks to cheap labor, and availability of many crucial resources, such as lithium and other minerals known as rare earths, which make technology such as hybrid car batteries and other wonders possible.

While recognizing the need for globalization in order to achieve the progress that humanity did so far, it is also sad that we have to acknowledge that we once again did things in a manner that addressed our needs and desires for the short to medium term, but did not think far enough into the future. It is at this point that we have to admit that by not listening to those advocating that trade deals be negotiated in a way that also would have addressed sustainability and human rights, we dug ourselves into a very deep hole. When asked by various activists, which some like to refer to as politically correct "granola munchers", whether they were ready to raise these issues, politicians mostly said that they would, but not condition trade deals on the above mentioned issues. By not dealing with the things that make them currently a very formidable competitor for capital attraction, thanks to the fact that we did not in the end demand that they deal with the above mentioned issues, we shot ourselves in the foot. Many talking heads characterized these crusaders for the greater global good as a nuisance who are trying to block human progress. Now that we are stuck dealing with the consequences of not having listened to them, we completely forgot the error of our ways. No one talks about the role, lower environmental and human rights standards play in attracting investments away from responsible societies, to the ones claiming, that since Europeans burned dirty coal to industrialize, they should now have their turn at damaging the environment as well.

The first victims of these policies that benefited the bottom line of many multinationals, and to some extent the poor of the developing world, were the lower skilled western workers. They suffered alone and largely ignored for about two decades, and then were joined by many high skill workers, many of whom had to face the humiliation of having to train their replacements from India, China or some other up and coming economic power. Small firms in our society, engaged in small-scale manufacturing or repairs, found it increasingly hard

251

to survive with products coming from cheap manufacturers from China. The wages paid someone to fix a product, as opposed to replacing it with a brand new one from China became in many cases a more expensive, less desirable alternative. The fact that an economic model based on discarding as quickly as possible an old product in favor of a new one is one that can create an unsustainable path for the world, escaped everyone's calculations. It also seems that governments failed to factor in the diminished capacity to collect revenues as fewer and fewer economic activities in our economy continue to remain viable. The service sector remained healthy, because as long as people were able to spend on credit, they were able to afford them, and service sector jobs are much harder to outsource. Now there is precious little left for us to compete on in the long-term. With a decline in economic activity, government is left with no hope of raising the needed revenues needed to cover their obligations.

Because of these trade policies, we have a high wage environment, but the opposite can be true when it comes to product quality unfortunately. Because of lower wages, factories in India, China and other low wage economies can afford to pay for the better patents, more quality control and to buy the better quality materials for their products. Western companies that try to compete in the market on price often skimp on those very vital inputs. I saw this personally when I decided to enter a Canadian textile factory warehouse in Winnipeg. Most products compared in price to import textiles sold in retail stores, but to my amazement, quality of workmanship and design of clothing was of inferior quality, and not at all in fashion.

In terms of productivity advantages, manufacturing ability per worker is not such a great advantage anymore either, because the workers of the developing world are almost as well equipped with physical tools, training and educations as their western counterparts are. The very narrow gap that currently exists, continues to narrow as the transfer of capital and knowledge progresses. The main result of all this is an increasing aversion on the part of major firms to build new manufacturing facilities in the US, Canada, or the EU. As I already mentioned, many companies only maintain production plants in the developed world because the need to have local producer credentials in many fields, like the auto sector. The increasing pricing pressures and the growing reliance of these companies on the developing world market will continue to erode the will of many companies to maintain factories here. The nature of the companies that helped build our standard of living is to maximize profits. The road to maximizing profits increasingly leads to Asia, and a few other locations outside the west.

As consumers, the importance of westerners is waning very fast. China is now the number one car market, number one cell phone market, and the number one computer and internet services market. The relatively heavily indebted western consumers, who are also stuck in mature, slow growing economies, cannot continue on their recent decade's trajectory of increasing leveraging. Real wages are stuck in a hold position, and recently, steady employment is hard to come by. The western consumer is in urgent need of de-leveraging. With manufacturing and consumers headed on a downward path for the foreseeable future, prospects of economic growth can be summed up as mediocre at best.

To make matters worse, there are global pressures on GDP growth potential caused by the cursed nature of our planet, which is that it is finite. I already expressed my personal opinion that a very crucial resource such as petroleum that most agree that we need, in order to sustain our economy, is in a production holding pattern at best, while the global economy needs it to grow. Given the current economic dynamics, it is to be fully expected for the developing nations to continue to cut into the share of energy being used globally. As there are very slim hopes of significant increases in supply, the only way that they will get what they need is to continue the very recent trend of pushing OECD consumption levels down, while the BRIC nations, the Middle East and other smaller players continue to increase their own consumption levels. A decreasing amount of raw materials available for our economy means declining economic activity. The only way to change this trend driven from multiple sources combining to cause the current trajectory is to act through the one unifying element at our disposal, mainly our elected governments. The question arises whether they are equipped to deal with these very real problems, that can potentially finish us of on the global stage as soon as 2020, and end all hope of us having a decent future at least, if not a bright one, which is very unlikely despite many political promises that suggest otherwise.

In order for our governments to have the ability to deal with these grave challenges that few can convincingly dispute that are in fact on our doorstep, they need to have resources. They need to have money to invest in new infrastructure needed to help us adapt to a much slimmer energy diet. We need to replace more road and air transport with rail transport, wherever feasible. Agricultural practices may have to be reversed to create more fossil input efficiency, by relying less on petrol and gas in the fertilizer and physical production process. The shortening of the distance traveled of the average food item also needs to be encouraged. In essence, a real decentralization needs to happen, turning away from factory farming that is costing us a great deal in environmental degradation, and general health of the human population. A more labor-intensive practice of farming will also help soak up an increasing volume of urban destitute that is already becoming an increasing feature of the urban lifestyle, even though we are just at the very beginnings of this trend. As unbelievable as a reverse in the urbanization trend sounds, it is increasingly equally stupefying to expect less than 5% of our western citizens to produce the bulk of the food we consume. If the current model were feasible for the long-run, then perhaps the massive farming subsidies would be unnecessary in propping up this system.

If we would have listened to the granola munchers many years ago, before we built this trading system that favors the hollowing out of government coffers, and a race to the bottom in human rights, and environmental protection, then perhaps we would not be in our current predicament. We would not be losing millions of jobs to less regulated countries who justify their abuses towards their people and the environment by pointing out the great strides they made in increasing prosperity for many in their society. Our governments would not be stuck with a smaller tax base due to the relatively lower wages that many who lost their higher quality jobs, and are now stuck working at McDonald's, or Wall-Mart are earning. More emphasis would have been put on reducing waste and improving efficiency, making the current commodities crisis a thing to worry about in a relatively distant future. Improving the rights of women in many countries would have done a lot to empower them to take control of their own reproductive life, which means that there might be a few hundred million fewer mouths to feed on this planet. It is really quite unfortunate that we failed to listen to those "granola munchers".

Are we already facing crisis? Is it too late?

A Malfunctioning society: The 2008 financial near-meltdown is only the first of many shocks to the system that should be expected to re-occur every few years in the near future, for reasons already given in our analysis of the financial system, investment trends and the natural resource situation. As the 2008 crisis did, future ones will also cost western governments far more than it did the developing nations. The many millions of newly unemployed have to be taken care of in order to prevent a social breakdown from occurring. Before the majority of these newly destitute can be soaked up into the labor force courtesy of some modest growth that will continue to occur following sharp downturns, new episodes of crisis will reverse the modest job growth gains and then some.

A vicious cycle is currently forming that will continue to cut into revenues flowing into government coffers, while costs of taking care of the increasing numbers of unemployed will continue to skyrocket. The US is currently running budget deficits in the 8-10% range and is forecast to more or less keep this average range for the rest of the decade. This forecast naturally assumes that the US economy will have robust average yearly economic growth of around 3-4% for the duration of this decade. Given the more recent trends, it is not outlandish to assume that the good periods will only register growth of 2-3%, or even less. There will most likely also be at least another down cycle lasting maybe two to three years that will see negative growth of perhaps as much as five percent, given that governments have few resources left to fight a recession like they did in the latest down cycle. It may be fashionable to underestimate the effect that government ramp up in deficit spending did for preventing a much deeper downturn, but it is highly unrealistic on the part of those who try to make it look like the government failed to help.

The combination of low growth and high deficit spending that looks to be inevitable at this point will increase the debt to GDP ratio in the next decade, leaving the governments vulnerable to outright catastrophe. Once the levels of debt are at certain heights, all it takes is a reassessment of risk levels that will cause the rates of borrowing to go much higher, at which point default through either outright cessation of payments, or through forced currency devaluation, leading to eventual hyperinflation is inevitable. If this seems like such an outlandish outlook on the current situation, especially since we are talking about many AAA rated nations, perhaps it is time to step back and reconsider a few things. Many of the sub-prime mortgages were also rated AAA by the same rating agencies, as we saw in the chapter on failed institutions. These ratings agencies can only keep a rating on an asset a certain way due to political considerations for so long, before their ratings reputation comes under increasing attack, endangering the credibility of all asset classes if a serious, and honest re-evaluation is not done on most assets, given the economic climate.

It is very important to understand the real cost of our governments incurring these debts in order to keep the economy afloat. Aside from yearly interest payments, which should increase even if rates remain very low, there is also the problem that we are likely to experience if economic growth does go into a robust phase. That is usually associated with a strong performance of the stock market, which siphons investment away from the bond market. If the debt to GDP ratio is very high, then we run the risk of higher deficits to cover the higher interest payments. This is despite the positive effect that economic growth would have on government revenues. There is of course also the possibility that government would keep deficits stable through spending cuts, but that can cause an economic slowdown that would otherwise be premature in the economic cycle.

Following the 2000-01 dot.com bust, half trillion-dollar budget deficits became the norm in the US, as a structural part of the economy for the rest of the decade. Spending less on the part of the US government would have meant a much deeper recession. Now that we are supposedly in another recovery following the housing and financial bust, there is a new structural yearly deficit, which is staring all in the face, which is roughly double, perhaps even more than double if economic growth will disappoint as it is currently looking to do. There is absolutely no doubt in my mind that when the next downturn will arrive, which can be anywhere from now to near 2020, the US government will be faced with two choices only. The first choice, which was the favorite one up to now, to stimulate a new recovery, where one was not supported by the fundamentals, and therefore had to be created and maintained through increased government borrowing, will be the most tempting. This first choice is inconceivable at this point given that the structural deficit will already fluctuate around the one trillion mark, or worse. The idea of a two trillion dollar structural deficit being accepted by the government and the markets is insanity. This choice would lead to extreme measures to devalue the currency in order to be able to deal with the large increase in debt.

The second choice as an alternative to the unrealistic deficit spending levels is similar to the one that is frowned upon by the students of the great depression, but is the more likely one to be taken due to circumstances. This is a very painful choice to have to make, especially in a society, which is no longer properly adapted to deal with harsh economic conditions, and it will likely be seen in hindsight similarly to the year 476, when Rome was sacked once again, and it officially ended the last remnants of an era. We are very likely to be just one more deep recession away from complete financial disaster in the western world, because it is now increasingly obvious that our government balance sheets can no longer resist another shock. A recession where a government is pulling back spending to match the drop in revenue, exactly when economic stimulus is needed, will most likely turn into depression.

European nations are not looking much better with average EU deficits running in the 7% range, and a recent effort to tighten the belt is being met with hostility from the masses and with lots of anxiety on the part of many Keynesian economists who feel that this is endangering the recovery. Some members of the EU are looking to be already beyond any long-term hope for recovery. The Greek debt crisis is the poster child of the overall problem faced by Europeans, but many others, such as Spain Portugal, Italy, Ireland, Britain, the Baltic States, Bulgaria, Romania and Hungary are all on shaky ground in terms of their fiscal situation. Even other nations that are not considered to be headed in a very negative direction currently have very large debt to GDP ratios, such as Belgium. Unlike the US, the EU is already weighing its choices, and acting to prevent further deterioration of the overall situation. Plans meant to reinforce the 3% deficit ceiling mandated by EU legislation by 2013 are forcing all European governments to restructure their economy.

It is unclear at this point whether they are likely to succeed, but given their other already mentioned structural advantages they poses, such as government programs that are fat, and relatively easy to trim, and a physical infrastructure such as better planned urban areas that will make economic hardships easier to bare, there is a possibility that they will. The EU economy is among the most energy efficient in the world. Their energy use per unit of GDP is only half that of the US. A decline in car ownership for example would affect the overall quality of life far less in a European town that is capable of providing public transport to 80% of its population compared to most American towns where most of them would be hard-pressed to provide it, even for half their residents.

The main danger to the Europeans is their lack of cohesion as a unit. Unlike the United States, the threat of an eventual ceasing of the union is just one major political disagreement away. In addition, there are the endless arguments in regards to relatively narrow interests that various members push within the union. The lack of ability to enforce cross union discipline is obvious from the fact that for years now the fines meant to discourage EU members from crossing the 3% deficit threshold have not been levied on the many countries that failed to comply over the last decade. Currently, only four or five nations in the entire 27-member union are able to bring their state budget in line with the rather restrictive 3% threshold. In the 17 member, Euro currency club within the EU there is the very real prospect of the relative health of the currency and the Euro denominated bond market becoming sort of a much used and abused public good, where some members will leave it to others to remain the pillars of stability. That role is currently being filled by Germany and a few other nations that are careful to prevent infrastructure and social programs from ballooning past the point of sustainability.

Recently, there was a great deal of dissatisfaction on the part of many German citizens who found themselves in the position of having to help bail out Greece, where the debt became unsustainable at a rate of 115% of GDP (After austerity measures, it is actually over 140%, and Greece has now effectively gone through default). Dissatisfaction in this case is very understandable because in Germany they are currently discussing raising the retirement age to 67, while in Greece they only raised it to 62 as an austerity measure in 2010, while previously it was 55 for many. Like all public goods, the health of the Euro and the Euro denominated bond market may become a good that soon no one will want to contribute to if it will repeatedly fall on the same shoulders to carry the burden. It is like having a public park in a city where only a small fraction of the population contributes to the cost of maintaining it, while everybody uses it nevertheless, despite many not having contributed to it[4].

Given the relative generosity of the European social programs in relation to the US system, which is completely devoid of any meaningful benefits to the average contributor to the budget, it is easy to imagine how the Europeans could get out of this in a much easier fashion. They can implement a higher retirement age wherever necessary, and cut maternity leave where it is more than one year. Millions within the EU are employed under the table; therefore, care should be taken to ensure that everyone pays their dues. There are also various social programs that encourage a culture of overdependence on government aid, which have to be looked at seriously. Some minor tax increases that target job exporters from the EU for instance can add more funds to their budgets. The overall situation is not that bad, if the will to solve these fiscal problems is to be found in the near future among the political ranks in Europe. Room to cut, combined with some modest room for tax increases, with increased efficiency in government operations and a good endowment of infrastructure that makes Europe one of the most efficient economies in the world can overcome the difficulties related to competition from the developing world. An aging population and a lack of domestic self-sufficiency in natural resources are however weighing them down. The current population is very hostile to many of these necessary changes, therefore without a better education of the masses in regards to the future; there is only a very slim chance that Europeans will avoid disaster.

The more painful decision that needs to be made within the EU organization is a reforming of the nature of EU membership itself. Generally, there are many preconditions that need to be met when joining the union as a new member. There are rules ranging from basic human rights principles, to financial responsibility. The regulations meant to deal with any of these potential sticking points are lacking in ways to reprimand those that break the laws and regulations and fail in the expectation of being responsible members of the union, once accepted as part of the club. The Greek example is just the most recent situation where a complete breakdown in member responsibility is currently threatening the very viability of the EU as an organization. To deal with such a lack of responsibility, and to prevent the re-occurrence of such situations, the EU has almost no levers at its disposal, in other words there is no real way to deal with it. When the Greek financial crisis came to the fore, the EU members realized that they were in fact on the hook for the toxic Greek bonds, and there was not much that they could do about it, except to pay up and shut up. The Greeks even had the audacity to attack the Germans over the historical past, suggesting that bailing them out was the least that the Germans could do in light of the wars of the 20'Th century. At this point, as in the recent past in regards to the behavior of other members, there were a few politicians in the EU who were asking themselves; why there is not a mechanism to suspend members who prove to be completely inconsiderate of the common good of the union?

The Europeans have some things going for them, which can be the difference between a complete collapse, or the eventual acceptance of a relatively more modest lifestyle, and an even more diminished global role. The United States of America, which is favored by financial analysts as a leaner, meaner global competitor, in reality has a lot further to go to deal with its shortcomings than Europe. The US government is running 8-10% structural budget deficits, yet they do not even provide a fraction of the social programs that Europeans are known for. By far the biggest social program that the US government provides is care for the retired and elderly. Social Security and Medicare make up almost half the US budget. As the population ages and arguably is also becoming more frail health wise, due to unhealthy life styles, this is going to be an increasing burden on US society. Unlike Europe, in the US very few social programs can be cut in order to meet other needs. The US has no maternity benefits and few healthcare obligations for those under the age of 65, which is the current retirement age. This retirement age level, in most cases is the limit of what can be expected of a person to contribute, especially given the many health problems that many face by then, and the fast-paced change in technology, finance and other fields that makes their knowledge and abilities obsolete in many cases.

The political right in the US generally favors cuts in the elderly programs that the majority depends on. The political mainstream still lacks the courage to come out clearly and state this, but their more radical wing, currently known as the Tea Party movement makes no effort to sugarcoat their stance. They want to do away with most government programs and regulations, even the ones that often relate to public safety. One of the main leaders of this loosely organized movement; Sarah Pallin, comes from Alaska, so perhaps she took the idea from the ancient Inuit tradition of allowing the elderly to expire by the campfire when they were no longer able to care for themselves. Trying to imagine a society that will allow its members to expire like that, just because they were not born in the few privileged families, flies in the face of any concept of human compassion. Incredibly, they increasingly manage to convince the very people that will be hurt, namely the poor and lower middle class that these sorts of schemes are a good idea.

In the event that the Palin movement, which Americans should thank senator McCain for making her part of the US political scene, will not grab power in the near future, there is still the issue of the over one trillion dollars in yearly deficits that Americans will have to deal with. The politically safe stance that most mainstream politicians in the US take is to condemn wasteful spending and earmarks. The reality is that most efficiency corrections and cuts in special earmarks will only save a hundred billion or so. The budget deficit for 2010 is roughly 1.3 trillion dollars, or almost 10% of GDP. The cuts in wasteful spending, and special earmarks, some of which are actually crucial infrastructure projects, will be a drop in the bucket and therefore not a real solution. The only true solution in the absence of the will to put out a large portion of the elderly into the cold, and leave them to their fate, is a tax rate increase. That may be easier said than done however as Americans are more allergic to paying taxes than Europeans are to cutting services.

Currently the total Federal taxation rate of the US economy is roughly 17% of GDP. Raising that rate to about 25% would take care of the bulk of the budget gap, and leave only a relatively healthy 1-2% deficit rate. The political support for such a move is non-existent, so this is very unlikely to happen. In a way, we cannot blame the American people for their aversion to taxation, because unlike their European counterparts, they seldom see that money benefiting them directly. In the past decade, they saw a large chunk of that money used to support two largely unnecessary wars. This lack of a real government safety net is the main aspect of American life that is responsible for the US not being the greatest country in the world when it comes to the overall standard of living.

Those two wars were largely unnecessary, but still supported by a large proportion of the population, and the same people support allocating about 15% of the total budget to military spending. The military budget is also heavily supported by the very strong roots it has in society. Weapons manufacturers and military bases are strategically placed all over the US, making it very hard for senators and congress members to support deep cuts in the military budget. The cessation of the military hardware industry would also unmask the real shape of manufacturing in the US. Without the many military programs, and the spin-off demand it creates from other industries, the US manufacturing base would be almost insignificant.

Given that the tax hikes are impossible to achieve politically, the other direction, of deep spending cuts will eventually prevail. When those cuts will be sufficient to redress the budget situation, the US will most likely have a standard of living similar to many developing nations such as Poland currently enjoys. Tea Partiers will argue that it will not be the case, because low taxes will lead to economic growth that will keep the masses happy, but they continue to rely on a presumptive hypothesis that given money to invest, companies will invest in the US. Recent evidence suggests that money availability plays no role in investing in the US as I already expressed. Companies that are currently sitting on large piles of cash, mainly earned from shutting down many unviable operations in the west, are not looking to re-invest here. They are simply waiting for the developing world to continue development opportunities to absorb this money. The very system that the Tea Partiers worship is one that favors the profit-maximizing firm. In this case, being patriotic and investing at home is not a profit maximizing solution. Deep budget cuts at this point will most likely have a downward spiraling effect on US economic development.

The Tea Party movement advocates the gutting of the already relatively flimsy US social safety net as a way to stimulate job creation, especially coming in the form of small and medium sized business reinvesting the money given to them through tax cuts, but the reality is that the opposite is likely to happen as a result. They leave out from their calculations a very important ingredient that is necessary to encourage job creation, which is especially crucial to small and medium sized local businesses. Unlike big business that tends to be very international, small business depends very much on local consumer demand. To date, none of the Tea Party elites, or their supporters asked themselves the important question of what will happen to consumer demand if the basic social safety net is gutted.

Remember what we established about the nature of wages, and how they tend to reflect individual immediate needs, rather than long-term needs. So, the expectation in my view should be that if individuals perceive that they have to take care of their own wellbeing later on in life, while their wages tend to only cover the perceived needs we have today, people will change their spending habits in such profound ways that the current way of life will be no more. Entertainment will be the first victim. People will switch to cheaper ways to entertain themselves, such as downloading movies, rather than going to the cinema. Restaurants will also suffer, because eating at home is much cheaper. These two items alone, if they were to see dramatic cutbacks would gut locally supported jobs, and let us not forget their vicious cycle effect.

Cutting back on entertainment would not be the end of it either. Two car households might become one-car households. Dealerships and mechanic shops would likely suffer. Home maintenance, decoration, and upkeep would be cut back drastically. People might buy fewer clothes, and make their wardrobe last longer. The list of cutbacks that most would likely engage in is literally endless, and the end result is that all who have a job that is dependent on local consumer demand would be affected. The resulting job loss and lack of demand, which would likely force business to cut wages, would result in a feedback effect, whereby the resulting lower income coming in for most families would make people cut back even more. The last time such a cycle took root, it took a world war to break it. I'm not exactly sure what it would take this time, because another world war is certainly not an option given our ability as humanity to auto-destruct.

The Tea Party cry for all power from the government to the markets is possibly the most misguided policy idea since living memory at least. They want to transfer power to Wall Street companies that increasingly only desire the hollowing out of the west and pushing into debt the government and "main street" Americans. The intentions of the ones with the financial capital are clear as day. For many such companies, the main markets are no longer the US, but rather China, India, Brazil and a few dozen smaller countries that are currently on a tear, economically speaking. The interest of companies such as GM and Caterpillar is increasingly for these trends to continue. As such, US continuation of its policies is imperative. If the trends will not continue however, the next best thing will be to transform the US into a country that will be as competitive as China, as soon as possible.

The competitive aspect sounds good at first, until one looks at the details of what that means. Wages will have to drop considerably for the average worker. The average family income today of roughly $50,000 per year will become something more like $20,000 per year. Medicare, Medicaid, Social Security and any other social safety nets need to disappear. EPA, FDA and other protection measures meant to regulate firms are equally harmful to competitiveness; therefore, they can only exist on paper. Worker protection measures will become a thing of the past as well, because it is such a hindrance to think of their safety, health concerns related to work related exposure to things, and those nasty rules on having to pay them overtime, provide health insurance and other headaches. Public schools are not in the constitution either. If those things, which the Tea Party movement detests, are gone, there will be a good chance that the budget will get balanced, and manufacturing will become almost as profitable in the US as in China or India. There is still one big difference however. The combined government and personal debt will remain, and on a debt to GDP ratio scale, it will become insurmountable. When the average family in the US will only earn $20,000 per year, the GDP level of the country will be cut by half. A fast crumbling infrastructure is generally also not conducive to a desire on the part of business to invest. This is something that did happen in the great depression, but back then, people and governments had far less debt.

Taking stock of what western politicians have on offer for us as the main solutions to our economic problems, I came to the conclusion that between the current left and right of our political spectrum all paths may seem very different, but they all end in the same place. That place I called death, because social collapse in both cases resembles a terminal disease. The disease may be different, but the fact that they both lead to death remains the constant.

The current brand of politicians in power offers us death by cancer, which is perhaps in some ways better than the massive heart attack that would have already finished us off, if the only serious alternative in the form of the US Tea Party would have been in power a few years back when the economic crisis started. Radiotherapy as well as chemo might not be very pleasant, and it is doing damage to the body, but at least we are still alive, and as long as that may be the case, there is always hope in the form of a miracle cure. Instead of chemo and radiotherapy, the current government engages in fiscal and monetary stimulus to prevent us from going under. At some point however, the prolonged effects of cancer treatment will make the body unresponsive to it, and the cumulative damage to the body may become too much to bear.

We may fail, but let us at least try

Comparing the Tea Party proposals and the option of staying with status quo ideas, with the one I put forward, in the form of the sustainability tariff, it is becoming clear that the political system and environment, within which we currently operate, does not stand much of a chance to produce any solutions of positive relevance to our current problems. The strongest alternative to the status quo in the US is in fact a group that offers nothing but an accelerated path towards economic disaster. Their government shrinking policy suggestions would do nothing except to speed up the process of the hollowing out of their country, in favor of taking the capital out from there to chase other markets with better prospects. My proposal on the other hand would bring back a healthier economic situation, including a chance to create new industries that can produce goods needed across the globe. We westerners are still the most innovative culture on the planet; therefore, we can easily introduce new products on the global market as long as there is potential investment for us to produce those goods. The redressing of the economy, fueled by the manufacture of new products, with new and improved techniques would not erase the giant deficits overnight, but give it a decade or so, and we could free ourselves from this vicious cycle. Despite the obvious advantages of my proposal, there is currently no political movement anywhere that is actively proposing this or any other solutions that would have an actual chance to correct our current wrong economic path.

To do this, we need the opposite of what Tea Partiers and like-minded counterparts in Europe are proposing. We need a strong government to steer us in the right direction. We need the investments in research, education and infrastructure, just like US president Obama often states. The difference is that with the level playing field in trade that my tariff idea would encourage, there would also be money available to achieve those things. We have to recognize that without the means to get things done; passionate rhetoric on ushering in the new economy, as Obama is known for will remain only rhetoric.

Developing nations would cease to pursue an exclusively export based development of their economy, with their internal consumers playing only a secondary role. They would have no choice, as they would be faced more and more with an increasingly competitive developed world, so they would have to also change the way they do things. This change would have to include a turn away from corrupt practices of the past, which is highly characteristic of the countries that are using their low wage, no regulation status as a substitute for clean, competent leadership. In a more competitive environment, everyone would have to do better than they are doing now, and therein I put my hopes for a decent future for us westerners and for human kind.

Part 4

Importance of culture for survival and relative success

As I already mentioned, I was born in Ceausescu's communist Romania, one of the most brutal, nationalist and closed regimes in Europe, during the cold war era. I was ten years old when the regime collapsed. My family moved to Canada when I was thirteen, and that is where I lived most of my life. My wife, who is originally from Romania and I, currently live temporarily in The United States, because she secured a post-doctoral position here, which we could not renounce. I am also ethnically Hungarian, so between all these experiences, interacting within these various places and backgrounds, I managed to observe many subtle cultural differences, and as I apply these observations to understanding the reasons for different ways that all these cultures I experienced so far, adapt to the global economic environment, I am becoming more and more convinced that we need to stop focusing on the much needed technological revolution, to save us from our current economic predicaments. We need a new leap in cultural development. We need something that would rival the European Enlightenment era; because anything less means that we are very likely to face disaster in the near future, given the sad state of our economic affairs, as I illustrated in previous chapters.

When faced with a great challenge, nothing is more important for society than to have within it the right values needed to adopt the right path. If those values are missing, then there needs to be enough wisdom to identify the right path, and the cultural elasticity to re-adapt society's values and views in order to be able to form the appropriate consensus. To better illustrate these points, I chose an example from the former communist countries of Eastern, and

Central Europe, where countries recently had to adapt to the post communist reality, which started more than twenty years ago, following the collapse of communism. Some countries fared better than others in these past twenty years of re-adaptation, and there have been many reasons already proposed to why this might be so. I am of the opinion that the root cause of why some countries were less able to adapt than others stems from their cultural inheritance, which is contradictory to the currently dominant theory that the infrastructural inheritance is the main factor. The cultural factors that I identified, which are not the sole explanation for the relative failure to adapt of some people living in the region, might be surprising to most, and most likely a very much disliked explanation for most who consider themselves part of these cultures, which is not to say that it may not be accurate.

Given the lessons that we westerners can learn by examining a situation that most are relatively unconcerned about, I decided to include this comparison. Most westerners do not have many preferences towards where the blame for failure needs to lie in this particular case; therefore we can stand a better chance to remain impartial. Maybe we can learn to appreciate the lessons we can learn from the folly of many unwise decisions made by these countries in the past twenty years, which are mainly due to their cultural perceptions, which promote a view of current reality that can be highly distorted and devoid of proper perspective. Using that part of the world as a reference, we can identify our own misguided decisions, and more importantly, we can start talking about the true meaning of the events we have seen so far, and what this all tells us about the most likely scenario for our future.

In undertaking this exercise in cultural analysis we can draw our conclusions in regards to whether we are capable of coming up big as a society in demonstrating that we can recognize our true challenges, and once we admit that we have these problems, we have within us the ability to work through them. If we do not, then we have to realize the consequences, and start thinking of our own individual well being within a new world order. To do that, we should be conscious of what are the things that are likely to remain of value from the debris, and make sure that we have a claim on those possessions.

10

The former communist states of Eastern Europe

(A case study of the difference that cultural norms make in adapting to the economic environment and the difference that some seemingly irrelevant facts, from an economist's point of view can make in how well a country's economy does.)

To illustrate the power culture has to influence a society's economic well being; I decided to use the example of the varying differences in success that East European countries had in re-adapting themselves to a democratic and free market system following the collapse of communism more than 20 years ago. To simplify the example somewhat, I excluded all former soviet nations, although the inclusion of these countries would not change the overall trend, just the complexity of the argument. To further bring insight and clarity, I took advantage of the fact that I was born in Romania, which is one of the countries that did not adapt very well in the past twenty years. As I mentioned already, I am ethnically Hungarian, and Hungary is one of the countries that did somewhat better with its transition to a market economy relative to Romania and a few other countries. Being familiar with both countries which for cultural reasons that I shall explain, belong in two different categories in terms of their adaptive success, gives me unique insight into what are the factors that made the difference. I should also admit that there is undoubtedly a measure of bias which possibly altered my conclusions, which is unfortunately natural, even though I tried to stay as objective as possible. I will focus my comparison on these two countries as a case study.

To start, we have to recognize that not all countries started from an even playing field economically speaking, but nevertheless, culture seems to have played a bigger role in their current situation and future outlook. In comparing some of these countries, I refer to

270

the per capita GDP rankings that measure overall wellbeing of the population, as well as the relative level of economic development of a country. The latest year that is available publicly is the 2010 ranking of nations. To illustrate the effect of culture on the economy, I decided to compare the development in the past 20 years of former communist states to see the difference between Balkan nations compared to non-Balkan nations. In this case, the Balkan nations are represented by; Bulgaria, Romania, Serbia, Macedonia, Bosnia-Herzegovina, Montenegro, and Albania. Croatia and Slovenia are sometimes included in the Balkan category due to their former Yugoslav past, thanks to the redrawing of the regional map after the end of the first world war, but historically speaking, for many reasons that I will discuss in detail they are culturally in fact non-Balkan, central European countries. The other central European nations, besides the two above mentioned former Yugoslav states, are Hungary, Slovakia, The Czech republic, and Poland. Incredibly, there is a very clear demarcation line, between Balkan and non-Balkan nations in terms of their position in the GDP per capita rankings, with absolutely no overlap.

According to the IMF, Slovenia has the highest per-capita GDP in this group, with $28,000. Slovenia is ranked 31'Th in the world in this ranking. From the non-orthodox, non-Balkan nations, Croatia is the poorest former communist state, with a GDP per capita of $17,700. Croatia ranks 48'Th globally. Slovakia, Czech Republic, Hungary and Poland all fall in-between, within this range. The highest ranked Orthodox-Muslim, former communist, Balkan country is Bulgaria, which comes in at 65 on the global rankings, with a GDP per capita of $12,800. The poorest member of this group comes in at 95'Th place, with a GDP per capita of $7,400, and that state is Albania. Romania, Serbia, Macedonia, Montenegro and Bosnia all fall in-between. As we can see, not only there is no overlap, but the difference between the poorest, mainly Catholic former communist state in Europe and the Richest Orthodox state is rather significant.

The obvious lack of overlap in rates of development and standard of living cannot be denied. The relatively level starting point is not as easy to argue; after all, it is hard to compare Czechoslovakia in 1990, with Romania in many respects. The Czechs have a much closer proximity to the western markets, they were also technologically far more advanced. Romania did have the one advantage over most of these countries, which was its debt free status, but that advantage evaporated very fast. Various former Yugoslav countries also suffered the ravages of a nasty war in the 1990's, now known as the war in the Balkans. One of the countries hardest hit by this war was in fact Croatia, despite that it is firmly entrenched in the central European camp in its level of development, as should be expected, given that culturally they are not a Balkan state, even though politically it belonged there when it was part of the former Yugoslavia. Overall, one finds more similarities than differences in the level of development and circumstances among Central European and Balkan countries, than there are differences at the starting point in 1990.

Similarities that were advantageous as a good starting point for all east European nations, Central Europeans and Balkan nations alike, were in fact many. A well-educated workforce goes right to the top of my list. On balance, east European workers were as capable in terms of technical skills as their western counterparts were. Finance may have been one exception as east European accountants and economists were educated within the centrally planed economic system. East European schools continued to perform relatively well throughout the 90's in comparison to their western counterparts. Some obvious exceptions are some of the war torn areas in the Balkans. The second most important advantage in my view is the physical infrastructure that all these countries inherited, such as rail lines, highways, ports, airports, and means of industrial production. Although some inheritances were more, obsolete than others in this instance.

Arguably, the third most relevant advantage is their proximity to a body of nations that have shown remarkable success in ensuring regional stability since the end of the Second World War. The benefits of this proximity are evident in such countries as Greece, the Balkan country I left out of the discussion, because it escaped the fate of the other Balkan nations of being a Soviet satellite, due to its political position as a country firmly embedded in the western sphere of influence during the cold war. Greece was ranked 28'Th in the IMF, per capita GDP ranking, which makes it the exception to the no higher than 65'Th rule that the rest of the Balkans falls under by that ranking. Part of the relatively high ranking can be attributed to the historical endowment of the ruins of the ancient world, which makes it a natural tourist magnet, together with its tropical climate, and many beaches. The other part is obviously thanks to Greece's economy being dragged along by the fast-paced growth and stability that Europe has enjoyed.

Interestingly, if one compares Greece to the other states that enjoyed freedom in Europe after the Second World War, they did not do very well either in terms of their development. Despite all those advantages, somehow, Greece has managed to miss the opportunity to build a solid base for their economy, and they are now the sick man of Europe. Aside from the US collapse of the sub-prime mortgage market, Greece has been the biggest threat to global financial stability during this latest crisis. In the absence of an international, IMF led bailout, Greece would now be insolvent, especially because devaluation is not an option for them, given their use of the Common Euro currency. The austerity measures that have to be implemented in Greece are certain to drag it down many notches in their GDP ranking in the coming years. This proves that the third element that is in the favorable column for these still developing western nations from Eastern Europe is no guarantee of long-term economic success. In fact, there is a case to be made for the hypothesis that joining the EU is a dangerous thing for countries that are not entirely ready to be members. Greece's joining of the common currency may be just one such situation.

The main structural disadvantages of these nations are also shared in a large measure. The main disadvantage in my view is that all of these countries failed to keep up with technological innovation starting from the 70's, until the communist system's final collapse. Here, a slight advantage has to be acknowledged to have benefited the central European states. Poland, Hungary, Czechoslovakia, and the Western part of Yugoslavia made up of Slovenia and Croatia, which were more advanced technologically than Romania, Bulgaria, Albania and the Balkan half of Yugoslavia; namely, Serbia, Montenegro, Macedonia and Bosnia-Herzegovina. As I mentioned already however, I am of the opinion that Romania for instance may have been more technologically impaired in comparison with its central European neighbors, but it was also debt free, and I should also mention that it is perhaps the richest in natural resources. If we take things in greater detail, we also have to acknowledge the fact that Serbia for instance was not really all that far behind technologically compared to Hungary, Croatia or Slovakia. When all is put into balance, at least some of the Balkan nations should have been capable to develop as well as the central European countries, which themselves it can be argued could have done somewhat better in transitioning to the market economy.

The other main aspect of the situation communally faced by the transitioning east Europeans in 1990 is the lack of developed institutions in place meant to deal with many of the new challenges posed by free market economics. Here, there are some countries, which were at a definite disadvantage even compared to their peers, but again there is no clear central Europe/Balkan divide. The main institution in place that was needed to be more successful in transitioning was the general familiarity and similarity to a market economy. In the former states of Yugoslavia, there was a great deal of familiarity with the market economy. Small businesses were in existence before the 1990's, and collectivization never occurred on a large scale. That is actually better than Hungary Poland and Czechoslovakia where with the exception of Poland, there was full collectivization, and private business ownership was almost non-existent. Romania on the other hand was perhaps the most centralized and controlled state by the end of the brutal Ceausescu regime.

My Grandfather is the only person who I know to have in fact been running a small self-employment operation in Romania during that period. He built a paprika grinder in the countryside in the western region of Banat to provide this service to the many peasants who were growing the peppers in their small plots of land awarded to them for personal use. Some of the farmers were able to sell a few kilograms of the spice on the market to city dwellers, and that is as far as private entrepreneurship went in Romania during that period. I am not personally very familiar with the Eastern part of Romania, but from most accounts, there was far less freedom in that part of the country than in the more multi-ethnic regions of Transylvania and Banat in the west of the country. Aside from a segment of the population in the west that felt that their historical place is in the west as a culture, Romania was possibly the most unprepared to embrace the market economy from all the countries in question, with the possible exception of Albania.

The industrial and agricultural capacity in Romania was effectively run as one large conglomerate, controlled from Bucharest. That is in contrast to the situation in Hungary to the west, where by the end of the 80's industrial entities were still government owned, but were being managed as independent entities in a similar fashion to private enterprises in a market economy. In this instance, there is a clear advantage that a Central European country had over a Balkan counterpart, but again I should stress that Romania was one of the richest in resources and started off the restructuring process debt free, while Hungary was the most indebted nation in the region as a percentage of GDP.

The rest of the differences that led to this discrepancy among countries belonging to two different geographic and cultural regions aside from the relatively small ones already identified are certainly cultural. There is no other way to explain that all members in one region developed without exception better than all members of the other region in question. The most obvious difference that I chose to focus on is religion, because it is the main cultural feature, which separates the two regions. Religion is rather obvious to those who know anything about the history of Europe and religion's effect on its development. The reformation is perhaps the most important factor that shifted economic power from the Mediterranean to the north of Europe centuries ago. The link between the rise of Holland, England, and eventually Germany towards the end of the medieval period and the protestant revolt against papal rule is clear as day. Protestant culture was clearly more dynamic than the Old Catholic culture. A clear divide developed then between the mainly protestant cultures I mentioned above and mainly Catholic countries, such as Italy, Spain, and etc[1]. Assuming that current Orthodox Christian culture may have some drawbacks compared to the mainly Catholic countries of central Europe is not therefore a bad place to start our analysis of what may be responsible for the wide differences observed in per capita GDP.

The Turkish Ottoman occupation and rule to some extent is also responsible for diluting the western values and attitudes that allowed

Europe to rise to the top of the global pecking order in the past 500 years. It cannot be denied that wherever Ottoman occupation was of longer duration, typical European culture could not penetrate. There is very little evidence that Renaissance culture that started in Italy in the 1300's was present at all in the Balkan region that was occupied by the Ottomans as long as Ottoman occupation was present. In some parts of the Balkans, the occupation lasted until the beginning of the twentieth century. The fact that Hungary and Croatia, which also had a period of Ottoman occupation as part of their history, are laggards in economic development, compared to their central European peers, is also an indication that Ottoman occupation has likely affected culture in the region in a negative way.

Aside from the fact that I was born in Romania, so I am quite familiar with the way people think and analyze things, I also met many people from the former Yugoslavia region, and must admit that the absence of Renaissance thinking is definitely there. Western elites were discussing ideas coming from Voltaire, Russo, Hobbes, Adam Smith as well as the classical period thinkers, a few hundred years ago. The discussions, arguments and analytical thinking evolved from there into what it is today. There were no such thinkers in the Balkan region. The conversation never took place. The result as I noticed it is that on social issues especially, they tend to reject complex arguments. They like to keep things far more simple by bunching issues together, and neglecting to differentiate circumstances.

There are many examples that I can think of, where arguments are reduced to a far more simple equation. One that is personal to me is in regards to the ethnic Hungarian minority that lives in the regions of Transylvania and Banat. Romanians generally try to equate the way that they should be treated, with the rights of immigrant communities living in North America or Western Europe. Those communities do not receive any special rights, such as the right to an education in their own language, regional autonomy, or any other such privileges, so why should Hungarians. They are living in Romania, they therefore should learn in Romanian according to the view of the majority there. The fact that the region where they live was only awarded to Romania in 1918, and the Hungarians who lived there for 1100 years were never asked if they wanted to be part of Romania is left out of the conversation. They conveniently neglect to also mention that in most circumstances in Europe, North America, and even elsewhere, where there is a historical minority in place, such as the French Canadians, they have far more rights and avenues to preserve their culture and cohesion than Hungarians in Romania do.

The inability to differentiate between a historical minority and a migrant one that chose to move to a new country, and therefore should rightfully accept the conditions they find, extends into most other areas of discussion. They fail to see the difference in why a Rroma (gypsy) child is unlikely to achieve a high level of education, given their background; because after all, school is in theory as accessible to them as it is for the majority Romanians. The fact that they were kept as slaves until 150 years ago, and when they were freed, they were never given a real chance to integrate by the state as well as the people, is also not part of the conversation, because that would raise a host of issues, including having to discuss their historical misbehavior. This is an issue that they should pay particular attention to, because the Rroma minority, which probably makes up roughly 10% of the country's population. They have a birthrate that far exceeds that of the majority, which is in fact rapidly shrinking thanks to a birthrate of 1.2 per woman, and a fast-paced outmigration of the youth population.

This lack of eagerness to analyze an issue more in debt also extends to questions of economics and its relationship to the state. There is a serious problem of corruption within the ranks of public servants. The simple argument goes that they steal because they are corrupt, so what is needed is to elect some people who are not. Many argue (wrongly) that all over the world, public officials are equally dirty, thus excusing the dirty nature of public employees, starting from the central government, and ending with a gate keeper at a school dorm, who also asks for his kickback. Few people, even from among the higher educated classes tend to accept any argument that relates to how the administrative system as it is set up is in large part responsible for a large portion of the corruption cancer that eats their country. I tried often to point out to many people, that the highly centralized administrative system that concentrates most revenues into the hands of the central government, and only then is in part re-distributed to regional officials can lead to a conflict of interest. This is especially true given that the funds flow back to regional councils mainly on an ad-hoc basis, rather than by utilizing a redistributive formula, such as the kind used in Canada's system of fund transfers. The most common response I received was that local officials are corrupt as well, so there is no point delegating more revenue raising power to them from the central authorities.

I tend to disagree with such an argument, because I believe that the best way to reduce corruption as well as inefficiency in administration is to make the link of responsibility as clear and as direct as possible. Imagine a Romanian council member asked to make a decision on building a new bridge in the county. Two private contractors enter a bid. One costs $10 million, the other $20 million. The $10 million bid comes with no kickbacks, and is overall more efficient. They will also create 100 jobs for the four year duration of the project. The $20 million bid comes with a fat kickback, and is less efficient, as such it will in fact provide for 200 local jobs. The money to finance the project comes in large part from the central government, so it makes little difference to an official elected locally, how much the project costs. The kickback does make a difference to his/her personal bottom line, and there is also the matter of the extra 100 jobs created, which provides more political capital for a possible re-election to the local council. By sharing a chunk of the kickbacks with legal entities, as well as central government representatives, the local officials can make sure that the money will be allocated from the central coffers, and no inquiry will be forthcoming to investigate why the more expensive bid was chosen. There is nothing to lose by being corrupt in this case, by neither party. Given that firms tend to gain access to the contracts by being able to offer kickbacks, they stop concentrating on efficiency altogether, and make sure to network with public officials instead.

The problem with presenting a description of such a long chain of causes to the problem is that people tend to black out, and that is more so the case within Balkan people than with others. The only solution left to deal with corruption, and mismanagement either willful, or through incompetence is to try to catch them. That however only happens on rare occasions, because the whole network of public officials is corrupt, or simply unwilling to stand up to the system for fear of reprisals in the form of job loss, or worse. In such an environment, the best solution would be a de-centralization, where local officials would have to secure funds for their projects in large part from local tax levies. At least this would give local officials an incentive to fight for efficiency, because we all know that people resent taxes, especially so if they see the money squandered. Any official hoping for re-election would want to do the best with the money collected from locals. This would be on top of the fact that local politicians would finally be able to try local strategies for development, which is generally the best reason to have a more decentralized system of governance.

There is of course the other reason that people tend to dismiss this idea, especially if it comes from me, or any other individual of my ethnicity. I am ethnically Hungarian; therefore, any talk of a more decentralized system as a way forward usually brings about a very hysteric reaction on the part of most Romanians. The charge is that we (Hungarians) want to tear the country apart, or that we want to create a country within a country. It is true that most ethnic Hungarians living in Romania want to see a more decentralized system, where they can have more influence on a local scale. Despite a sustained effort on the part of the Romanians to assimilate and colonize Transylvania and Banat, where roughly half the population was non-Romanian at the time when it was awarded to them at the end of World War One, there is still a relatively large Hungarian presence in some parts of Transylvania. Some counties like Harghita and Covasna, still have a Hungarian majority, while in others, they make up in some cases somewhere between 20-40% of the population.

This underscores the fact, which is that while ideas on social and economic issues, which the era of enlightenment produced in Europe, never penetrated the Balkans; there is one ideal, which did penetrate, despite the continued presence of the Ottoman Empire. The ideal is that of nationalism, and its deep penetration within Balkan society is due in large part thanks to the Orthodox faith. The Orthodox Church embraced this ideal, by embedding itself into it through its one feature that sets it apart from other Christian movements. The effect of it is still very powerful today, setting Balkan nationalism apart in its flavor and some may argue also in its intensity from nationalism brands found in other cultures.

All Balkan countries are majority Orthodox Christian, or a mix of mainly Orthodox and Muslims. It is a religion that differs from Catholicism in some ways, most of which is largely irrelevant to our discussion, albeit very interesting in some ways. To name a few of some of the more obvious ones are the attitude towards marriage, where the Catholic Church forbids it for its priests, while the Orthodox Church actually requires it as a prerequisite of becoming a priest. There are some other differences, such as differing beliefs in iconoclasm, where the Orthodox believe in the power of religious images, while the Catholics see the images officially as only teaching tools, although many of the faithful from the Catholic ranks in reality seem to have a deeper relationship with iconoclasm. Other than differences of this variety, there is one major and very important difference in the hierarchical structure of these two Christian denominations. The Catholics have one international structure, and therefore do not look at ethnicity or nation states as important aspects of their existence. The Orthodox Church on the other hand is a national church, in other words the Romanian Orthodox Church is a completely different and almost unrelated entity to the Serbian Orthodox Church. This very important difference has played a major role in creating very deep cultural divides between the Balkan nations and the Central Europeans, who are majority Catholic, with some Protestant influence.

At first glance, one might think that such a difference may not play such an important role in the collective cultural psyche of a nation, which would lead to differences in economic development. As a person of Hungarian ethnicity, born in Romania (also married to a Romanian), I had the benefit of observing both cultures, as I speak both languages fluently. For that reason, I will focus on comparing these two countries, since I am most familiar with their situations. One observation over the years that I made is how this changes the way that people see themselves in terms of their identity. At first glance, looking at the recent history of both peoples, one can easily see that both nations have a very strong sense of national identity, and both are certainly capable of exhibiting strong nationalist tendencies. The biggest difference is the source, and that makes the whole difference in how it manifests itself. In the case of Romanians, as is the case with all other Balkan Orthodox Christians, the church is a major source, while the Hungarian brand of nationalism is more ethnocentric oriented, similarly to west European brands.

Romania & Hungary

Hungarian national self-identity is rooted in history, and mainly shaped by the events. Hungarians (Magyars), arrived and settled into the Carpathian Basin in 895AD, by most accounts. Between the years of 1000 and 1500 AD, they played a major power role on the European scene. The kingdom of Hungary comprised in addition to modern day Hungary, also Croatia and Slovakia as vassal peoples who where not really conquered, but they saw a benefit to their safety by becoming a part of a bigger entity. The regions of Transylvania and, Banat, which is where I was born, and which are currently part of Romania, were also a part of the Hungarian kingdom until 1918. These regions have a very complex history, and few are willing to tell it with honesty. For our purposes, it is sufficient to know that its ethnic makeup has changed almost constantly in the past 1000 years, and it has changed perhaps most dramatically in the past 90 or so years, since it became part of Romania. Additionally, there are some significant lands that were lost to Serbia, and Ukraine, where some Hungarians still live today as a result of being on the losing side of the First World War.

Given the grand historical past of the Hungarians in the medieval period, which puts it on par with the other great kingdoms of that period, it is very hard to swallow the current situation, where Hungary has in fact become a rather insignificant country, relatively speaking. Three main, disastrous events shaped this current situation. First, there was the Mongol invasion, in 1241, when roughly half the population of Hungary was massacred. As a result, the Hungarian king decided to settle some of the more heavily depopulated regions such as Transylvania with Saxons, Cummans and Romanians (Romanians dispute this version of events). The second event that contributed to its current situation is the defeat at Mohacs in 1526, where the king of Hungary was killed, and a prolonged civil war ensued, with the

Ottomans and the Habsburgs both picking sides, which decimated large areas of the kingdom. Freedom was first tasted in 1918, but only for two thirds of the Hungarian population, as large parts of the former kingdom were distributed among Hungary's neighbors as a result of the French vision of an East European group of natural allies for its next confrontation with the defeated Germans. Hungarians were seen as natural allies of the Germans; therefore, they tried to make the new Hungarian state as weak as possible. Because of this, one third of the ethnic Hungarians ended up living as a minority in another country.

It is this loss of territory and more crucially one third of the ethnic Hungarian population, some of which was justified but some of it was not; on the principles of ethnic boundaries, that shapes most nationalist views among Hungarians. The subsequent, constant oppression and humiliation that most of the three million Hungarians living as a minority have had to endure as an ethnic minority is also a big part of it. This also shapes their sense of who they are historically. A people who could have been more, but were dealt a raw deal due to the political and strategic interests of others, and the predatory attitude of its neighbors. The result of this is a sense of national trauma that has befallen the Hungarian people. Among the Hungarians living as a minority, there is a sense of having to preserve their identity at all costs, not unlike the attitude of many Jewish communities spread throughout the world. Among the Hungarians of Hungary, there is a frustrating sense that they live in a neighborhood surrounded by potential enemies. Ironically the enemies were created by others, through the awarding of lands to its neighbors, which included areas inhabited by ethnic Hungarians as the majority population. There is the frustrating feeling that they are no longer strong enough to take on these newly created enemies, in order to bring justice for themselves or to defend the Hungarians living across the borders.

Romanians have a completely different view o themselves through history, because they claim their historical heritage far beyond a point that can clearly be traced as historical fact. They see themselves as the inheritors of Dacian history and culture, which takes their origins myth back to more than two thousand years in the region. Here, the church comes in and helps by claiming that it can trace its roots back to the first century AD, when the apostle Andrew Christianized the Dacians (who the Romanians claim as their ancestors along with the Roman settlers, who were settled there by the Empire once Dacia became a Roman province)[2]. As such, the Romanian Church and Romanian ethnic identity are given parallel paths as far back as two thousand years. There is very little evidence that such a population lived in present day Romania during the early medieval period, between 400 and 1100 A.D. Most archeological evidence points to mainly Slavic, Germanic, and various Asiatic inhabitants of present day Romania during that period. The presence of the Latin speaking Vlachs, living south of the Danube in present day Bulgaria, Serbia, Macedonia, Greece during that period, in addition to evidence of migration by these people north, plays no role in Romanian's view of themselves[3]. Presently, the theory of continuity of the Daco-Romans is supported by the presence of Christian artifacts from this period, which automatically is accorded to belong to the proto-Romanians, despite ample evidence of Christian missions to the Germans and Slavs during that period. Here the church again helps to reinforce nationalist myth.

The migrating peoples that settled the region during the early medieval period, including the ones that are still represented today in the ethnic makeup of present day Romania are seen as mainly a nuisance that interfered with Romania's manifest destiny. Ironically, there is ample evidence that shows that a nomadic group from the East known as the Cummans may have founded the first two Romanian principalities. They may have in fact been the population that formed the bulk of their nobility in the medieval period. This is a theory, which has been embraced by very few Romanian historians, such as Neagu Djuvara, but the vast majority is still vehemently opposed to any such suggestions. It seems that they not only strive to purge their sacred land of foreign elements, they also have to do so with their history books.

The relative backward nature of the country is also often attributed to the migrant peoples of the first millennia, of their supposed existence as a nation, because their pure civilized European qualities were corrupted. That view is especially ironic, given that the most advanced regions that eventually formed present-day Romania were in fact Transylvania and Banat, which up until 1918 were mainly under Hungarian and German influence. This false view of history, has an overall negative view that Romanians have towards all things foreign, including the one and a half million Hungarians living in western Romania. Despite having roots of over 1000 years on the land they inhabit, they are still talked of as migrants from the Asian steppe (which is also historically false due to a confusion of Hungarian origins as the antecessors of the Huns). If one traces this one thing alone back to the past twenty years and looks at how it affected the transition period from Communist rule to a market economy, it shows what a difference the evolution of Romanian's sense of their own identity has made in regards to their recent economic situation, due to decisions they made as a result.

Going back to December 1989, when an ethnic Hungarian priest and his followers sparked the revolution in the city of Timisoara in the Banat region, there was already a negative reaction towards Hungarians, because of the simple fact that, it was a Hungarian, who has affected their "sacred path". Only a few months after the revolution ended, which overthrew one of the most brutal regimes in Europe, its main spark, pastor Laszlo Tokes was attacked as a traitor, especially after he denounced the past crimes committed against Hungarians by a very nationalist communist regime, which strived to erase Hungarian identity in Romania completely. As the Hungarian minority started to demand that some of the past deeds, such as closing down Hungarian language schools, and erasing of their history and culture be reversed, it ended with Romanian spirits heating up, manifesting itself in a brutal Romanian backlash in the city of Tirgu Mures (Marosvasarhely). In March 1990, the Hungarian community there was attacked by armed peasants bussed in by some radical organizations, with the support of the Romanian authorities. The street fights that followed were broadcast internationally, making Romania look like an unstable country, more in line with what one might expect from an African post colonial state, newly formed along the lines of former colonies. Similar, and in most cases far more brutal events marked the rest of the Balkans as many may remember during the 1990's.

The economic impact of this was visible in the way that serious investors, such as car and machinery manufacturers and others, largely stayed away from Romania, during the better part of the

1990's. This should not come as a surprise given the way that modern companies operate today. Naturally, following the collapse of communism in Eastern Europe, many companies in the west were eager to invest in production facilities in order to take advantage of the low wage, and high capability environment offered by these countries. Industrial manufacturers invested heavily in transferring production of goods and components to many of these countries, providing jobs for at least some of the millions who lost their previous position as many non-performing sectors of East European industry were shutting down. In Romania, there was in fact very little investment of this nature in the first decade of transition from 1990 to 2000. The main investors were opportunists looking either to buy the privatized national companies on the cheap, through a bribe, or simply in order to shut down production in order to gain market share for their already existing operations. This was the case with the company where my father worked until 1991, when he left for Canada.

Given the uncertainty in Romania during the period caused by many factors, including the display of extreme nationalism made by Romanians in Tirgu Mures in 1990, it should not be surprising that western investments shied away. The new post-communist Romanian constitution, also ensured that Hungarian and other languages would never have an official status in any region of the country, including in areas where they are the majority population. The same constitution forbids according any level of autonomy to regions inhabited by other ethnic groups, or even if inhabited by a Romanian majority currently, as is the case of Banat, where I was born. From my understanding of current laws, a municipal government does not even have the authority to change a street name, which means that the centralized aspect of government there is taken very seriously. These are all provisions that are continuing to add tension within the country's society to this day. When companies make a serious decision to invest, especially when we are talking about high value, high capital investments, they first analyze the risk involved. In the case of Romania, among many other perceived risks, ethnic tensions were among them, which fall under the category of geopolitical risk. For many of the potential investors, the perceived benefits were outweighed by the perceived risks.

Besides the loss of investments, which would have been so crucial at the time, the current inefficient administration of Romania also has its roots in the brand of nationalism that evolved out of the marriage of national church and modern nationalism. Currently, Romania operates under a highly centralized administrative system. Tax revenues are collected from the forty-one counties, and then a large chunk is redistributed for local county and town councils to spend on local initiatives. There is no incentive within this arrangement to choose cost effective ways to function on the local scene, because the money spent is coming from a common financial pot. In fact, there are many incentives to behave in a splurging manner, because local spending at all levels of government is highly beneficial in encouraging job growth. To make matters worse, the money distributed from the central authorities is in a large measure reflected in the political allegiance of local councils. This creates a clientele situation, where local council success, is in fact in large measure dependent on being in bed with members of the central government. All this is made possible because the church reinforces a false historical myth about historical land inheritance that is sacred, and not to be divided, especially if some regions would possibly have a foreign, non-Romanian, and non-Orthodox ethnic and religious administrative influence. The need to have complete, undisputed control over this land is so ingrained in the psyche of the Romanian people, that there is little chance that they will manage to get this done before it will be too late to save themselves from impending disaster.

The Hungarian minority in Romania is constantly advocating more local autonomy for the entire country, but the mind of Romanians is wired in a way that automatically equates the word autonomy with separation. Given the manifest destiny, view they have of their current territory, regardless of whether some regions were, or are still currently inhabited by another ethnic minority, this should be no surprise. Even when a group of local intellectuals and officials from the city of Timisoara from the western Banat region, which is now majority Romanian, sent a letter to the capital requesting a decentralization of the administrative machine in 1990, right after the collapse of communism, they were branded as traitors. Not even the fact that the people petitioning were mainly ethnic Romanians saved them from the scorn of the government and the Romanian people from around the country. That was another opportunity missed, and given the current mindset of the Romanians 20 years later, I see no chance of them redressing the current unhealthy political situation any time soon. A stronger local direction for economic development, partly financed through locally collected funds, which would reflect local needs and competence would be essential for a country like Romania, given its size, and cultural and economic variation from region to region. Instead of considering all options however, people there are more likely to be driven by their nationalist zeal, aided in its current form by the church.

The Romanian government and many ordinary people as well, realize the fact that a need for more decentralization is urgent and perhaps crucial to the country's long-term well-being. As a result, there was just in the summer of 2011 a new initiative started by the country's president to re-organize Romania into eight regions. He could not help himself however to refrain from proposing a re-organization of the current map in a way in which at least 80% of Romania's Hungarian minority would have found themselves in a new administrative entity, with a much smaller percentage of Hungarians living within the new entities, compared to the current counties. In fact, none of the three new counties that would host the ethnic Hungarian population would have more than 30% of the population belonging to this ethnic group. As I mentioned already, currently Harghita and Covasna have a solid Hungarian majority, while Mures County has a 40% Hungarian minority and Satu Mare has 35%. Given that, the bill needed the ethnic Hungarian vote to pass, the initiative failed. The initiative started by the country's president would have passed if it would not have contained within it an attack on the right of the ethnic Hungarians to maintain some influence in local administration, which would have allowed them to have a voice in their own local affairs. There was no logical economic reason to choose the latest initiative over many other options for decentralization, which would not also be an attack on the ethnic Hungarians.

The Hungarians in Romania have seen this movie before, and they know that it ends badly for them. During the communist period, the regions of Romania were reorganized into what is the present administrative shape in a way that attacked the cohesion of the Hungarian community. What happened next was that the state authorities made good use of the weakened natural cohesion in order to make colonization of Hungarian inhabited towns and regions easier. For instance, Mures county was formed by chopping a piece away from what was then known as the Sekler region, also known as the Hungarian Autonomous Region (Autonomous only in name), and they attached it to a nearby region inhabited by a clear Romanian majority. Given that the new region no longer had such a clear Hungarian identity, a sustained program of colonization over many years was not as noticeable. Nor was the presence of an increasing number of ethnic Romanian dominated administrative apparatus, more Romanian schools, and decreasing Hungarian ones, which themselves were increasingly Hungarian only in name, because an ever-increasing number of courses were no longer being taught in Hungarian.

This instinctive drive to continue with the slow process of eradication of ethnic Hungarian elements still present on their land is at least in part connected to the display of this mindset by the church. The Romanian Orthodox Church is currently one of the main actors still pushing for colonizing the few areas of Transylvania where Hungarians are still in the majority. In the counties of Harghita and Covasna there have been many recent developments, including one, where a Romanian priest erected a commemorative monument in his village, remembering over 100 Romanians who were martyred in 1848, when the region belonged to Hungary. Local Hungarians got word of the situation and they investigated, and found that no such incident took place. They confronted the priest with their findings, and yet he still went ahead with his monument, even after admitting that he had no evidence to support his claims. His only concession was no longer to refer to the martyrs as the village martyrs, but to Romanian martyrs in general.

Romanian priests from this region also regularly call openly for the suppression of the Hungarian language in order to make the Romanian population, which makes up 20% of the whole more "comfortable". Given that 80% of the population in those two counties is Hungarian, they complain about language barriers that prevent the believers in their Orthodox faith from settling there among the Hungarians, and thus they call on the central authorities to do something. That something is of course placing curves on the use of the Hungarian language by locals. This effectively creates a perverse distortion in perception in Romanian public opinion, where it is not the ethnic minority within Romania that needs to be protected from assimilation, but the few Romanians that live among these people. To add some perspective to the situation, officially over 85% of Romania's population is ethnically Romanian, and yet the argument that they are under threat of assimilation still sticks.

The central authorities have done quite a lot, by maintaining a central civil service dominated by Romanians, including police, bureaucrats, and they funded the building of many Orthodox churches in the region, including in places where none are needed, given the current ethnic composition of certain places. A report that a government official from the Republic of Moldova, which is also mainly inhabited by Romanians, called a local official in Covasna County to enquire about the plan to settle some of their citizens in the region, may be an indication of why so many churches were built there recently. The fact that in Romanian society, in the 21'Th century, the concept still predominates that some sort of ethnic purification needs to be implemented to finalize the job started in the 20'Th century, which forever changed the cultural fabric of Transylvania, says a lot about their level of cultural backwardness. This program saw the Romanian population in the region of Transylvania rise by 250%, while the Hungarian population there dropped by one quarter, and the formerly third largest ethnic group, the Germans all but disappeared from the scene. The Transylvanian region will probably become homogenized ethnically and culturally by the end of the current century, unless things change urgently.

The latest failed initiative to reform the state in 2011 is yet another opportunity missed to save Romania from a potentially disastrous future that most people it seems are still largely unaware of. In the minds of most Romanians, the big catastrophe would come in the form of the loss of the lands they gained in 1918 to the "irredentist" Hungarian menace. Few of them are aware however that aside from a few die-hard Hungarian nationalists, most Hungarians realize that the Transylvania they lost is not the Transylvania of today. In 1918, they lost a land where roughly half the population was Romanian, a third was Hungarian, and about 12% was German (with regional variation within). Now Transylvania is a place where over 70% of the population is Romanian, less than 20% is Hungarian, while the German community was largely replaced by the Rroma minority, which as I will clarify in this chapter are the exact opposite of what it means to have a German population in place. For Hungary, this would mean that almost a third of the population would become ethnic Romanian and its own problematic Rroma community would more than double, while the ethnic Hungarian population would grow by only about 15% because of repatriating the 1.5 million ethnic Hungarians from Romania. As I shall explain, Hungary in my opinion has plans that are more practical in place, which does not include territorial expansion.

This wish for ethnic purity on the part of Romanians is extremely out of place with the needs of that society. Hungarians only make up roughly 7% of the country's population, but in the Transylvania-Banat region, they are 20% of the population, and this region makes up one third of the country's economy, and represents over 40% of all goods produced for export. Given the current attitude that predominates among Romanians, which is that Hungarians are just historical interlopers, in their quest to achieve what has always been manifest destiny to control the current lands that makes up modern Romania, there is a chance that young Hungarians will do what Romanian nationalists have chanted for decades now. They may just decide to move to "their country" Hungary. A trend towards this eventual new reality is already noticeable, and due to recent moves on the part of the Hungarian government, it may accelerate. The part that needs to be addressed to understand the context in which the majority of Romanians dream of achieving this homogeneity is what makes it inappropriate not only morally but also practically, is the demographic situation.

In the past twenty years, Romania lost roughly three million of its inhabitants to migration, out of a total initial population in 1990 of almost 23 million. The vast majority of them are currently either permanent immigrants who settled throughout the EU and North America, or are currently abroad on work visas of various duration. A large number of them work on short duration contracts, then they go back to Romania for a few months, and then they leave again.

Bottom line, Romania is in the process of loosing its workforce. There is an especially high rate of migration of its qualified people. This is hardly a sustainable situation given that its birth rate is now at below 1.3, per woman, which means that even without migration; this country's population is set to shrink in the near future by a relatively fast rate.

Add in a high rate of migration set to happen in the future, given that the demographic damage done in the past 20 years is in fact a great contributing factor to lack of future prospects, and a demographic disaster is brewing. This is especially the case since Romania joined the EU and Romanian nationals have full rights of seeking work elsewhere within the EU. Average EU wages are about four times higher than the Romanian average, so it is hard to keep the workforce when the discrepancy is so high. Despite all of this, many still entertain dreams of pushing the Hungarian minority living there to emigrate, potentially exacerbating the poor situation of Romania even more. Given that in some regions of Transylvania, Hungarians make up a sizable chunk of the population, a fast paced out migration could create economically dead zones in the country, causing a spiral effect, where a worsening economic situation can lead to a chain reaction that can potentially cause even more migration than the current trends are registering. If there was ever a good example of a mismatch between the reality of the economic situation, and cultural norms that are meant to adapt a society to its environment, this is it. The Romanians do not see things this way, because according to their simple analysis of the past decades, when they had an expanding population, it should be expected that the young Hungarians moving away from this hostile environment will be replaced with Romanians. That is after all what happened during most of the twentieth century, when they managed to eradicate countless Hungarian and German communities.

The Hungarian government is showing signs that it is currently better adapted to facing the challenges of the present and the future. Like most European nations, Hungary is currently copping with low birth rates, threatening to cause an imbalance in the economy through an overabundance of living quarters, and a poor ratio of pensioners to workers. Unlike Romania, the Hungarian economy did advance just enough to preserve its workforce much better, and there is the additional potential of gaining some of the youth from the neighboring countries, where as I mentioned almost one in three Hungarians currently live. As painful as it is for Hungarians to accept the diminished role they now play in Europe, as well as the injustice that the allied powers imposed on them after the First World War, it seems that it is easier nevertheless to accept, given the absence of the semi religious manifest destiny aspect of Hungarian nationalism. It hurts to admit that the 1100-year presence of Hungarians in Transylvania is close to ending, but the former German inhabitants made peace with their fate in Transylvania as well. They left behind 800 years of history, including great cities like Brasov or Sibiu, which even now are among the most visited cities in Romania. They left the region of Banat, which was by far the most developed region in the neighborhood, at the time that it was handed over partly to Romania, and partly to Serbia. Hundreds of thousands of them left for a more peaceful and prosperous life in Germany or Austria in the last few decades, leaving only the elderly behind. A once vibrant and solid community of over 700,000 that lived in Transylvania and Banat for hundreds of years now, numbers less than 60,000, mostly elderly people.

The prospect of making this move is a lot more disturbing to the 1.5 million Hungarians that still live in Romania than it was for the 700,000 Germans. Transylvania for ethnic Hungarians is a place where many aspects of Hungarian culture developed. During the period of Turkish and Habsburg occupation and use of Hungary as a battleground for almost two centuries, Transylvania was the only place where Hungarian autonomy from these forces was possible economically, politically and culturally. The individual decisions will likely determine the collective one however, and the fact that roughly 100,000 Hungarians from Romania chose to move to Hungary on a permanent basis in the past 20 years already, is a beginning of what can end up becoming a trend setting phenomena.

As of January, 2011, all people of Hungarian descent will have the right to apply for Hungarian citizenship even if they do not set up residence in Hungary. Officially, this is touted as a move on the part of the Hungarian government to give back something that was taken from the three million Hungarians forced to live as a minority under other people's rule. In reality, this is more likely a move meant to signal a welcoming policy for those of Hungarian descent, as well as making it more practical for young people who might consider emigrating from one of the neighboring countries. They are not doing this because they want to create an exodus, but because they recognize the value of attracting these people. It is a way for Hungary to stabilize its demographic situation, which in Romania is already potentially beyond repair, and headed for disaster as out-migration of its potential workforce continues at a relatively fast pace. Given the apparent desire to convince young people to consider a move to Hungary displayed by the current government, Romania may have fresh competition for a portion of its current and future workforce. The continuing opposition on the part of Romanian society to accept an accommodation that would ensure the future viability of a Hungarian minority in Romania almost assures that there are potentially another million, or so people who might decide to take off and find a home somewhere else in the next few decades.

The suspicious neighbors of Hungary have largely greeted the new citizenship law with some amount of unease, thinking that they are in fact trying to create new realities on the ground in order to re-take some of the lost territories in the future. At least officially, none of the official or non-official voices of Romanian society seems to recognize the Hungarian government's real objective of adapting to present realities, which I find surprising. Given current trends, failure to recognize the name of the game in the Europe of the 21'Th century can potentially be fatal. The low average birth rate throughout Europe means that the fight to attract young blood, especially the better-educated, more productive type, will likely intensify. Even some of the countries that managed to do better with their development such as the Slovenes, the Czechs, and those who developed to a lesser extent, like Hungary, Poland, and Slovakia are likely to lose some of their potential future workforce to western competition. Countries like Romania and Bulgaria, both of which are far less attractive in terms of average living standards offered, are likely going to become even more inhospitable as future living prospects for many, as a result in some part to the already large percentage of their potential workforce having been lost. Joining the EU, which could have potentially led these countries on to the path to prosperity, has in fact opened them up to intensified human resource recruiting by other EU members.

The desire on the part of the EU to recruit from Eastern members and some non-members as well should come as no surprise. Letting in fellow European migrants is a far more comfortable direction than the more physically and culturally different, potential migrants from Asia, Africa, or The Middle East. First, the culture really is far closer, and for the other part, just because we pretend to be color blind, it does not make it reality. Besides, the fear of colonization is a very real and justified concern for the long-term from the European perspective. Not just Europeans are observing this potential reality. Libya's president Ghadafi also made some comments recently, expressing his pleasure at the very real prospect of Europe being taken through Muslim migration, which is an achievement that eluded the Muslim world, when they tried to take it by force in past centuries.

The absurdity of the mentality still predominant within Romanian society that continues to make their country an unwelcome place for many, given their demographic issues is astounding. Unlike many other problems that Europeans face today, the demographic challenge is actually obvious. I grant this much, that in many urban areas within Romania, this reality may not be as obvious in everyday life yet, given that they are still experiencing an inflow of rural youth making the move into the large urban centers. Parts of the countryside are increasingly starting to look like settlements for the elderly. When I went to the community of Balint-Bodo in 2010 for instance, one of the town's preachers told me that in a whole year he only had to perform one christening, in a town of over 1600 people. Bodo, which is an ethnically Hungarian town separated by mainly Romanian Balint by a soccer field, has shrunk to half its population size in the past 60 years, and most who are left are old. Many people from the nearby city of Timisoara are buying up properties to make themselves a summer home as the local population continues to age and die out, given that there are few young people left to carry on.

I went to kindergarten there, because my grandmother lived there, and I still have a picture of the class of that year. It is true that some of the other children were also there because their grandparents lived there and they were sent there to learn Hungarian from the city, where it was not always possible to attend Hungarian language schooling, or interact with other Hungarian children. Now there is almost no reason for the building to exist anymore. The few students that attend school in this rural community go to the larger Balint facility, once they finish grade four. Many of the young have either moved to the city, or have emigrated from the country altogether. The overwhelming majority of the population is made up of senior citizens. Looking at that picture of my kindergarten class, taken less than three decades ago, I am amazed at how fast that community changed.

Even with this influx of the youth from the countryside, in a country where roughly 40% of the population still lives in a rural setting, some of the urban areas are shrinking as well. The city where I was born, in Resita has shrunk by roughly 20% since 1990. There are also a few cities that actually expanded in population, but most are currently in stagnation mode, and given the decreasing rural to urban migration that until recently was still able to make up for the natural decrease of the population, and the large outflow of the country's labor force, they are set to shrink as well. It is within this sad environment that many Romanians still want to see an outflow of the Hungarian population, which is already starting to flow to Hungary, as well as to other places, not just for the reasons that Romanians have to migrate, but also because of the hostile environment.

The government still promotes a version of history that vilifies the Hungarian community, mainly through shameless historical distortions that are taught to kids in schools. It is true that part of the reason that this practice is still alive and well, is because after generations of this practice of transforming the history lesson into a nationalist tool of propaganda, it is very hard for the public to accept anything less than the Cinderella version of historical events. Nevertheless, the government's failure to change this policy of vilifying some of the ethnic minorities through the very programs it sponsors is a reflection of their overall inability to adapt to the new realties of this world.

The many ironies of Romania and Hungary

The birth rates for Romania and Hungary are 1.3 and 1.4 per woman, respectively. If we are to exclude the Rroma population that resides within both countries, which is rather important as I shall explain later, the birth rates are likely closer to 1.1, and 1.2 respectively. What these birth rates mean essentially is that the population of these countries is set to shrink rapidly. In effect, each reproductive generation, which is considered to be 25 years in length, is set to shrink by almost half. If you calculate an approximate trend for Romania, which currently has a population of 20 million, by around 2100, there will be only about 30-40,000 new, non-Rroma births every year, compared to over 350,000 being born every year on average, between 1965-1990. I am not even including the effects of migration in this calculation. With the rapidly shrinking birth rates, and the rapid aging of the population as a result, there might actually be an accelerated rate of migration of the youth, given that the increased burden of caring for so many elderly people will mean a reduced standard of living all around.

Their situation is already desperate in these regards, given that they already have more people collecting pensions than there are wage earners. There are currently over five million people collecting pensions, while only 4.5 million people are officially employed and paying taxes. There are an additional 2 million people who are officially employed in agriculture, but they are not net tax contributors. Despite having such a high percentage of the potential workforce employed in agriculture, Romania is a net food importer. It is also believed that as many as 1.5 million people may be working under the table, at least occasionally. Their potential workforce of roughly 9 million is currently shrinking by at least 100,000 per year from natural demographic effects. In the period between 2030, and 2040, this loss will accelerate to about 250,000 per year. If one is to consider yearly migration as well, the rate of loss is much higher.

It is possible that the situation in Romania is already beyond repair. In the absence of a miraculous repatriation of their labor force that they already lost, and a parallel jump in economic activity that would absorb them into the economy, I do not have any reason to doubt that they are in the best case scenario looking at a very tough century. The state of the economy however is a reflection in large part of the hyper-centralized state that their leaders convinced them to accept. The main tool they used to convince the populous to accept this state was the continued reinforcement of the chauvinist version of their history, collaborated by the church. In effect, they are becoming victims of their own lies and intolerance they disseminate through their society. Poetic justice that makes up a little for the wounds I received myself, and feel for other fellow ethnic Hungarians in Romania, but on balance cannot be truly happy about. There are also decent, people living there, who are smart enough not to swallow what is on the propaganda menu. They certainly do not deserve their fate, but nothing can be done about it, because it is probably too late to salvage something from that society. Romania is likely headed for a demographic disaster that will similarly affect many countries in the region. Only the ones with leadership that possesses enough wisdom and vision will survive the current century, which might bring hope for overall long-term survival, if enough time is given for cultural change that might redress the current demographic trends.

The irony is that the people who got them into this mess are too often credited for being the saviors from the Hungarian "irredentist" menace. The people who went to whack Hungarians over the head twenty years ago in Tirgu Mures (Marosvasarhely), over such issues as Hungarians demanding education in their own language, the right to put out signs and inscriptions in Hungarian and worst of all, daring to celebrate their history, which is what truly set them off, are heroes. They put Hungarians back in their place, and even now, many Romanians like to threaten with a repeat of those actions whenever Hungarians raise the issue of their rights. The Illiescu regime that took over after communism collapsed in 1989 is also credited with resisting decentralization of the administrative structure of the state. The general population has been well-trained to believe that any move towards local administration of affairs is in fact a threat to national security. As such, these are their heroes, and so are the Priests who in subtle ways still instigate for a colonist state of mind when it comes to the regions that still have a significant ethnic Hungarian population.

Ironically, they may be less paranoid if 90 years ago they would have resisted the urge to incorporate territory that had in many cases a Hungarian Majority. Leaving those regions out of their territorial expansion, would have left only a few hundred thousand ethnic Hungarians on current Romanian territory, while admittedly a few hundred thousand Romanians would have remained as part of Hungary as well. Even so, this extreme paranoia about the Hungarian minority in Transylvania is quite illogical. Currently over 70% of the population of that region is Romanian as I already mentioned, while ethnic Hungarians make up 20% at the most. Furthermore, the region that is still solidly Hungarian in its ethnic composition, the Szekler region is right smack in the middle of the country; therefore, there is no chance of separation. This is a great example of what it may mean to fail to gain an appropriate collective perspective as a society, when it comes to identifying their main problems.

I have my suspicion that the fear of separation of Transylvania is in fact not, what is driving many Romanians to oppose a decentralization of the country, or most of the initiatives to protect the Hungarian minority. Their main point of grievance and unease is in fact the cessation of the communist regime's ethnic purification drive in the region, which they had to end due to their desire to become part of Europe. They may have succeeded in eliminating the German minority, which made up 12% of Transylvania's population, but Hungarians still make up a significant part of the current population. The very fact that many there speak a different language, have a different religion (Hungarians are mainly Catholics and Protestants), celebrate a different history, and observe different cultural traditions is an offence to their sacred inheritance. The present territory of Romania, and the territory of the Republic of Moldova, which is also inhabited mainly by Romanians, is in their view sacred land that they think they inherited from the kingdom of Dacia two thousand years ago. In the absence of Hungarians willing to be assimilated, their very presence is an affront to their sacred land. Thus, the presence of the Church in Romanian's national consciousness makes itself felt in their culture, to their detriment in this case. They may have been able to dig deep and find a way to adapt, if it were not for this manifest destiny version of history, encouraged by the church, which shapes their identity. They may indeed succeed in keeping their feet on the throats of the Hungarian minority, but the price they are paying; I doubt they would be willing to pay, if they would actually realize what they are doing to themselves.

In the scheme of things, the biggest jackpot that the state and people of Romania could ever have hoped to win was the annexation of Transylvania and Banat. Two regions that, were rich in their natural as well as cultural and infrastructural endowment, were gifted to them by historical circumstance. The region of Banat for instance was as developed and advanced economically as the Austrian region was before the Habsburg Empire collapsed in 1918. The difference could not possibly be greater today. Average wages are now five times smaller in Banat compared to Austria. The cultural inheritance was perhaps the greatest thing they squandered, because historically Transylvania was part of the western cultural framework until 1918. For Romania, it could have been a cultural bridge towards Western Europe, but with the massive colonization of the region with Romanians and the Rroma from the regions of Moldova and Wallachia, and the exodus and assimilation of large proportions of the Hungarian and German people who lived in the region, there is no longer a chance of that happening. To make matters worse, they are so obsessed with squeezing their lottery winnings with both hands, that they do not have any more free hands to work on other things, leaving them paralyzed in the current disastrous situation. In many ways, they are the same as the many famous cases of lottery winners who through a twist of irony, ended up in the poor house because of their squander.

The big picture, if one is to look at the strategic situation in terms of demographic issues, the clear potential winner of Romanian intolerance towards the Hungarian minority there is the Hungarian state. If it is to survive the current century, Hungary must use its traumatizing historical misfortune to its advantage. Unlike its EU peers to the west, Hungary cannot attract through economic incentives the productive and potentially reproductive individuals to re-settle among them. Relying too heavily on that is potentially dangerous, because at some point it may lead to cultural colonization by others. That is not a worthy goal for a nation state. While there is no doubt about the fact that the great territorial and demographic losses suffered by Hungary over ninety years ago negatively affected its development since, there needs to be recognition of the effects of the changing circumstances. The positive effect that cannibalizing the almost three million strong communities of ethnic Hungarians who were condemned to live as a minority at the hands of its neighbors can have is not to be ignored. It is true that this would forever end their historical presence of over a millennium in many of the places that they would abandon. These are places, which played a crucial role in their history, but it should be recognized that it is more important to secure a future.

The prospects of continued survival for the very long term for the Hungarian minority in Romania and elsewhere are not very positive anyway. Therefore, whether the process will be sped up by the continued absorption of many of the young by the Hungarian state, or whether they will simply wait for the slow process of assimilation to take its course, the result will be the same. In Romania, the point where this process will be sped up is fast approaching. The moment as I see it, is when the overall proportion of the Hungarian minority there will hover around 5% of the entire population, which is only about two percentage points lower than in the present. At that point, they will lose all political leverage to protect the institutions that currently still guard their communities from the overall hostility of the Romanian majority. When that happens, it will become entirely clear to most of the population that they have no future in Romania as a people, speeding up the process of moving out. The Hungarian government will of course hope that they will be the recipients of a large proportion of this outflow. Whether that will be achieved or not remains to be seen.

Ironically, the political party that represents ethnic Hungarians, which Romanians often like to demonize, is the only political group in Romania that has within its platform a way to give Romania a chance to survive. Their platform, which includes a plan for a decentralization of the country's administration, is relevant for the entire country, not just for the areas inhabited by ethnic Hungarians. It would provide more incentives for local development strategies, as well as a greater level of accountability for the way that government spends the country's revenues. It is not something unconventional or bizarre as it is no different from the way that Germany, Canada, Spain and many other countries approach their administration. The reason that this party indirectly finds itself fighting for the survival of

Romania is because they are looking for ways to ensure the survival of the ethnic minority they represent within it. They are in fact opposed to the goals of the Hungarian government, which no longer sees the survival of the ethnic Hungarian communities from outside its borders as their main concern, but the survival of the Hungarian state instead. They certainly do not want to see them assimilated, but they do see an opportunity to consolidate the Hungarian population, which improves their own chance of survival as a state in the region. The young people that the Hungarian government is hoping will consider the move to Hungary are also the electorate of the UDMR (RMDSZ), so they are now the only ones truly involved in trying to preserve the Hungarian community in Transylvania[3].

The Rroma people (also known as gypsies)

I left out the issue of this minority living in the region from the above conversation for a very good reason. This is a minority, which behaves very differently from the majority, and its inclusion in the previous considerations would distort the reality. They make up roughly 5-10% of both Romania's and Hungary's overall population. Unlike the majority Hungarians and Romanians in their respective countries, the Rroma have a positive birth rate, in other words, they are having more kids than is necessary for achieving the replacement rate, i.e. 2.1 kids per woman. One might rightly be tempted to jump to the conclusion that this is in fact a good thing, because it lessens the impact of the extremely low birth rates exhibited by the majority populations in this region. Unfortunately, for these countries, the Rroma population is by no means a blessing. It is often very hard to get good reliable stats on the situation of the Rroma in these two countries, but what is known about their situation paints a picture of them being a curse rather than a blessing.

By numerous accounts, it seems that most Rroma are hardly what one might be able to consider literate currently. The majority of them do not even graduate from high school, and only 2-10% of them go on to graduate from a secondary school institution[4]. Recent efforts to involve them in the regular education system have had some success, but not enough to turn the current trend. The trend I

301

am referring to is the one, where most young Rroma kids tend to end up doing what their parents before them do or did. That thing usually involves following a life of petty criminal activities, and since the end of communism, also taking advantage of any welfare and aid program that they can access. By many accounts, as much as 80% of the adult Rroma population is unemployed. This in effect means that they are a net drain on the host society, and by no means a net contributor. They take advantage of most facilities and programs that these governments make available to the public, yet very few of them actually contribute.

In addition to being a drain on society, due to their veracious appetite for social assistance services, they also contribute a great deal to the overall criminal activities levels in these countries. That means that many economic activities, including tourism are affected. More law enforcement and judicial system demand is also created due to their activities. The prison system is also obliged to accommodate the increased levels of criminal activity, therefore it adds to the overall costs of accommodating this minority. Here I should specify however that in my own personal view, they are not the main drain on society due to their criminal activities, even though they are the most visible face of criminal activities.

Begging, prostitution, fraud, pick pocketing, small-scale theft, smuggling and other petty crimes do not compare in terms of overall losses to the regional economy in both Hungary and Romania, when compared to the billions of dollars that are being lost to corruption, and ineptitude on the part of government employees. That is especially the case in Romania, where the level of corruption is beyond what can be considered workable as a situation that still permits for the functioning of a modern economy.

If nothing changes in respect to the current demographic trends, both Romania and Hungary are likely to have their national identity changed as the minority Rroma increase in numbers, while the majority population decreases at a disastrous rate. By my rough estimate, the Rroma can become the majority population in both these countries before this century is up. That is a strange proposition however, because if the Rroma do not change their behavior in a manner that allows them to become contributors to society's needs instead of a drain, it is hard to envision a country where they would make up more than a quarter of the overall population, much less them becoming the majority. That is especially so in countries like Romania and Hungary, where the economy is already hard-pressed to deal with the fact that these are fast ageing societies, giving them enough dependents to worry about, without having to deal also with an ethnic minority that is engaged in an opportunistic and parasitic state of existence.

There is only one realistic solution to the problem of the Rroma. They have to be brought in to the modern economy as contributors and full participants in the economy and society. The unfortunate reality of the past 20 years of post-communism is that thus far; no realistic project of integration was suggested, much less implemented. Various political and human rights organizations from the west simply sized up the problem as one that is simply a result of discrimination by the majority population. The problem with that of course is that it is only half the story. The other half is the reality that at this point the Rroma population is already well-adapted to life on the fringe. Their leadership is most often fearful of any positive change within their community, because they need the poor masses of their community to continue doing the footwork that makes their criminal dealings possible. The Rroma are also very fearful of any attempt at integration, because their experience tells them that it usually involves a program of assimilation. They have a very strong view of their distinct culture; in fact they see the world divided in two camps, Rroma and Gadje (non-Rroma).

Based on their assumption that the main problem with the lack of integration of the Rroma in the wider society of the host nations is mainly tied to discrimination, the west pushed for social aid programs as well as measures to be taken to integrate them in the education system. Thus far, the welfare programs only served to supplement their income. Not by any stretch of the imagination, can it replace their reliance on their traditional, mostly non-legal means of supporting themselves. As for increasing their rates of attendance in public schools, they mainly do their best to attend the minimum necessary to qualify for aid, whenever it was designed in a way that made attendance in schools for their kids a prerequisite of qualifying for the welfare programs.

The one thing these programs did not do was to increase the rate of participation of these people in the workforce, and there are three main reasons for that. First, there is a barrier for them to being hired in the form of discrimination and distrust on the part of those doing the hiring. The second reason that the participation rate of the Rroma did not improve is the relatively poor state of the economy in the region. In Romania especially, millions of young people had to leave the country to find work. It is hard to imagine under such circumstance how one can go about absorbing a mainly unskilled and culturally not familiarized with work ethics population into the workforce. There is also the third reason, which continues to be a major barrier, which is a demonstrated lack of interest on the part of the majority of the Rroma population in earning a living through holding down a steady job. After generations of living on the fringe of society, the lifestyle becomes ingrained in the community, and it gets passed down through the generations.

To be able to move a large group of people culturally out of an anti-social stance, cultivated through the generations, it would have to be a concerted effort on the part of the majority. My best guess is that the states in question do not have the resources to do this on their own now. They would need EU help, which is something they can only hope to gain if they were to present this proposal as a solution to the problem together with all other central and eastern European countries that have a significant Rroma population. That is the only way that they can muster enough political influence to get something done.

The solution as I see it is to act together in order to simultaneously eradicate their organized crime syndicates, and provide them with an alternative to earning a living, by creating work programs for them. I would also cut out most social assistance programs, in order to encourage labor participation. As I already said however, the economies of central and Eastern Europe are not strong enough to absorb hundreds of thousands of new labor participants in a short period of time; therefore the west would have to participate by issuing temporary work visas specifically for Rroma who may wish to work. This effort would have to be sustained for a few decades perhaps in order to change their social behavior enough to be able to expect them to seek out a place within society, instead of at the fringes. My hope is that in seeing their parents hustle to earn a living in a conventional fashion, the children of these communities will try to ensure that they can write their own ticket upon reaching adulthood by earning basic skills through education. I currently have little reason to hope that such an initiative will ever take place; therefore, the issue of the Rroma people in Europe is likely to become a more and more bitter situation for all involved, given that they are the fastest growing ethnic minority in Europe.

The hope of Romanian society in dealing with this issue was that they would be able to get back at the westerners for pestering them to integrate the Rroma, by unleashing them upon the rest of Europe as soon as they were incorporated into the EU in 2007. "Let us see how well they will fare in incorporating them" was the general slogan favored by most Romanians when talking about this issue. Sure enough, the Rroma were unleashed on the general population of Europe, and they did not like it one bit. In fact, some countries like Italy and France went as far as breaching EU law by engaging in the deportation of many of them back to their country of origin, namely Romania. Many other countries within the EU also took measures to express their displeasure with the state of Romania, because so many Rromas ended up on their doorstep. The way it looks now, west European countries have no intention of integrating Romania's Rroma into their own society, because they are after all Romanian citizens. It turns out that Romanians were very naïve to believe in European naivety. They did very little to integrate this population thus far, and currently they are the poorest member of the EU, meaning they now have few resources to do so. They have the largest Rroma population in Europe, and they are the least integrated into their society, which is a very grim situation indeed. Worst of all, they lack the cultural ability to understand why it is such a crucial thing to deal with this issue even though it is hard and complicated.

The Rroma situation in Hungary is not much better. Labor participation rates for their Rroma population are not much better than for those in Romania, and school attendance is only a little better as well. There is no doubt that the Hungarians have almost as much to do on this issue as the Romanians. I have reason to believe however that they are at least starting to move on the issue internally and externally as well. During their six-month rotating EU presidency in the first half of 2011, they made the issue of the Rroma inclusion in society one of their top three issues on the EU agenda. They most definitely failed to propose anything resembling the kind of solution that I suggested here, but at least they are trying.

After the most disastrous governing regime in the post communist era in Hungary, which lasted for the better part of the last decade, with the Socialist party at the helm, Hungary is looking to rebuild the economy. The center right FIDESZ party granted the right to citizenship to all Hungarians living in the territories lost 90 years ago, giving them the opportunity to harvest a chunk of the productive and re-productive Hungarian population. In conjunction with this move, they stated a clear goal to create a million new jobs by the end of the current decade. That would be an increase in the total people working by a quarter, given that currently, 3.8 million people work for a wage in that country. It is certainly a very ambitious goal, and I personally think that even in the best-case scenario, they will only achieve half of their stated goal; especially given the turbulent global economy we are in. They currently do not have half a million people officially unemployed, and one always has to factor in frictional unemployment that shows up in the statistics. I therefore foresee that about half of the 500,000 new jobs created would have to be filled by new participants in their labor market. A large chunk of the new labor force can come from ethnic Hungarians looking for opportunities from all the neighboring countries, most of which received a generous chunk of land, including regions inhabited by ethnic Hungarians. In order to fill higher skilled positions, they would have no choice but to rely on attracting some of these people. There will be also lower skilled positions that will have to be filled, and that is where there is an opportunity to involve the Rroma minority in filling some of those positions. The finance minister of Hungary, Gyorgy Matolcsi, recently stated that given that there are a large number of unskilled people in Hungary, he would not mind attracting some low skilled jobs in order to re-educate and reintroduce segments of the idle population into a working culture. He did not refer to the Rroma in this case, but the description certainly applies.

If the Hungarian government can integrate the Rroma population to an extent that future generations will grow up seeing their parents earn a living in an honest fashion, they can only benefit from such a change and turnaround from current trends. Not only is there an obvious economic benefit from turning a net draining population into a net contributor, but there are also demographic benefits. The much younger Rroma population can greatly enhance the overall workforce. Then there is of course the other benefit, which is that the Rroma population would most likely stabilize in the absence of an idle lifestyle. Their families would most likely adopt a similar way of thinking to ours, which is that one should invest in fewer offspring who will have more opportunities if enough attention and financial resources are invested in them. Thus, Hungarians can avert the possibility of becoming a minority in their own country.

There is no chance whatsoever that Romania can tackle this problem in my view. The idea of having the Rroma minority flood the rest of Europe, and thus making them someone else's problem was such a sweet dream for them that they now have a hard time getting back to reality. I should emphasize here that we are not talking about two different countries, where one has a more tolerant society than the other is, and therefore they can better deal with this issue in a more enlightened way. On balance, I believe that Hungarians are just as intolerant towards Rromas and other people. The difference as I already emphasized is the flavor of the intolerant currents running through society, just as the flavor of their nationalism differs, due to the sources it comes from. Here again I believe that in addition to the regular sources of xenophobia, there is an unconscious undercurrent of having to purge all that is not Romanian, including another nomadic arrival in the region aside from the Hungarians. They have the notion of their manifest destiny interrupted by nomadic tribes that came from the east so ingrained in their national consciousness, that they currently have no ability whatsoever to come to grip with their own historical past. It is a past, which may in fact include a brief period, when they themselves were probably living somewhat of a nomadic lifestyle almost a thousand years ago. Most archeological studies suggest that proto-Romanian culture was absent as a distinct entity on the territory of present day Romania from the third century when the Roman Empire retreated, and until they made their presence in the medieval period around the eleventh century. Therefore, a migration from the south of the Balkan region is a very plausible and probable historical reality.

Going back to this one historical myth of daco-roman continuity, which is intertwined with the myth of religious continuity of the Romanian Orthodox Church dating back just as far, is important in understanding what makes the Romanians misfire culturally as a collective entity in the 21'Th century. When nationalism and religion act in unison, to protect their common position, there is nothing that can stand in the way, not even the need for cultural re-adaptation to new realities. The unfortunate thing is that we all have to live in the current century and deal with the current realities. Being well adapted as a culture to dealing with challenges presented by modern trends is perhaps more important than ever. The sad case of Romania is a case in point. It may even be too late for them as the damage they have done to themselves by allowing the loss of such a high proportion of their workforce and reproductive population in an environment where birth rates are much lower than the minimum requirement to have a stable population is paramount to national suicide. Their continued hostility towards the ethnic Hungarian minority may exacerbate an already disastrous situation as more and more young Hungarians may give up on staying put in the face of such hostility, in order to preserve their cultural and historical endowment of over a thousand years in Transylvania. Failing to find an avenue to integrate and include the troublesome ethnic Rroma minority in their society is likely to be a threat to their long-term social stability that may be just as dangerous as the rest of the demographic situation.

Conclusions

If times were better globally, Romania's situation might still have a good chance of being salvaged through urgent, intelligent, well executed reforms. In the current environment, and with the lack of cultural ability to adapt as a collective, there is no chance in my view that they can come up with a viable plan for the future. As a nation, they may have already condemned themselves to extinction, they just may be too oblivious to it, and even the few who see it, point the finger to all the wrong places. Hungarians on the other hand were condemned already over 90 years ago, mainly by others to have a rotten future by dismembering large parts of its territory and ethnic Hungarian population. This ensured that all its neighbors would see what was left of the state of Hungary and the ethnic Hungarian minority they became host to, as an enemy that needs to be suppressed. It is hard to explain to others what it means to be put in such a situation, but from my experience as an ethnic Hungarian that was born in this role; I can say that it really is a very unpleasant thing to experience so much hostility[6].

Given the current environment, there is a unique opportunity for the Hungarian state to press home a potential advantage that none of its neighbors has. They have a relatively large pool of potential migrants of productive and re-productive age who they can rely on to cushion the blow that all European countries are likely to feel because of the potentially disastrous demographic trends happening there. It is a very rare historical moment that rarely presents itself for a group of people who all thought that they are likely forever beaten down, and are most likely to stay down, to actually turn the blow dealt to them generations ago to a relative advantage. The cultural maturity demanded to grab on to this opportunity is such that I do not necessarily see leadership on steering their flocks towards the right direction. The sacrifice demanded is to relinquish forever their claim to historical lands, where ancestors have built a cultural presence and have been buried for over a thousand years. It also takes a mature Hungarian population in Hungary to welcome and embrace new arrivals as equals, rather than looking down on them as some tend to do. It would take a mature governing regime to realize the need to create opportunities for a constant inflow of young talent coming from neighboring countries, which needs to be sustained for decades.

The long-term benefits include a long-term advantage over Hungary's neighbors in stemming a disastrous demographic decline and overall aging that will likely afflict most of its neighbors. For the young ethnic Hungarians, making the move from the neighboring states would mean a permanent respite from being treated with hostility by the majority population. A younger, more stable population would be a better magnet for investments in the region, giving them a unique opportunity to achieve something that few have done before in Europe. They could transcend the East-West rift that took place centuries ago, and they could in fact have an opportunity to compete in affluence with the western states. The future may not look very promising for most of the world, but it is important to be able to secure a relatively decent life within that world. As things are set to become harder due to our global predicaments, survival itself may end up being an issue, so there is a lot at stake.

With the benefit of being detached from the region, I have the unique opportunity to view the situation there from a more pragmatic perspective that allows me to analyze the situation in a passionless way. This however may not mean that people living the events there currently may have the same perspective. Given the realities of today, a young Hungarian in Romania should logically respond to any attacks of his/her heritage, culture, language or traditions by considering a move to Hungary or elsewhere, the next time the need or desire to look for a job arises. It would in fact be the ultimate revenge given the already sorry state of Romania's demographics. I do not expect such a mentality to take root among local people there however, because the natural response is to resist the desire by others to destroy one's community. This ironically facilitates the abuses, because they are devoid of any negative consequences, given the current demographic reality.

I am equally convinced that the desire of the Romanians to purify their sacred land will override logic. They already have a template in realizing what this may mean to the region. They already lost the somewhat smaller German minority that used to make up 12% of Transylvania and Banat's population. The consequences to the region's economy are grave. The ethnic German communities were among the most prosperous historically, and even after they left, the towns where they used to dwell are still among the most important engines of growth in western Romania. The rural German communities were also an important part of the local economy. Those communities are now mostly inhabited by the Rroma minority, which is less than eager, or culturally able to contribute. Given the overall size of the Hungarian community and the very desperate demographic situation of that country as well, they are setting themselves up for even more severe losses. I most definitely do not expect most Romanians to understand this.

11

Our own cultural problems

Romanians & Americans

I would like to begin this chapter by analyzing whether there are any cultural parallels between the above-analyzed Balkan culture that seemingly has a hard time adapting to new realities of the world and the leading western culture and economic power. On the surface, there seems to be little doubt that there is no reason to expect similarities, especially given their historical pasts, which could not be more different. The US was founded on 18'Th century enlightenment principles, and Americans have a very strong sense of respect towards the founding principles. That on its own would be a good enough argument to be able to claim that there cannot possibly be a similarity between American culture that was at the forefront of enlightenment and Romanian culture that can be argued that it never had the opportunity to experience enlightenment.

Main reason I have to question the American commitment to enlightenment comes precisely from their reverence of the ideas of enlightenment. Remember what the meaning of enlightenment was to western culture. It has everything to do with a cultural shift, where at least the intellectual elites are able to make and in turn accept a complex analysis. In other words, they have the ability to make multistep assessments of cause and effect. The ideas of the enlightenment were themselves advanced and in many cases appropriate to the time, but since then many things have changed, and the arguments that were relevant then, are obsolete or inappropriate to current circumstances. So the increasing trend of pledging allegiance to founding father principles and ideas coming from enlightenment era thinkers such as Adam Smith are in fact a sign that complex analysis culture is being abandoned in favor of simple answers that conveniently fit within crafty political and ideological slogans. I believe we are witnessing convergence of western culture towards Balkan culture, and that should worry us all.

Further proof of this cultural convergence comes in the form of the marriage of American patriotism and nationalism, with the evangelical movement, which is also both increasingly politically active and increasingly inclined to fan the flames of US nationalism. This marriage is a dangerous one, especially given the also semi—manifest destiny aspect of it, which threatens to impair people's ability to recognize logic. In the case of the US, this marriage may not lead to xenophobia as it does in Romania, but it seems to re-classify what it means to be an American, by claiming that allegiance to a specific set of values is necessary to be identified as such. The level of hostility towards the ones who do not share these values is steadily ratcheted up. Any attack on the values that these people share is an automatic attack on god and America. This marriage may manifest itself differently than the one in the Balkans, but the negative consequences can easily be as grave in the end.

Are we culturally prepared for our challenges?

The lesson for western society that can be gained from looking at the above example of cultural mismatch due to historical and religious circumstances is that we have to be careful not to allow such a mismatch to happen to us. We are lucky to be the inheritors of culture stemming from European renaissance and enlightenment, but perhaps we need to realize that sometimes we cannot simply rely on a cultural revolution from our increasingly distant past to keep us competitive in this world forever. We have to remain culturally relevant. Things change and circumstances require new adaptations. We have to keep up not just technologically but also culturally. In fact, culture dictates technological innovation and deploys it as it sees fit. If there is, something that we can learn from the case of Romania is that our faith in technological innovation alone is by no means a guarantee of positive results. Romania certainly has access now to most technological innovations available to most of us. In spite of this, their per capita GDP is only one third of the

EU average. The average wages are even less competitive, while many prices for consumer goods and services are similar to the EU average. If technology transfer alone would have been enough, then this sad situation of the Romanians would not be the case.

If we were well adapted to the present, and ready to deal with the challenges of our future, we would not be in our current rut either. We would be able to compete with the newly rising economic powers, without being faced with the prospect of having to throw our less fortunate, elderly, as well as our environment under the bus, in the hope of preserving a few extra jobs, which would otherwise be transferred to the developing world. Nor would we be faced with a future that demands us to strip our workforce of the rights they earned over the past decades, including protection from unsafe work conditions, benefits, and the right to collective bargaining. Europe would not be on the brink of demographic disaster, and the US would not be contemplating giving up on their average standard of living of its people just to save some jobs. The lessons of the past decade show us that we are perhaps almost just as badly equipped culturally to deal with our economic problems, and perhaps it is our very culture, which is in fact preventing us from thinking outside the box, in order to come up with, and embrace new ideas. I fear that history shows that asking for a cultural revolution in order for society to prevent its demise is asking much more than what should be expected of us. Perhaps others see it as well, and that is why we prefer to concentrate on the next big technological breakthrough, as the next big hope, so we can avoid having to face up to admitting that cultural change may be necessary, but it is no easy task.

Some argue that Karl Marx was not wrong in his vision of a socialist utopia where, ownership of capital would be abolished, and transferred to the ones doing the work. Those who still support his ideas, claim that he was just far too ahead of his time. The failure was in fact cultural and not technical, where human nature to be greedy for power, prestige, and the right to consume more than others, which is in fact what capitalism banks on, and therefore is the system still standing, undermined an ideal that perhaps could have changed our future forever. It might have ushered in an era that would have taken us down the path envisioned by the creators of the

Star Trek show, but it was never realistic to expect this of humanity, because it is unfortunately, not the way we are.

I can testify from personal experience that the system I was born into in Romania had almost nothing to do with the ideals of Karl Marx, once it was implemented. Essentially, it is important to understand that ownership of capital was never abolished. It was concentrated instead into corporate conglomerates that took the shape of nation states. The communist party elite became the new de-facto owners, corporate CEO's and board members. As it turned out, they were extremely bad at running these mega-conglomerates, which is a reflection of the human quality that formed the new elite. Personally, I do not see any circumstance in which we will become culturally advanced enough to be able to make such a utopian system work and therein lays Marx's folly, because I doubt we will ever be capable of taking such a big cultural leap.

The Cultural Revolution that I envision to be necessary for us to adopt new ways of doing things, such as the sustainability tariff, is not nearly as dramatic as what Karl Marx expected people to achieve, to his own discredit as a judge of human nature. It is however no less intense than the enlightenment, which ushered in the modern age. The fact that I place my hopes on a repeat of a cultural revolution, which would have to be just as strong and groundbreaking as the one that sent us into our current era of success is asking a lot more however, than what should be expected from our society in most circumstances. There are few examples of a culture creating a revolution that ushered in an era of relative prosperity, and then undertaking another one to prevent its decline. I believe the only reason that we should be hopeful is that unlike the Marxist, environmental, humane movements of our times, my idea does not rely on naïve utopist expectations. It instead relies on us realizing our own self-interests and proceeding in implementing a new international trade policy that does not necessarily restrain our natural greed, it just regulates it better by changing the parameters of the game. Expecting people to act in their self-interest is by no means something that should be unexpected; I therefore hope that we can reach the cultural sophistication that will permit us to re-define what our long-term self-interests are.

Their SOB's, or ours? (Changing the political culture)

Before we contemplate any move to try to save ourselves, from the likely disaster we are headed towards with accelerated speed, we have to take care of one important detail in our political environment. There is absolutely no chance in my view for the current political environment to produce the kind of leadership that is needed to steer our path in a better, healthier direction. That is unless we get our own politicians. What I mean by that is the following: The elites already have their politicians. They paid for the greatest part of their campaigns that got them elected. Furthermore, the bulk of the politicians themselves belong to the elites; therefore, they are likely to be naturally inclined to pushing for their narrow interests to begin with. I am not suggesting that we start voting in less educated politicians. That would be a very big mistake, as I personally witnessed the results of uneducated hoards of people running a country, I can testify to its folly. The communist regime in Romania was often eager to advance not so educated people into high positions; the results were catastrophic for the economy and society as well. We need to hire the best and the smartest to run our governments, but like I said we need them to work for us and the country they represent.

There is only one way that this can be achieved and that is through publicly funded campaigns. At this point, it would be the best government spending initiative I can think of. For a mere few hundred million dollars and Euros per year, we could potentially save hundreds of billions that will no longer be granted to special interests who currently fund campaigns throughout the western world. Currently, most big business leaders think that the best investment they can make is to fund politician campaigns, which will in turn return the favor by granting them privileges of all sorts, and generally protect their interests. There is no reason why we should not think the same way, in fact we should learn from them, because they did not get where they are, by being stupid or naïve. We need to stop spending so much money on shortsighted initiatives that produce some gain for some private interests, who happened to invest a little of their money into political campaigns.

Now more than ever, we need to spend all our resources as efficiently as possible. We also need an overall long-term strategy to re-tool our economy and society in a way that will make us competitive again. We cannot afford to give veto power for those much-needed strategies to some fat cats who happened to be opposed to those strategies on grounds that it may personally affect their wealth, or business, and therefore they use the advantage of being the ones funding campaigns for politicians to squash those initiatives. The cost to each individual would average no more than $1-5, per year. If we are foolish enough as a society, to refuse to pay this small price to get us government that works, we probably do not deserve to survive as a society, and it is increasingly obvious that we will not, unless we change.

Re-introduce meritocracy

With a proper decision making apparatus in place, there is a chance that we can make better decisions that hopefully will put us on the right path to becoming competitive again. The place to start after taking care of the inefficiencies caused by politicians that cater to the individual and corporate interests of the elites is to remove the equally detrimental practice that many may not know about, but it is costing us a lot in direct and indirect costs through loss of economic efficiency.

The official version of the cultural description that people like to equate our system to is a meritocracy. The idea is that even if a person is born in a poor family, there is a good chance that he/she can still make it, if he/she works hard enough, and gets an education, and has the natural abilities to do a certain task well. It is with sadness that I have to admit to myself and to the reader that, this is increasingly no longer the case. The real description of our culture is more accurately referred to as nepotism that is increasingly openly practiced in our society, and is no longer frowned upon. Based on the increased presence of advice for those who look for work coming from media and even government officials to engage in such practices, I would have to say that it is now the new normal. Christine Romans on CNN does not in any way shy away from suggesting that one should

316

"network" in order to find a job, or get a promotion. I have often heard that even government employees, working with unemployed people encourage the job seekers they work with to "network" in order to find a job. It is good advice indeed for individuals looking for work, given that by some accounts 80-90% of jobs are now landed in this manner. It is unfortunate that no one stops to consider the ramifications of such practices to our economy.

It is often pointed out by academics that one of the main factors that differentiate successful and thriving economies from the laggards is the quality of their human capital. I question therefore the wisdom of encouraging our present and future workforce to concentrate on cultivating networking skills and important contacts as a path to success, rather than cultivating their professional skills. If this is, the path we encourage it will likely be the path that most will take, because after all, we all want to succeed. The ones who still believe in making it through hard work are made to feel like suckers, because it is no longer rewarded. Seeing the path of hard work and applying one-self to honing technical skills and knowledge as the path to being thought of as a loser is sure to turn many people off that path. If this persists, it is only a matter of time before we will no longer poses a capable, well qualified, knowledgeable workforce, but a mass of "networkers", who will increasingly resort to bribing in order to land a good position, as simply making an acquaintance will no longer be enough to get an edge over others. I lived in such a society already; I strongly urge this one to keep from sliding into such a poisoned cultural environment.

The costs of this cultural decay: I have a good math teacher friend who lives in Northern Canada. He lives there, despite the fact that his wife is down south. Despite his master's degree in math, the only teaching job he was able to get was up north, on a native reservation. For years now, he has been trying to get a position down south or within a 2-hour driving distance from his wife, without any success. Despite applying for every job that is posted, he rarely even receives a call back. I find it hard to believe that all the math teacher jobs filled since in the area, were filled by more capable and better-educated people than he was. He is in fact the only math teacher I know of, who has a master's degree, because most who get that far, end up doing a PhD after, therefore they go on to bigger, better things.

Some might be tempted to argue that it is actually a good thing that better qualified teachers are being sent to teach harder to reach kids, such as the ones typically found on native reserves in Canada. Such a statement is politically correct, therefore fashionable, and I should add, equally unfashionable to challenge these days, but as is often the case, it is very flawed. The reality of it is that few children in that community ever finish high school. Many of them end up having children before they reach eighteen[1]. After years of teaching there, he is yet to have the opportunity to teach pre-calculus to even one student. This should come as no surprise, given that out of dozens of children who reach maturity each year, only three or four of them graduate high school. The reality is that the level of math that most students attending high school there end up learning is not beyond the teaching ability of even a fresh high school graduate, with higher than average math skills. Many more potential teachers, like my friend end up doing substitute teaching forever, because they do not know someone. Most of the rest of us in North America are then left wandering, why is it that the rest of the world is steadily catching up and surpassing the quality of education that we are achieving, despite the fact that we spend so much more money than they do? This could be a big part of the answer

Do not be fooled into thinking that just because the scale of the possible negative side effects of the situation that I described may seem relatively small on its own, this is a small problem. This example is just a small piece of a much bigger problem that has more negative side effects than most may imagine. First of all, as many as nine out of ten permanent, career positions that are currently being filled in North America, are being filled not because the right person has been found through careful examination of CV's, and subsequent interviews, but through "networking". It is true that many of those positions still require a minimum level of qualification, but I know from reliable accounts that many in graduate studies are now increasingly squeezing through, by using their strong socializing skills as well. I also know through personal interaction with others that many people who are talented and capable are often people who have rather awkward personalities, and therefore are most likely left fighting for the remaining 10% of positions that are filled through the principle of meritocracy.

I do not know about the rest of you, but I would rather have an architect, engineer, accountant, economist, lab technician or people of any other specialty on the job that got the position, because they worked hard at learning and building the necessary skills to understand the job. Thanks to our newfound tolerance for nepotism practices, someone who is good at networking, or simply knows someone thanks to family, friends, or ethnic ties, is the more likely to get in through the door. To better illustrate the negative effects of such practices that are already affecting our society, I chose a few quotes found in *media matters.org,* in reference to the handling of the occupation of Iraq in the aftermath of the invasion[2]:

"Many of those chosen by O'Beirne's office to work for the Coalition Provisional Authority, which ran Iraq's government from April 2003 to June 2004, lacked vital skills and experience. A 24-year-old who had never worked in finance—but had applied for a White House job—was sent to reopen Baghdad's stock exchange. The daughter of a prominent neoconservative commentator and a recent graduate from an evangelical university for home-schooled children were tapped to manage Iraq's $13 billion budget, even though they didn't have a background in accounting. *"

"The decision to send the loyal and the willing instead of the best and the brightest is now regarded by many people involved in the 3 1/2—year effort to stabilize and rebuild Iraq as one of the Bush administration's gravest errors."e

"To recruit the people he wanted, O'Beirne sought resumes from the offices of Republican congressmen, conservative think tanks, and GOP activists. He discarded applications from those his staff deemed ideologically suspect, even if the applicants possessed Arabic language skills or postwar rebuilding experience"

The examples I found on this site, go on and on with many such examples, which if we weigh carefully in terms of their consequences, it probably cost the US Taxpayer more money than the 2008 stimulus package meant to save the US and global economy from catastrophe. For those who are not familiar with this issue,

James O'Beirne was a White House liaison to the Pentagon, and was deeply involved in shaping the administration of Iraq in the months after the occupation. The information is out there, available to all, yet very few know about this, therefore we tend to underestimate the size of this problem, and its consequences.

It is amazing that here we have a clear case of nepotism practices within the US government, which possibly cost the US taxpayers hundreds of billions, due to the initial failure of the administration of occupied Iraq, which later led to the heightened level of violence and yet there is precious little outrage on the part of the public. Yet when it comes to issues such as money for the unemployed, health care, education, food-stamps, infrastructure and other useful initiatives, everyone is outraged about allocating a few billions more, or not being willing to cut deeper. This should give us all cause to worry about the cultural state of our society, because it seems to me that we have very little collective ability to put things in proper perspective.

The more dangerous effect of nepotism practices becoming widespread in our society stems from social reconditioning, which happens inevitably, when the value structures are modified. No longer is it important to work hard and get noticed through competence as I already mentioned. One can go much further, by honing his/her social skills, and maintaining important contacts within society. Just like natural selection happening in nature, we select for people who are good at networking through society, so increasingly people learn that one's value is measured by those skills. Through this process, hard work and honing one's talents become an increasingly pointless pursuit. Many still do it only because of their realization that their natural abilities and the means to network are not present in their bag of tools they poses for this competition, so they give up and hope to compete for the few remaining positions left untainted. As for the ones who are aware of their skills and means to network, they can just do the minimum required to be considered qualified, because the network will take care of the rest. Better yet, when they receive the leg up, they can make sure that they hire a few capable people, who are less equipped to network, to work under them, so he/she can claim responsibility for the work that they do.

Many competent people are brushed aside through this process and marginalized. This happens because of lesser social skills, fewer important acquaintances, and many other factors such as ethnic ties, which may qualify one for affirmative action rules, or simply allows people to rely on other members within the community, who already secured a high position for themselves. Usually, the ones who were born into less affluent families end up working part time during school and full time during the summer in order to make ends meet during their attendance of a higher education facility. I still remember the frustration I often felt while in school, when I heard from many about the many benefits of "volunteering" in order to build contacts for later on when it comes time to start looking for work. While I was in school, I did not know how to go about fitting in more hours at work in order to be able to pay for tuition and living expenses. So much for the much-trumpeted social mobility aspect of society, that everyone brags that we have, while other societies do not. Between having poor parents, and being smart and ambitious, or having rich, well connected parents, but having few abilities and poor work habits, chances are that the one with the rich parents is still the more likely to succeed in this society. A net loss for the gifted and hardworking individual, and for society as well, in favor of the one born in privilege, who is kept in privilege despite not deserving to be.

I am sure that this is not a new phenomena, and many can surely point to plenty examples in the past where nepotism was alive and well. Then they can argue that it is acceptable, because after all, we are still on top for now, therefore they can argue the, "if it ain't broke why fix it" clause. The fact that CNN contributor and correspondent Christine Romans can go on television and openly encourage people to try to find help in seeking favor, means that we no longer have the luxury to even pretend that we are a straight forward, honest society, based on meritocracy. The fact that it is now in the open, means that it is accepted, and no one needs to fear any retribution for engaging in it. It also means that young people are being taught certain values that they now feel they should adopt in order to be successful. The danger is that we are raising the next generation to be one of networkers, who will be eaten up by our competitors such as the Chinese, Indians, Brazilians and other up and coming

321

economic powers. In fact, we are already losing out to them. We have been threading water for at least a decade now.

CNN contributor Christine Romans and other like-minded individuals have a vision for our society, where we all try to kiss up to someone, in order to get ahead. That is the society she envisions to be the best adapted to take on increased economic competition coming from abroad, and our collective human challenges that need to be dealt with, such as convincing the world that we need to do more for environmental protection. The thing is that we are already in the middle of trying out her vision, and we seem to be sinking deeper and deeper into the big pile of problems previous generations and also we accumulated. Maybe this CNN reporter should be assigned to do a report on the cost of nepotism in the administration of Iraq. At least then, the story will finally be publicized as it deserves to be, and she might learn some important lessons as well.

My vision is that of a society that continues to grow, through embracing and implementing ideals that we only preach, but we do not follow. Meritocracy is reinforced as an ideal we live by, and thus we propel forward the ones that are truly the best and the brightest in our society. By eliminating nepotism, we increase our efficiency as an economy, because the education and skills that our people have accumulated can finally be put to their appropriate use. Our young people can confidently aspire to work towards becoming good at doing what they desire to do in their future; without the constant worry that others who concentrated on being socialites will beat them. Perhaps in the future, we will have advisors to our leaders, who will recognize the dangers of such misadventures as the US had in Iraq. If not, then at least we will send in better administrators, who will create a more stable society, which will be less prone to violence, thus cutting the cost of invading and occupying other countries.

Just like the inefficiency created by our tolerance for our elected politicians to be comfortably placed in the pockets of a few elites who are mainly geared towards defending their narrow interests that often are directly opposed to our interests as a society, so does nepotism create similar inefficiencies. Thanks to such practices that plague our society, we are most likely loosing hundreds of billions of dollars and Euros every year. Our infrastructure capital is diminished due to government waste generated by the legal loophole we left open for the haves to bribe our politicians through their campaign contributions. Our human capital is also diminished by the same process, thanks to lack of funding for education in many cases, which is further exacerbated by poor choice in hiring teaching staff, as I exemplified through the case of my friend in Manitoba, Canada. Even the quality that we do get out of our educational system is under-utilized heavily through the job selection process that now depends heavily on potential employees having the right connections, rather than the right professional and natural abilities. Maybe this is one of the reasons why many of our best and brightest in the financial world, who regularly collect multi million dollar bonuses for their work, did not see our current financial disaster coming. In fact, many failed to recognize it even as it was unfolding. Maybe many of them were good at networking and thus made it to the top, rather than being good at their job. It is also possible that they may have learned all the neat financial analytical skills at prestigious universities, such as Harvard, but perhaps they failed to learn many of the basics about our world, past and present in their high school years. It is possible that the teachers who taught them about our world were disinterested individuals who may not have very well developed teaching skills and subject knowledge, but they knew someone, so they got in.

If more than 80% of people who land a new job these days got it through nepotism, it is certain that a large proportion of those are under-qualified. They likely lack in education and experience, as well as natural abilities and work habits, in comparison to what the result of the hiring process would have brought through a fair process in terms of human capital applied to the tasks needed to be done. It is entirely possible that a few good advisors and technocrats would have saved the US the fiasco of the aftermath of the Iraq war. Better yet, some analysts could have predicted the difficulties of succeeding in such an adventure, and therefore would have advised against the whole misadventure before it got started. The result instead, is that we have a bunch of incompetent individuals who got to work in the early administration of Iraq, who now have a better CV, than those who were passed over, but would have been much better suited to the task. The result of course is that we now have incompetent people who have the necessary credentials in the shape of work experience, while those who should have been hired often end up doing jobs that they are overqualified for in both education and skills. The initial act of nepotism actually leads to the wrong people being promoted throughout the system.

Alarm bells ringing, and the natural reaction of denial or looking to the ideal past for solutions

The unfolding disaster on Easter Island was easy to see. There was no need for a complex analysis of the situation by the elites or the people to understand the crisis they were heading into. When that society collapsed, there is evidence that suggests people knew what was responsible for their predicament in the form of evidence that they took their anger out on the big stone heads that they built. More often than not, the problems facing a society that may be threatened with major calamity is not very obvious to the average person, even after clear signs of trouble. When Rome was sacked for the first time in 410 A.D, there seems to have been very little in terms of a strong reaction on the part of the elites or the masses, in terms of demanding a reorganization of the empire that by then was facing challenges on many fronts. Historian Peter Heather, who is an expert on this subject, describes in one of his books a society that still believed in its destiny to bring Christianity and general order to the world. We have the benefit of hindsight, and we also have a different understanding about societies tackling their problems, therefore we cannot be faulted for being tempted into seeing their choice of no reaction as foolish. We tend to think also that we have the tools in place to deal with the kind of changes that the Romans went through in an effective and ultimately successful manner. We see ourselves as superior in our adaptation to circumstances.

The Romans cannot be faulted for not understanding what was happening to them, because their information network did not in fact permit a dissemination of a clear picture of the situation. The empire was vast, and far beyond the comprehension of most in terms of the significance of each development within or outside its borders. Therefore, while we may be tempted to think when examining the historical evidence that alarm bells should have been ringing, it was in fact normal for them not to. Let us not forget also that seeing the problem coming our way is one thing, but as the Easter Islanders have demonstrated to us, doing something about it is another thing altogether.

We do have the necessary means of communication to inform ourselves with the necessary information. Information can travel across the world in an instant. Logic dictates that we should therefore be aware of our actual predicaments and act accordingly to fix things. Reality is however that the relevant information does not filter through the massive volume of relatively insignificant information to a sufficient degree to matter in terms of public opinion. Even when some bits and pieces filter through, the information tends to be hijacked and distorted into a form that benefits the messenger's agenda. The end result is that we are offered solutions to our problems that make no sense whatsoever when put to the test.

This trend is most obvious in the US, which is by far the largest western economy. The prevailing argument currently, which is sweeping the nation, is that they need to go back to small government, and let private enterprise handle most things. To a lesser extent, there is the same opposition to change coming from Europe's left, which argues that the sometimes overly generous government programs can be maintained. Can they be right? Will the US prevail through a radical shift towards a more purified version of its *laisez faire* mentality that the country was founded on? Will the EU survive without addressing the very grim reality of having to give up some of the cherished social safety nets that may indeed make it a very humane place, but certainly not a sustainable one? Is it not more likely that they are hanging on to old habits and ideas that are way past their prime and have outlived their usefulness long ago, just like Romania's sense of identity, fueled and reinforced by its national religion? Are we refusing to undergo drastic cultural, social and administrative re-tooling, just like the Romans did as they collapsed under pressures that were by no means insurmountable? Perhaps I am completely wrong and our society does not need a drastic change in order to survive the future as it is being handed to us. If that were the case, then there would not be so much apprehension about our future as a planet in general and as westerners and our way of life in particular.

Alarm bells are ringing from all sides and increasingly for good reason. The peak oil movement warns that we cannot keep raising global output of a finite resource forever. The Tea Party movement warns that the US is going bankrupt, and near anarchy achieved through shrinking the size of government beyond what is realistically needed in modern times, is the only savior. There is also preacher John C. Hagee, who thinks that the US is in terminal decline, and the only way to save it is to run all aspects of government, internal and external, according to the teachings of the Old Testament. For further instruction on his ideas I recommend the book he authored *"Can America Survive?"* I will bring up only one of his recommendations, as a sample of what he thinks is our most pressing problem. He thinks we need a confrontation with Iran, because we need to ensure the safety of Israel. He is convinced that if we do not attack every potential enemy of the chosen people, God will forsake us, and we will collapse. The fact that a war with Iran is probably unnecessary because Israel certainly has the means to defend itself, courtesy of 200 nuclear warheads, as well as the most sophisticated conventional military in the region, courtesy of $3.5 billion in yearly aid, courtesy of the US taxpayer, is lost in this proposal. The fact that if the US will undertake a new military adventure that might be even more costly than the Iraq debacle, which might be catastrophic financially at this point, is also left out. My question in this case is whether America can indeed survive, given that individuals like Mr Hagee can mislead millions in regards to what our most pressing needs truly are?

Countless political leaders of the EU believe that major reform needs to happen in order to prevent Europe from loosing its competitive edge in relation to the rise in economic power occurring in other regions of the world, although the majority of the population it seems is still not up to speed yet. I have to say though that I do admire some aspects of past and present European decision making that gives them a distinct advantage when it comes to energy efficiency. The current global environment is far from rewarding fully such achievements however, so given the downsides of stringent energy and environmental rules on investment, the net effect may be negative on the economy.

Assuming that we can agree at least on the fact that we likely have some major problems here, then the next question is where can we start in bringing us back on track and transform ourselves into an entity that can compete on the global stage within the new environment? We have to deal with the fact that others can now produce most of the goods that we can for a cheaper price due to lower wages and environmental & worker protection standards. We have to deal with the fact that our consumers are aging, and are more indebted than most consumers around the world are. We have to deal with a world where there is increasing competition for renewable and non-renewable resources, some of which are destined to experience a decline in availability, while the global economy as it is currently structured requires a steady increase in the supply of most of those same resources in question. Through all of this, we also have to find urgent solutions to the problem of increased pollution worldwide, and convince the rest of the world to go along with us. I think that at this point it is hard to find many reasonable and informed individuals who would counter that solving all the potential issues on this list is not essential to our wellbeing. Many other things could go on the list perhaps, but just the number and gravity of tasks that we need to take care of on this list are more than enough for us to tackle. Unfortunately, they are not likely to be solved if we do not take steps to change course in the near future.

False Saviors: (An important ingredient in any collapse of past societies)

There are plenty of people out there that recognize some of the same problems, which I believe we need to tackle with haste, if we want to have any hope for a decent future for our children and ourselves. Unfortunately, I am yet to see a solution or set of solutions come forward that is likely to truly deal with our present and future predicaments adequately. It is very unfortunate that in dealing with this issue of paramount importance, we have to deal with refuting claims of solutions to our problems that come from as far from reality

327

as the solutions that are being proposed by pastor Hagee, who bases most of his ideas on Old Testament scripture. It is sad that someone like him and other evangelicals can confuse millions into believing in a way of thinking that is likely to cause complete failure of our society if implemented. I do not intend to deal with the ideas coming out from that segment of society, but I will point out one thing. Just like Romania, which I used as an example of a society that is failing miserably to adapt culturally to deal with 21'Th century problems due to factors that keep it stuck with 19'Th century nationalistic ideals, so are these evangelical movements in the US helping do the same for US society. If anyone believes that running our 21'Th century society according to the teachings of the Old Testament is a good idea, it must mean that they also think that it is a good idea for us to achieve the same standard of living as the people living in biblical times enjoyed more than 2000 years ago. I just do not see how we can get anything else but that, if we choose this route.

The biblical solutions are in many ways just as inappropriate to our reality as the extreme left that advocates a return back to utopist hunter-gatherer principles to run our society. If 19'Th century mentality is not adequate to run 21'Th century Romania, Stone Age cultural values centered on the need to organize small bands of 50 to 100 people is just beyond any plausibility. Some more reasonable proposals come from the likes of the Tea Party Movement, who advocate a return to Adam Smith principles of *laisez faire*, which is a very strong argument actually, because many elements within that concept are in fact the elements that drive our current economy forward. While elements of Smith's theory are indispensable to modern economics, it should not be taken to mean that moving towards a complete embrace of his theories will necessarily make things better, but they insist that it will despite the fact that we no longer live in a mainly agrarian society, for which Adam Smith tailored his ideas.

Tea Parties & Status Quo Politicians: (Role of Government)

In his book *"The Wealth of Nations"* Adam Smith made the best argument to date for free market economics, and for the limited role of government. He argued that allowing each individual to pursue his or her own self-interest unhindered by government intervention, allows everyone to benefit. We see that in every day life as well. For instance, a person with a lot of money to invest decides to build a food processing plant in your local neighborhood, causing economic activity to occur. The investment is especially attractive given that there is no government interference through regulation, and therefore the money invested is done so in a way that will maximize profits, just as Adam Smith prescribed. The economic benefits to this investment are obvious. The operation will mean jobs thanks to the initial investment, as well as indirect jobs thanks to the multiplier effect. The company also provides a crucial service since none of us like to slaughter the animals we eat, nor is it practical for us to do so, for many reasons. The owner of the company becomes super rich, and therefore spends a lot of money in the community, creating even more economic activity. The individuals working in the plant are likewise eager to spend their wages, on whatever they may think will be crucial to bettering their lives, creating more demand for goods and services and therefore more jobs. The government is staying away from the whole thing, therefore the owner and the workers keep most of their wages, only surrendering the minimum needed to provide for public safety and defense. So far, Adam Smith seems to have been a genius.

The problem with this picture of course is that even though small government seems at first glance beneficial to encouraging business; employment and therefore economic prosperity, there are some problems that do not come into consideration. First, things have changed a lot since Adam Smith's era. If this food processing plant had opened 250 years ago, the cattle, or any other needed raw materials, would have simply been brought in by farmers overland. Now we need rail and/or road transport infrastructure to get the raw materials to the plant. As an example of this in modern terms, Mercedes recently announced that they chose to build a factory in Hungary instead of Romania, because of infrastructure related issues. Government cannot provide those things without a tax levy. Government also effectively provides a workforce with the right level of education to run such a plant. A thing that was not nearly as

329

crucial given the level of education needed to perform adequately in Adam Smith's days.

Tastes have also changed greatly in the past 250 years. We demand a certain level of safety in our everyday lives on a level not even imagined back then. For one, we demand food safety and regulations in the western world. Without government involvement, it is inconceivable that the demands made by us would be followed. Regulations tend to be the enemy of profit maximization, therefore in their absence; private enterprise would find it in its interests to cut corners. I should specify here that it is in my view overkill on the part of government to regulate small independent farmers who market their products directly to the end consumer. I do not believe that a farmer should be prevented from selling me un-pasteurized milk for instance. Government does have to prevent farmers from engaging in practices such as the one that led to the tainted baby formula scandal in China, which made many infants sick. This is where we need to make sure that we have competent and diligent administrators, who can recognize the very important difference between the dangers of un-pasteurized milk, and tainted milk due to greedy behavior.

The economic cost of regulating and inspecting the food industry is something that we have to accept as something that we have to pay for through taxes, and a cut in the company's profit margins, due to demands of proper business operations. The toxic or potentially disease spreading waste created by such a meat processing plant needs to be disposed of in a manner that satisfies safety to the community and to nature. The cheapest and most cost effective way for the company to rid itself of its waste would be to dump it on the edge of town, and let nature and wild dogs do their bidding. The danger to human safety, and probably to the environment as a whole would probably be unacceptable. The smell of rotting food waste would also be something that has to be considered. After all, who would want to live beside such a dumpsite? As a result, government interferes further; to make sure that the plant's owner allocates enough funds to dispose of the waste in a manner that does not create discomfort, or risk people's safety.

Since the US declaration of independence, this country's population increased roughly 200 fold (excluding the natives). It went from a population of roughly one and a half million back then, to a population of just over 300 million people. Industrial output per person also increased since then by a few hundred times, from its original point, when this country came into existence. So, overall industrial production increased about one hundred thousand times the original level of output, when the US was born. The nature of output also changed dramatically. The chemical industry was born for instance, with all its various applications. The capacity of industry to affect negatively the environment and our health, if it was to go un-regulated would be unthinkable. The reason that I bring this up is that it is a good visualization of the absurdity of the political right in calling for a constitutional government. In other words, a government that only does the things that are written in the constitution. There are no provisions in the constitution to deal with pollution as far as I know. There is also nothing in the teachings of Adam Smith to deal with these negative externalities, because these were just not major issues back then, compared to the present situation. The scary thing is that an increasing number of people are being convinced of the benefits of these extreme right wing ideas, which do not even stand up to basic introductory year economics teachings.

The overall growth of government as a percentage of GDP in the past century is a common trend observed in the developed world. Canada's share of government spending as a percentage of GDP for instance has gone from 13% in the 1920's to roughly 40% in the past decade. This trend has nothing to do with Government flexing its muscles, or trying to crowd out private enterprise. It is a natural evolutionary adaptation of the evolving situation. Consider the change in lifestyle for people moving from a mainly rural setting as the average norm, to the hyper-urbanized situation we witness today. At the beginning of the 20'Th century, the majority of the western world was still composed of a rural dominated demographic. Taking a closer look at what this meant in practice, it means that the majorities of the population had a plot of land as an asset, and as such most were self-employed. Things have changed drastically in the past 100 years however as people moved to the city and gave up their productive assets, such as farmland, mills or other common features of the rural economy, and exchanged them for selling their labor, and purchasing non productive assets such as an urban house, or renting.

The urbanization trend gave rise to an increased need for a social safety net, which I think should be obvious. We examined this already as we learned of Bismarck's career. A farmer could work the land until age no longer permitted such exertion. The last remaining years of life were easily taken care of by renting out the land, selling it, or relying on the inheriting children to take care of them as the duties and privileges of the land were transferred over to them. For the increasing labor selling population, the point when the body and the mind no longer allowed for an adequate ability to earn a living left them with nothing to support themselves with, except with what they could put away from their earnings. Saving up from what tends to be the going wage in a society was never plausible for everyone however. The wage floor in most societies is always somewhere close to what a person needs from paycheck to paycheck for the most basic necessities. Pensions were set up because there was no other way to get the majority of private enterprises to pay enough to allow people to do more than survive. The taxation introduced to fund those pension funds effectively meant a wage increase for most people, because firms still had to pay a net wage that was enough to allow people to survive after the deductions. Even those who have the ability to allocate a part of their wages to a private pension fund are by no means able to guess how much in savings is adequate. An unemployment insurance scheme is also necessary to keep the urban population from experiencing extreme hardships. All of this is necessary because the nature of firms is to be profit maximizing, therefore many employees end up receiving the minimum necessary to keep afloat while receiving the regular checks from the employer. Stashing away for a rainy day or for retirement is just never an option for a large segment of the population. Establishing a minimum wage is also a way that Governments can offer stability, which is needed.

One might ask why we should care about creating a stable way of life for individuals. Aside from our lack of appeal for seeing misery all around us, there are also many practical reasons. For instance, it allows for creative destruction in industry to occur with far less resistance, and fewer side effects. Having some stability within a community also allows the housing market to prosper, because the appearance and disappearance of some industries in a region will no longer cause entire communities to go through extremely dramatic demographic boom and bust cycles. Examples of that are resource extraction based communities and manufacturing sites such as Detroit, Flint and numerous towns in Ohio, in the US. It is hard to imagine a town like Flint after many car-manufacturing jobs disappeared rather suddenly and no government support system in place to at least, minimize the effects.

Aside from a social safety net that allows for a normalization of life, we also need to increasingly, develop our human capital, which is one of the main factors that separate us from many underdeveloped countries. Government is the most effective means of expanding the naturally occurring talent found within our population through making education available as much as possible, regardless of a child's economic means. After all, naturally talented and smart kids are not born only to wealthy families. The need to have a workforce far more educated than was the case in the time of Adam Smith is an absolute given. We need an environment, where people's talents and abilities are given the opportunity to shine and enrich our lives through helping advance our way of life towards improvement. This too is something that requires the government to step in and facilitate, which is something that they can only do through taxation and spending.

Government has to play a role whenever there is a situation where a good consumed is a public good, or non-excludable. For instance, few private firms would engage in building sidewalks. The thought of having to charge everyone who used it, is quite absurd. It is true that private toll roads operate in many places around the world, and with improved technology, one day a toll system could be set up even for sidewalk use. Just think of the implications however. First, conditioning one's most basic right to physical mobility on one's ability to pay would be a chaotic and outright inhumane situation. Many people would be forced to choose between walking, and eating. Communities would be taken advantage of as the owners of infrastructure, such as a sidewalk, can easily use their monopoly power to extract fees as high as they want. If roads are similarly also privatized, the new owners can set whatever fee they deem to be in their interest, and given that most such infrastructure tends to gain some monopoly power, it is likely that some of us may end up becoming prisoners in our own homes, due to the inability to pay to move around. Those opting to move around more could bankrupt themselves through walking. So much for The Tea Party and other right wing slogans advocating freedom through the shrinking of government. When applied in practice, it is more like the imprisonment of the masses in the interest of the elites.

When me and my wife moved down to the US from Canada for her post doctoral, she wanted to celebrate her first birthday after we moved by having a picnic on a lake shore. This was not usually a difficult task in Canada, with its low population density, where we would have likely gone for a walk on the lakeshore, and would have had our picnic there as well. We searched the map for a nice big lake, we found one, and when we got there, we realized that the entire shore was sold for development of private cabins, and a factory, therefore there was no possibility of us enjoying nature the way that people 100 years prior would have been able to do. A similar thing happened when we wanted to go to the beach one time. As it turned out it was transformed into a gated community. There are still places where one can go to enjoy nature's beauty, but increasingly one has to pay, and in private hands these places can end up costing a lot. I went to Yellowstone Park in the summer of 2009, one of the most beautiful places I have seen in my entire life. The place is still accessible to the public courtesy of government involvement. I shudder to think what would happen to the place, if it were privatized to someone looking to maximize profits.

As it turns out, government interference keeps places accessible; therefore, they preserve our freedom, although business lobby is slowly winning the fight as our governments are becoming weaker, and are more likely to auction off more and more public land and assets. Tea Party initiatives may be applauded and most likely supported by the business elites who always support the monetization of things, and that may explain all the money they have to support their candidates. With the money donated, they convinced millions of people that if we sell ourselves to private enterprise, everything shall be peachy, and we will never be freer. This is just not true and if you are not convinced that I am right, check out what the privatization of water did in Bolivia, a very impoverished country, where most are poor. After the privatization of the water utility, the purchasing company Bechtel hiked the price for its services by 200%, making it prohibitively expensive for most to purchase the water. In order to force the population to buy the water, the government was pushed into outlawing the collection of rainwater, a very natural thing to do. So much for privatization bringing freedom to the people of Bolivia, which actually makes it look more like slavery.

Just because I used a poor South American country as example, do not be fooled into thinking that this may be just a poor nation issue. There are many states in the US where it is in fact illegal to collect rainwater, because apparently it actually belongs to the owners of the rights to underground aquifers or streams. This may not be such a major issue now, because water is still something that most can afford to purchase from the utilities. Just imagine however if you have no money to pay the utilities, and you are legally required to refrain from collecting rainwater to bathe, water a garden so you can eat, or even to collect it to drink. You would in that case have to choose between letting it flow by your house, or brake the law by doing something that up to recent times people were always naturally predisposed to doing.

These examples from the US are just a sample of the many false saviors that are currently floating around, making it increasingly harder to pinpoint the real issues and problems that we are facing, and the more realistic solutions are thus often lost under the noise. It is a real shame, because as the last decade was a bumpier ride, many people are now more engaged and want to be more aware about the prospect of maybe changing course in order to avoid a potential disaster, which is more and more clear that it is getting closer to our doorstep. The conversation is further drowned in the information overload that our society is constantly bombarded with and has to compete for attention with many other relevant or just seemingly relevant conversations that are being held in the larger social spectrum. The conversation is further diminished by the lack of ability on the part of the general population to understand the true scope of the situation. I despair every time I hear a politician praising the wisdom of the electorate. It is often in fact, the same politician praising them, which favored cutting school budgets, making it harder to teach our kids some basic background information in regards to our history, and other useful subjects meant to build a decent background for our future adults to better understand the issues. The truth is that most people do not understand the world we live in to a degree that is adequate for them to make decisions, including on voting day. Yet they are regularly asked to cast their ballot, which in the end gives the cover needed for our elites to hide behind the apparent will of the masses.

In his book "Collapse" which deals with the failure or survival of many cultures around the world in the past millennia or so, Jared Diamond came to a very important conclusion. After studying many cultures that collapsed in the past, he concluded that one of the main obstacles to making changes vital for re-tooling a society to be better adapted to new conditions is the entrenched narrow scope interest. Many of the elites within society fight to keep the status quo in order to prevent potentially losing out to competitors, or even in the hope of keeping the increasing trend of benefiting from the current system. Most often, this led to general collapse, which in the end also destroyed the elites who were obstructing change that might have also saved them. This obstruction is our main obstacle in trying to adapt to our present and future challenges. The elites are putting up these obstacles right now, and most do not realize it.

The Tea Party movement is just one such obstacle and it is most effective due to its misunderstood purpose for its existence. They claim to be for freedom, while in reality, they wish to enhance the ability of corporate America to exploit the lower classes, by removing government curbs on exploitation. They are against any progress on issues related to the environment, which also mainly affects the average Joe, because the rich can afford to buy mansions in pristine Montana and other such places, and they can afford to drink bottled water and eat organic. They are for eliminating public schools, because the rich can afford to go private, leaving most of the middle and lower classes to fend for themselves, and in the end they will likely end up with far fewer opportunities when they grow up, removing altogether any hint of social mobility that still exists. They want to eliminate any government involvement in health care, because the answer once again is that the rich can afford to look after their parents, who most likely are rich, themselves. They obviously do not care much for social security, what use would the rich have for that? Perhaps Sarah Pallin will teach us all the lessons she learned in Alaska about an old Inuit tradition to leave the elderly to freeze to death, when they were no longer able bodied. That lesson off course is only valid for the have-not segment of our society, because the rich can take care of their own elderly.

Despite the anti average Joe platform, that these Republican Party splinter group advocates push, they manage to crown themselves as the Populist Party, and the poor of America fall for it. The rich love them, because they represent a pro business lobby. If they would not, they probably would refrain from throwing so much money at them to support their political campaigns. In these conditions, the Tea Party will likely channel the populist energy of society exactly where the elites want it to be channeled, to the detriment of society, until it becomes clear enough that they are false saviors, which would take decades. That can prove to be way too late for us to save ourselves from what looks to increasingly resemble the fate that the Romans experienced 1600 years ago. This once again proves that democracy cannot produce any positive results as long as the voter is misinformed and the political campaigns depend on money fundraised from the ones interested in buying favor.

Because the electorate is being misled, it will never produce the kind of political outcome that will cater to anything else but the narrow interests of the elites, whose interests increasingly diverge from that of the average person and of the countries, we live in as westerners. The fact that we even bother to show up and vote in these conditions saddens me, because it just shows the debt of the delusion that we have as a society, thinking that it actually makes a great deal of difference in the larger scheme of things, and we believe that we have control. In reality, it is still the same employer who has most political parties on their books, they are the few and very affluent upper strata of our society. Expecting these politicians to stand up for the overall interest of their country, and to care about the interests of the average worker and the lower classes, is a lot like expecting an employee that is paid by Apple to do work for Dell. That will not happen, just as our politicians will never break their allegiance from their sponsors.

The politicians that Tea Party like movements in the vest promise to rid us from are increasingly the do nothing of major importance parties. They can afford to do just that, and thus avoid dealing with the real issues by creating false issues, and false solutions to the real problems. One of the best recent examples is the move to make it look like they are dealing with the heavy hemorrhage of jobs that we westerners are now subjected to in favor of the developing world. The easy answer that they found both in the US and EU was that this is in large part a reflection of the fact that China is artificially suppressing its currency, making it easier to attract investment by making their wages more competitive than ours. On the surface, it is a perfectly valid analysis of the problem, and a natural way to convince manufacturers from US and EU to stay put, or come back if they already left. Most importantly, enough people are willing to buy their argument, so the masses are temporarily impressed.

The reality however is that there is little reason to believe that Chinese workers will no longer be more competitive than US or EU workers if that country's currency would rise by 50%, or so. A rise in wages in China by 50% would likely just cut a little into the profits of the companies that outsourced there, while still making average wages there four times cheaper at least. The benefits of operating in China do not stop at wages either. In the case of the US, where the public health option is not present, companies also have to deal with health insurance costs, while no such costs exist in China. Environmental regulations and worker protection laws are so far behind in China in comparison to the west that they could compete in many fields just on that, without the wage advantage.

At first, I was puzzled that our politicians try to make such a huge issue out of this. Given that the Chinese already benefit in attracting investments to such a high degree, it is highly doubtful that their currency manipulation scheme is meant to compete against us. It is more likely however that they are doing it to compete with other rising economic powers in Asia and elsewhere, such as India, Vietnam, Indonesia, Brazil and many others who we are also losing out to. If they let their currency float freely on the exchanges, they would likely lose more jobs to some of the lower paid workers in some of these even cheaper countries, where they are also starting to close the worker ability and infrastructure gap with them and us. So then I realized that I should not be puzzled by this, because in the absence of a real solution to a problem, it is a classic political move to claim the problem is something that is not related to the economic structure itself. It is convenient to claim instead, that it is just something that needs to be dealt with, in this case through diplomacy.

What none of the politicians that make up mainstream politics, as well as some of the ones pretending to be the antidote to this political culture, when in fact they are all on the same team, are not telling us, is the truth of the situation we are faced with. Given current trends, we are likely destined to be headed for a leveling out of overall living standards across the globe. Furthermore, that relative level of standards of living is likely to be found as a correlation of availability of resources. To put into perspective what that means, if one takes a list of countries by per capita petroleum use, and you add up the population of the bottom 100 countries in per capita petroleum use, they add up to 4.8 billion people, and that number is still rising fast. Currently, the total petroleum use of those 4.8 billion people is still less than the amount of petroleum used by the US with only .3 billion people. If they would converge to the current US level of consumption, we would need to find 300 mb/d of extra production, or almost four times the current global production capacity. Even a convergence at roughly one quarter of current US levels of consumption would require a 50% rise in global petroleum production. These are some of the real issues facing us in the near future, because the process of convergence has already been underway for over a decade now, and there is still no one talking about it, and its consequences for us.

I chose to use petroleum in this book as an example, due to its special importance in the world economy, but this issue is in no way limited to just this one resource. We should also remember the fact that resources are being extracted with increasing effort. An effort which itself requires an increased share of resources to be allocated to it, due to the low hanging fruit aspect of our resource extraction patterns. The global population is also still in expansion mode. Technological innovation may help a little with alleviating the effects of having to live on less, and would alleviate the situation even more, if the global economic system would be such in nature, that it would encourage a faster switch towards efficiency. That has not been the case in the past and will likely not be so in the future either. So far, if you add up the net results of this convergence in the last decade between 2000 and 2010, the main results read as follows. The developing world has had a net gain in standards of living, with hundreds of millions being lifted out of absolute poverty. They increased their share of consumption of petroleum, from roughly one third of total to almost one half. They gained tens of millions of new jobs, and average wages rose somewhat, but that rise is tempered by the large masses of still very poor people. The OECD, mainly made up of western countries has seen stagnation in economic growth, no increase in net jobs. Millions of people became impoverished and net levels of debt to level of assets and GDP has increased dramatically. The OECD gave up on roughly 10% of its petroleum use, most of it not due to technological innovation, but because there are an increasing number of families that are being priced out thanks to an increase in price and a decrease in earnings for millions of people[3]. Given the large ballooning of public debt that was needed to keep us from even more dire consequences, the trend already witnessed will most likely accelerate even more in the coming decade. One bright spot is seen for the top 1% of earners in our society, who continue to prosper and increase their incomes quite nicely.

It is understandable that a politician in the EU or the US would not be interested in telling us that we are about to converge in our lifestyle with a country like India. In a worst-case scenario, we can even end up worse than some of those countries, especially if we end up going through default, which is a situation that looks to be more and more plausible given the large budgetary and trade imbalances we have with the rest of the world. There are already many countries, which are clearly in trouble in the west, and it is probably only a matter of a few more years of heavy borrowing before the truth will no longer be hidden behind feel good ratings of our bonds by rating agencies that after all belong to us. Iceland and Eastern Europe were hit first in 2008. Greece and Ireland got themselves into trouble, just in the following year. Portugal, Spain, Italy, Belgium and possibly a few more EU countries are in danger of suffering from financial attacks as well in the near future. A financial meltdown of the western economies would surely accelerate our downward drop into poverty as a society overall. Given the damage that the latest economic downturn has done to public finance balance sheets in the west, chances of a complete meltdown, including default on the debt either direct, or through massive devaluing of our currencies is a likely outcome in the next decade or two, unless things change fast. Change is exactly what we are not likely to get as long as we continue to have corporate sponsored politicians leading us.

If we are to succeed in this world, we really need to correct these inefficient practices. We cannot have so much self-interest working through the system and still expect it to work. We are the founders of the current global economic system and therefore we should know better than anyone that it is very unforgiving, and there is little room for making bad decisions, and tolerating inefficiencies such as nepotism. Aside from taking care of these two major inefficiencies above described, there is one more important thing that we need to address before taking on the harsh global competition that we face. This last cultural aspect is the most difficult to address in my view, because it has to do with creating a profound cultural shift. The problem that I am referring to is that of the uninformed electorate in a democratic system. I am currently trying hard to find an argument that would defend the democratic system in its form, as opposed to the autocratic regime in Beijing that is currently eating our leadership for breakfast in terms of ability to steer their country towards a more competitive form. The current political establishment embodied in the likes of former British Prime minister Brown, who suggests that we can compete if we just speed up R & D, allowing us to export to the growing and soon to be, the dominant market of Asia are misleading us. He suggests that our future lies in staying ahead technologically, so we can export high-tech products to Asia, Latin America, and other emerging markets. He neglects to specify how we can convince producers to manufacture these new products in our high wage, highly regulated environment, having to respect a whole range of norms that we care about, as opposed to manufacturing in Asia. Pretending that our R & D advantage is going to save us from our current predicament works quite well when the audience is kept in the dark about the reality of our situation. Because we believe in our leader's competence, and we believe their feel good stories of how we will export wander products in the future, they can afford to stand by and do nothing about our real problems.

As an example of where the true direction of trade is headed in such goods, just look at the trends for our wind turbine production. Turbines of similar capacity, made in China, are 25% cheaper, thus making the prospect of selling our turbines to them very grim. In fact, they are currently exporting them to us. Another good example of the likes of Mr. Brown being wrong is in the aerospace industry. It is true that Airbus of Europe and Boeing of US currently dominate the global market for passenger planes, with only a few small competitors on the fringe. However, manufacturers in China and Brazil are moving up fast. In fact, Airbus has agreed to build planes in China, and share technology, effectively ensuring that in exchange for a lucrative contract with the Chinese they sold their future, because a decade from now, they will have to compete with Chinese made aircraft that they helped design. This already happened to the Russians in a defense contract, where the Chinese gained valuable knowledge by making a similar deal of partial fulfillment of an import contract through home production. They recently launched a relatively similar fighter jet for export to the Russian version, but the cost is 1/3 cheaper. Under current trade conditions, we can innovate all we want, because in the end, production will still end up being done in the developing world.

The real future looks nothing like the one suggested by Mr. Brown and a host of other western leaders. The growth in consumption in Asia, Middle East, South America and Africa is not necessarily the great opportunity for us to sell to them, as they often like to claim. We may indeed continue to invent and improve products ranging from electronics, chemicals, drugs and machinery, but the rights to manufacture go to the lowest bid, and that bid is most certainly not ours. We may collect the royalties for our patents, and as long as we continue to own shares in the companies, we may profit from the sale of those products, as for the millions of jobs created from introducing these products on the global market, I hear Wall-Mart is still going strong for now.

Our biggest export currently is set to continue to be jobs. It is true that we have a definite cultural advantage in creativity, but as long as we are not willing to exploit our environment and workforce to the extent that it is being done by our main emerging market competitors, there is little we can do to regain the right to manufacture.

If you need more evidence of that, just look at what is happening in the renewable energy industry. President Obama was successful at whipping up enthusiasm in the youth of his country, painting a picture of Americans taking the lead in producing clean energy technology, and selling it on the global market. They believed it, and only three years later, China has now moved to restrict the rare earth metals export from their country, which is needed for the production of many energy efficient and renewable technology products. In fact, the Chinese are now producing more of those products such as electric car batteries, and a host of other products at a much higher rate than the US, and at a lower price. The gap will only grow as they also have the advantage of trillions of dollars in reserves and a fast decision making process at a central government level that deploys resources at lightning speed, compared to our current leadership. We, the people who elect our leadership have to be aware of these things, because it is important for us not to be misled. As long as this misleading of the majority continues, democracy might actually become a much hated hindrance to being able to compete.

12

What to do in the event of our collective failure

As I stated from the beginning, I am not very hopeful that we will be able to change course given the monumental task. This is not the kind of challenge that humans managed to solve in the past, which were often greatly celebrated. Landing on the moon, or decoding the human genome, both of which were great human achievements, are the kinds of tasks that we can feel rather comfortable in tackling, given the necessary investment and resources. The sort of challenge we are facing now are the kind that we humans failed to recognize in most cases, and in the rare event when we did see it coming, we failed to adapt, despite the fact that it would have been doable. The challenge we have in front of us in this respect is mainly a cultural one. We have to re-invent ourselves, and re-organize some core areas in our society that we have become accustomed to them being the way they are. That is hard to do, it saddens me therefore that I have to include this chapter.

My best guess in regards to how this situation we are in will end is that we are on the verge of global chaos. The western world is losing more and more of its core values, such as the concept of meritocracy, as I mentioned. We are also becoming financially unsustainable. We pilled on personal and government debts that require us to increase our wages, in order to cope. At the same time, we are being dragged towards lower real wages by increased competition from the developing world for jobs and resources. Given the strength of the pressures towards lower real wages, and benefits, the latter is likely to be the prevailing trend. In order to keep the entire system from choking on debt as real wages fall, with government revenues also diminishing accordingly, the US Federal Reserve and possibly the ECB will likely inflate, causing an eventual stabilization in stagflation mode. The severity of the situation will be mainly a consequence and in correlation with global resource scarcity levels.

The developing world will in this case face the problems that are already currently evident, including their inability to provide basic nutritional stability for their lower class citizens, who are the first to feel the effects of rising food prices. Social stability will depend on two main factors. The government's willingness to either provide subsidies, or in case of the inability to do so, or the lack of interest in such schemes, they will depend on the use of force on their own civilian populations. There are also likely to be further conflicts among nations in order to try to gain access to vital resources. There are already many such conflicts in the world. The Israeli-Palestinian conflict is in fact, in part about Israel wanting to keep access to the underground water aquifers in the West Bank, and access to the gas by the Gaza shore, therefore, there will likely never be peace, despite what some would have you believe. Israel depends on those aquifers from the occupied territories for 40% of its current water use; therefore, they cannot afford peace. Iraq was of course about oil, despite the image the initiators try to present us with. The African continent was always a battleground in large part because of various parties who wanted control of certain resources there. Proxy wars are likely to be an increasing trend there, as various powers, who would not dare face each other directly, will try to gain control through a clientele relationship.

The new political landscape

Democracy and the freedoms we currently enjoy are likely to suffer a great blow as the need to maintain regimes and stable societies will outweigh the desire and the benefits of a free society. Many of the developing countries that will succeed in deposing their leaders will be disappointed in the aftermath with the lack of change in their situation, despite the change in regime. In that case, there is the real danger that the state will likely collapse altogether, leaving behind a place controlled by the ones with the most capacity for violence, similar to Somalia. There is mounting evidence of that occurring right now in the aftermath of regime collapse in the

Muslim world. In Egypt for instance, people demanded better living conditions, including affordable food and fuel. In the aftermath of the regime collapse, there is now chaos, a contracting economy, mounting budget deficits, and a sharp increase in unemployment. Failure on the part of a new government to improve the people's living standards in the immediate aftermath of the revolution is causing even more bloodshed and chaos, giving rise to the possibility of an eventual collapse of basic order and stability.

In the formerly developed world, some form of authoritarian rule is probable, although it is likely to be far more sophisticated than the more naked violence oriented regimes that we presently observe in places like the Middle East. Violence would likely be more targeted towards stamping out dissent from the root, in the form of wrongful trumped up charges against key individuals. It is possible that we are already seeing this trend, in the case of Wiki leaks Founder Giulian Asange, which is probably just a more visible example of our current reality, rather than a first case, in other words; other, less visible individuals may have already been subjected to this kind of setup. To spell this out, we will have a form of repression that is likely to be stealthy in nature, beyond our collective ability as a society to recognize and cope with. Private enterprise is likely also to jump on the ship of destroying opposition in the form of ostracizing individuals who will be seen as inconvenient. Destroying the ability of people to earn a living as punishment for political activism is just as potent as detainment and violence can be. I am very certain that private enterprise will increasingly screen potential applicants for their political activities and views.

There will still be a significant number of people forming a middle class, who will also be interested in defending its position, so playing the poor against the well off is likely to be an important tool. The middle class will be kept in check through the threat of being demoted to the ranks of the increasingly harsh and growing ranks of the impoverished. The impoverished on the other hand lack the ability to fight back. There is already an admitted trend on the part of potential employers to do a search of the net for potential job candidates in order to screen them for potentially undesirable activity. That activity may easily include the voicing of opinions on political issues. Thus, the internet that was for a long time thought of as a tool for mobilizing the masses politically is now becoming a tool of oppression, not unlike the kind I witnessed during the communist repression. The democratic process will likely continue, although the choices will always reflect the interests of the same people, who just like now, will continue to sponsor all political sides. The thing that we can be certain of is that the authority of the corporate world over our lives is complete already through its domination of the political elites, and its ability to punish political activity that they consider undesirable, including perhaps those who write a book, is a reality[1].

Odds of continued economic stability for the long-term

Like I explained, in my chapter on finance, given a heightened risk of instability, interest rates are likely to rise, and lending will become much tighter. At this point, initial resource scarcity problems will give way to a lack of financial capital problems, including for funding resource exploration projects, most of which are now increasingly complex and expensive, because historically speaking, we went for the easy to get resources first. The much higher interest rates will make more and more industrial projects unfeasible, as well as consumer spending, which is likely to crash in the face of mounting interest charges. Government will likely feel the pressures from all sides. They will be pressured to tax less as people become less affluent. At the same time, the increasing ranks of the poor will likely demand more and more support. The first thing to suffer in this case is investment in infrastructure, education, and useful programs such as R & D work. It may be possible that under these circumstances, we might for only the second time in history be faced with a situation where net collective human knowledge will actually decrease. The first time this happened of course, was in the aftermath of the collapse of the Western Roman Empire. That may seem incredible, but do not forget that paying for all that infrastructure to educate, train and employ scientists is very costly, and it will likely be regarded as less important than immediate needs, such as feeding the hungry masses. Once we reach this level of hardship, we can forget about new ideas stemming from technological research saving us from our problems.

Our modern agricultural industry depends heavily on commodities mined from the ground. A spike in the relative price of these commodities, due to our diminished ability to continue opening up new frontiers in production can mean that farm production may lose its current productivity rate. To produce the current yields, farmers need to add substantial mineral resources, like, hydrocarbon based fertilizers and pesticides, as well as potash and phosphorus, the latter of which may have already peaked a while ago, and there may be serious shortages of mined resources of this substance in the not too distant future. The alternative to mining the stuff is to separate the phosphorus from human waste. We currently have no infrastructure or the will to deal with such an operation. We all would much rather see the stuff flushed and then forget about it. If we were to build such infrastructure, which might ultimately be the only alternative to mass starvation, it would add to the cost of food production massively. Without these very important mined resources, we would not be able to get even half the current yields from our land. The loss of these important chemical additives to our soil may in fact cause a lower yield per unit of land than we had in the pre chemical farming era. Soil exhaustion and depletion of naturally occurring nutrients is a well-known problem modern farming created. That is why many people are told to take supplements, because the nutrients that we should get from our crops are no longer present in their natural abundance. Remember, we have two billion people who are not getting adequate nutrition as it is right now. Hungry people can be very destabilizing to the world economy.

Of course, many will say, that a global economic meltdown could never happen. That is despite the fact that we were literally one bad decision away from reaching this point in 2008. In that moment, if we would have failed to keep some credit flowing through the economy, we would be living the scenario that I described above, right now. It is also important to keep in mind that if a similar, or even more intense recession will hit in the not too distant future, which is increasingly likely that it will, given the multiple sources of danger, our governments no longer have the same resources at their disposal to fight back. If we are to experience another economic breakdown before 2015, which is indeed very likely, we are still going to be in the middle of dealing with the damage caused by the 2008 breakdown. That damage includes continued job scarcity, a housing overhang, continuing problems dealing with the toxic financial assets that still float around within the financial system, and of course, ballooning government debt, and still very high deficits. Aside from the continuing problems with the financial system, there is of course the very immediate problem, which is already hitting some of the weak economies around the world such as Tunisia and Egypt, which is commodity price inflation due to lack of availability. Considering all these things, is it justified to deny that there is a good chance of a meltdown happening, perhaps very soon?

I think that odds are about 25% of it happening within a decade, 50% that it will happen by 2030, and a 75% chance that it will happen by 2040, when my son will be 30 years old, and I will be looking to retire, if the concept will still exist by then. The chances of collapse would likely diminish considerably, if a system of global trade, like the one I proposed in this book would be implemented promptly. History shows us however that we are unlikely to come up big in a situation like this, and fix the problem in order to let us preserve some of what we achieved so far.

How to prepare as an individual?

I intend to focus in this chapter on the western individual and what he/she should think about for their near term as well as long term future, given the above-mentioned summary of our most likely future as I see it. I assume in this scenario about the future economic and social environment that no such initiative will ever happen such as using trade to re-stabilize the world. Thus, there will be no effort made to solve the environmental, political, social, and economic ills that are threatening to end our past relative stability that westerners have enjoyed since the end of the Second World War.

The real bad news here is that the interests of the individual and the interests of the collective to continue our current path for as long as possible are complete, irreconcilable opposites, unless something is done to once again bring them back in sync. Continuing to play the role of the global consumer of last resort is sheer madness at this point, even though there is a chance that many may get away with it, unless government will step in to protect the interests of the wealthy, which is not out of character for them. Our economy is heavily reliant on people continuing to consume however, so stopping one's current spending habits can contribute to the hastening of economic collapse.

While continuing to accumulate debt, by spending most disposable income on trivial things that may enhance ones reputation, ego, and image of success may be a very foolish thing for people to do under the circumstances, it is vital for the continued viability of our economy. When an economy depends on the service sector for as much as 70% of GDP, as is the case with the US and many EU countries, which are close to it as well, the consumer is the most important thing. The collapse of the consumer would wipe out such a huge chunk of the economies of the west that they would likely collapse altogether. Nevertheless, as I said, while one is doing his/her patriotic duty by consuming, they are also doing irreparable damage to their odds for survival for themselves as well as their families.

I have some personal experience with a collapsing economy. Even though I witnessed it as a child, it is still a memory that one hardly can be expected to forget. The former communist block had very different problems and it was a slightly different situation, but many of the results can be expected to be the same. The one difference was that after the initial pain of the first decade of freedom from communist dictatorship, most of these economies re-oriented themselves to the exploitation of their low wage, high ability workforce. That eventually attracted many western as well as some Asian firms, who invested in enhancing their production capacity there, mainly to hit the western markets with the lower cost products made there. When the west will see its collapse, there will be no outside market and outside investors, which will be big and strong enough to help us to dig ourselves out and re-stabilize our economy through exports. This major difference is one of the most crucial ones that may be a big factor in how things will play out.

One of the first things that happened in Eastern Europe was the flight of capital out of the region. Many people who made money in the early 90's were eager to re-invest that money in more secure environments. Eastern Europe became the Wild East, where one went in quick, made money, and then got out of Dodge as fast as they went in. The net result was a constant flight of capital out of those countries, which crippled their ability to stop their freefall. Some countries that were more in tune with western culture, such as the catholic states that I mentioned in the cultural comparison chapter, re-adapted faster, and eventually became net receivers of capital, but for countries like Romania, where I was born, that did not happen until well into the second decade.

From this perspective, the similarity can be observed already as a fact on the ground, although it is happening under different circumstances, and therefore it has a slightly different form. In the west, we are witnessing the first stage of the flight of capital, in the form of the loss of manufacturing infrastructure. The second stage is just starting to unfold in the form of the shift in capital through the equity markets. Western investors are increasingly searching for long term investments in solid emerging economies that show a much better promise of returns. The capital tends to flow back to us in the form of bond purchases that are more attractive because of the perception that mature economies are more stable fiscally, which is now herd mentality more than anything. This is likely the beginning of the second phase of capital flight from the west, and it explains the reason why it takes 10% budget deficits for countries like the US to keep the economy from stalling out. US government bonds are seen as safe haven assets, because of the size and maturity of the economy, as well as the fact that the US dollar is the world's reserve currency. That too is likely to change however, because the US bond market is showing signs of early strain. The problem is found in the local bond market, where states and municipalities are at risk of default, due to their inability to print their way out of their hole as the federal government can. This will eventually move up the chain to the federal bond market, and at that point, the net outflow of capital can become permanent.

The consumer in the west is likely to capitulate permanently due to increased pressure on wages due to government cutbacks. In the US, state and municipal level governments are already threatening to deal the final blow to the strength of the consumer through layoffs and wage and benefits cuts that are likely to affect millions of consumers who will see their wages shrink or be eliminated altogether. This adds to pressure on the federal budget, because millions more will become dependent on federal handouts, and the federal government will have to ensure that there is some additional stimulus to pick up the slack due to local government cutbacks. Once the creditors, whether they may be internal or external become unable to justify continuing to fund the US federal deficits, the end of the US consumer will become a certainty.

The situation in Europe is not much different, because there are multiple forces that threaten to wipe out the consumer economy. The stagnated population there is probably the best example of what should be happening across the globe if we are to survive the situation that humanity is in without complete chaos. Yet this stagnation in population growth is seen as the greatest threat to the EU economy, because with it comes a stagnation in consumption. No speculator likes to invest in a stagnated market; therefore, Europe is seen as one of the least popular places to hold capital. Rich people from across the globe still keep their money in European banks, and they invest in Euro bonds, for many of the same reasons that they buy US bonds. Many European companies have also fled the west however, although it was very beneficial for them that they expanded the EU to include East European nations, because much of the capital has fled there, which is a lot closer to home, and still within the EU.

The European consumer is being hit hard already, because unlike the US, the EU cannot afford to print as much money, because the Euro is not the world's reserve currency. As a result, governments across Europe have already started implementing harsh austerity measures meant to stabilize their budget situation. The consumer in Europe will be hit especially hard because one of the austerity measures is aimed at keeping the elderly in the workforce for longer through raising the retirement age, and reducing incentives for early retirement. This means that the young people in Europe will have a much higher rate of unemployment as well as under-employment, because the elderly will crowd them out in the job market. Young people are the most likely to be the consumer that can be counted on to spend with few considerations for the future. They are the most likely to frequent restaurants instead of eating at home for one third of the price. They need to keep up in the latest fashion in order to play the mating game, so price is less of an issue. The already under-employed youth will have no chance to continue this important role in society. Not to mention the destabilizing effect that a large number of unemployed, discouraged youth can have on society, which can lead to a complete grinding of the economy to a halt, as recently being witnessed in the Middle East.

The western consumer is slowly but steadily being grinded down anyway, so if an individual feels the need to break away from the herd, and cautiously prepare for a possible turbulent future, he or she has no reason to feel guilty. Given the herd mentality of human beings, most will not do this anyway, so a few wise individuals who know better, should not have a major effect on the overall health of the economy. In economic terms, an individual who saves for tomorrow is in many ways no different in their economic behavior from entire societies that currently do the same. Emerging markets do this all the time. They invest a part of present national income in order to have the potential for greater enhanced consumption in the future. In the case of a breakdown in economic activity in the near future, those who may have saved may not have an opportunity for an enhanced level of consumption compared to the present, but in relative terms, they may have a greater right to consume in comparison with the new post collapse average. That may be a very important thing, when the average level of consumption may be measured in whether one still has shelter and adequate nutrition.

In the aftermath of collapse, some individuals will have an opportunity to move up the economic ladder. I have seen this in the immediate aftermath of the collapse of communism. Most who benefited were people who were at the top in the previous regime, but there were some new players as well. All one often needed was a relatively small amount of startup money, and the sense to get in early and the smarts to bribe the right officials. A likely scenario where there is a breakdown in our economic structure, some current economic elites caught holding the bag of everything that is toxic will likely end up dropping down the economic ladder. Those who are likely to have made significant contingency plans for such a scenario will end up becoming even more powerful. Some millionaires may end up becoming multi billionaires. In times of chaos, there is always an opportunity for some.

If you are convinced that you should indeed save in order to have something to fall back on, in the case that things are not as peachy as the current elites want us to believe, then there is still an important question. What kind of assets would have value in the aftermath of an economic meltdown? This is a very tough question, and no one can be sure of what the right answer is. Some elites who may currently know the answer, are unlikely to tell us, in fact they may do the opposite in order for them to be able to acquire some of those assets on the cheap. In such turbulent times, it is very hard to guess what the most likely things are, that will fly in the aftermath, but there are a few obvious things that we can count on to maintain their value and marketability.

My number one guess is that farmland will continue to have value no matter what the circumstances. Whether one chooses to lease the land to other farmers, or break with the current long-term urbanization trend and become a farmer oneself, the land will be valuable, because the elasticity of food as a consumer good is almost zero. People can go without most manufactured consumer goods for a while, especially non-essential goods like televisions and video games. We can go without most services, such as restaurants if need be. Giving up on consuming food means essentially that we give up on life. In a severe depression, I actually think that many of the minerals that enrich and protect our fields will become unaffordable, because the price of producing many of the mining projects will become higher than people will be able to afford to pay. In addition, we can expect poverty to cause violence and disruption worldwide; therefore, significant disruptions should be expected for many mineral resource-producing regions. That means that yields per unit of farmland are likely to drop, making the production of the land all the more valuable. There is also the likelihood that governments will drop all subsidies for the big farmers who currently dominate the western farming industry, making local small-scale providers more viable, for the additional obvious reason that a local provider will have smaller transportation costs.

You may have noticed, I like to take into account human behavior in certain circumstances that economists do not like to look at, because it does not fit very neatly within their theoretical models. They are often right to keep from factoring in human behavior of many sorts, because we are a very unpredictable species, but there are always some obvious givens. One of which is that if people who were used to eating well become hungry, they become violent. Another one, which should be expected based on past history, is that when government fails to compensate the public sector employees with a decent wage and benefits, it becomes only a matter of time before they resume the tried and tested method of survival through corruption. They also tend to become more careless when doing their duty. That is something that should be especially relevant to US citizens who are now seeing their public sector officials having their wages and benefits slashed. With that in mind, one should realize that retreating to some rural, lightly populated area of the world if possible, is not necessarily such a bad thing, given the poor prospects that one should expect in highly urbanized areas.

In considering making such a move as retreating to a rural setting, there should be one more thing to be taken into account. Depending on how desperate things in the big city become, violent behavior could hit rural communities especially hard as the urban masses decide that somehow it is not fair that rural people have so much food, and do not give it away as charity. If government remains strong enough, they would likely try to protect those who provide the nourishment to society. On the other hand, government officials may decide that it would be wiser to oppress the rural minority, in favor of appeasing the urban majority. There are many such precedents in history, so this can also be within the range of possibilities.

Ideally, I would personally choose areas, that are not as heavily populated, but still within range of the major towns, so one can still sell some produce, at least to be able to provide for some necessities, and for any property taxes that may be due. There is however a serious downside to living close to a large human population. In such situations, it can be expected that there will be a breakdown in environmental and sanitation standards, which is to be expected when providing for very strict necessities becomes the prime priority. With that in mind, an underground reservoir of water that one can tap into would be a very valuable asset. When purchasing property one should look ahead to assess the likelihood of contamination stemming from urban activities.

Some livestock alongside the farmland could provide more self-reliance because it would be a good source of fertilizer. If you happened to live in a colder climate, then building a hot house or two may be a good idea as well, in order to prolong the growing season. In addition, very importantly, try to find a community where, people tend to have a strong sense of local cohesion and solidarity. If you end up living among people who tend to eat each other alive, it can be very unpleasant, and it will provide very little protection from predatory behavior from outsiders.

If you happen to have currently a very good place of employment, you should consider keeping these things in mind, but it might be wise to wait with making the move to a rural setting until things are quite obviously going down the crapper. In the meantime, just make sure to save a good chunk of those earnings you are bringing in, and make sure that your savings are not exposed to too much risk through your investments. There is of course the eternal question then that pops up, which is what to invest in? One can buy farmland, if there is a good chance that the land can be leased on a yearly basis to other farmers, who might be willing to pay at least the equivalent of the yearly property tax on the land. The price of farmland might rise later, so there is a good chance that land might not be affordable later on.

A particularly good investment that is always likely to keep some value is gold. With 5,000 years of history as a means of exchange, it is by far one of the most stable currencies out there. The reason I chose to call it a currency, despite the fact that to my knowledge there is currently not one country out there that uses gold as a national currency is that on many levels it remains an important currency. Almost every country on this planet holds gold reserves as a reserve currency. I doubt that the offer of this precious metal in exchange for services rendered, or as a means to purchase, a foreign currency would ever be refused by another party. There have been recent moves as well to let people have gold denominated bank accounts, as well as to use gold as collateral for bank loans[2].

While I doubt that, we will soon have to carry gold with us to go shopping for groceries; gold remains a solid part of our global financial system. It is the only currency that cannot be devalued, because there are physical limits to how much of the stuff can be mined, while there is no limit to how much money can be printed on paper or electronically. In the event of economic hardship, central banks will most likely resort to increased printing of money. The recent result that can be observed just now, is the inflation of certain assets, including gold, petroleum, and most importantly food, which is responsible for much of the political instability seen recently in the developing world. Economists mistakenly state that there is no inflation, because they measure it through the cost of manufactured goods, such as televisions, washing machines and other items. They forget however to take into account the price of food and gasoline to a sufficient degree. Gold is the only currency that has kept up with the increase in the price of fuel and food. In the interest of full disclosure, I own some gold, as well as some silver. Thus, far I think it was a much better investment than a flat screen TV, or some other ultimately perishable good.

The stock market is another place where one could park some money, but judging by trends from the last decade, only a certain type of investment strategy is likely to bring back positive returns. Short-term investments, buying and selling mainly on rumor and momentum is the kind of investment that was successful in providing returns for some perceptive investors. Buy and hold was rather disastrous for most people, and most institutional investors who invested on the behalf of individuals and pensions. As I write this, we have regained a good chunk of the losses, and are now far above the lows of the recession, but we are still not very far ahead of levels seen in 2000. The next recession is likely to bring average stock price levels back to below year 2000 year levels as well. That effectively means that investors who poured money into the market around the year 2000, will likely not see any net gain if they were to sell into the next recession, which can easily happen if one is about to retire for instance. Same goes for people forced to sell because they might be among the ones who may have lost their job due to the recession, in fact they will likely incur a loss.

Remember that none of these considerations have even taken inflation as a factor to be reckoned as part of the overall situation. I do not believe that people investing in most western markets right now, will see a different result than they did in the last decade. Emerging markets have great potential, but they are very vulnerable to food and energy inflation, therefore it is very risky to invest there. So unless you are one of the few skilled traders who know how to make money in any environment, including during market declines, I recommend that you stay away from traditional buy and hold, except for an investment avenue that should not be shunned.

If you happened to have a retirement plan from work, where the company matches your contributions, it is worth investing in it, only for the fact that you automatically double your money, even before it is invested. There is also a chance that the current elites can actually hold this madness together beyond the point of your retirement, whenever that may be. In that case, it would be wise to have some money invested into a retirement plan, because it is increasingly clear that governments will not be able to fund their retirement schemes. In fact, I do not expect that governments will do much of anything in the future, beyond perhaps providing some form of judicial system and perhaps some law enforcement, and of course defense. Having said all that, I should emphasize that by holding it together, I do not mean to say that they will be able to provide the same current standard of living that we currently enjoy. It is more likely to be a sort of a two tier society, where a proportion of society, probably a minority of the entire population will still live well, while the majority of the people will be encouraged to aspire to join that minority, while their condition will be quite miserable. That pattern is emerging in the US already, where the top 10% of the population own more than two thirds of the total wealth, and the bottom 90% of households only earn about $31,000 per year on average. That compared to the top 1% who earn over a million a year, and the next 9% who earn over $100,000 per year[3]. In such an environment, I still think that one should mainly focus on getting out of Dodge, because things will become rather gruesome, as the poor will most likely turn on each other to fight for scraps. I say that only as a guide if you live in the US, because by now people are very well trained to think that one should never turn on the rich and affluent, because that is communist thinking. That is not really the case in Europe of course. I expect people to take it out on the rich there, even though income inequalities are not as severe, and the social safety net provides the poor with services and aid to a far greater degree than the US does.

All this goes back to the issue of global convergence remember, which we looked at before, where there is precious little left to justify the wages we earn, given the shrinking advantage we maintain in human and physical capital compared with many regions in the developing world. If we do nothing, given the current trends of globalization, we will converge to a lower level of consumption, where most of the developing world will see a slight improvement, while most of us will see a large drop in real incomes and standard of living. As most stats show, some stand to benefit from this, by becoming even wealthier. The middle class as we know it is no longer a sustainable possibility. If you think that you can stay in the mix and join the few who are very prosperous and are able to stay there once reaching that goal, it is worth keeping yourself in your current environment. If you think that you are like the majority who will likely make up the bulk of the newly impoverished through the current process, you are better off using the few years there are left in your capacity to earn a far superior wage by global standards to get your hands on some assets that are truly of value.

I am not sure how long there is left for us to do that, but signs of the current system cracking are emerging everywhere. One thing that is for certain is that with every recession from now on, more people will be leaving the middle class, than those who will join during the subdued boom times, with the obvious effect of a net loss with every cycle that we will go through. The length of the cycles will most likely become shorter and probably more severe downturns will be followed by weaker and, in effect increasingly jobless recoveries. It is likely only a matter of time before you are either laid off, or unable to find any other meaningful equivalent work, or you remain in your place of employment, but you are forced increasingly to swallow more and more injustice from your employers. They can do that, because they can replace you at any time, given the large number of people looking for work. Real wages cannot but drop in such an environment. You may not feel that right now personally, but as the average gets worse, chances increase that you cannot stay safe from this forever.

Personal responsibility

I know that it seems very hard to put some money aside, especially given the constant bombardment with suggestions for you to spend any money that may be left over after the basic needs are met. There are always new neat gadgets that seem like a must have after a robust advertising campaign to promote it, makes you scared that not having it may leave you behind the times. The people who employ their credit to help them get things may make you feel poor if you try to live within your means. It is however possible to put money aside and to invest it if you show some common sense and discipline.

In the last decade, I managed to get through university, get married, have a kid, and I owned a car since I was seventeen. I went to Europe twice in the last decade, and had many smaller vacations within North America. In other words, I lived a relatively normal life, yet I have zero debts, and I even managed to invest in a few ounces of gold, which has so far been a very good move on my part, especially because at this point, there is little chance that I will actually lose money on that investment. It is true that my parents helped by letting me live with them until I was twenty-five, but they did not give me any financial help of any sorts. I come from a modest family, so I was not able to ride the gravy train as many spoiled brats got to, in the past decades. In the course of the last decade, I never held a job that paid more than eighteen dollars per hour, yet I managed all this. It is true that I currently do not own a home, and will not until after me and my wife are both done with searching for our career paths. Still, given that no free money came my way, and that I had to pay tuition for university, and had to sustain myself for the past years after I moved out from my parents, it is a lot that I can say that I do not owe any money to anyone.

I am by no means perfect, but I do have an important trait that helps me in this case. I do not like getting into debt. I like the freedom of not having to make payments. That is why, to date my first three cars that I owned were used, and I paid cash for all three of them. When I started university in 2000, I bought my second car for 6,700 Canadian dollars, and still had a relatively good cushion of cash. In the end, I did borrow 6,000 dollars in student loans, which I paid back within a year of graduation. I first got a cell phone after I moved out from my parent's place, and it was mainly, because I did not get a landline. During my years in university, I worked weekends, which helped me keep out of trouble. I was psychologically able to do so, because in the three years prior to signing up for courses, I partied wildly, so I got that out of my system. By the time I started classes in university, going bar hopping became such a boring event that I hardly craved it.

I never bought expensive furniture; most of it was second hand. Designer clothes always seemed like a rip-off to me, because I am a firm believer that if it says CK (Calvin Klein) on my T-shirt, they should pay me for wearing it, because they get to advertise as I wear it in public. Besides, I think the best way to look good is to keep in shape, not by buying expensive designer clothes. When you are in good shape, most clothes will look good on you. I did spend money on going to Europe twice, but unlike most people headed to Eastern Europe on vacation to see relatives, I did not splurge on a car rental. I still remember my Uncle in Canada horrified at the concept that I will not rent a car, making all my relatives and acquaintances think that I am a complete failure (unlike everyone else who usually does so when going there). I am not sure how my relatives and friends there see me, but one thing that I am certain about is that the thousands of dollars I saved by not renting a car while I was there is a good investment, since it went into purchasing gold. The peace of mind I get from knowing that I can provide my newborn son with the necessities for some period, in case that things go wrong in terms of work and income in the near future is priceless. Most definitely, it is worth more, than impressing some people I only see once or twice per decade.

I find that it is precisely this desire to impress that gets us in trouble financially most often. I myself did make this very mistake in my younger years. I could have opted to pursue a trade instead of going to university. Electricians in Manitoba, where I lived most of my life earn roughly $35 per hour. The best part is that unlike most university graduates who can only dream of earning that much, firms in Canada actually offer sign up bonuses for journeymen. Most of you who have finished university, regardless of field of study, know that it is nowhere near as easy to get a job after graduation.

Even those with post secondary degrees often end up out in the cold. Master's graduates in biology related fields in Winnipeg, earn on average $35,000 a year working in a university lab, which is barely half of what a plumber can make in a year. There is of course the stigma that is attached to working with one's hands and getting dirty. I remember, it was often the case, that after a hard day's work, when my clothes were sometimes a little dirty, if I happened to stop by in a store, people always looked at me as if I was some poor destitute washout. These looks often came from people who earned only half of what I used to earn working in construction, yet in their eyes, I was the destitute one. There is no doubt in my mind that I would have done far better for myself financially in the past decade, if I had resisted the urge to impress through earning a university degree. It is not yet clear whether I will regret this for the rest of my life, but unless I end up doing something spectacular with my degree in economics/history and anthropology, chances are that over a lifetime, most trades' people will earn more money than I will. That is most likely true in Canada anyway.

We all make mistakes, but the important thing is to try one's best to learn as much from them as possible. I have many friends who have struggled with their debt load in the past and present. Between having to make car payments, monthly phone bills, which tend to get expensive if one is not careful, and some who did not realize in time that a credit card limit and student loans, does not mean that it is free money, it can become quite a struggle to stay afloat. A good friend of mine asked me a few years ago, with tears in his eyes, "what it feels like not to be in debt". Poor guy has been in debt constantly since he turned eighteen. The reason that he cannot find out is because he does not understand that finding out involves a more or less permanent change in behavior. He struggles for years now to get out from under debt, but always falls off the wagon. I tried to explain to him that it is not about tightening the belt until you cannot breathe. It is about making permanent decisions to make sure always that you are using the money only on things that are truly important to you. As I said, I went to Europe twice, because I love the cultural atmosphere, the history and still have some relatives and friends that I enjoy seeing. Other than that, I have visited almost every major town in Western Canada. I also spent some money to see some of the natural wonders of North America, such as Niagara Falls, Yellowstone Park, Banff, Jasper and other places. I love natural beauty, thus I found it worth my money to spend it on experiencing this. I, on the other hand do not even have a cell phone right now, I never bought a new car, or a gas-guzzler, and my TV is not a flat screen. I also seldom eat out, and I buy clothes based on how well they fit, not on some sort of twisted notion of brand allegiance. All the trips I took I paid for in cash, and it was not by any means the kind of deal, where I neglected to pay my other obligations as a result.

It is possible to live a normal life and still maintain some measure of fiscal discipline. Once you manage this, you will have more freedom than the likes of the Tea Party, who in fact want to deliver you as slaves to the few affluent, promise to give you if you are an American average Joe. Having had the experience of living under a brutal dictatorship, I find freedom to be a very important thing. Financial freedom is by far among the best kinds that one can taste. Unfortunately, too many people are tricked into thinking that freedom is about not having to pay some taxes in order to provide health coverage for all (which actually ends up being a benefit for most, because a public health care option is more efficient than the private US system, based on insurance). Some think it is about doing away with environmental regulations and protection, so firms can have the freedom to exploit nature, and destroy it for profit. The freedom of the elites, which is the only kind that they (Tea Partiers and likeminded organizations) care about, is completed through engaging in some union busting, in order to diminish the right of the average Joe to associate, and unite in order to stand a better chance at negotiating with the big boys. Regardless of how much you earn, if you manage to live within your means and remain debt free, you can be free as a human is meant to be.

Ironically, it is the people living in the supposedly most freedom-loving nation, where the average person is least able to live free from financial debt, and that country is the US. The main reason that it is almost impossible to do so here in the long term is because they insisted on having the least developed social safety net in the developed world. Millions of families here have no health insurance for instance. Millions more are regularly denied coverage for various reasons that insurance companies are able to find, despite individuals and their employers paying for the policy. That is because insurance firms are behaving just as any good profit-maximizing firm should do. Education related costs also have the effect of saddling people with a high rate of debt, as there is no subsidy for college education in the US, except for community college. In this environment, it is not enough to keep a disciplined monthly budget. Some may indeed manage to keep their family budget balanced for years, and they may even manage to put a little bit aside. A medical emergency or the loss of coverage due to job loss may blow all that hard work away as if it never even happened. Medical related bills are the number one reason for personal bankruptcy in the US.

Having a child is also one of the main dangers to one's fiscal balance, because the governments here do not provide maternity leave, unlike most other civilized countries. Having one of the parents drop out from work and as a result lose his/her job altogether is a real shock to a family's finances, besides the added costs related to taking care of a child. Despite all this, Americans are having more kids than almost any other developed nation on this world. I guess religion directed at the preaching of the right issues does have its political uses after all. Most European countries would see a complete collapse of their already suppressed birth rates, if such a brutal measure were to be implemented. The difference of course is that unlike in America, society there has become mainly secular in nature. American families however soldier on, piling on more and more debt. They are convinced that freedom is not financial, but it is freedom from having a potent government. They are constantly told that this is so; therefore, they do not seek the freedom that I describe here as being an essential part of the truest form of it.

A win-win proposition

As time passes, opportunities to earn enough to be able to put some money to the side, and invest it in things that are likely to hold value, are likely to diminish. With those opportunities becoming harder and harder to come by, the likelihood that you can get caught unprepared will rise. Note that you are not losing all that much by saving some part of your income. Even under the rosiest scenarios currently floating around about the future, there are likely to be major issues with retirement funding by governments, especially in the west. Having some assets stashed away for the golden years, cannot be a bad thing even if I happen to be wrong about my assessment in regards to our most likely future. Having worked as a night shift manager in a high income retirement home, I can say with some authority that it can take a lot of money to buy some comfort and dignity for our last years of life. It is also expensive for families to provide such a nice environment for their loved ones who may not be able to function in society anymore due to the onset of mental illness. In conclusion, the only ill effects you may have from listening to me, if I happen to be wrong is that you may have a more comfortable retirement.

As the Roman Empire was collapsing in the west, the large landowners of the empire, gradually gave up on urban life, and increasingly concentrated their efforts on creating a sustainable life in the countryside, on their large properties. The increasingly impoverished urban masses either ended up the victims of urban misery, or they formed the beginnings of generations of serfs, who were in many cases no better than slaves, who worked on either the farms set up by those Roman landowners who fled, or under the ownership of a new landed aristocracy formed from the barbarian warriors. The former cool urban dwellers and generations that were spawned from them afterwards were condemned to a miserable life, where security was almost non-existent, and the constant humiliation and lack of social mobility became a nasty norm that most could expect. Some continued to inhabit the cities that did not disappear entirely, but their lives were quite miserable.

Our situation is in many ways similar in case that our system breaks down, except for one major difference. Our population density, and technological know how, even in the absence of the fossil fuel and other mineral inputs that currently go into farming would not require nearly as high a percentage of the overall population to work the land as was the case in early feudal Europe. With exceptions such as Canada, most western societies would end up being comprised from large masses of urban poor. Most of them would end up bankrupt due to the high levels of debt that they carry, unless governments decide to inflate the current debt away, in which case the value of a home that currently sells for a million, will be worth something like a hundred thousand in real terms. That essentially means that real wages could drop by as much as 90% in the urban areas of our society. The situation of the urban poor, unable to secure the right to earn the nourishment needed to sustain them, unless they are willing to work in the most horrible conditions is a depressing situation to be in. This is perhaps the greatest danger that one should watch out for and prepare before it is too late.

Rural & urban options

Having observed Romania's society as a child growing up right when the system was no longer working, I made some very important conclusions that I can now reference. I remember the gladness I felt whenever I travelled to my grandma's place on weekends, or on school breaks. She lived in the countryside, and even though there was a lack of some modern facilities, such as indoor plumbing, it was nevertheless a pleasant place for me to go to. Among other things, there was adequate daily food that I was able to consume, which was no longer the case in the city in the closing years of the dictatorship. It is true that the rural folks were in many ways being exploited similarly to the urban people by the government. There was one important difference however. A small piece of land that was not part of the collective system was allocated to each family, out of which they were able to not only feed themselves, but were often even able to raise some extra cash by selling their products in the city. They were also able to raise some farm animals near their property, which made healthy proteins readily available to them. By the end of the communist system, there is one thing that can be said. The rural population of Romania had a tendency to be far healthier. Most people grew up to be larger and stronger, which was visually obvious especially among the young people who reached maturity during the 1980's. The urban population was starting to show signs of malnourishment. I myself remember that most of my growth spurts occurred during the three-month summer vacations I spent in a rural setting.

It may be the case that governments may be harsh in exploiting the rural population, because they need a source of revenue, which can only come from people who produce something in the economy. Governments have often resorted to confiscation of food from the farmers, as was the case in the Soviet Union in the 20's. In our case, especially given that, there is a high degree of danger given the level of firearm availability among North American farmers; government may decide not to cross the line that might lead the rural population to rebellion. Even if they believe that they can win, they may not be able to afford a possible disruption in the food supply that might result from conflict. Failure to provide some level of nourishment standards in the urban areas may lead to an even greater problem for governments. They may decide to turn the urban masses on the rural minority however, which could be disastrous, but that would most likely happen only in drastic circumstances.

Regardless of how we will do in adjusting to the future, even if we were to surprise the course of history by coming up big with a solution similar to what I suggested, which would provide the right incentives for the market to get its direction from, food will still be a very valuable commodity for the foreseeable future. Even if global population growth were to be tempered from its current trend, there is still the issue of demand for higher quality food that requires more land and energy inputs to produce, such as meat. Investing in prime, sustainable farmland cannot be a losing proposition under almost any scenario. In the best-case scenario, it will be a piece of land that can produce some income if you lease it out to other farmers. In the worst-case scenario, it could be a place of retreat for you and your family, although in some drastic scenarios, one might also have to defend that land from many who might want to lay their hands on it, one way or another. Food has always been the most important product that we ever produced; we just lost sight of that important fact for a few generations now. Its importance is highlighted especially by recent events in the Middle East, where one can see the consequence of its absence from that market, at an affordable price. I doubt that people would have taken to the streets if the price of I-pads, cell phones, video games, televisions or any other products we seem to hold as having great value to us, would have risen in price beyond affordable levels as food did.

I am fully aware that it is very un-glamorous to do the job of a farmer. Cool dude coffee shop guy, earning minimum wage, tends to be held in higher regard than someone who is responsible for feeding the masses by owning and operating a food producing operation. If one is further up the social and pay scale ladder in the urban environment than a coffee house waiter, such as an engineer, or financial expert, then there is no question that giving it up in order to go shovel some manure and drive a tractor on the fields during a hot sweaty, dusty day is not an option. The problem is that we have already witnessed a situation just a few years back where credit almost stopped flowing through the global economy. If the next crisis will manage to shut down the financial system, it may be the case that the cool dude, coffee shop guy, the engineer, and the financial expert may all end up working for the farmer. We can all hope that we will be the farmer, but that privileged position will only be available for a small minority of people.

If you cannot find it within you to make such a step, which is understandable because this may be a situation that may not come to pass for a few decades yet, although there is a small chance, it could even happen in the immediate timeframe, there are a few practical investment alternatives that may serve a similar purpose. Gold is an obvious one, because it could always be exchanged for some piece of land, albeit at a less advantageous price if you wait too long. Some foreign investors may find their way into the local market, such as the Chinese government; because let us face it; they need a lot of food if they are to keep their billion plus population from outright revolt. If that were to happen, it would be very difficult for a small bidder such as an average western citizen to get in on the action by the time it becomes obvious that things have gone bad.

Getting involved into merchandizing is another good possibility that may provide a very good living, without having to move to the countryside. Rural-urban trade would become very important under such a scenario, because the urban masses need affordable food, while the farming communities need manufactured products. In this field, however you have to be very good at seizing the moment, and understanding the direction. There are already many people involved in merchandizing, and they are already well established in the community. All they have to do is adapt to new trade flows, which should not be hard. Many merchants who currently operate in our communities are not debt free however, and in the absence of an inflationary bout that would take care of their debt loads, they would likely end up bankrupt given the reduced level of revenue and profit that the new environment will be able to provide. Depending on how indebted the competitors are, a person with fresh capital to invest could end up being one of the last ones standing after the weaker competitors would be pushed out.

There could be some benefits to owning certain manufacturing facilities, but it is hard to assess which specific facilities would be the best. Here, once again the most successful enterprise would be the kind that would cater to the rural-urban trade flow. Farmers will most likely become more self-sufficient than they are now, but they will still lack the ability to provide themselves with certain goods and equipment. Welding supplies would probably be in high demand, specifically the portable type that can easily be used in various modes. Glass or ceramic items could be a good industry to be in as well. Metal tools of various sorts, which would be too time-consuming for many farmers to produce themselves, are also a possibility. Once again, the key here would be to have a debt free status that can allow one to survive the downfall of our economy.

This may not be such a big issue in Manitoba, where I grew up, but some places will likely see high demand for independent electricity generation capacities such as wind or solar. Owning a company that produces or installs such products for individual households, or in some cases for small communities can have a bright future as well. The reason that a place like Manitoba may not see such high demand for such infrastructure, is because the area already has a very high installed capacity to produce hydro power, therefore most people can expect to have reliable electricity supplies in the absence of violence related disruption. In other places around the western world, most farmers will want to have a reliable electricity source to do work for them, as well as to provide them with the basic comforts that they are used to.

An industry with definite potential is the service of septic tank servicing. Most rural people will prefer to keep that service even at a relatively high cost, as opposed to what the alternatives could be. This may be a dirty business, but someone has to do it, and someone could see a steady income derived from this business even in the presence of a deep economic downturn. This industry relies heavily on fossil fuels, but it could be one of the few industries, which will generate enough revenue to afford that fuel. Similarly, to all other currently established businesses, this one should see a shaking out of weaker, heavily indebted competitors. Keep in mind here, that once again, if you want to be the successful one, just as is the case with all other possible industries of success, this one requires that you be debt free, and with some capital to spare, if you want to be among the few successful people of the future.

There are probably many other opportunities that I overlooked, which could be a successful occupation for many who through luck or perceptive personal financial ingenuity will be positioned to take advantage of the new opportunities. One thing you do not want to position yourself as for the future, is the person willing to sell his labor, with no other fallback position in case that labor is no longer in demand at some point. Your future as a past consumer of relatively worthless goods in the big picture of things is one of destitute existence along with the majority of today's global population. It is true that you may still have some time to enjoy this lifestyle, but there are already many people in the western world whose future is set. The millions of relatively well paying jobs that are not being replaced, or are only replaced with low paying jobs that do not allow for any significant levels of saving to take place, especially for those who already have a large debt burden, made sure that for millions of westerners it is already too late. Any one of us could be the next on the chopping block, as the stage is already being set for a much deeper recession to occur, as soon as this decade, most likely sparked by commodity shortages. Being over—invested in these current trends of buying expensive gadgets, paying for expensive services, and having a big mortgage on a property that is likely to lose its relative value at some point in the future is not an appropriate plan for the current environment. It is however the way that the system wants and needs most of us to behave, if it is to survive for a while longer.

There is also no future in being a future pensioner, expecting the public and private pension systems to carry you for twenty years or so. Those who are already retired, or close to it, may have a good chance of receiving what is owed to them. People who are ten or more years away from retirement should consider an alternative plan. These funds continue to rely on a relatively robust long-term performance from the markets, which is already showing signs of not coming to fruition. The political battles that are taking place in the US that mainly target the worker's right and ability to associate in order to negotiate a set of benefits that the employer should provide, is effectively an admission coming from the right that the very system they defend no longer has the ability to provide those things.

The right wing politicians in the US are in essence fighting on the part of some wealthy interests who want to see an end to the current labor environment that demands things such as pension plans and health benefits. At the same time, they are fighting any plans which might provide a government funded solution to these employee needs, because that would eventually mean that they would have to pay more taxes directly, or indirectly. Remember that the current state of labor relations demands that the employer provide a level of compensation for employment, which allows the employee at the minimum to cover short-term family budget needs, such as food, shelter, clothing, transport, hygiene and other miscellaneous items that may fall within this category. Even if the government were to fund its needs through increasing payroll taxes, the rich would indirectly be on the hook, because nobody will work for less than what is needed to cover the above-mentioned costs through their net pay. This situation is indicative of the fact that the benefits that many think that they will receive, are likely to be missing in action in the not too distant future.

High paying jobs that we became accustomed to taking for granted as our birthright as citizens of the western world are likely to be increasingly missing in action, making it harder to make ends meet, never mind trying to save. Saving now, while there might still be some time left, before your real wages are slashed, or replaced with unemployment insurance, welfare, and food stamps is not such a bad idea. I cannot emphasize enough the fact that even if I happen to be wrong, and it will be business as usual for the next few decades, or even for a century or more, there is nothing wrong with putting some wealth aside for a rainy day. If those of us who pointed out lately the unsustainable nature of our current trajectory happen to be right however, then you might be very glad to have a small financial cushion to help you and your family weather the hard times. In the process, you might benefit from doing some soul searching, to find out what are the things that can go on the personal financial chopping block, as opposed to the things you cannot part from, and therefore continue spending on them.

Some Parting Thoughts

It would be very nice if we did not have to worry about making such decisions for our future, and that of our children. Making sure that we are among the ones who will be best positioned to keep some of the present assets that will be valuable to survival in the perhaps not so distant future is a grim prospect. The unfortunate reality however is that every indication suggests that there is very little reason for us to think that we are likely to solve the problems that threaten our way of life as we know it and gotten used to living. There are very few cases in history, where a culture managed to change their time honored beliefs and ways of doing things when these guidelines no longer served them well. Most of the time, there was a need for a great calamity to change people's minds, and often even that is not enough, as there are always enough people with vested short-term interests in protecting the status quo. The interests of the few but powerful may win out over the interests of society as a whole. Even in the absence of the ability to project brutal force due to the constraints of societal structure, they still have the power of persuasion, which usually targets the less educated and uninformed as their likely political allies. This is not a unique event in human history; it has been done before in the past. Perhaps the most famous of these manipulations happened as the result of the rich and powerful bet on Hitler as the savior from the red menace that was threatening their wealth with the danger of expropriation.

In our case, waiting for the calamity to happen, most likely in the form of continued price spikes in the commodity market due to inadequate supply needed to meet demand, is likely to be a fatal decision, because as we already witnessed in the aftermath of the 2008 recession, we are becoming weaker and weaker with every such event. The difference I believe lies in our inability to recover from the damage fully, before the next negative event hits. As I write this(2010-11), there is already a very real danger to the fragile recovery in the form of global unrest triggered by food prices initially, and now is followed by financial risks related to a growing risk of petroleum supply disruption, causing prices to spike once again. Remember that this is only three years after the first oil and food price spike we witnessed in 2008, which is still debated among many, as to what effect or role it may have had in the recession. Contrary to economist's beliefs, that shortages give rise to alternatives and harder to access sources of a commodity as prices surge, it is increasingly evident that if one factors in the human impulse to rebel against situations of hardship, and financial constraints created through recessionary forces due to sudden price spikes, the opposite is the more likely scenario. The short duration we witnessed of price spike to price crash is also a phenomenon that makes it unlikely for the economy to adapt to supply constraints. In times of crisis investing into infrastructure is low on the priority list, compared to the most pressing need, which is to keep the masses docile, so government is also unlikely to have the capacity to save us if we wait too long.

Investment in renewable energy is likely to take a beating due to cutbacks in government funding. Water supplies are threatened in the US due to our desperate need to bring new sources of energy on-line in the form of Shale Gas. Food supplies are threatened by our quest for bio-fuels to supplement our thirst for liquid fuels. They are also threatened by our environmentally damaging behavior, such as deep water drilling for oil as well as our consumption of the fuels that leads to greater dangers of crop failure due to likely changes in weather patterns caused by greenhouse gasses in our atmosphere. Then there is of course the increased danger of unrest in developing countries many of which are responsible for a big chunk of supplies of natural resources ranging from oil to phosphorus.

Economists also have the wrong idea about the low hanging fruit pattern of long-term commodity production. They assume that as we move up the tree, all the fruit in the orchard will still be available to the end consumer. They neglect to count all the fruit trees that had to be cut down in order to build the ladders needed to reach the higher branches. They also neglect the fact that the workers climbing up those ladders are now expending more energy per unit of fruit collected, they therefore have to eat more of the fruit themselves to provide them with energy to do work. The obvious result is that there are smaller quantities of fruit left to be sold to the end user, who will bid up the price of the fruit, because they have to compete with other potential customers for the energy and vitamin rich nutrient.

Our planet is in many ways no different than the orchard example, except that in an orchard, trees that are cut down to build ladders can be re-grown in time, while many of the resources we produce are non-renewable. The bottom line is that we are now steadily increasing the amount of commodity input that goes into producing other commodities as the low hanging fruit was picked first, leaving less and less to the end user, and it becomes more expensive for us, as the level of inputs rises. The best example of financial analysis applied to finite, non-renewable, and non-substitutable resources, gone wrong is the flawed assumptions made by finance experts, who only a decade or so ago were predicting such an abundance of crude oil supply hitting the market. They predicted that the poor markets would have a hard time keeping prices from dropping by half from the then price of $15 or so. They said that this low price environment was likely to be the situation for decades perhaps.

Far from dropping as low as seven dollars, we are now unable to keep prices below $70 in the absence of a deep recession. The problem is that the market economy that we have had in place basically unguided for the last few decades left us the inheritors of infrastructure that is more appropriate for an environment where prices would be closer to $7 rather than $70, or even higher. At some point, prices may move down for a long period, if not forever. At that point, there is a complete economic meltdown, and petroleum exploration as well as mining of other commodities will become a small-scale venture, providing only small amounts of the stuff that is only absorbed by some remnants of stable society. Effectively, many of the resources that we now think that we will produce, will never be produced, or at least not until a new social reorganization will happen as it did 1000 years following the collapse of the Roman Empire, which might take society to new heights.

Perhaps it is time for financial and market analysts to consider other factors besides their theoretical models that they use to predict the future. We after all live in a physical world, not a paper or electronic one. It would help perhaps some, if these Harvard graduates would have had a greater understanding of past human history, but the future generations are likely to understand less as they will only be trained for math and science, which it seems, is now accepted to be the only useful material that is to be kept in our public education system. I am not underestimating the need for us to learn those important subjects; I just think it is not enough, because we first have to understand who we really are, before we decide what we should do.

Part of our collective human identity is a history of many societies establishing some norms of conventional wisdom, and then resisting all challenges to those norms until they are proven wrong without any doubt by a complete breakdown that makes that norm obsolete, since the society that supported it, is no more. One of those norms is that there are only two solutions to our economic organizational needs. One is the much discredited command economy, and the other is the free market economy, which performs best with the least interference by government. The center tends to argue for a hybrid system to a varying degree, and that is the full spectrum of choices we are presented with. I hope that one of the things I accomplished here was to demonstrate that there are other choices, including changing the environment in which the invisible hand of the market, and governments operate in. It may not be the perfect answer, and it would take courage and sacrifice to see it implemented. The break we would have with the current direction is likely to cause some significant pain in the short-run for society as a whole, and it is likely to hit some important interests around the world, therefore it gives me reason to think that such a solution will never be implemented despite many of its practical features.

The many problems it would solve are already on the mind of many, but unfortunately, most are betting on people across the world giving up rational selfish behavior in favor of behavior conducive to the common good, in spite of having to forego many opportunities for selfishness. Now that we have the benefit of having observed all sorts of initiatives ranging from the Kyoto protocol, to calls to mobilize the masses to voluntarily give up the pleasures of certain activities such as eating meat, fall flat on their face, we should be ready to recognize its failures. We also know from basic economic definitions of the firm that it is solely interested in the generation of profit; therefore, it will always choose the people and the places that allow it to profit the most. In this case, obviously the dirtiest, least human rights friendly place wins out as long as they have the physical and human infrastructure necessary to do the job, because that is the most cost effective in most cases, especially when it comes to manufacturing. When we see this to be unfolding before us, we should stop acting surprised and full of indignation. This is what the system we accept creates; therefore, this is what we have to live with.

Fixing this current flaw in the market that encourages the race to the bottom mentality globally, which is becoming more and more evident if you look at the current political environment in places like the US, is imperative if we are to keep from imploding. There is no force other than trade, which can fix this problem; therefore, I chose trade as the logical tool that should be re-shaped to eliminate some of these very destructive features of our current global business environment. Rigging the system to automatically reward countries that provide an environmentally and human friendly environment over those which do so in a lesser manner, can reverse the current trends and put us back towards a race to the top in terms of efficiency, clean environmental policies and respect for human dignity and rights. That is why I chose to name my solution appropriately "The Sustainability Tariff". I sadly have to admit however that the odds of seeing such an initiative be taken globally being realized in my lifetime, or even my newborn's lifetime are low, even though it should be obvious to most by now that we are headed in the wrong direction in the long-term. I do not think we have reached such a level of cultural maturity, nor am I sure that we ever will, which might see us achieve such a great feat as changing direction in order to save ourselves from disaster. This is the one point on which I urge anyone, or everyone to prove me wrong, because then, we will no longer have to contemplate with an aching hart, the world that we are leaving behind for my son and all others of his generation, across the globe.

Notes

Introduction:

1) The IEA is an organization tasked to advise OECD developed nations on energy related issues. In their *World Energy Outlook* yearly report released in 2010, they admitted that conventional crude production, which makes up 80% of all liquid fuels, reached a permanent plateau in 2006, but they nevertheless claim that unconventional sources such as oil sands, Natural Gas Liquids, ethanol can make up the difference during the period in question going to 2035. They also make the very dubious claim that this plateau in conventional crude can be maintained beyond 2035.

2) C.R. McConnell, S.L. Brue, T.P. Barbiero: *Macroeconomics*, 10'Th Canadian edition, McGraw-Hill Ryerson. 2005. p 3.

Chapter 1:

1) As the economic power of many developing nations is increasing, so is their ability to impose their views. China's increased ability to neutralize the Dalai Lama internationally through pressuring foreign governments to shun him is one such example. When the 2010 Nobel peace prize was a awarded to Chinese imprisoned dissident Liu Xiaobo, China was able to claim that it has 100 countries on its side in opposing the prize, and in the end about one third of countries that received invitations for their officials to attend the ceremony, turned down the invitation. This is just the beginning of what is likely in store in the absence of major global changes coming soon.

2) According to a Stanford study done by Steven Davis and ken Caldeira, on CO_2 emissions, which includes a measure of how much each country is responsible for when including imports of many products that led to the emission of this greenhouse gas due to the production and transport process, much of the recent improvements, including in Europe show up as increased imports that

the population consumes, which essentially means that the emissions did not disappear, they were outsourced (together with the jobs).

3) In his budget proposal for the fiscal year of 2012, president Obama made no provisions for the funding of a cap and trade scheme, making it unlikely that he will do so during his first term in office (which may turn out to be his only term).

4) Proceedings of the Paris 2008 degrowth conference, April 18-19. I used Mister Schneider's presentation as a sample of the basic intellectual inclination. Degrowth theorists do a decent job of explaining the unsustainable aspects of our current global economic system, but do a poor job of presenting us with an alternative, because of their insistence on voluntary persuasion of the righteousness of their ideas, as well as their anti-western bias.

5) According to EIA data, North America and the European Union currently use about 35 million barrels of petroleum per day. Europe is already on a fuel diet, which causes them to use ½ as much petroleum per capita as North Americans, so there is already little room for drastic reductions there in the absence of the effect of a deep recession of very long duration. In North America, the infrastructure and community planning necessary to make such drastic cuts in consumption just aren't there.

6) Parreto efficiency theory is available online, as well as in many economics textbooks.

7) Lack of perfect information in the marketplace is one of the many factors that cause market failure. Market failure is the result of not being able to achieve a perfectly competitive economy, which exists only in theory, but cannot be applied in practice, for reasons such as the human inability to provide perfect information.

Chapter 2:

1) *Pax Romana* refers to the period of relative peace and stability created in the region due to Roman military dominance, which allowed the region to flourish economically, which can be considered the peace dividend of its time. Since that period, historians as well as economists tend to make reference to the periods

379

of *Pax Britania*, which is considered by many to be the period of British naval dominance worldwide, which faded away to make room for *Pax Americana*, which refers to the twentieth century period, and is considered to be still valid today. Some people, with me included, believe that *Pax Americana* is now ending, and there might not be a replacement waiting in the wings. Others believe that it might be replaced by the Chinese Peace.

2) Peter Heather provides a great description of Roman society in his book *"The Fall of the Roman Empire"*.

3) According to Peter Heather, the time it took for a message to be transported from on part of the empire to another, often made the message irrelevant. It often took weeks or even months for a message to make it from a province to the emperor, or vice versa.

4) My description of the collapse of Easter Island is mainly influenced by Jared Diamond's theory of what happened there, found in his book *"Collapse"*.

5) Based on basic microeconomic theory that the main goal of a private firm is to maximize profits, combined with the labor economics model of the worker's choice of trading off work versus leisure time, depending on wages offered, I assume that in the absence of minimum wage legislation, the minimum take home wage that employer and employee will agree on is close to the approximate amount that a person needs to live on modestly. There is little or no spare income to dedicate to savings or insurance to cover unforeseen difficulties. That person will live from paycheck to paycheck. If an employee possesses a skill or qualification that is scarce, the wage will be bid up from that minimum point.

6) Robert Solow quote on club or Rome is available on Wikipedia.

7) Elasticity of consumption of a product in the face of price increases is dependent on two main features. One is whether there is an alternative desirable substitute. The other factor is the level of consumer dependency on the product.

If the consumer good in question is Pepsi as an example, a slight price increase in the absence of a similar increase from the competition, leads them to losing customer demand fast, because there are many alternatives as close substitutes, and it is not a vital consumer good, because most of us can get by without Pepsi.

If the consumer good in question is food, then it is an entirely different matter. There is no substitute for food, and we need it to live on. Consumer reaction as a result of a price increase may be to switch to lower quality food, or give up on a portion of all other consumer goods that are not vital, in order to make up for the price increase.

Chapter 3:

1) A study made by Alex Chakhamkhchev and Peter Rushworth, entitled *Global overview of offshore oil & gas operations for 2005-2009,* gives us data for discovery of oil and gas during this period. Total discoveries amounted to no more than 27 billion barrels of oil equivalent in the best year, while the worst year yielded fewer than 20 billion. Total global consumption is about 45 billion barrels of oil equivalent per year if we add oil and gas together.

2) This is a claim made by the late Mathew Simmons, and there are others who seem to think that the Thunderhorse project may have been overhyped. Jean Laherrere, a long time peak oil supporter examined the field's production history and came to the conclusion that based on current production decline rates, it will possibly yield less than the officially booked reserves would suggest.

3) The Data on production I used for these countries comes from the Energy information agency, or EIA. The data sourced for the 21 graphs represents production as the EIA measures it. Reserve data can be found through the CIA factbook online, the BP global reports, and many other sources.

4) The USGS study looks at technically recoverable resources with current proven technological tools available. It neglects the economical aspects of it, as well as above ground issues, such as access to land to drill, due to population distribution in the region. A nasty accident that might contaminate the underground aquifers that provide water to millions of people in the region might also make this resource unavailable due to a popular backlash. On the other hand, technological improvements might enhance recoverability.

5) Natural Gas Liquids are often counted as oil liquids reserves and production. Compared to crude oil, it only contains 2/3 of the energy content per barrel.

6) According to the IMF, UN and other data sources, Global average GDP per capita stands at about $7,000, while the EU average is about $35,000. At an average global real growth rate of 4%, and taking into account the UN population prediction of nine billion people on the planet by 2050, average global per Capita GDP should be about $35,000 in today's dollars.

7) This study was done by the *Center for German Army Transformation, Group for "Future Studies"*. It is easily accessible online, and I recommend reading it for anyone interested, who has not been made aware of it yet.

8) There is another great difference, which is the health care system, which in the US tends to extract a greater toll from potential manufacturers of a product, because providing partial coverage, of 50% for instance to employees for health insurance can easily cost a firm about $6,000 per year, per worker. The German universal health coverage system costs 12% of the country's GDP, compared to 18% in the US. This in fact may be a greater cost difference than anything else.

Chapter 4:

1) A UN report from 2009 claims that oceanic fisheries may be completely depleted before 2048, given current trends.

2) This is just a rough estimate based on a study commissioned by the International Bottled Water Association that in the US, the total energy involved in producing and transporting bottled water was .14% of total US energy consumption.

Chapter 5:

1) Phosphate rock production reached a peak already in the 1980's, but it may still surpass that, unless Morocco and China, who jointly poses 60% of phosphate rock reserves decide to curtail production.

2) In the period of 1980-1990, average increase in grain yields per hectare of land was 2.5%, from 1990-2000, it was only 1.5%. The last decade, ending with 2010, was about the same as the previous one. It seems clear that the green revolution is coming to an end according to the UN and USDA data.

3) Jared Diamond provides a detailed explanation about the problem of increased soil salinity in Australia, in a chapter dedicated to that country's challenges of sustainability in his book *Collapse*.

4) According to data compiled by the UN, the global food price index hit a record 213.5 in June 2008. The global recession tempered demand until December 2010, when food price index hit another record high of 214.7.

5) Recent Canadian government stats show that the Canadian white male population is in fact underrepresented in government jobs as a result of current government hiring policy. There is also very little empirical evidence to suggest that visible minorities need a helping hand due to discrimination, because government stats show that certain visible minority groups do rather well, while others less so, which can better be explained by cultural adaptation to the environment rather than discriminatory practices. The broad consensus of Canadian society towards this situation is one of acceptance, which testifies to this society's commitment to being an attractive place to emigrate for non-European migrants.

6) Jared Diamond's theory on the Rwanda genocide differs from the standard view of ethnic friction caused by pure hatred. He presents the evidence of genocide within the same ethnic group in some communities, mainly driven by an increasing lack of farmland available as evidence of economic considerations being the drivers of hatred as an excuse and a symptom, rather than a cause.

7) The median age in the Middle East is about 25 years, which means that half their population is under 25, and due to economic pressures, they are underemployed in some countries.

Chapter 6:

1) The multiplier effect of money pumped into the economy is mainly determined by the marginal propensity to consume (MPC). So if the MPC is .8, in other words people save 20% of what they earn, the calculation of the multiplier effect is equal to 1+.8+.64+.51 . . . ., which is in fact just an approximation because money leaks through other avenues as well, besides only savings.

Chapter 7:

1) The Hungarian government missed the mark by running a 4.2% deficit, but it is still one of the lowest rates in the western world, and 2011, and 2012 are not looking so bad either, despite the current global economic difficulties.

2) The justification for the higher rating of the US and GB government debt is in part due to their size, and their long-term history as stable financial entities.

Chapter 9:

1) I wrote this before the August 2011 S&P downgrade of US debt, so in essence my view of this is turning out to be correct, unfortunately it happened before I managed to publish.

2) Texas is a good example of this sort of economic strategy for an administrative entity in the present that undermines other states such as California. Texas is in the process undermining the state's education system by underfunding it. It also provides one of the flimsiest social safety nets, which would kill consumption if it was applied nationally in the US. Texas is however freeloading from other states by importing educated workers from other areas, and they also depend to some extent on consumption made possible in other states through their more generous safety nets.

3) The top tax rate has been halved since the 1950's.

4) A public good is a good that cannot be owned by a profit seeking firm, because it cannot enforce a fee collection for its use. A private firm would only build and maintain a sidewalk if it is paid to do so by a government entity that collects taxes in order to support the cost. Public goods have a tendency to be abused by those not wanting to contribute, but would still like to benefit.

Chapter 10:

1) Gabrowski et all, have a somewhat different view on the role of religion as the driver towards more economic development. They argue that nationalism and inter-nation competition was a more important factor that explains the rise of some European nations during the renaissance period.

2) the Apostle Andrew may have not even existed, and there is furthermore little evidence that the people he may have Christianized in the region are the ancestors of the Romanians, because from that event, and to the point where Romanians do appear in the historical record as an entity identifiable as living in present day Romania, there is a 1000 year gap.

3) Contemporary Hungarian state records indicate the migration of a proto-Romanian population from the region of Macedonia, into the old kingdom of Hungary during the 14'Th century. Furthermore, it is well documented that the Ottoman empire repopulated the historical region of Banat, which was also part of the Hungarian kingdom with proto-Romanians, from their occupied territories in the Balkans, due to the earlier depopulation of the mainly Hungarian inhabitants which occurred due to the fact that the region was a battleground between the Ottoman empire and the Hungarian kingdom for about a century.

4) Recent statements made by Romania's UDMR party leader Kelemen Hunor, shows that he and others are concerned about the effect that the granting of citizenship to ethnic Hungarians living in Romania will have on the community there. He declared his desire for the Hungarian government to try to prevent the trend of migration of young educated ethnic Hungarians from Romania to Hungary.

5) The reason for the large level of uncertainty in regards to the education level is due to the fact that many members of this community do not declare their ethnicity. That is often the case especially with those who succeed in moving up the social scale.

6) Even as I wrote this chapter, I pondered the potential hostility coming from many members of the Romanian community, including those who are close.

Chapter 11:

1) The cost of living on a native reserve is low, because they receive free housing, and they receive a small amount of money as a result of being treaty people members. Having a few kids further enhances one's financial situation in a place where not so much money is necessary, because the government provides welfare payments of around 400 dollars per child. Many children on the reserve end up having children of their own as a result of these incentives.

2) Media Matters: For America, Published September 19, 2006: It is a review of a Washington Post report written by Rajiv Chandrasekaran written on September 17, 2006.

3) 2011 data shows that in the decade of 2001-2010, median household income in the US fell 7%, which matches a roughly similar drop in petroleum consumption rates.

Chapter 12:

1) Jeff Rubin comes to mind in this case. Repression through taking away one's means of earning a living is just as effective in a world where most of us are dependent on selling our labor, as are other more naked forms of represion witnessed in other parts of the world.

2) JP Morgan decided to accept gold as collateral for certain transactions, which puts gold on equal footing with AAA rated bonds that are also accepted as collateral. Gold is also accepted as a common collateral asset for consumer loans in India. Gold denominated bank accounts are available in Asia, Europe and North America.

3) An article by Dave Gilson and Carolyn Perot entitled "*It's The Inequality Stupid*" is a very good highlight of the widening income inequalities in American society. It was published on February 25th, 2011. Recent census data from the US is also a good place to go for information on this phenomenon.

List of Abbreviations:

BP. British Petroleum.
EIA. Energy Information Agency, which is a US government entity that concerns itself with energy related issues and statistics.
EPA. Environmental Protection Agency of the US.
EU. European Union.
HDI. Human Development Index, is a ranking of nations' by living standards measured by a set of indicators.
IEA. International Energy Agency, is an international entity tasked with giving guidance to OECD countries in regards to present and future energy availability prospects, which came into being as a result of the 1973 OPEC embargo.
IMF. International Monetary Fund, created to provide global financial stability.
GDP. Gross Domestic Product, which is currently the most common measure of an economy's relative health and trajectory.
GB. Great Britain.
GE. General Electric, a multinational corporation.
GM. General Motors, a multinational corporation. **mb/d.** Million barrels per day
OECD. Organization of Economic Cooperation and Development. It is a club of the developed world.
OPEC. Organization of Petroleum Exporting Countries.
R&D. Research and Development.
UDMR or RMDSZ. Political party in Romania, representing the ethnic Hungarian minority living there.
UN. United Nations.
US. United States of America.
USDA. United States Department of Agriculture.
USGS. United States Geological Survey.
WTO. World Trade Organization.

387

References

Barbiero P. Thomas, Brue L. Stanley, McConnell R. Campbell. *Macroeconomics: 10'th Canadian Edition.* 2005.

Becker Antoaneta. *China Closes in Around its Rare Earths.* IPS News. November, 2010.

Benjamin Dwayne, Gunderson Morley, Lemieux Thomas, Riddell W. Craig. *Labor Market Economics, Sixth Edition.* 2007.

Bradford Jason: *Oil and Food Prices.* January 2011.

Brown Lester: *Data highlights on the global food supply.* Grist. February, 2010.

Brown S. Alan. *A Shift in Engineering Offshoring.* Mechanical Engineering magazine.

Cameron Rondo, Neal Larry. *A Concise Economic History of the World: From Paleolithic Times to the Present.* 2003.

Chakhmakhchev Alex, Peter Rushworth. *Global overview of offshore oil & gas operations for 2005-2009.* Offshore-mag.com.

Diamond Jared. *Collapse: How Societies Choose to Fail or Succeed.* 2005.

Forbes Wallace. *Bracing For Peak Oil Production By Decade's End.* Forbes.com. September, 2010.

Gail the Actuary: *Peak phosphorus: Quoted reserves vs. production history.* The Oil Drum. October, 2008.

Ghosh Pallab: *Report: Urgent action needed to avert global hunger.* BBC News. January 2011.

Grabowski Richard, Self Sharmistha, Shields P. Michael. *Economic Development: A Regional, Institutional, and Historical Approach.* 2007.

Hagens Nate. *Unconventional Oil: Tar Sands and Shale Oil—EROI on the Web, Part 3 of 6.* The Oil Drum. April, 2008.

Heather Peter. *The Fall of the Roman Empire: A new history of Rome and the Barbarians.* 2006.

Hughes David. *New USGS Marcellus Shale analysis drastically cuts DOE estimates.* Postcarbon.org. August, 2011.

Irwin Neil. *Aughts were a lost decade for U.S. economy, workers.* Washington Post. January, 2010.

Jamail Dahr. *Gulf spill sickness wrecking lives.* AlJazeera.Net. March, 2011.

Long R. Gary, Morehouse F. David, Wood H. John. *Long-Term World Oil Supply Scenarios: The Future is Neither as Black or Rosy as Some Assert.* EIA Home. August 2004.

Kageyama Yuri, Kinetz Erika. *Ford's Massive' Asia Expansion: Automaker Makes Big Push in India, Thailand.* HuffPost Business. August, 2010.

Kopits R. Steven. *EIA: Hard Core Peak Oil Forecast.* Econbrowser: June, 2010.

Laherrere Jean. *Deepwater GOM: Reserves versus Production Part 1: Thunder Horse & Mars-Ursa.* Theoildrum. September, 2011.

Matthews Steve. *Poverty Rate in U.S. Rose to 15-Year High in 2009.* Bloomberg Businessweek. June, 2011.

Mills Robin. *Peak oil theory has peaked and there is no apocalypse now.* The National. August, 2010.

Oak Robert. *GM offshore outsourcing U.S. jobs.* The Economic Populist. May, 2009.

Palmer Doug. *Analysis: Hu addresses U.S. stress over China high-tech drive.* Reuters. January, 2011.

Siklos L. Pierre. *Money, Banking & Financial Institutions: Canada in the Global Environment, Fifth Edition.* 2006.

Perot Carolyn, Gilson Dave. *It's The Inequality, Stupid.* Speaking Truth to Power. February, 2011.

Rapier Robert. *Leaked Study on Peak Oil Warns of Severe Global Energy Crisis.* The Energy Collective. September, 2010.

Rapier Roper: *Cellulosic Ethanol Reality Begins to Set In.* Oil Drum. December, 2010.

Rembrandt. *A Primer on Reserve Growth—part 1 of 3 (Revisited).* The Oil Drum: Europe. October, 2010.

Robertson Roy: *Doubling food production by 2050 'doable'.* Southeast Farm Press. Jan 2010.

Simmons R. Matthew. *Twilight in the Desert: The Coming Saudi Oil Shock And The World Economy.* 2005.

Swartz Spencer, Oster Shai. *China Tops U.S. in Energy Use.* The Wall Street Journal.
July, 2010.

Timmer John. *Europe outsourcing CO_2 emisions to developing economies.* Arstechnica.com. March, 2010.

Weber Tim: *Davos 2011: Why do economists get it so wrong?* BBC News. January, 2011.

Media ignored front-page Washington Post report that White House hampered Iraq rebuilding efforts by hiring unqualified individuals based on "loyalty to the Bush administration". Media Matters, for America. September 2006.

China warns of pressure on food supply in next 5 yrs-paper. Reuters. January 2011.

New threat to global food security as phosphate supplies become increasingly scarce. Peak Oil message board. November, 2010.

India/China to contribute majority of world middle-class population by 2030. Peak Oil Message board. June, 2011.

World food prices at fresh high, says UN. BBC News, Business. January 2011.

Mid-East: Will there be a domino effect?. BBC News, Middle East. February 2011.

The Chinese Coal Monster. Peak Oil News and Message Boards. June, 2011.

ProPublica's Guide to Fracking. June, 2011.

US Wind Energy Installations Collapsed in 2010. March, 2011.

Major reports point to oil supply turmoil and price volatility. Peak Generation. August, 2010.

A Review of Shale Gas Plays in North America. GLG News. August, 2010.

How Much Energy Does it Take to Get Our Energy? Peak Oil News and Message Boards. June, 2011.

Obama gives up on cap-and-trade to curb climate change. Monsters and Critics. February, 2011.

Report links fracking to tainted drinking water. Reuters. May, 2011.

Revitalizing Old Fields. www.chevron.com.

Saudis Will Stop Exploring for More Oil. Wallst.com. July, 2010.

International Energy Outlook 2010, with projections to 2035. Center for Strategic and International Studies. May, 2010.

Interview with Art Berman Part 1. ASPO-USA. July 2010.

E.I.A: International Energy Statistics, Production, Consumption data.

United States Geological Survey: World Petroleum Assessment 2000—Description and Results.

United Nations: food production statistics.

2008 conference on degrowth, Paris. PDF version of the presentations available on-line.

Index

A

a mass of "networkers", 322
a poisoned cultural environment, 322
a warming trend may provide some extra farmland, 170
abuse of basic human rights, 1
Adam Smith, 12, 280, 316, 333, 334, 335, 336, 338
ad-hoc sacrifice, 156
Africa, 1, 43, 60, 76, 79, 97, 139, 154, 172, 177, 179, 185, 188, 189, 217, 298, 348
agricultural subsidies, 35
Alaska, 137, 265, 342
Albania, 275, 277
Algeria, 114
American Wind Energy Association, 191
an increasingly competitive developed world, 271
Angola, 113
anti average Joe platform, 342
anti-western bias, 45,
apparent will of the masses, *341*
Asia, 1, 43, 154, 168, 177, 185, 223, 224, 257, 298, 344, 347, 348, 389, 392
austerity measures, 277, 357
Australia, 64, 142
available cropland, 170
Azerbaijan, 118, 134

B

baby boomers, 237
Balkan nations, 274, 276, 277, 284
Baltic States, 262
Banat, 278, 280, 283, 285, 288, 289, 290, 294, 296, 303, 315, 388

Bangladesh, 10
Barnett shale play, 137
basic economic theory, 13
Bechtel, 340
Belgium, 346
benefits of outsourcing to dirtier and more inhumane places, 242
best and the brightest, 107, 210, 324, 327
Biblical and Koran times, 34
Bill Gates, 43
Birzava River, 162, 163
Bismarckian moment, 207
Boeing loyalty to American workers, 234
Bolivia, 340
Bosnia-Herzegovina, 275, 277
bottled water as an alternative to tap water., 161
BP disaster, 95
Brazil, 43, 77, 83, 112, 171, 226, 227, 229, 234, 236, 268, 344, 347
BRIC nations, 257
brick and mortar operation, 239
bubble economics, 201
Bulgaria, 140, 262, 275, 277, 287, 298
Bush, 9, 53, 103, 138, 164, 202, 203, 214, 230, 235, 324, 393
buy and hold investing, 238

C

Canada, 85, 88, 137, 150, 272, 282, 289, 305, 336, 339, 366, 367, 368, 371,
public transport infrastructure, 18, 19
19'Th century, European offshoot, 64
Canada Immigration; economic incentives for, 70, 185
increasing Chinese interests and influence, 76
petroleum production and reserves, 99 - 102

Jeff Rubbin, 107
use of natural gas in oilsands
production, 130
per capita energy consumption, 142
environmental situation, 153 - 155
loss of farming capacity to oil
production industry, 168
effect of climate change on food
production, 170, 176
Chinese interest in purchasing
Canadian farmland, 182
loss of manufacturing to cheaper labor,
232, 233, 256
nepotism, 323, 328
evolution of share of gov't spending as
% of GDP, 1900 - 2000, 336
cap and trade, 37, 38, 383
capital gains tax, 240
capital intensive farming, 172
capitalism induced prosperity, 8
capitalism inspired monetary
redistribution, 239
car culture, 18
careful examination of CV's, 323
carrying capacity of their environment, 33
Central banks, 197
Central European, 274- 278
centrally planed economic system, 276
Chernobyl, 164, 169
China, 30, 36, 37, 109, 135, 157, 162, 199,
212, 243, 250, 251, 268, 269,
growth in energy and commodities
consumption, 43, 229, 230
contribution to the disposable economy,
50, 51
urban social safety net, 70
grab for global resources, 76 - 78
doubling of petroleum consumption
2000-10, in face of rising price, 83
petroleum production, 96 - 98
need for improvement of energy
efficiency, 143
environmnetal carelessness as tool for
atracting investment, 157
farmland colonialism, 182
effect of sustainability tariff, 218 - 220
population size impediment to wage
increase, 226, 227
outsourcing to China, 232, 234
Shanghay stock index, 236

export driven economy (no social
safety net), 243,
hypothetical example of manufacturing
advantage Vs US, 245 - 248
cheap products killing developed world
industries, 255 - 257
tainted baby formula, 335
western misrepresentation of effects of
China currentcy manipulation, 343
producing the products of the future,
347, 348
choking on debt, 349
climate change, 14, 22, 23, 32, 126, 153,
169, 170, 172, 176, 394
Clinton, 39, 254
CO_2 emissions, 33, 101, 148, 150, 216,
383
coal to liquids, 126
collapse of the consumer, 355
collective bargaining, 318
collective goodwill, 25
collective utility, 14, 15
collectivization, 278
colonization of Hungarian inhabited
towns, 292
commenda, 195
commodity price fluctuations, 215
Commodity price spikes, 221
common financial pot, 290
competent people are brushed aside, 326
complete seizing up of credit, 208
constitutional government, 336
consumer confidence, 68
consumer demand, 2, 48, 66, 185, 267, 268
consumer driven economy, 68, 174, 207
consumer satisfaction, 10, 14, 16, 49, 50,
52, 151, 166
consumers of the environment, 156, 166
continued job scarcity, 353
conventional gas, 139
convergence, 10, 140, 142, 143, 144, 168,
170, 175, 184, 226, 248, 316, 344, 345,
364
corporate conglomerates that took the
shape of nation states, 319
cost of nepotism, 327
Covasna, 283, 291, 292, 293
creative destruction, 338
credit based economy, 13
Credit Default Swap, 216

credit default swaps, 215
Credit markets, 207
credit-based economy, 203
Croatia, 275, 277
Crops with natural resistance to pests and
   disease, 173
crude oil production, 74, 123, 146
cultivating networking skills, 322
cultural mismatch, 317
cultural revolution, 42, 317, 318, 319
culturally relevant, 317
currency devaluation, 33, 42, 260
Currency fluctuations, 221
currency instability, 218
Czechoslovakia, 277
Czech Republic, 275, 277

D

debound, 41
debt to GDP ratio, 81, 260, 269
decentralization of the administrative, 291,
   302
declining trend of yield growth, 172
deep-water exploration, 112
default rates, 207
defense spending, 234
degrowth, 40, 41, 44, 52, 383
demographic damage, 295
demographic disaster, 295, 301, 318
deprived of basic rights employees, 25
deregulated playing fields for multinational
   corporations to play in., 23
deregulation of emissions standards, 23
derivatives, 214
developed world, 1, 9, 141, 142, 162, 168,
   227, 244, 251, 257, 336, 351, 369, 390
developing market exchanges, 236
developing nations, 21, 34, 40, 43, 49, 78,
   79, 83, 127, 158, 162, 190, 203, 236,
   251, 257, 259, 266, 383
developing world, 2, 41, 126, 181, 183,
   184, 212, 231, 232, 234, 254, 255, 256,
   318, 348, 349, 362,
   low paid, well trained workers, 10, 11
   convergence in poverty, 16, 364
   market guidance to emulate western
   living style, and consumption paterns,
   18, 170

demographic reality, 22
benefits of globalization, 25
dangers of environmental degradation,
27
role of religion in population growth,
33
neglect of people and environment as
strategy to atract investment, 40
gain in manufacturing jobs, 42
increase in commodities ocnsumption,
43, 85
decrease in poverty, transfer of
technology, 78 - 81
paradox of better adaptation to rising
commodity   prices, 83
increase in afluence, growing middle
class, 132, 168
hypothetical convergence to our
standard of living, and what it would
take, 140, 141
low crop yields, subsistence farming,
172
convergence in education and
infrastructure, 226
absence of social safety net, and access
to education, in favor of keeping costs
low for investors, 243, 244
switch from debtor to lender, 250
a more atractive place to invest for
western companies, 264, 267
China currency manipulation to
compete with developing world peers,
343
correlation between growing
developing world middle class and
increasing poverty in west, 345
discouraging the use of contraceptives,
(religion), 34
disposable economy, 51
double counting, 102, 168
durability kills consumer demand, 19
durable economy, 52
duties and privileges of the land, 337

E

East Europeans, 9, 278
Easter Island, 3, 58, 62, 329, 384
Eastern Europe, 4, 8, 43, 86, 171, 182, 211,
   274, 277, 289, 346, 355, 366

ecological collapse, 155
ecological footprint, 34, 150
ecological reasons for people to migrate, 155
economic cost of regulating, 335
economically dead zones, 295
educated electorate, 25
efficiency based economy, 27
Egypt, 26, 205, 350, 354
EIA, 90, 92, 99, 103, 106, 120, 123, 131, 384, 385, 390, 392
elasticity of food as a consumer good, *359*
emerging markets, 103, 128, 144, 347
energy diet, 258
energy input to output ratio, 89
energy return on production inputs, 21
environment as a natural resource, 156
environmental and labor deregulation, 26
environmental damage, 9, 17, 156, 180, 190, 203
environmental degradation, 1, 11, 17, 166, 187, 243, 258
environmental footprint, 13, 33, 34, 52, 179
environmental protection, 23, 25, 40, 43, 44, 156, 157, 158, 164, 166, 167, 178, 254, 258, 327
Environmental regulations, *344*
environmental responsibility, 44, 156, 242
Environmental sustainability, 29
EPA, 23, 38, 138, 268, 390
ethanol, 10, 21, 86, 119, 120, 161, 162, 383
ethnic identity, 287
ethnic purification, 293, 302
Europe, , 55, 58, 60, 61, 64, 66, 67, 70 79, 128, 147, 171, 185, 202, 208, 247, 270, 330, 331, 364, 365, 366, 368, 371,
policy of encouraging energy efficiency, 19 - 21, 157, 229
history of ancient Rome, and 19'Th century Europe
Ghadafi comments on muslim colonization of
gas imports from Russia, and Caspian region, 133
industrial revolution, and advances in environmental protection since, 154
purchase of foreign farmland, 177
industrial revolution & coal, 189

birth of modern finance, 193 - 195
financial bailout, 208
birth of the stock market, 223 -227
effects of outsourcing, 231, 232, 234
failure of proposed common EU corporate tax rate (race to the bottom), 253
EU sovereign debt crissis, 263, 264
Balkan Vs Central European adaptation to post- comunist economic reality, 272, 275, 276, 277, 278, 279, 280, 283, 288, 296, 297, 298, 302, 303, 309, 311, 314, 318
Airbus transfer of technology to China, 347
economic headwinds, 356, 357
European Enlightenment, 272
European Union, 28, 36,
Expecting people to act in their self-interest, 319

F

false saviors, 340, 342
family planning, 184
farm subsidies, 216
farmland, 67, 70, 126, 153, 155, 164, 169, 170, 171, 175, 176, 177, 178, 182, 186, 204, 216, 337, 359, 361, 372
fast rail transport, 242
FDA, 268
Federal Reserve, 197, 201, 208, 213, 349
Finance reform, 230
financial crisis, 1, 26, 83, 198, 211, 215, 264
financial squeeze faced by local governments, 161
financially unsustainable, *349*
finite resources, 1, 74, 84, 173, 190
finite world, 13, 83, 190, 206, 217
Fitch Ratings LTD, 209
Food prices, 146, 181, 216
food production, 24, 72, 73, 125, 169, 171, 173, 176, 178, 183, 184, 189, 216, 243, 353, 393, 395
food rioting disrupting the status quo, 243
food safety, *177, 335*
forced to choose between walking, and eating, 339
fossil fuels, 21, 143, 181, 189, 190, 191, 375

France, 195
Francois Schneider, 41
free enterprise, 230
free market, 1, 20, 35, 274, 278, 334, 381
free market economics, *278*, *334*
frequent trader program, 238
friction over farmland availability, 186
fuel efficiency, 18, 21, 142, 144, 148, 157, 161
fuel efficiency of providing drinking water via pipeline, 161
fuel efficient infrastructure, 21
future energy supplies, 103

G

gated community, 339
Gazprom, 133
geopolitical risk, 290
George Bush, 33
George Soros, 215
Germany, 3, 19, 29, 148, 149, 154, 218, 219, 220, 227, 263, 279, 296, 305
Ghawar, 93
global convergence, *364*
global economy, 2, 12, 16, 28, 33, 37, 42, 46, 86, 89, 128, 144, 150, 164, 179, 190, 191, 192, 228, 257, 310, 325, 332, 373
global resources, 14, 26
global trade, 1, 2, 3, 36, 46, 233, 254, 354
globalization, 10, 38, 168, 223, 224, 254, 255, *364*
GM bailout, 232
GM crops, 172, 173, 177
gold standard, 79, 196
Goldman Sachs, 209
Government flexing its muscles, 336
government interference keeps places accessible, 340
government subsidies, 35, 172
granola munchers, 255, 258
Greece, 206, 216, 221, 263, 276, 287, 346
green revolution, 174, 386
greenhouse effect, 22
greenhouse gases, 23
greenhouse gasses, 37, 242

H

Habsburg, 65, 296, 303
Harghita, 283, 291, 292
HDI index, 30
health insurance costs, 343
heavily indebted western consumers, 257
Hedge funds, 214
Henry Ford, 68
herd mentality, *356*, *358*
high deficit spending, 42, 260
high wage environment, 49, 256
highly centralized administrative system, 281, 290
historical reference to measure the true effects of tax cuts, 253
honing technical skills and knowledge, 322
human dignity, 203, 242, 382
human rights, 2, 25, 29, 30, 34, 35, 37, 39, 40, 49, 179, 220, 221, 243, 245, 248, 254, 255, 258, 264, 307, 382
human rights disparity gap, 35
Hungarian Autonomous Region (In Romania), 292
Hungary, 262, 274, 275, 277, 278, 285, 286, 292, 294, 296, 297, 299, 300, 302, 304, 305, 307, 310, 313, 314, 335, 388
Zalaegerszeg public transport system, 19
Kolontar industrial accident (environmnetal disaster), 165, 169
Sovereign debt credit rating, compared to AAA rated Britain, and US, 210 - 213
punishment for its stance on making banks share in the pain of recesion,(questioning political motivation of credit rating agencies), 250
Post-communist cultural capabilities to adapt, in comparison with Romania and other Balkan states, 274, 275, 277, 278, 285, 286, 292, 294, 296, 297, 299, 300, 302, 304, 305, 307, 310, 313, 314
hydrocarbon based fertilizers and pesticides, *353*
hydrocarbon-based fertilizers, 73
hyperinflation, 206, 260
hyper-urbanized, 337

I

Iceland, 346
IEA, 6, 18, 20, 77, 103, 191, 229, 383, 390
IMF, 210, 211, 250, 275, 277, 386, 390
important acquaintances, 326
increase in soil salinity, 175
increased rate of environmental
    exploitation, 159
India, 30, 37, 43, 76, 77, 83, 135, 144, 174,
    223, 224, 226, 227, 229, 231, 233, 236,
    255, 256, 268, 269, 344, 346, 389, 392,
    394
Indonesia, 43, 165, 226, 344
industrial farming, 174, 175, 180, 181
infinite growth, 13, 41
infrastructure investment, 20
initial stock offer, 225
International Energy Agency, 6, 18, 390
invisible hand, 9, 10, 15
Iran, 95, 107, 132, 133, 134, 135, 136
Iraq, 77, 87, 102, 103, 107, 110, 126, 139,
    324, 325, 327, 328, 350, 393
Ireland, 262, 346
Israel, 96, 134, 135, 185, 350
Italy, 195, 262, 346

J

Japan, 31, 32, 167, 229, 232, 254
Jared Diamond, 7, 186, 341, 384, 386, 387
Jeff Rubin, 84, 107
jobs versus environmental protection, 23

K

Kashagan, 116
Kazakhstan, 76, 116, 134
Keneth Defeyes, 123
Keynesian, 1, 261
Kolontar, 165, 169
Kuwait, 105, 106, 107, 142
Kyoto, 22, 25, 31, 33, 36, 381

L

labor selling population, 337
laise fair, 150
laise faire, 330, 333
leaked German Army report, 145

leaving most of the middle and lower
    classes to fend for themselves, 342
legal tender, 196
less stringent environmental rules, 25
leverage, 208, 245, 304
liberalization of trade, 38
Libya, 60, 115, 118, 152, 298
limitless economic expansion, 200
LNG, 119
local cohesion and solidarity, 361
local economic sacrifice, 156
long-term urbanization trend, 359
loss in nutritional quality, 174
loss of natural habitat, 23
lower taxes, 128, 243

M

Macedonia, 275, 277
Mad Max, 208
Malthusian, 73
Manifa, 93
manifest destiny, 287, 290, 294, 296, 303,
    312
manufacturing jobs, 26, 31, 42, 79, 80,
    231, 338
Marcellus Shale, 137, 392
market economy, 3, 4, 13, 162, 192, 226,
    274, 278, 279, 288, 380, 381
Marxist, 12, 65, 319
Mathew Simmons, 92, 122, 123, 124, 385
mature, slow growing economies, 257
maximize profits, 23, 65, 225, 257, 334,
    339, 384
Medicare, 265, 268
Mercedes, 335
Meritocracy, 321, 327
Mexico, 26, 88, 95, 98, 99, 111, 112, 232
Middle East, 185, 245, 348, 358, 373,
    growth in commodities demand, 1, 229,
    257
    geopolitical disruptions of petroleum
    export, 16
    cultural values, contrast with west, 30
    birthplace of agriculture in the old
    world, 54
    Eatern Roman Empire, 61
    petroleum industry, 89
    water desalination and energy use, 131,
    136, 141

nuclear weapons (Israel, Iran), 135
doubt about petroleum reserve, official
estimates, 139, 146
unrest triggered by high food prices,
youth unemployment due to high
population growth, 151, 186
purchase of foreign farmland, 177
problem of religion and demographic
presures, 217
migration to Europe, 298
authoritarian culture, 351
minimum wage, 338, 373, 384
mismatch between the reality of the
economic situation, and cultural norms,
295
momentum trading, 214
monetary liquidity, 195, 196
monetization, 340
money lending, 193, 194, 195, 197
monopoly power, 339
Montenegro, 275, 277
Moody's, 209
mortgage backed securities, 202
mortgage backed securities"., 202
mortgage brokers, 208
most drinking water supplies contain toxic
chemicals, 163
motorized farming, 73
Mr. Buffet, 43
Muhamar Ghadafi, 115
multinational corporation, 223, 390
Muslim population is set to double by
2030, 34

N

Nabucco, 134, 136
Nabucco pipeline, 134
NAFTA, 29
naïve utopist expectations, 319
narrow interests of the elites, 342
narrow scope interest, 341
national church, 284, 290
national identity, 284, 307
national or regional competence, 34
nationalist tendencies, 284
nationalist zeal, aided in its current form
by the church., 291
Natural gas, 130, 134, 139
Natural Gas, 100, 120, 130, 131, 132, 133,

383, 385
negative externalities, 336
nepotism, 66, 321, 324, 325, 326, 327,
328, 346
net return on energy, 190
new renewable technologies, 126
newfound tolerance for nepotism, 324
Nigeria, 109
non fossil energy, 129
non-Balkan nations, 274
non-renewable, 13, 124, 156, 332, 380
North America, 1, 79, 98, 101, 137, 139,
169, 184, 224, 226, 227, 229, 231, 232,
280, 295, 323, 365, 368, 384, 389, 394
North Sea, 117, 125
Norway, 111, 112, 117
nuclear power, 135, 164

O

Obama, 37, 38, 202, 230, 233, 270, 348,
383, 394
obscene concessions, 1
OECD, 77, 127, 226, 227, 229, 230, 257,
345, 383, 390
oil prices, 18, 20, 26, 207
oil sands, 21, 87, 90, 100, 101, 167, 168,
169, 383
old Inuit tradition to leave the elderly to
freeze to death, 342
on the verge of global chaos, 349
OPEC, 88, 92, 95, 102, 106, 108, 109, 113,
114, 115, 146, 390
Orthodox Church, 283, 284, 292, 312
Otto Von Bismarck, 3, 66, 71, 252, 253
outsourcing firm Infosys, 233
outsourcing of jobs, 69

P

Pakistan, 135
Pareto efficiency, 46, 47, 48, 49
Pax Romana[1], 54
peak oil, 6, 120, 122, 123, 124, 147, 331
Pemex, 98
pension funds, 209, 237, 337
pension plan, 69
per capita petroleum use, 344
perceived risks, ethnic tensions, 290
perfect information, 51, 384

Petroleum Intelligence Weekly, 105
Petroleum production, top twnety nations:
  Algeria, 114
  Angola, 113
  Azerbaijan, 118
  Brazil, 112
  Canada, 99 - 102
  China, 96, 97
  Iran, 95
  Iraq, 102 -104
  Kazakhstan, 116
  Kuwait, 105 - 108
  Libya, 115
  Mexico, 98, 99
  Nigeria, 109
  Norway, 111
  Russia, 90, 91
  Saudi Arabia, 91 - 93
  United Arab Emirates, 104
  United Kingdom, 117
  United States, 94
  Venezuela, 108, 109
petroleum reserves, 88, 97, 105, 134
phosphate production, 168
poisoning of the underground water, 138
Poland, 275, 277
political campaigns depend on money
  fundraised from the ones interested in
  buying favor, 342
political reserves, 134
politicians that cater to the individual and
  corporate interests of the elites, 321
poor ratio of pensioners to workers, 296
population density, 153, 155, 186, 339, 371
population growth, 10, 33, 34, 72, 157,
  170, 184, 185, 186, 357, 372
positions left untainted, 325
post collapse average, *358*
Portugal, 262
predatory behavior from outsiders, *361*
price paid by the environment and the
  human collective, 33
price signal, 18, 23, 144
private enterprise, 68, 77, 85, 199, 233,
  330, 335, 336, 340, 351
private toll roads, 338
privatization bringing freedom to the
  people, *340*
pro business lobby, 342
productive and potentially reproductive

individuals, 304
profit maximization, 144, 335
profit maximizing, 23, 65, 226, 233, 267,
  337
promissory notes,, 196
proposal for a viable solution, 1
public good, 22, 262, 338, 388
public land and assets, 340
public schools, 308, 342
public transport, 14, 19, 126, 262
publicly funded campaigns, 320

Q

Qatar, 132, 136
quasi-state institution, 224

R

R & D, 33, 347, 352
race to the bottom, 1, 4, 23, 26, 30, 39, 44,
  158, 242, 252, 253, 254, 258, 382
rating agencies, 202, 209, 210, 211, 212,
  260, 346
raw materials, 73, 74, 220, 257, 335
Reaganomics, 252, 253
real price on all goods, 33
re-balancing of the global economy, 33
rebound effect, 41
Recovery rates (petroleum fields), 105
regime collapse, *350*
religious organizations, 33
removing government curbs on
  exploitation, 342
Renaissance, 62, 279, 280
renewable energy, 348, 379
renewable resources, 84
Republic of Moldova, 293, 303
required reserves (banking), 198
Reserve depletion, 101
reserve ratio, 208
resource nationalism, 16, 75, 76, 133,146
resource scarcity, 4, 35, 36, 39, 40, 75, 77,
  84, 148, 349, 352
risk assessment, 208, 212
Robert Solow, 73
Robin M Mills, 122, 125
rock fracturing, 138, 164
Romania, 58, 140, 147 , 262 , 356,
  1989 revolution, 8, 11

agriculture, 47
falsified production reports, 108
textile production handicap versus
China, due to EU environmental rules,
157, 158
pollution, 162
un-utilized farmland, 171
cultural shortcommings in adapting to
current global economic environment,
272 - 317
communist system (state capitalism),
319
advance of inept people through the
communist system, 320
national identity, shaped by national
religion, outdated, keeping culture
stuck in 19'th century, 330, 331, 333
lack of physical infrastructure, barrier
to investment, 335
communism, malnourishment in
1980's, rural versus urban situation,
371
Rome, 3, 54, 55, 56, 57, 58, 59, 61, 71, 73,
74, 195, 261, 329
rural dominated demographic, 337
Russia, 76, 90, 91, 109, 132, 133, 134,
170, 234, 236

S

S&P, 209, 212, 250, 387
Sarah Palin, 265, 342
Saudi Arabia, 75, 88, 91, 92, 93, 105, 123,
124, 125, 142
Saudi king Abdullah, 93
Securities and Exchange Commission, 209
securities trading, 239
Sekler region,, 292
self-employed, 337
self-interest, *334, 346*
Serbia, 275, 277, 285, 287, 296
shale gas, 23, 101, 137, 138, 139, 140,
141, 164, 167, 168, 169, 191
Shale Gas, 136, 137, 138, 379, 394
slick day-trader investment environment,
240
Slovakia, 275, 277
Slovenia, 275, 277
small government, *252, 330, 334*
social mobility, 326, 342, 371

social reconditioning, 325
social safety net, 3, 42, 65, 66, 67, 68, 69,
70, 71, 81, 128, 207, 243, 253, 267,
337, 338, 364, 369
social security, 342
Social Security, 265, 268
socialist utopia, 318
South America, 1, 139, 348
sovereign debt, 206, 215
Spain, 262, 346
special interests, 25, 320
specialization, 47, 48, 49, 228
stagnated market, *357*
stagnation in consumption, *357*
standardized tariff system, 27
starting point of the wage negotiation, 69
state subsidies, 34
status quo, 4, 22, 25, 52, 136, 166, 221,
234, 244, 249, 270, 341, 378
Steven Chu, 36
stock ownership, 225
stop loss option, 240
sub-prime fiasco, 212, 213
sub-prime mortgage, 209, 277
sub-prime mortgages,, 209, 251
surplus environmental carrying, 155
survival through corruption, *360*
sustainability trade tariff, 1, 2, 3, 4, 46,
216, 148
sustainable development, 12
Sustainable farming, 180
synthetic crude, 21, 100, 101
synthetic materials industry, 86
systemic risks, 146

T

T Boone Pickens, 130
tainted baby formula scandal, 335
taking it out on the poor, 250
tax cuts for the wealthy, 230
Tea Parties, 334
Tea Party, 208, 265, 267, 268, 269, 270,
331, 333, 339, 340, 341, 342, 343, 368
the going wage, 337
The Limits to Growth, 73
the low hanging fruit, 140, 345, 379, 380
The National, 122, 392
the planet's newest consumer, 235
the rich can afford to go private, 342

the right to manufacture, 79, 251, 348
The Wealth of Nations, *334*
the western consumer, 40, 71, 234, 244
the western consumer economy, 71
theoretical economic models, 51
Thomas Malthus, 34, 72
tolerating inefficiencies such as nepotism, *346*
toxic financial assets, *354*
trade agreements, 3, 25, 27, 28, 31, 32, 39
transport infrastructure, 244, 335
Transylvania, 278, 280, 283, 285, 288, 292, 293, 294, 295, 296, 302, 303, 313, 315
Turkmenistan, 76, 134
Twilight in the Desert, 92, 124, 393

U

Ukraine, 133, 164, 165, 285
unconventional petroleum, 108, 130
Unemployment insurance, 69
union busting, *368*
United Arab Emirates, 104
United Kingdom, 117
United States, 94, 105, 137, 184, 262, 264
unlimited supply of labor, 2
un-pasteurized milk, 335
urban working class, 66
urbanization trend, 258, 337
US defense department, 129, 234
USGS, 99, 105, 106, 137

V

Venezuela, 108, 109
Vietnam, 10, 344

W

wage floor, 337
water and soil pollution, 23, 29
water desalination, 131, 141
western eating habits, 170
western governments, 27, 31, 42, 128, 148, 231, 250, 251, 259
wisdom of the electorate, 341
women's rights, 34, 35
work hard and get noticed through competence, 325

worker protection laws, *254, 344*
worker's unions, 38, 39
World Bank, 250
world's reserve currency, *356, 357*
WTO, 28, 32

Y

Yellowstone Park, 339, 368
yields, per unit of farmland, 171
Yugoslavia, 277

Z

Zalaegerszeg, 19